781.3Ca

THE ACT OF MUSICAL COMPOSITION

SEMPRE Studies in
the Psychology of Music

Series Editors

Graham Welch, *Institute of Education, University of London, UK*
Adam Ockelford, *Roehampton University, UK*
Ian Cross, *University of Cambridge, UK*

The theme for the series is the psychology of music, broadly defined. Topics will include: (i) musical development at different ages, (ii) exceptional musical development in the context of special educational needs, (iii) musical cognition and context, (iv) culture, mind and music, (v) micro to macro perspectives on the impact of music on the individual (such as from neurological studies through to social psychology), (vi) the development of advanced performance skills and (vii) affective perspectives on musical learning. The series will present the implications of research findings for a wide readership, including user-groups (music teachers, policy makers, parents), as well as the international academic and research communities. The distinguishing features of the series will be this broad focus (drawing on basic and applied research from across the globe) under the umbrella of SEMPRE's distinctive mission, which is to promote and ensure coherent and symbiotic links between education, music and psychology research.

Other titles in the series

Musical Creativity: Insights from Music Education Research
Oscar Odena

Advances in Social-Psychology and Music Education Research
Edited by Patrice Madura Ward-Steinman

The Musical Ear: Oral Tradition in the USA
Anne Dhu McLucas

The Act of Musical Composition

Studies in the Creative Process

Edited by

DAVE COLLINS
University Centre, Doncaster College, UK

ASHGATE

Published by
Ashgate Publishing Limited
Wey Court East
Union Road
Farnham
Surrey, GU9 7PT
England

Ashgate Publishing Company
Suite 420
101 Cherry Street
Burlington
VT 05401-4405
USA

www.ashgate.com

British Library Cataloguing in Publication Data
The act of musical composition : studies in the creative process. – (SEMPRE studies in the psychology of music)
   1. Composition (Music) – Psychological aspects. I. Series. II. Collins, Dave.
   III. Society for Education, Music and Psychology Research.
   781.3'111-dc23

Library of Congress Cataloging-in-Publication Data
The act of musical composition : studies in the creative process / edited by Dave Collins.
      p. cm. – (SEMPRE studies in the psychology of music)
   Includes bibliographical references and index.
   ISBN 978-1-4094-3425-2 (hardcover)
   1. Composition (Music) – Psychological aspects. I. Collins, Dave, 1952–
   ML3838.A27 2013
   781.3'111–dc23
                                                                      2012018275

ISBN 9781409434252 (hbk)
ISBN 9781409434269 (ebk – PDF)
ISBN 9781409471318 (ebk – ePUB)

MIX
Paper from
responsible sources
FSC® C018575
www.fsc.org

Printed and bound in Great Britain by the
MPG Books Group, UK.

Contents

List of Figures

List of Tables

List of Music Examples

Notes on Contributors

Freya Bailes is a senior research fellow at the MARCS Institute, University of Western Sydney. She received her PhD in the Psychology of Music from the University of Sheffield in 2003. Her principal research interest lies in musical imagery, or imagining music in the 'mind's ear', but she has also published widely on topics that range from aural training to compositional archetypes: the perception of contemporary musical forms (e.g. electroacoustic works and microtonal music), musical expertise, cognitive and social processes in performance, music and emotion, and the dynamic analysis of music. Freya remains actively involved in music as an oboe player.

Joe Bennett is Head of the School of Music and Performing Arts at Bath Spa University, UK. As a teacher of popular music, he was awarded a National Teaching Fellowship in 2004 by the UK Higher Education Academy. In 2004 he founded the UK Songwriting Festival, a week-long event now held annually at the University, and in 2007 launched the University's Masters degree in Songwriting – the first of its kind in the world. He is listed on the Music Publishers' Association Register of Expert Witness Musicologists, advising publishers and songwriters on copyright disputes involving possible plagiarism in songs.

Laura Bishop is a doctoral student at the MARCS Institute, University of Western Sydney, Australia. She has degrees in psychology from the University of Toronto and the University of Sheffield, and completed the ARCT in piano performance at the Royal Conservatory of Music in Toronto. Her research focuses on musical expertise and the production of performance expression, and she is investigating the roles of imagery and perception in the planning and monitoring of expressive performance.

Andrew R. Brown is Professor of Digital Arts at the Queensland Conservatorium of Music, Griffith University in Brisbane, Australia. His previous academic positions include Research Manager for the Australasian Cooperative Research Centre for Interaction Design, and Professor of Music and Sound at the Queensland University of Technology. He is an active computer musician and computational artist whose work explores the aesthetics of process and creative interactions between humans and computer systems. His research interests include designing creativity support tools, developing new processes for algorithmic music and art, and investigating computational models of musical intelligence.

Pamela Burnard is a Senior Lecturer in the Faculty of Education at the University of Cambridge. She manages and lectures on Doctoral and Masters programmes in Educational Research and in Arts, Culture and Education. She also supervises PhD students and teaches courses on creativity, creative teaching and learning, musical creativities, and creative partnerships. She is co-convener of BERA: SIG Creativity in Education and is co-editor of the *British Journal of Music Education*. She has published extensively in books and academic peer-reviewed journals including including *Musical Creativities in Real World Practice* (Oxford University Press), *Practices in Arts Education* (Springer), *Documenting Creative Learning* (Trentham) and *Music Education and Digital Technology* (Routledge).

David Cope is Professor Emeritus of the University of California, Santa Cruz and founder and director of the annual Workshop on Algorithmic Computer Music. He has written extensively on computer music composition, including the books *Virtual Music* and *Computer Models of Musical Creativity* (2001 and 2005, MIT Press), *Computers and Musical Style*, *Experiments in Musical Intelligence* and *The Algorithmic Composer* (1991, 1996, and 2000, A-R Editions). He is also recognized as a composer with many books/recordings available and numerous performances worldwide.

Steve Dillon[1] is a senior lecturer in Music and Sound at Queensland University of Technology in Brisbane Australia, Director of Save to DISC Research Network and project Leader of the International Network Jamming Research Group. He studied music education at the University of South Australia, before completing a Master of Music Education and a Doctorate of Philosophy at La Trobe University in Melbourne. He has combined a career as a professional singer-songwriter with school music teaching. His research interests are in arts education and participation in community arts practices.

Nicolas Donin is head of the Analysis of Musical Practices team, a joint research group of Institut de Recherche et de Coordination Acoustique/Musique, Université Pierre et Marie Curie and Centre National de la Recherche Scientifique in Paris. His work focuses on contemporary musical practices, particularly composition and performance, using both a musicological and a cognitive approach. He co-edited with Rémy Campos *L'analyse musicale, une pratique et son histoire* (Droz/Conservatoire de Genève, 2009), and with Laurent Feneyrou *Théories de la composition musicale au XXe siècle* (Symétrie). His recent work has been published in *Contemporary Music Review, Genesis: Revue Internationale de Critique Génétique, Intellectica* and *Music Theory Online*, as well as in various edited collections in French and English. He also co-authored several documentary films on the creative process of composers Georges Aperghis, Luca Francesconi, Philipp Mainz, Roque Rivas and Marco Stroppa.

---

[1]   Since the inception of this book, Steve Dillon sadly passed away in April 2012.

Shira Lee Katz is interested in the process by which novel ideas and creations emerge. She holds a Doctorate in Human Development and Psychology from the Harvard Graduate School of Education, where she studied with Howard Gardner. In her dissertation, she identified prototypes of inspiration among new music composers. Since 2000, Katz has managed research projects on social and emotional learning, moral development, bullying, at-risk kids, arts education and digital learning. Currently she holds the position of Director of Digital Media for US-based non-profit Common Sense Media. At Common Sense, Katz directed the research and creation of an innovative K-12 online digital literacy and currently heads a team that rates and reviews digital media for learning potential and age appropriateness.

Aaron Kozbelt is Professor of Psychology at Brooklyn College and The Graduate Center of the City University of New York. His research foci lie at the intersection of creativity and cognition in the arts, particularly on the nature of the creative process, archival analyses of lifespan creativity trajectories and self-evaluation in classical composers, and the psychological basis of skilled artistic drawing. He is the author of approximately 50 journal articles and book chapters on these and other topics, and serves on several editorial boards. He has been the recipient of the American Psychological Association Division 10 Daniel Berlyne Award for Creativity Research and the International Association of Empirical Aesthetics Alexander Gottlieb Baumgarten Award for Creativity Research; some of his current research is funded by the National Science Foundation.

Raymond MacDonald is Professor of Music Psychology and Improvisation at Glasgow Caledonian University. After completing his PhD at the University of Glasgow, investigating therapeutic applications of music, he worked as Artistic Director for a music company, Sounds of Progress, specialising in working with people who have special needs. He has published over 70 papers and co-edited four texts: *Musical Identities* (2002), *Musical Communication* (2005), *Musical Imaginations* (2012) and *Music Health and Wellbeing* (2012). He is Editor of the journal *Psychology of Music* and Associate Editor for *The International Journal of Music Education, Musicae Scientae, Jazz Research Journal* and *Research Studies in Music Education*. As a saxophonist and composer he has recorded over 50 CDs and toured and broadcast worldwide.

Eduardo Reck Miranda is a composer and Professor in Computer Music at Plymouth University, UK, where he is head of the Interdisciplinary Centre for Computer Music Research. His research interests include composition (including algorithmic, computer-aided and electroacoustic), sound synthesis, brain–computer music interfacing and evolutionary computer music. Professor Miranda's compositions are informed and inspired by his research into Artificial Intelligence. His music has been broadcast and performed at festivals and concerts worldwide. Recent publications include the book *A-Life for Music: On Music and Computer*

Models of Living Systems (2011, A-R Editions) and the CD *Mozart Reloaded for Piano and Electronics* (2011, Sargasso).

Simon Rose is a professional musician and a performer on baritone and alto saxophones with a specific research interest in improvisation. He completed a Best Practice Research Scholarship for his MA in Professional Practice, at Middlesex University (2008) and is currently working towards completing his PhD thesis, concerning improvisation in music and learning, at Glasgow Caledonia University. Publications include the chapter 'Free improvisation in education,' in *Investigating Musical Performance* (Ashgate, 2012). Simon is based in Berlin and London.

Geraint A. Wiggins was educated in Mathematics and Computer Science at Corpus Christi College, Cambridge, and then completed a PhD in Computational Linguistics at the University of Edinburgh. He took a second PhD in Musical Composition at Edinburgh, in 2005. Since 1987, Geraint has been conducting research on computational systems for music, with a strong emphasis on cognitively motivated approaches. He is Professor of Computational Creativity in the School of Electronic Engineering and Computer Science, Queen Mary, University of London.

Series Editors' Preface

There has been an enormous growth over the past three decades of research into the psychology of music. SEMPRE (the Society for Education, Music and Psychology Research) is the only international society that embraces an interest in the psychology of music, research and education. SEMPRE was founded in 1972 and has published the journals *Psychology of Music* since 1973 and *Research Studies in Music* Education since 2008, both now in partnership with SAGE (see www.sempre.org.uk). Nevertheless, there is an ongoing need to promote the latest research to the widest possible audience if it is to have a distinctive impact on policy and practice. In collaboration with Ashgate since 2007, the 'SEMPRE Studies in The Psychology of Music' has been designed to address this need. The theme for the series is the psychology of music, broadly defined. Topics include (amongst others): musical development at different ages; musical cognition and context; culture, mind and music; micro to macro perspectives on the impact of music on the individual (such as from neurological studies through to social psychology); the development of advanced performance skills; musical behaviour and development in the context of special educational needs; and affective perspectives on musical learning. The series seeks to present the implications of research findings for a wide readership, including user-groups (music teachers, policy makers, parents), as well as the international academic and research communities. The distinguishing feature of the series is its broad focus that draws on basic and applied research from across the globe under the umbrella of SEMPRE's distinctive mission, which is to promote and ensure coherent and symbiotic links between education, music and psychology research.

Graham Welch
Institute of Education, University of London, UK
Adam Ockelford
Roehampton University, UK
Ian Cross
University of Cambridge, UK

Preface

One of the very first thoughts to enter an editor's mind at the early stages of book production is, 'what title best expresses its aims and scope?' In this respect, the chosen title, *The Act of Musical Composition: Studies in the Creative Process* was not long in gestation, since the very earliest intention was to focus upon the 'in the moment' process of musical composition: the real-time creative act of making a musical product.

Little attention has been paid to this particular form of musical creativity other than directly through biographical and autobiographical narrative and anecdote, or indirectly through analytical and theoretical approaches, and, whilst not attempting to deal with the vast domain of human creativity, it is hoped that the reader will observe in this edited volume a range of experts grappling with notions of creative thinking in the context of musical composition. As such, there is no single view of musical creativity offered here, nor any attempt to construct a global theory or model: each author presents an intriguing facet of compositional creativity, which may be described in terms of cognitive aspects or, for example, an environmental/social/cultural aspect of creative thinking. As editor, I have welcomed this diverse multi-view approach, since single-view approaches, as Robert Sternberg suggests, have led to a narrow and unsatisfactory understanding of creativity. He comments that 'the cognitive work on creativity has tended to ignore or downplay the personality and social system, and the social–personality approaches have tended to have little or nothing to say about the mental representations and processes underlying creativity'.[1]

Such a multi-perspective view allows the reader, as Wyndham Thomas mentions in his introduction to a related text, to be able to read chapters in any order without 'affecting the cumulative experience … [and] … the old cliché of the whole being more than the sum of its parts is true … regardless of how the parts are assembled'.[2] The 11 chapters here represent a move away from the traditional experimental paradigm; the methodological stance adopted in many of these chapters reflects what Persson and Robson describe as the researcher providing the opportunity to 'meet the musicians in an environment where they feel at ease, and

---

[1]   Robert J. Sternberg and Todd I. Lubart, 'The concept of creativity: prospects and paradigms'. In R. Sternberg (ed.), *Handbook of Creativity* (Cambridge: Cambridge University Press, 2003), 9.

[2]   Wyndham Thomas (ed.), *Composition, Performance, Reception: Studies in the Creative Process in Music* (Aldershot: Ashgate, 1998).

listen to what they have to say about their own music-making'.[3] Thus, some of the underlying research stances here include the voice of the composer, disrupting the conventional isolation between a researcher and their 'subject' and, in some cases the voice of the critical observer/author is also the voice of the composer/artist.

To a greater or lesser extent, the existing literature in this still young field of study tends to sit in the genre-context of 'classical music'; however, the chapters in this book offer not only a mix of theoretical and empirical approaches, and engagement with digital technology as both a compositional and an analytical tool, but also a diversity of compositional genres described in case-studies and autobiographical accounts – contemporary classical music, music for video-games, popular song, jazz improvisation, turntablist composition and algorithmic computer-based composition.

The book opens with Nicolas Donin's chapter proposing a methodological approach that hybridises activity/observational analysis and genetic analysis – sketch studies of unfolding compositions. Donin outlines a series of coordinated studies that share a particular methodology, namely, the reconstruction of compositional process through a composer's 'traces' – manuscripts, sketches and digital elements, together with situation simulation videotaped interviews. Donin offers that, 'within a given window of time, particularly if it contains a sufficiently varied accumulation of data, the significant characteristics of a composer's cognition can be identified … within a determined physical and cultural environment, personal history and socio-historical context'.

Donin's study of contemporary composers' compositional practice is counterpointed against Aaron Kozbelt's chapter, which highlights the variability in the ways that different major classical composers have approached the problem of musical composition. He links his discussion to current theories of creativity, specifically the traditional distinction between generating and elaborating musical ideas and recent typological distinctions of conceptual vs experimental innovation. Using qualitative and quantitative methods Kozbelt offers a convergence onto a theoretical account that relates individual differences at two very different levels of analysis: the nature of individuals' creative process and their lifespan trajectories.

The study of extra-musical influences upon the compositional process is taken up by Freya Bailes and Laura Bishop, who suggest that our current understanding of conscious, endogenous representations of music – musical imagery – is rudimentary, and that the study of its relationship to imagination and creative musical practice has barely begun. This chapter reviews psychological understandings of the role of musical imagery in musical imagination, firstly as a phenomenon limited by both our musical experience and our cognitive mechanisms and, secondly, as a creative tool, in which re-presentations are manipulated to new ends. A case-study of occurrences of everyday musical imagery offers a window into the seemingly spontaneous mental generation of musical patterns in ordinary life.

---

[3]   Roland Persson and Colin Robson, 'The limits of experimentation: on researching music and musical settings', *Psychology of Music*, 23/1 (1995), 39–47, at 42.

Bailes and Bishop suggest that the act of musical composition is not a disembodied, de-contextualised cognitive function, and this is considered in the following chapter by Steve Dillon and Andrew Brown, who discuss the notion of a socially constructed, embedded worldview, where the composer's life world, constructed through personal, social and cultural contexts, is incorporated into what they term a 'meaningful engagement matrix'. Notions of meaningful compositional engagement and a resultant taxonomy are based on interviews and observations of creative processes with five professional composers.

The distinctive (and often idiosyncratic) nature of composition is articulated in the chapter by Pam Burnard, who explores questions around how diverse types of music creativities are recognised and practised by composers. In exploring three characterisations of creative practice, Burnard distinguishes between the different meanings of musical creativity as they have developed and been historically mythologised. The compositional practices featured in this chapter include those of a turntablist (DJ) composer, a contemporary classical composer and a media composer, and Burnard concludes with an argument for expanding the notion of musical creativities, for widening practice in school-based learning, and for radically rethinking professional music training.

In many respects, much of the related empirical work to date has assumed the composer to exist as a lone, autonomous creative, disconnected from and disengaged with their social and cultural world. Joe Bennett challenges such a notion in his chapter by exploring the creation of the Anglo-American commercial popular song in collaborative contexts, a compositional practice that has generally only received attention in terms of individual songwriters. Bennett outlines the tightly constrained musical form of the popular song, and in doing so he returns to one of the themes within this book – that of determining an appropriate methodology for exploring the compositional process – through the presentation of a case-study in which he situates himself as researcher/co-participant in the collaborative song-writing process.

Knowledge about the creative process has increased dramatically over the last century, with a burgeoning literature on creativity[4] together with a growing amount of research on the composing process.[5] Despite this, Shira Lee Katz argues in her chapter that there is still a gap in understanding the prototypical ways in which musical compositions come to fruition. What role do non-musical factors play? Are composers even aware of the factors that influence their work? If composers do employ non-musical models as they compose, what is the role of this material in their work? In other words, there has been little investigation

---

[4]   See, for example, Robert S. Albert and Mark A. Runco's overview 'A history of research on creativity'. In: R. Sternberg (ed.), *Handbook of Creativity* (Cambridge: Cambridge University Press, 2003). Albert and Runco describe the present research field as 'explosive'.

[5]   See Oscar Odena and Graham Welch, 'A generative model of teachers' thinking on musical creativity', *Psychology of Music*, 37/4 (2009), 416–44.

around the factors that inspire composers or about how initial ideas are synthesised as compositions develop. Katz observes three composers drawing inspiration from content domains characterised by strong visual elements which are identified as providing a structural roadmap for their compositions.

The role of improvisation within the compositional process has not yet received a great deal of attention from researchers, and in their chapter, Simon Rose and Raymond MacDonald argue that there is a need to reassess how improvisation aligns with notions of composition. The participants in Rose and MacDonald's study speak of forming what they term 'real-time composition' through the embodied act of improvisation. Employing an idiographic, hermeneutic approach by means of interpretive phenomenological analysis, themes are distilled from the analysis of text from 10 interviews with experienced improvisers, including socio-musical location, learning in improvisation, autonomous expression and self-assertion, and spontaneous composition. This chapter thus contributes to the broadening understanding of the significant, developing relationship between musical composition and improvisation.

At this point the theme of the book moves towards aspects of human creativity and computer-based music composition, with three chapters from Eduardo Miranda, Geraint Wiggins and David Cope, who interrogate quite differing aspects of this more recent phenomenon. Paradoxically, despite the fact that computing technology is now ubiquitous in a number of creative tasks, the notion of using computers to generate music is largely associated with adjectives such as artificial, mechanical, or even non-musical or anti-creative.

Nonetheless, the emergence of computer technology is increasingly affording composers unprecedented levels of symbolic processing power and automation. Whereas this is beginning to impact in the compositional practice of a number of composers, one can also observe an increasing number of composers who despise the notion of using a computer as a partner in the creative process. Eduardo Miranda argues that the methods of composing with pencil on a blank sheet of paper and through computer-based algorithms are not incompatible, but are manifestations of creative processes that have become increasingly polarised in our brain through evolutionary history. This chapter draws from research into the brain sciences to articulate the notion that computer technology enhances such polarisation, whereby objective formalisms and subjective metaphors can complement each other in creative compositional processes. Miranda draws upon examples of his own compositions, which use computational models of evolutionary post-Darwinian processes.

Reflecting a theme that other authors have made explicit or implicit, Geraint Wiggins suggests that we need to demystify creativity in order to better understand what happens in the act of musical composition, and offers what he terms a hypothetical mechanistic cognitive framework in which musical inspiration can take place through both conscious and non-conscious processes. Wiggins argues that situating a simulation of music-compositional creativity in the context of higher-level processes that simulate conscious reasoning may ultimately lead to computers that can compose as well as a better understanding of how humans create. He concludes, however, in the context of applying such frameworks to computational rule-based systems, that it is hard to see how a rule-based system can start from a blank page, and it is this idea that informs much of the final chapter, by David Cope.

Cope argues that rules, tactics and strategies (RTS) represent some of the most important basic processes used by composers when they compose music: rules, whether conscious or not, constrain the number and type of choices available. Tactics solve immediate problems created by such rules and provide successful local control of the compositional environment; strategies then involve more global goals indicating where – and to some extent how – a composer can achieve these goals. Since RTS seems more typically and traditionally associated with games, Cope begins this chapter by presenting a computer program showing how RTS can be used to successfully play board games (mathematical game theory) and follows this by using the same program to compose effective tonal counterpoint (musical game theory). By way of example, he concludes the chapter with an overview of the processes involved in the production of a movement for string quartet.

In conclusion, the breadth of the chapters in this book suggests that it would be unwise to attempt to offer a single over-riding theme, or a superordinate theory of the compositional process. However, the diverse multi-perspective view offered by these 14 authors represents a further and significant contribution to our understanding of this wonderfully unique aspect of human creativity.

Dave Collins
July 2012

Chapter 1
Empirical and Historical Musicologies of Compositional Processes: Towards a Cross-fertilisation

Nicolas Donin

The study of compositional processes is often deemed a poor relative of the psychology of music. Yet, if included in the general domain of musicology, would this judgment continue to hold? One particular branch of musicology – sketch studies – has devoted itself over the last half-century to documenting the creative processes of many nineteenth- and twentieth-century composers. These reconstructions, being almost exclusively based on archived collections containing the material traces of a composer's activity, seldom, if ever, include commentary from the composer or any other real-time-generated data. Consequently, they rarely bear any resemblance to the results of an empirical study of a present-day composer's creative process. Nevertheless, the nature of these two types of study is essentially the same: a complex creative activity involving various cognitive skills and emotions, embedding technical and (nowadays) technological artefacts, which then produce tangible public outcomes (like a consistent musical text) that go on to become part of a culture, influencing the subsequent creative cognition of other composers.

Can empirical and historical musicologies merge, or at the very least confront their respective findings regarding creative processes, despite highly differentiated sets of approaches? In this chapter I will plead for a cross-fertilisation, and demonstrate how these subfields of musicology might establish a common ground upon which concepts, results or methods could be exchanged. I would propose that, in order for knowledge about musical creativity to move forward, it is necessary to imagine how a general musicology of the compositional process could benefit from both a historical approach and an empirical one. I shall begin by discussing the difficulties faced by those who seek cognitive analyses of present-day composers that are comparable in detail to the ones found in history regarding great musicians of the past. I will then present a research method based upon musicology's historical and empirical branches, and further elaborate upon the types of knowledge such a method might offer. I will conclude this chapter with the presentation of a collective project in which an integrative epistemological approach is used to study the creative processes of the past and present.

Studying Compositional Practices in the Real World?

Prior to discussing the present, let us briefly focus on the past. In line with nineteenth-century philological tradition, musicologists have sought to identify and compile every written trace left behind by great composers of the past. Critical editions of masterworks, *Urtext* scores, and the publication and commentary of Beethoven's sketchbooks are all the results of such a heritage. Sketch studies of composer's studies truly gained momentum as a musicological discipline in the 1970s in the United States.[1] These comprehensive genetic studies are similar in aim and in method to *critique génétique* (genetic criticism) studies taking place at the same time in literature studies, in France and elsewhere. Both seek to define a corpus of *avant-textes* or pre-texts (sketches, drafts, etc.).[2] The most successful of these studies, from a musical analysis standpoint, demonstrate how elements of the compositional process determined qualities such as the coherence or the novelty of a final opus; each draft, deletion or legible alternative is then interpreted as a possible window into both the composer's mental processes and the variation space surrounding each musical element included in the final work.

However, a model of creative cognition (defining its possible patterns, time-scales, variability, balance of divergent and convergent thinking, etc.) governs even the most limited rendering of a sequence of compositional actions. As long as this model remains implicit (and undoubtedly linked to the analyst's personal experience as both a musician and a writer), no serious discussion can afford to satisfy questions linked to cognition, and the study of the creative process keeps focusing on philology and music analysis . In order to analyse composition as a creative act, documents drawn from the creative process should not only be considered with respect to the final musical product; they should also be viewed as temporary components of a cognitive act-in-progress, as they interact within a specific, constantly evolving environment. A number of authors, from Bahle to Harvey,[3] have sought to use accounts of past creative processes in order to build models of creativity. Although we shall not describe this approach in detail, we must stress the difficulties inherent to any secondary data analysis that

---

[1]   See 'Studies in Musical Genesis and Structure' series, published from 1985 by Clarendon Press/Oxford University Press.

[2]   Jed Deppman, Daniel Ferrer and Michael Groden (eds), *Genetic Criticism: Texts and Avant-textes* (Philadelphia, PA, 2004). Two issues of *Genesis: Revue Internationale de Critique Génétique* were devoted to music: 4 (1993) and 31 (2010). Genetic criticism and musicology have began coming together recently, see William Kinderman and Joseph E. Jones (eds), *Genetic Criticism and the Creative Process: Essays from Music, Literature, and Theater* (Rochester, NY, 2009); and, currently in preparation, Nicolas Donin, Almuth Grésillon and Jean-Louis Lebrave (eds), *Genèses musicales*.

[3]   Julius Bahle, *Der musikalische Schaffensprozess. Psychologie der schöpferischen Erlebnis- und Antriebsformen* (Leipzig, 1936). Jonathan Harvey, *Music and Inspiration*, ed. Michael Downes (London, 1999).

involves verbal materials heterogeneously collected and situated within a variety of cultural contexts (musical, historical, geographical). The models of creative cognition emerging from this approach are severely limited in scope, coherence and extensibility.

Despite its abundance, documentary evidence alone is unable to provide all the necessary insight into mental processes, so it seems natural to shift our attention towards present-day composers. However, as little of their work is conserved in libraries or museums and they themselves often avoid divulging their own creative processes, their practice often appears even more mysterious than that of past composers.[4] How then might one collect significant data regarding their compositional processes? Both an oft-cited chapter in John Sloboda's text, *The Musical Mind*, devoted to composition and improvisation, and an essay from the same author[5] concluded that the psychology of composition is fraught with difficulties. Composition was deemed too complex and personal to realistically be subjected to a scientific research programme. More recently, Collins's exhaustive literature review[6] illustrated the scarcity of work carried out in the past century: only a few studies have presented the work of expert composers, featuring most often the compositional outputs of students and novices. Although Sloboda's resistance is an extreme example, in many case studies the mystique of the lone creator, not to be disturbed under any circumstance, is seemingly difficult to relinquish. This seems odd, at a time when musicology seeks to deconstruct the founding myths of western musical tradition.

Nonetheless, there are some exceptions: a small number of relatively unknown studies have been carried out across a variety of disciplinary backgrounds, most often unaware of each other's existence. These include Thomas and Mion's seminal study, at the GRM,[7] which focused on the compositional process of Parmeggiani's *De Natura Sonorum*, a study inspired by Piagetian psychology and Nattiez's musical semiology, in addition to Jean-Pierre Richard's (literary) thematic critique.[8] Several years later, another GRM

---

[4]   These traces are tricky as: (1) they are mostly personal documents, private in nature and likely to be used in subsequent creative processes; (2) composers use digital technologies for a large part of their compositional work, thus changing the nature and permanence of such data; (3) contemporary composers are more than ever aware of the academic attention their creative practice attracts.

[5]   John A. Sloboda, *The Musical Mind: The Cognitive Psychology of Music* (Oxford, 1985), chap. 4; and 'Do psychologists have anything useful to say about composition?', in *Analyse et création musicales, Actes du Troisième Congrès Européen d'Analyse Musicale, Montpellier, 1995* (Paris, 2001), 69–78.

[6]   David Collins, 'A synthesis process model of creative thinking in music composition', *Psychology of Music*, 33/2 (2005), 193–216.

[7]   Groupe de Recherches Musicales, Paris.

[8]   Philippe Mion, Jean-Jacques Nattiez and Jean-Christophe Thomas, *L'envers d'une œuvre – De natura sonorum de Bernard Parmegiani* (Paris, 1982).

study by Delalande, compared the creative processes of composers working with identical musical tasks and identical compositional environments.[9] Surveys led at the University of Sheffield from questionnaires and activity analysis (inspired by cognitive ergonomics) focused on the role of computers at different stages of the composition process.[10] We also see Roger Reynolds's collaboration with a team of researchers led by Stephen McAdams on the topic of both the perception and composition of his *The Angel of Death*.[11] A number of composers have also chosen to analyse their own individual creative processes. Choosing to forsake more traditional styles of theoretical writing or aesthetic manifestos, the few published texts more closely resemble compositional journals,[12] essays[13] or occasionally a combination of both.[14]

The scarcity of such attempts should come as no surprise given that they are inevitably confronted by the evanescence and irreducibility of the creative act. As Pascal Dusapin, a noted contemporary composer, describes in his inaugural address before the Collège de France:

> How might one bear witness to musical creation as it took place? Can we indeed convey a composition-in-progress? I do not believe so. Composing has taught me that the invention of sounds is a phenomenon one cannot distil into an exposé. (…) Describing the procedure through which a work of music evolves cannot capture the essence of the creative act as it occurs. It is only a description.[15]

Dusapin's choice of vocabulary – 'convey a composition-in-progress' or 'describe the procedure' – voluntarily and accurately mirrors the cold and distanced posture musicologists tend to adopt when discussing particular composition processes. Nevertheless, such an approach is not inevitable: one might imagine *analysing* an *activity*, instead of 'convey(ing)' a 'procedure'. To 'analyse' is to use relevant criteria in breaking something down, in order to understand the logic that governed its construction. To do so with regards to an

---

[9]   François Delalande, 'Towards an Analysis of Compositional Strategies' [first published 1989], *Circuit: musiques contemporaines*, 17/1 (2007), 11–26.

[10]   See, for instance, Ralf Nuhn, Barry Eaglestone, Nigel Ford and Mark Clowes, 'Do composition systems support creativity?—An evaluation', in *Proceedings of the International Computer Music Conference* (La Havane, 2001), 22–5.

[11]   Stephen McAdams, 'Problem-solving strategies in music composition: a case study', *Music Perception*, 21/3 (2004), 391–429.

[12]   Robert H.P. Platz, *TOP Skizzentagebuch*, ed. Stefan Fricke (Saarbruck, 2009).

[13]   Robert Saxton, 'The process of composition from detection to confection', in Wyndham Thomas (ed.), *Composition – Performance – Reception. Studies in the Creative Process in Music* (Aldershot, 1998), 1–16.

[14]   Jean-Luc Hervé, L'image sonore: regard sur la création musicale, PhD dissertation (Lille, 1999).

[15]   Pascal Dusapin, *Composer. Musique, paradoxe, flux* (Paris, 2007), 21.

'activity' distinguishes it from a closed procedure, as the former presupposes an free, open-ended and hardly formalisable process.

These difficulties are further complicated by researchers' attempts to strip their object of any subjectivity and avoid provoking a disturbance in the creative activity, otherwise known as, according to Dusapin, the centipede syndrome: 'as soon as this small crawling creature begins to question the mechanics of its own motion it ceases to move forward'.[16] Similar statements exist in both the empirical literature and other composers' writings, and their concerns seem legitimate. If the production of knowledge about composition implies its disruption or even its failure, then one might understand a reticence to develop such knowledge. Yet, this frightening danger may be no more than an illusion. In any case, one thing is certain: all composers do not value this emphasis on spontaneity vs reflexivity, which essentially likens them to animals. For instance, Jonathan Harvey believes that artistic activity, as opposed to a craftsmanship, possesses a specific dynamic, which begins with the raised awareness of what was once only a semi-conscious thought and leads to the latter's subsequent development.[17] Therefore, if the phenomenon described by Dusapin exists, it is neither documented nor widespread.

An approach that accounts for the epistemological and methodological aspects of such a dilemma remains to be determined. Obviously, the scientific approach and the studied activity are both implicitly subject to interference when the composer is involved in collecting data in order to produce specific knowledge of his/her own activity, known for its private and tacit nature. However, interferences between the observer and the observed occur often in both the social sciences and the humanities, as well as in experimental 'hard' science. Therefore, the implementation of guidelines meant to control and evaluate this obstacle is essential to the empirical study of composition as an activity. In other words, composers and analysts need to establish observation methods that provide reliable data without crippling or distorting the creative compositional process.

In their introduction to *Musical Creativity*, Deliège and Richelle point out that the refusal to approach creativity as anything other than an inherent global aptitude measurable through standard empirical studies involving a group of subjects has deprived the cognitive sciences of information about this very phenomenon.

> It was assumed [by Guilford] that a special aptitude, labelled *creativity*, is measurable *per se*. The obvious fact that creativity is always in one specific domain, using a certain material, resulting in some type of product, was ignored.

---

[16]   Ibid., 27.

[17]   [Irène Deliège and Jonathan Harvey], 'How can we understand creativity in a composer's work? A Conversation between Irène Deliège and Jonathan Harvey', in Irène Deliège and Geraint A. Wiggins (eds), *Musical Creativity. Multidisciplinary Research in Theory and Practice* (New York, 2006), 397–404, at 398.

> As a consequence, individuals with high scores in tests of creativity were reputed
> to be creative, irrespective of their creative activities in real life.[18]

In order to reduce the existing gap between creativity as studied in a laboratory
and real-life creative activity, these same authors suggest that we 'look at those
behaviours that eventually lead to novelty in a given field of arts or science' and
'account for them by identifying the processes involved'; hence the authors'
proposal to 'get rid of *creativity* and look at *creative acts*'.[19]

Such a proposal offers new perspectives that can intertwine, on the one
hand, psychological research which focuses on the general creative potential of
a population of 'ordinary' subjects across a variety of competences, and, on the
other hand, specialised fields (literary criticism, art history, musicology) that only
study the life and work of history's most noteworthy creators. We endorse Deliège
and Richelle's will to transgress, or at the very least blur, the line between the study
of induced (and presumably replicable) phenomena and that of socio-historically
situated ones, selected because of their exceptional nature – a difficult task since
epistemological doubt occurs on either side of this line. Even in literary genetic
criticism, we have yet to witness a large study devoted to monitoring the creative
process in real time or selecting creative cognition as its target. If we expect to
develop a scientific discourse that justly reflects the wealth and complexity of
composition, then we must free ourselves of existing psychological, musicological
and artistic *doxa*.

Delineating Creative Cognition

In light of the aforementioned challenges, what methodological framework and
what type of composer–researcher interaction would best encourage the emergence
of suitable knowledge of a composition's cognitive logic? Sigmund Koch and his
Boston University Aesthetic Research Project[20] offer an interesting proposal. In
the 1980s, through a series of extensive interviews with artists, the psychologist-
led studies were devoted to the common characteristics of creativity across the arts
and supporting some rather unorthodox – at the time – ideas on the psychology of
creativity:

> First, artists have a large repertoire of tacit knowledge concerning their
> creative activity, including the genesis of skills, modes of working, and artistic

---

[18]   Deliège, I. and Richelle, M., 'Prelude: the spectrum of musical creativity', in
Deliège and Wiggins, *Musical Creativity*, 2.

[19]   Ibid.

[20]   See Margery B. Franklin, 'The artist speaks: Sigmund Koch on aesthetics and
creative work', *American Psychologist*, 56/5 (2001), 445–52. Virgil Thompson and Milton
Babbitt were among the composers encountered.

objectives. Second the view from "inside" – that is, the artist's account – must be privileged as a source. Third, under appropriate conditions, artists can render explicit considerable portions of their tacit knowledge; although they may not spontaneously engage in the kind of differentiated description requisite for advancing understanding into creative work, they can be guided to do so through informed, focused, and sympathetic questioning. Fourth, […] other methods do not provide material for the kind of fine-grained experiential analysis that is the prime path to genuine understanding of creative processes.[21]

Koch devoted four, two-hour interview sessions to each artist-participant, which he prepared for by immersing himself in their work. Although he had a pool of questions on hand, he expected the interviews to more closely resemble casual conversation. As opposed to being a 'subject', Koch viewed the artist as a collaborator, hence his preference for the term 'research conversation' instead of 'interview'.[22]

Unlike Koch's approach (whose originality and epistemological novelty are of greater interest than the scientific results it provided), a qualitative study of creative cognition requires more than just a timely and knowledgeable interviewer in order to render valid results. It demands concrete, material and singular evidence of the activity in question, such that even the manner in which those involved in the inquest refer to it is transformed. In other words, a methodological aim is to avoid the random digressions and trivialities that often surface when composers are asked to broadly discuss such an intense, strategic and heterogeneous activity. In the kind of subjective encounter favoured by Koch, the exchange is based upon a degree of intuition and persuasion, and it does not allow of silent introspection. The focus is then hardly on the composer's creative activity as it happens during the making of his works. Instead of a 'research conversation' (as Koch defined it), where great minds meet and exchange freely, we imagine a collaborative inquiry into creative activity that rests upon a foundation of relevant artefacts pertaining to that activity. Soliciting both the composer's memory and point of view, then, does not necessarily imply that one should take his or her word, nor assume his or her omniscience (or omnireminiscence).

A systematic and rational approach to compositional cognition requires a certain level of openness with regards to the essence and the internal organisation of a composer's activity. In order to reveal the cognitive categories in the compositional process – from the classic distinction between convergent and divergent thought to modular notions of problem-solving, or even the model of the creative process as a series of discrete stages from incubation to the revision of drafted copy, the data collection methods need not contribute to an experimental manipulation that would isolate variables in order to provoke anticipated phenomena. Cognitive categories must, however, withstand being

---

[21]   Ibid., 448.

[22]   Ibid.

tested against the collected data. The framework that governs the researcher and composer's collaboration should match the studied activity's specific internal logic even as it unfolds. This type of reconstruction requires the composer to verbalise every aspect (including the implicit) of every stage of the creative process under scrutiny. Although this last condition appears impossible in real time (expressing thoughts/actions out loud while working),[23] it should be feasible *a posteriori*. Such an undertaking is at risk of becoming the sort of retrospective self-interpretation frequently found in interviews, in which the composer might be tempted to depend on an oft-repeated representation of self, whose elaboration began with his or her professional career. The verbalisation should derive from a coherent re-enactment of parts (or essential components) of the creative process within a realistic simulation of the creator's work environment, including every available trace of the past compositional activity. When such conditions are met a 'situation simulation interview based on documentation'[24] can then take place. As an expression of the successive moments, operations and situations that substantiate cognitive and artistic characteristics, the collected data allow us to reconstruct – up to a certain point – the compositional process. Subsequent analysis may explore questions such as: what does the creative subject select from their environment (a private, personal work space)? What impact do their actions have on this environment. How does this in turn affect subsequent compositional situations? Can recurring traits in their activity be identified? To what extent do they manoeuvre their own activity?

Such an approach would be a hybrid of two distinct fields: activity analysis and sketch studies (genetic analysis). Specifically, methodological and epistemological elements stemming from genetic criticism, musical analysis, psychology of creativity, ergonomics and cognitive anthropology are selected and brought together. The implementation of such an aggregate was the focus of a study of the internationally renowned composer Philippe Leroux and, led by Jacques Theureau and this chapter's author,[25] over several years, it examined the composer's actions/

---

[23]   McAdams (2004) refuses to consider speaking-aloud as a possible method toward elucidating the creative process, whereas Collins, ('Real-time tracking of the creative music composition process', *Digital Creativity Journal*, 18/4 (2007), 253) noted the success of immediately retrospective verbal reporting alongside computer-based musical data collection.

[24]   Nicolas Donin and Jacques Theureau, 'Theoretical and methodological issues related to long term creative cognition: the case of musical composition', *Cognition Technology and Work*, 9/4 (2007), 233–51.

[25]   Researcher Jacques Theureau at the *Centre National de la Recherche Scientifique* (now retired) was one of the first to introduce cognitive anthropology into his field of origin, ergonomics. In 2003, we cofounded the team *Analyse des pratiques musicales*, within which we designed and led a number of collaborative projects focused on contemporary musical activities (see http://apm.ircam.fr/).

cognitions based upon two of his key works: *Voi(rex)* and *Apocalypsis*.[26] We shall briefly present its methodology and its results, as well as its contribution to the main issues at the heart of this chapter.

A Study with Philippe Leroux

The first study spanned from 2003 to 2004 and focused on Leroux's *Voi(rex)*, for voice, ensemble and electronics, composed during 2002 and first played in January 2003. The research aimed to reconstruct the work's compositional process based on specific elements and traces – manuscripts, studies, sketches, drafts and digital elements that the composer had kept. After the event data collection enabled us to document the process at its own pace: in-depth interviews, carried out around a table, replicated Leroux's usual work environment (all available traces[27] were duplicated and laid out identically to his studio), which included his own computer (equipped with the same files and programs) and his speakers. In this 'real-world' environment the composer was then able to recall the compositional approaches he had progressively implemented while writing the score. Each session contained three phases: firstly, pre-texts involved in the passage or movement in question were extracted; secondly, each was dated and commented on according to the passage's state at the onset of the period of compositional activity considered; thirdly, the succeeding compositional operations whose impact on the initial state transformed the considered passage into its final version were reconstructed. The situation simulation interviews, which lasted approximately five hours per movement (five movements), were videotaped and transcribed (the transcription included the verbalisations as well as (a) areas within the compositional sketches the composer pointed to, (b) his gestures and singing, and (c) other useful information with regards to his activity and the terms of his recollection). Based on these transcriptions, a detailed reconstruction of the composer's 'course of action'[28] became possible.

---

[26]   See Nicolas Donin and Jacques Theureau, 'L'activité de composition musicale comme exploitation/construction de situations. Une anthropologie cognitive du travail de Philippe Leroux', *Intellectica*, 48/1–2 (2008), 175–205, in terms of cognitive studies; and Nicolas Donin, 'Genetic criticism and cognitive anthropology: a reconstruction of Philippe Leroux's compositional process for *Voi(rex)*', in Kinderman and Jones, *Genetic Criticism*, 192–215, in terms of musical studies.

[27]   Sketches, drafts, computer files, marks in a personal calendar, printed email exchanges with performers, and the manuscript.

[28]   Jacques Theureau, 'Course-of-action analysis and course-of-action centered design', in Erik Hollnagel (ed.), *Handbook of Cognitive Task Design* (Mahwah, NJ, 2003), 55–81; and Jacques Theureau, *Le cours d'action: méthode développée* (Toulouse, 2006).

A second study focused on the genesis of Leroux's *Apocalypsis* (from 2004 to 2006). In this case, the compositional unfolding of the work was regularly monitored (as opposed to retrospectively) from the project's onset to the score's completion. According to the previously established mode of data collection, both paper and video recordings were regularly collected over the course of the creative process. This allowed us to document the process in much greater detail than the previous study with an interview every month and a half over a period of 20 months). Two aspects distinguished the resulting data from the study of *Voi(rex)*: firstly, at our request the composer kept a journal, which was then used as the basis for our interviews; secondly, facsimiles of all of the composer's working documents were made during each session. It became possible to chart the evolution of most drafts and sketches as they related to the day-by-day details of the creative process.

In each of these studies the timeline of the creative process was used to organise the transcribed interviews. Based upon the latter, we can determine recurring issues (for example, preparing a specific movement, drafting the general outline, working on a specific instrument or parameter), together with methods of handling compositional matter (self-borrowing with or without variants, filing elements according to emerging categories, imagining contrasted notational implementations of a musical idea). Within a given window of time, particularly if it contains a sufficiently varied accumulation of data, the significant characteristics of composer's cognition can be identified in accordance with both its dynamic and its situated aspects (it manifests and transforms itself based upon a determined physical and cultural environment, personal history and socio-historical context). Specific categories, inspired by Peircian semiotics, allow for a fine-grained 'course of action' analysis. These include the 'experimental unit' (that is, course-of-experience units as identified by the subject), the 'anticipatory structure', the '*representamen*' (significant disruption occurring within the anticipatory structure) and the 'referent' (previous knowledge and experience the subject calls upon in the considered action/perception).[29] These categories help to highlight a number of different types of knowledge-in-action: from implicit to the explicit, from unsubstantiated to confirmed, from unconscious to voluntary. This approach offers both a cognitive and a musicological perspective on data, from collection to analysis.

What have we learned from these endeavours? Naturally, to begin with, there is a wealth of knowledge crucial to the understanding of the analytical and aesthetic qualities of Leroux's work and art, for instance, the marked focus of his strategic considerations on the opening sounds within a movement or a whole work, as compared with his relatively lesser concern for the ending; the impact of the calligraphy of letters of the alphabet on the melodic writing of several passages in *Voi(rex)* and on the design of the structure of *Apocalysis* as a whole; the importance of work on the sequencer in generating polyphonic material intended

---

[29]   See Theureau, *Le cours d'action*, chap. III–6.

for staff notation, to be ultimately played by the instrumental ensemble; and, as regards musical form, variety and innovation primacy over directionality and the processes' immediate perception.

The in-depth analysis of the creative process of specific parts of the work metonymically provides, without being compared with other occurrences, the key to understanding the composer's cognition at a more global level. Such was the case for the reconstruction of the obstacles encountered by Leroux in completing *Voi(rex)*'s fourth movement. This had been formally designed according to a graphic pattern that defined a series of blocks and the transitions between them, each intended to contain distinct, specified musical matter. A contradiction between the categories of musical material programmed by the composer and the contrasts he sought locally within a relatively long section appeared from the first attempts to implement this formal notion. Although there were seven categories of musical material at hand stemming from the drafts, the composer established a binary opposition between two instantiations of one of the seven categories, thereby favouring a strong local contrast. This decision to stray from his predetermined typology and radically enhance his palette diminished the chances of the listener identifying the seven categories (meant to reappear in the same fashion throughout the movement). At a compositional level, the inclusion of such differences in the movement's realised, as opposed to planned, form implied at least two types of consequences: first, they acted retrospectively on the drafted outline and the terms of its fulfilment; second, they increased the possibility for variations in the way the composer would implement his predetermined musical categories.[30] Beyond the questions raised by the analysis of the categorisation process undertaken by Leroux, we are faced with the issue previously identified by Julius Bahle, a pioneer of the psychological study of musical composition, namely that, during the act of composition, interactions and adjustments occur that bear upon both the planning process of an abstract entity and local shaping of the musical material.[31]

Toward Broader Issues in Compositional Cognition

Beyond demonstrating properties specific to Leroux's individual cognition/ action, the analysis revealed features that might apply to the activity of composition in general. Some seemed particularly noteworthy as they appeared repeatedly throughout the data. For example, one could clearly distinguish

---

[30] See a detailed account in Nicolas Donin and Jacques Theureau, 'La composition d'un mouvement de *Voi(rex)*, de son idée formelle à sa structure', *L'Inouï, revue de l'Ircam*, 2 (2006), 62–85.

[31] Julius Bahle, *Eingebung und Tat im musikalischen Schaffen. Ein Beitrag zur Psychologie der Entwicklungs- und Schaffensgesetze Schöpferischer Menschen* (Leipzig, 1939), 292–319.

between a preparation period (during which musical ideas are developed alongside the technical constraints that define the projected final work) and a writing period (during which a musical manuscript is written and computer files are produced). By Leroux, these periods are comparable in length. Composition throughout these two successive periods of preparation and writing reveals itself to be an activity that first *constructs* the elements of compositional situations and then *exploits* these situations.[32] Although construction commands the preparation period, it continues during the writing period; similarly, although the exploitation of compositional situations is decisive during the writing period, it takes root in the preparation period. There are also phenomena specific to the area where these two periods merged. For instance, when the comprehensive review of the main sections' important drafts took place, we noticed that connections between scattered ideas were created or strengthened, particular elements gained importance (or became part of another element), audio files were placed into a ranked order and some were occasionally even sequenced as they were replayed.

Let us discuss further the transition from preparation to writing. Requirements and expectations from the former are entered into the movement's drafts and formal outlines, and become *writing guidelines*. However, these are often steeped in contradictions and partial redundancies and should thus not be seen as a set of criteria the composer might simply follow in order to proceed with his writing. Instead they more closely resemble a series of stimulants that allow for new composition problems to surface during writing. Therefore, although the work's form has often been previously laid out in detailed plans, it may also be partly determined during a given writing situation. This type of phenomenon would be complicated to analyse, or even detect, if our experimental system were based upon a theory wherein action is viewed as a chain of simple tasks leading towards a goal. We feel closest to situated action theories, in conformity with the distinction between two 'views of action' once put into words by Lucy Suchman:

> The first, adopted, by most researchers in artificial intelligence, locates the organization and significance of human action in underlying plans. On the planning view, plans are prerequisite to and prescribe action, at every level of détail. (...) The alternative view (...) is that while the course of action can always be projected or reconstructed in terms of prior intentions and typical situations, the prescriptive significance of intentions for situated action is inherently vague.[33]

---

[32]   See Donin and Theureau, 'L'activité de composition comme exploitation/ construction de situations'.

[33]   Lucy Suchman, *Plans and Situated Actions. The problem of Human-Machine Communication* (Cambridge, 1987).

Like Suchman, we believe here that, although plans unquestionably contribute to action, they do so only as elements of a cognitive repertoire: 'plans are resources for situated action, but do not in any strong sense determine its course'.[34]

Other related phenomena with the potential for extrapolation may also be mentioned. Let us consider one example. The numerous ties that bind the preparation period to the writing period rest upon time dedicated, in the latter period, to *(re) reading/(re)listening* – inner listening to composed pages, obviously, as well as listening to sound sequences and patches on the computer. There are different modes of (re)reading/(re)listening (which we will refer to as 'reviewing').[35] Firstly, Leroux's plotting out of the content of the score's forthcoming bars implies a recent review of those already written. Reviewing also takes place at *predefined strategic* moments, such as the beginning of composition of a movement or a movement section. Such reviewing considers previously written pages (which it validates), as well as drafts and notes related to the present (whose significance is updated with respect to the current state of the work); it leads to measures such as the recalculation of certain sections' and ensuing movements' scheduled lengths, as well as modified details (pitches, rhythms, and so on) in previously written passages. Reviewing can also take place when the creative process encounters a critical situation, at *strategic* but *non-predefined* moments, with significant consequences on the areas preceding and succeeding the passage being written when the crisis was ascertained.

This chapter was not intended to synthesise the results of several years of collaborative work with Philippe Leroux. My current emphasis on the role of (re) reading/(re)listening in the considered creative process is based on my belief that this phenomenon exemplifies what is at stake in Leroux-like approaches to musical creativity. Because the only traces this reviewing process leaves are handwritten (and hence undistinguishable from any other acts of writing),[36] the analysis of the 'pre-texts' would not have sufficed to reveal the importance of such practices in Leroux's work. When musicologists study the processes of past creators, they abide by a methodological precept based on common sense: composers' most important and obvious ideas – intuitive premises, basic principles – never appear in drafts or outlines because they are certain never to forget them. There are undoubtedly

---

[34] Ibid., 52.

[35] Donin and Theureau, 'L'activité de composition comme exploitation/construction de situations', 179–80.

[36] In this case, a comparison with literature is of interest: genetic criticism has always perceived a draft's progressive completion – with its notes and alterations – as the product of the reviewing process as much as the writing process. Why such a difference? Let us offer up a hypothesis: even if musical and literary manuscripts have a number of points in common, the overwhelming presence of 'vertical' dimensions (harmonisation, counterpoint, orchestration, variations) in music makes it more difficult to identify the contributions of a transformative review process that might unambiguously appear in literature given the linear quality of verbal text and its grammar's conventional nature.

numerous other facets of creative activity that are also not visible within the pre-texts. Thus, how may a musicologist make room in their research for these archival silences? How might they distinguish such silences from those owing to lost, dispersed or destroyed documents? Beyond raising the dead or fabricating sources, the musicologist could apply knowledge drawn from the study of living composers to offer new dimensions to their model of compositional activity, ones that might have otherwise eternally remained a scientific *terra incognita*. Hence the analysis of Leroux's practices allowed us to distinguish between the previously discussed varieties of (re)reading/(re)listening acts. We were also able to determine the frequency of their respective occurrences, their consequences and, among the latter, the types of entries to which they give rise, all opportune details regarding that aspect of creative activity, as decisive as it is poorly documented.

Having shown how investigation mechanisms might be released from the inherited opposition between psychology and musicology – studying the skills of 'normal' subjects' vs studying the life's work of exceptional subjects – our focus will now shift towards applied cross-fertilisation. I will introduce our current work programme and more specifically an attempt to establish the notion of continuity between empirical and historical investigations.

An Attempt at Cross-fertilisation:
The Coordinated Study of Past and Present Processes

The matter collected for analysis in our two previous studies was exceptional for a number of reasons: it was rare (no composer of equal standing had ever accepted as thorough a study of their cognitive processes), abundant (containing hundreds of documents) and coherent (both artistic projects and both methodologies shared enough common ground for the analysis to be applied to all of the data). Although it is quite common for intellectual discussions to take place between composers and researchers in the fields of computer and contemporary music, it is however unusual for a known composer to devote a significant amount of their working time to an in-depth study, thereby opening up their archives and their working methods and allowing researchers to explore their practice.

Although this study may appear very difficult to replicate, it nevertheless remains necessary: questioning and critique are the key to methodological improvement. Our goal is thus to develop a body of data and analyses significant enough to progressively enable us to transversally apply certain questions, and identify mechanisms or options common to several (if not all) processes. In other words, to constitute a broader knowledge of composition that extends beyond individually documented cases.

In previous studies, our data collection methods prevented us from recognising the composer's degree of innovation (from a historical perspective). For example, an opus like *Voi(rex)* or *Apocalypsis*, whose global logic is designed through parametric and perceptive aspects (registers, nuances, degrees of inharmonicity, noise/voice balance, types of musical gestures, etc.), then described in detail in '*plans généraux*' (general outlines)[37] that are themselves made up of parallel layers full of verbal and graphic annotations, bears witness to a work method common to several composers – and specifically common to spectral composers such as Gérard Grisey[38] or Jean-Luc Hervé.[39] Was it the result of individual thought processes, or an apprenticeship aside Grisey or other experienced composers, or simply a professional proximity to spectral composers of Leroux's own generation? More importantly, from a cognitive analysis standpoint, does this work method have a similar outcome in the work of other composers who plan in a comparable fashion? Plans are like any of the composer's tools and know-how, even the simplest ones: they conceal layers of history and their concept often stems from older creative practices that may be traced back generations. These deep roots in a multi-layered past must be investigated as part of our understanding of present-day compositional practices. This accentuates the reciprocal significance of studying past and present creative activities: cross-referenced corpuses might provide the basis for an analysis of current practice rooted in historical know-how. Conversely, unsuspected and often undocumented practices (such as the art of 'reviewing') might be used, at least on an experimental basis, to enlighten more obscure aspects of past processes.

The creation, in 2009, of our research programme entitled 'Musicologie des Techniques de Composition Contemporaines' (Musicology of Contemporary Composition Techniques) was guided by the above considerations.[40] The programme aims use the in-depth study of several examples of twentieth- and twenty-first-century western art music creative processes to question and document specific compositional methods and techniques. In order to precisely record the interaction between an artistic project and its cognitive conditions (mental and technical tools), we selected creative processes that involved specific technologies from the onset. The chosen processes span a 60-year period that begins in middle of the twentieth century. Analyses of creative processes substantiating existing research (Boulez, Jarrell and Murail) completed the

---

[37]   See a reproduction of the 'plan général' of *Voi(rex)* in Donin, 'Genetic criticism and cognitive anthropology', 200–01.

[38]   See François-Xavier Féron, 'Gérard Grisey: première section de *Partiels* (1975)', *Genesis: Revue internationale de critique génétique*, 31 [*Composer*] (2010): 77–97.

[39]   Hervé, L'image sonore: regard sur la création musicale, 16–18 and 66.

[40]   The MuTeC project was financed by an Agence Nationale de la Recherche grant from 2009 to 2011 (projet ANR-08-CREA066). It allowed me to assemble a team of researchers from IRCAM (Laurent Feneyrou, François-Xavier Féron and Samuel Goldszmidt), the Université de Lille-Nord de France (Noémie Sprenger-Ohana and Vincent Tiffon) and the Université de Technologie de Troyes (Marie-Christine Legout and Pascal Salembier), in collaboration with the Haute Ecole de Musique/Conservatoire de Genève (Rémy Campos with Raphaël Brunner and Antonin Servière).

Table 1.1   Overview of the MuTeC project

Creative process of:	Dates	Definition	Data	Researchers
Gramigna Stefano Gervasoni	2009 to date	Cycle, for cymbalum and ensemble	SSIBD, traces of the activity called upon during the SSIBD	Nicolas Donin François-Xavier Féron (IRCAM)
Tobi-Ishi Jean-Luc Hervé	2006, 2009 to date	Generative music designed for a public garden	Sketchbooks, direct observation, SSIBD	Marie-Christine Legout Pascal Salembier (UTT)
L'Esprit des Dunes Tristan Murail	1994	Mixed music with live electronics	Sketches, SSIBD, IRCAM documentation	Alireza Farhang (associated with IRCAM)
Trei II, Congruences Michael Jarrell	1983, 1988	Elaboration of a source-piece; MIDI-flute	Sketches, itws/ SSIBD, IRCAM documentation	Antonin Servière (HEM/CG)
Traiettoria Marco Stroppa	1982– 1988	Piano + Music V programme	Manuscripts, notes, teaching materials, itws/SSIBD	Vincent Tiffon Noémie Sprenger-Ohana (UdL and IRCAM)
Les Espaces acoustiques Gérard Grisey	1974– 1985	Acoustic models, sonagrammes	Esquisses (Paul Sacher Stiftung.), itws, institutional archive	François-Xavier Féron (IRCAM)
Requiem für einen jungen Dichter B.A. Zimmermann	1968	'Lingual' with multi-track tape	Composer's library; implementation plans for the tape; different versions of the tape	Laurent Feneyrou (IRCAM)
Pli selon pli Pierre Boulez	1957– 1962	Deduction of formal constraints extracted from a poem	Sketches (Paul Sacher Stiftung), commercial recordings	Raphaël Brunner (associated with the HEM/CG)
Charles Koechlin, music for the soundtrack of *Victoire de la vie* (Cartier-Bresson)	1938	Koechlin's first composition for a film	Sketches, writings, correspondence, press articles, institutional archive	Rémy Campos (HEM/CG)

Note: SSIBD: Composition situation simulation interview based on documentation; itws/ SSIBD: interviews resembling an SSIBD; HEM/CG: Haute Ecole de Musique/Conservatoire de Genève; IRCAM: Analyse des pratiques musicales research group, from the Sciences et Technologies de la Musique et du Son laboratory (IRCAM–CNRS, Centre National de la Recherche Scientifique–UPMC, Université Pierre et Marie Curie); UdL: Centre d'Etude des Arts Contemporains, Université de Lille-Nord de France; UTT: TechCICO laboratories, Université de Technologie de Troyes.

exhaustive study of previously unpublished material (Hervé, Gervasoni, Stroppa, Grisey, Zimmermann and Koechlin).

Any twentieth-century scholar could locate each of these composers (at these respective moments in their careers) on a map or family tree of contemporary musical aesthetics. However, could one position them according to their technical workshops, their methods of appropriating new tools or their manners of integrating constraint during the creative process? Aesthetic distance is not necessarily synonymous with distance in creative methods, and vice versa. As it were, the similarities and differences that exist between the various composition techniques compared within the MuTeC's framework appeared progressively. These were the fruit of several notions and transversal rules that merit a brief introduction:

- Each study aims for an accurate reconstruction of the composer's course of action during the entire creative process, resting systematically upon traces of this activity.
- Composition simultaneously develops a piece and an *atelier*, which interact with each other. Here, *atelier* is defined as all the materials and the procedures of action and perception, available and built during the compositional process.[41] This notion therefore includes not only the composer's library (if used during the creative process), but also all papers created for the work in progress.
- From its inception, each studied project is specified according to certain explicit constraints. The latter, technical or technological, are used to analyse the process; they successively influence the way the commission is expressed, the choice of means, the composer's personal and collaborative learning process, the intrinsic organisation of his creative approach, and so on.
- Each process involves its own share of reflection, prior to, during or post-composition. This reflexivity may manifest itself by the existence of notes expressing the project's aesthetic intentions, thoughts formalised as sketches, the composer's involvement in situation simulation interviews based on documentation (if they are still living), or any other responses to their own activity. The study incorporates these elements as parts of the creative process at large.
- Each study identifies a number of likely themes for further analysis. Those that appear over several studies are favoured.
- Whenever possible, each study exploits existing musicological and psychological studies that directly or indirectly document characteristics of musical composition relevant to themes identified for analysis.

---

[41]   Nicolas Donin and Jacques Theureau, 'La coproduction des œuvres et de l'atelier par le compositeur. (A partir d'une étude de l'activité créatrice de Philippe Leroux entre 2001 et 2006)', *Circuit: Musiques contemporaines*, 18/1 (2008), 59–71.

- Each study favours ways of archiving, analysing and publishing data that would facilitate both their adoption by several disciplines and the future accumulation of results.

Although they may be considered as a constraining set of principles, they do not aim to dictate the precise mode of the investigations in advance; rather, they can be interpreted or adapted according to each creative process's specificities. Let us take three very different examples.

The study of the creative process of Stefano Gervasoni's *Gramigna* began after part of the work had already been composed and was continued in parallel with the composition of another portion.[42] Depending on the number of available sketches (which varied according to the movements), it required a method of reverse role-play verbalisation (in which the researcher played the part of the composer while the latter walked him through the process, as he remembered it), as well as composition situation simulation interviews based upon traces. The study of Gérard Grisey's *Les espaces acoustiques* faced entirely different obstacles: a number of preparatory documents existed, but they were not dated and the composer had passed away without leaving indications as to their nature and function. However, the reconstruction was able to draw upon a number of personal and public documents (diaries and correspondence; *l'Itinéraire* archives), in addition to the testimony of those who had witnessed the composer's work during the 1970s. This enabled the interpretation and dating of various stages of the work's genesis. Finally, the study of Marco Stroppa's *Traiettoria* presented a scenario somewhere in between the above empirical (Gervasoni) and historical (Grisey) approaches: on the one hand, the composer was living; on the other, it is a long time since the work became part of the history of electronic music (Stroppa, now 52, composed *Traiettoria* in his twenties). Moreover, although his archives contain few sketches, they include a number of pedagogical or analytical documents generally produced *after* completion of the opus that were used in order to formalise some of its aspects. Therefore, methods developed for *Voi(rex)* or *Apocalypsis* could not be directly replicated for the creative process at stake. The composition simulation interviews were able to call on Stroppa's memory based not only upon the traces of *Traiettoria*'s composition, but also upon other media crucial to his cognition: numerous notebooks from his apprenticeship (which include musical computing class notes and lecture notes) from the same period, as well as the OMChroma library currently being developed in OpenMusic under the composer's leadership, which extends and re-implements many of *Traiettoria*'s musical components.

---

[42]   As I write this chapter only the first version of *Gramigna* (September 2009) has been premiered. More recent movements (composed in 2010, one of which is currently unfinished) are to be completed and played as part of a second, final(?) version.

Emerging Issues in Compositional Cognition

Synoptic Planning vs Heuristic Ideation

Broadly speaking, the working methods of these composers can be split into two directions. In the first, *synoptic planning*, a composer defines the project around one or several global concepts that command the material's characteristics. The piece's form is then designed around one or more charts upon which different projected variations (parametric, ontological, stylistic) are plotted on a time axis (metric or chronometric). The development of musical material can also be programmed digitally via patterns of evolution or the application of sound processing. The second direction is the *primacy of heuristic ideation*: a composition's essential properties emerge throughout the writing process, as a result of recurrent or accumulated local compositional procedures, or as influenced by ideas (melodic, harmonic, parametric, organological) that operate continuously throughout every stage of writing.

Although each of these can be distinguished within a specific (studied) process, neither ever exists alone as such. Composers whose project is rooted in an acoustic approach to the material (that is, deriving compositional components out of objective properties of sound) often proceed according to synoptic planning, making use of the objective, technically manipulable properties of one or more selected sound models (cf. *Les Espaces acoustiques* or *L'Esprit des dunes*). In contrast, those whose project uses material that is deduced, varied or extrapolated from a generative element, a pool or even a serial-like matrix, usually proceed according to the primacy of heuristic ideation during the preparation and/or writing stages (cf. *Pli selon Pli, Trei II, Gramigna*).[43]

Generating Rules in the Course of the Music Writing

Gervasoni's *Gramigna* provided an extreme case, with regard to our previous point, where no specific precompositional work, either drafts or sketches, took place prior to the work's first pages. In addition, any pre-texts pertaining to an entire movement addressed only one musical parameter, upon which they created a framework (for example, a harmonic grid or successive ratios of a variation technique to be applied to the entire piece). However, composition simulation sessions were able to demonstrate essential and unsuspected characteristics of

---

[43] This duality can obviously exist within a single process: although a series of closely followed (quotes to be read and recorded were annotated and extracted from texts; the polyphony of linguistic and sound archive interventions was detailed) preparatory documents exist for Zimmerman's *Requiem* on two quadraphonic tapes, the serial counterpoint of purely instrumental sections seems to have been achieved without any specific pre-compositional formalisation.

Gervasoni's cognition as he wrote the score, which notably included the ongoing production of rules that formed the evolution of pitches or rhythms.

These rules governed the direction of musical motion (ascending or descending, step-by-step or disjunct), the type of pace between two occurrences, and so on. At each new iteration of one rule, the rule itself could be modified, disputed or stopped. Rules could pile up or even contradict each other. We thus observed an overflow of underused rules, whose lifespan was often too small for the listener, or even a patient analyst, to permeate their mechanisms.[44]

Although this mode of cognitive operation is evidently not a constant in Gervasoni's past works, the genesis of *Gramigna* provided a well-suited terrain upon which to study the logic specific to a type of creative approach, one in which construction principles were essentially self-generated from the onset, and where the reliability of structure was both experienced and tested until the end of the writing process. As with Leroux's 'reviewing' process, one lacks evidence from other corpuses to decide whether this must be seen as a widely disseminated characteristic of compositional cognition. Future research might use this knowledge as the basis for questioning a similar cognitive logic in current composers.

Cycle Development and the Concern of Coherence

Several of the works studied have a cyclical quality: Gervasoni's composition presents itself as a cycle of miniatures in progress; Grisey's is a cycle of pieces, composed over a decade, which can be played separately or linked together using a growing instrumental ensemble; Stroppa's is a group of three pieces for piano and tape, composed over several years and able to be played separately or in random order; Jarrell's constitutes two steps in the rhizomatous development of a short original piece (*Trei* for a solo voice); Boulez's was built around two of his own *Improvisations sur Mallarmé* using material and procedures established in the years immediately prior to the cycle's completion. These are so many different cases of pieces that share at least a common aim, ensuring coherence at the levels of both the single opus or movement and the whole cycle to which it pertains.

In such examples of new music each piece must confront the issue of coherence. The above works provide a privileged position from which to observe such an issue, since the composer is faced with the question of coherence either from the onset (if the project is defined as cyclical from the start) or during the course of the creative process (if the idea of combining several pieces into a cycle appears after one or more of these have been produced). We can therefore analyse this series of pieces as they are developed into a cycle: the way some early pieces

---

[44]   See Nicolas Donin and François-Xavier Féron, 'Tracking the composer's cognition in the course of a creative process: Stefano Gervasoni and the beginning of *Gramigna*', *Musicae Scientiae*, 16/3 (2012), forthcoming.

were written was influenced, partially or totally, by the demand for them to fit the cycle's own logic, or occasionally the direction of a new piece would even be defined as fulfilling a missing part of the planned cycle.

There are two remarkable phenomena worth mentioning with regard to this compositional strategy of 'cycle development' ('*mise en cycle*'). The first pertains to the emergence of categories and techniques: a cycle is often the result of compositional ideas stemming from a first piece that compel further elaboration. Here, the cycle initiates a heightened consciousness of notions and techniques neither fully noticed nor mastered within the (first) piece where they emerged. These are then included in the composer's *atelier* as they are applied, over the course of the cycle, to successive pieces through replication, variation and designation, or even theorisation. For instance, Marco Stroppa initially intended to compose short solo piano studies harnessing the instrument's resonance. Once the project was re-characterised as a work for untreated piano and purely synthetic electronics, the composer began to forge musical concepts abstract enough to be applied equally to both the pianistic writing and to the technical and digital implementation of synthetic sounds. During the composition of *Dialoghi* (the second of *Traiettoria*'s three pieces), the notion of EIM (*Elément d'Information Musicale* or Musical Information Element) started to appear in his drafts. It was later renamed Musical Information Organism during the composition of the third piece, *Contrasti*. Thus, the somewhat conscious experimentation with an emerging notion in *Dialoghi* led to the elaboration and mastery of a concept that was then rigorously reproduced in the first section of *Contrasti*'s piano solo. Therein we have identified a self-learning mechanism that is more or less obviously present in every creative activity.

This leads to our second striking phenomenon: the interaction between production and theorisation during the creative process. Once the cycle logic is triggered, the production of pieces and their associated discourse are simultaneously revived. The latter enhances the genesis of new pieces, articulating their contribution to the global design of the cycle-in-progress. Once described, the cycle's internal necessity acts directly upon the terms used by the composer to express their project for new, forthcoming pieces of the cycle. For example, once the concept of Grisey's *Les Espaces acoustiques* was defined, all of the cycle's subsequent pieces would be structured around a low *E* spectrum. Compared with its limited role in the first piece composed, it took on a unifying function. The discourse of the cycle's unity led Grisey to a retrospective bias in his later writings. Notably, Grisey had argued that the cycle *Les Espaces acoustiques* was entirely based upon the sonagrammatic analysis of a trombone's *E*. Yet our analysis of the many steps that shaped his compositional techniques during the course of the cycle's genesis tended to contradict such affirmations. It therefore remains essential to keep in mind that theorisation makes up a sometimes massive and strategic part of the compositional process and needs to be taken into account when collecting and analysing data, as well as when considering the degree of critical distance to be maintained throughout every stage of research (especially *vis-à-vis* a composer's discourse in reference to his past work).[45]

Creative Borrowing as a Crucial Part of Creative Cognition

Finally, in the context of MuTeC the parallel analysis of different collections of musical works revealed a noteworthy fact that transcended aesthetic boundaries between the selected works and composers: *the frequent re-use of pre-existing material*. This runs contrary to the popular ideology that clearly defines postmodernism through its practices of collage, quotation and self-quotation, as opposed to modernism, defined by its tendency towards a complete language overhaul with each new piece. Composers often draw upon elements belonging to their personal archives or library, which can range from discrete recycling to the obvious borrowing of a found object; from a melodic fragment's re-use to that of several previously published pages. For example, Boulez re-used *Notations* (then unpublished) in *Pli*. Grisey inserted a section of *Dérives* into *Périodes*. Jarrell elaborated an aesthetic of interrelated, cross-referencing works. Gervasoni used *Gramigna*'s miniatures alternately as departure and arrival points for parts of other scores (past or in progress).

As noted by Sallis in an article devoted to György Kurtág's use of recycling, the practice of using self-quotation, paraphrase and parody was, until the late eighteenth century, quite commonplace, and generally perceived as 'an indication of the borrower's respect for the "modèle"'. It demonstrated the former's acknowledgement of tradition, and the acquisition of technique. During the nineteenth century:

> there was a drastic change in the judgement affecting the use of a "modèle":
>
> originality became the cornerstone of the new romantic aesthetic and borrowing from the past was a sign of mediocrity. [...] With this new aesthetic paradigm, as well as the gradual establishment of the copyright's legal framework, imitation became a disgraceful practice some went to great lengths to hide.[46]

Although the moral ban on imitation undoubtedly reduced its practice, it most certainly made it less detectable. Sallis developed the following suspicion:

---

[45]   Regarding examples presented in this paragraph see, respectively, François-Xavier Féron, 'The emergence of spectra in Gérard Grisey's compositional process: from *Dérives* (1973–74) to *Les espaces acoustiques* (1974–1985)' and Vincent Tiffon and Noémie Sprenger-Ohana, 'The Creative process in *Traiettoria*: the genesis of Marco Stroppa's Musical Thought', *Contemporary Music Review*, 30/5 (2011), respectively 343–75 and 377–409.

[46]   Friedemann Sallis, 'Fleurs recyclées: Sur les traces de relations souterraines dans l'*Officium breve in memoriam Andreae Szervánszky* opus 28 pour quatuor à cordes de György Kurtág', *Circuit: Musiques contemporaines*, 18/1 (2008), 46.

Although the practices of imitation, re-use and re-composition have now been pushed back behind the closed doors of composers' private ateliers, they remain nonetheless an important component of compositional technique for beginners and mature composers alike. There is little doubt (however impossible to prove) that they are as important to 20th century music as they were to music of past centuries.[47]

Only recently did the importance of these practices become a topic of research in itself. In addition to Sallis's work on Kurtág, quoted above, let us cite the identification of systematic procedures of melodic parody in Messiaen[48] and Xenakis's inter-opus assembly techniques,[49] as well as the bonds forged between Boulez's finished and unfinished pieces[50] – a few among many cases of modern composers in whose activity this dimension was unsuspected until recent years.

MuTeC allowed us acknowledge this phenomenon ourselves, corroborating Sallis's insight. In this case, empirical study contributes to reinforcing a historical research topic first deemed unlikely, undoubtedly owing to composers' and musicologists' guilty silence when faced with it. Beyond pointing out anecdotal occurrences of re-use procedures, we felt it necessary to integrate this dimension into our models of composition; a composer's creativity not only involves creating original sounds and structures but also extends to finding subtle ways to incorporate pre-existing texts/sounds – their own as well as those of others – into new ones. The degree of literality in this recovery must then be assessed, by differentiating borrowing strategies, rewriting, derivation and so forth. Finally there was also a methodological lesson to be learned: in studying the composer's cognition on the scale of several works (an *atelier*'s period as opposed to the genesis of a single piece), we were able to identify how the activity of composition continuously connects several compositions and corresponding creative processes.

Conclusion

This chapter has summarised the steps taken in the past decade towards a cross-fertilisation of empirical and historical approaches towards musical composition: firstly, the renewal of research tools focused on creativity based upon a hybrid

---

[47]   Ibid.

[48]   Yves Balmer, Edifier son œuvre: Genèse, médiation, diffusion de l'œuvre d'Olivier Messiaen, PhD dissertation (Lille, 2009); Christopher Brent Murray, Le développement du langage musical d'Olivier Messiaen: traditions, emprunts, expériences, PhD dissertation (Lyon, 2010).

[49]   Benoît Gibson, Théorie et pratique dans la musique de Iannis Xenakis. A propos du montage, PhD dissertation (Paris, 2003).

[50]   Pascal Decroupet and Jean-Louis Leleu (eds), *Pierre Boulez: Techniques d'écriture et enjeux esthétiques* (Genève, 2006).

of psychology, ergonomics, genetic criticism/sketch studies and musicology; and secondly, the construction of an integrated framework that encompasses a relatively large time scale (eight decades) for the empirical and historic study of learned music, or contemporary music. This last approach (still at an embryonic stage) is limited in its application to corpuses able to sustain the pre-defined methodology. Admittedly, it is unable to display a level of coherence equal to that achieved in our research with Philippe Leroux, in which the studies were strictly contiguous in their selection of objects, methods, timing and participant. Nonetheless the obtained results demonstrate the potential of a transversal questioning process that is oriented towards more general hypotheses regarding the nature of composition as an act.

Through these steps, we have described a research programme that features the following characteristics: study of the compositional process under real-world conditions (instead of 'realistic' or 'plausible') in the composer's normal environment; accounting for the technically, culturally, socially situated quality of composition; a method that enables the composer to express/describe past activity rather than disclose only what they believes it generally involves; adjustment and retrospective evaluation of the researcher/composer interaction, even during the interviews; data analysis via a detailed reconstruction of the composer's course of action, considering the cognitive impact of material and cultural resources at their disposal; and finally, the ability to compare results from this and other existing (about past creative processes especially) or future (belonging to the same research programme) analyses. Empirical studies that conform to such properties make it possible to shed new light on a series of pivotal contemporary pieces, better understand the relationship between creativity and technology and highlight particular characteristics of musical cognition through the thorough analysis of one of its most expert and least studied forms. Thus, continuing this programme is a way of broadening the epistemology of musicology, encouraging and contributing to a closer dialogue with the cognitive and social sciences.

Translated from French by Karen Brunel-Lafargue

References

Bahle, Julius, *Der musikalische Schaffensprozess. Psychologie der schöpferischen Erlebnis- und Antriebsformen* (Leipzig: Hirzel, 1936).

Bahle, Julius, *Eingebung und Tat im musikalischen Schaffen. Ein Beitrag zur Psychologie der Entwicklungs- und Schaffensgesetze Schöpferischer Menschen* (Leipzig: Hirzel, 1939).

Balmer, Yves Edifier son œuvre: Genèse, médiation, diffusion de l'œuvre d'Olivier Messiaen, PhD dissertation (Lille, 2009).

Collins, David, 'A synthesis process model of creative thinking in music composition', *Psychology of Music*, 33/2 (2005), 193–216.

Collins, David, 'Real-time tracking of the creative music composition process', *Digital Creativity Journal*, 18/4 (2007), 239–56.

Decroupet, Pascal and Leleu, Jean-Louis (eds), *Pierre Boulez: Techniques d'écriture et enjeux esthétiques* (Genève: Contrechamps, 2006).

Delalande, François, 'Towards an Analysis of Compositional Strategies' [first published 1989], *Circuit: musiques contemporaines*, 17/1 (2007), 11–26.

Deliège, Irène and Wiggins, Geraint A. (eds), *Musical Creativity. Multidisciplinary Research in Theory and Practice* (New York: Psychology Press, 2006).

Deppman, Jed, Ferrer, Daniel and Groden, Michael (eds), *Genetic Criticism: Texts and Avant-textes* (Philadelphia, PA: University of Philadelphia Press, 2004).

Donin, Nicolas and Féron, François-Xavier, 'Tracking the composer's cognition in the course of a creative process: Stefano Gervasoni and the beginning of Gramigna', *Musicae Scientiae*, 16/3 (2012).

Donin, Nicolas and Theureau, Jacques, 'Theoretical and methodological issues related to long term creative cognition: the case of musical composition', *Cognition Technology and Work*, 9/4 (2007), 233–51.

Donin, Nicolas and Theureau, Jacques, 'La coproduction des œuvres et de l'atelier par le compositeur. (A partir d'une étude de l'activité créatrice de Philippe Leroux entre 2001 et 2006)', *Circuit: Musiques contemporaines*, 18/1 (2008), 59–71.

Donin, Nicolas and Theureau, Jacques, 'L'activité de composition musicale comme exploitation/construction de situations. Une anthropologie cognitive du travail de Philippe Leroux', *Intellectica*, 48/1–2 (2008), 175–205.

Dusapin, Pascal, *Composer. Musique, paradoxe, flux* (Paris: Fayard, 2007).

Féron, François-Xavier, 'Gérard Grisey: première section de Partiels (1975)', *Genesis: Revue internationale de critique génétique*, 31 [*Composer*] (2010), 77–97.

Féron, François-Xavier, 'The emergence of spectra in Gérard Grisey's compositional process: from *Dérives* (1973–74) to *Les espaces acoustiques* (1974–1985)', *Contemporary Music Review*, 30/5 (2011), 343–75.

Franklin, Margery B. 'The artist speaks: Sigmund Koch on aesthetics and creative work', *American Psychologist*, 56/5 (2001), 445–52.

Gibson, Benoît, Théorie et pratique dans la musique de Iannis Xenakis. A propos du montage, PhD dissertation (Paris, 2003).

Harvey, Jonathan, *Music and Inspiration*, ed. Michael Downes (London: Faber, 1999).

Hervé, Jean-Luc, L'image sonore : regard sur la création musicale, PhD Thesis (Lille, 1999).

Kinderman, William and Jones, Joseph E. (eds), *Genetic Criticism and the Creative Process: Essays from Music, Literature, and Theater* (Rochester, NY: University of Rochester Press, 2009).

McAdams, Stephen, 'Problem-solving strategies in music composition: a case study', *Music Perception*, 21/3 (2004), 391–429.

Mion, Philippe, Nattiez, Jean-Jacques and Thomas, Jean-Christophe, *L'envers d'une œuvre* – De natura sonorum *de Bernard Parmegiani* (Paris: Buchet-Chastel, 1982).

Murray, Christopher Brent, Le développement du langage musical d'Olivier Messiaen: traditions, emprunts, expériences, PhD dissertation (Lyon, 2010).

Nuhn, Ralf, Eaglestone, Barry, Ford, Nigel and Clowes, Mark, 'Do composition systems support creativity? – An evaluation', in *Proceedings of the International Computer Music Conference* (La Havane, 2001), 22–5.

Platz, Robert H.P., *TOP Skizzentagebuch*, ed. Stefan Fricke (Saarbruck: Pfau, 2009).

Sallis, Friedemann, 'Fleurs recyclées: Sur les traces de relations souterraines dans l'Officium breve in memoriam Andreae Szervánszky opus 28 pour quatuor à cordes de György Kurtág', *Circuit: Musiques contemporaines*, 18/1 (2008), 46.

Saxton, Robert, 'The process of composition from detection to confection', in Wyndham Thomas (ed.), *Composition – Performance – Reception. Studies in the Creative Process in Music* (Aldershot: Ashgate, 1998), 1–16.

Sloboda, John A., *The Musical Mind: The Cognitive Psychology of Music* (Oxford: Clarendon Press, 1985).

Sloboda, John A., 'Do psychologists have anything useful to say about composition?', in *Analyse et création musicales, Actes du Troisième Congrès Européen d'Analyse Musicale, Montpellier, 1995* (Paris: L'Harmattan, 2001): 69–78.

Suchman, Lucy, *Plans and Situated Actions. The problem of Human-Machine Communication* (Cambridge: Cambridge University Press, 1987).

Theureau, Jacques, 'Course-of-action analysis and course-of-action centered design', in Erik Hollnagel (ed.), *Handbook of Cognitive Task Design* (Mahwah, NJ: Erlbaum, 2003), 55–81.

Theureau, Jacques, *Le cours d'action: méthode développée* (Toulouse: Octares, 2006).

Tiffon, Vincent and Sprenger-Ohana, Noémie, 'The Creative process in *Traiettoria*: the genesis of Marco Stroppa's Musical Thought', *Contemporary Music Review*, 30/5 (2011), 377–409.

Chapter 2

Process, Self-evaluation and Lifespan Creativity Trajectories in Eminent Composers

Aaron Kozbelt

Introduction

Western classical composers are among the best documented creators in any domain.[1] The basic facts of their lives and works are known to even casual classical music listeners: the prodigiousness and untimely deaths of Mozart, Schubert and Mendelssohn; the ambition of Wagner to create a total work of art, culminating in his 15 hour *Ring* cycle; the audacity of Schoenberg and Stravinsky in bucking musical tradition; occasional 'one-hit wonders' among notable composers; the old-age flowering of Haydn and Verdi; the deafness of Beethoven, and so forth. Aspects of composers' creative processes are likewise fairly common knowledge, for instance, in the contrast between the extreme facility of Mozart or Schubert vs the titanic labours of Beethoven or Brahms.

While such anecdotes enrich classical music lore and legend, they are varied and idiosyncratic. Can such information be put together into a coherent account that lends itself to rigorous empirical study and meaningful comparisons across composers? Could such an explanation inform the phenomenon of creativity in very general terms? I think the answer to both questions is yes. Properly operationalised, many aspects of composers' creativity are amenable to quantitative analysis, especially in terms of documenting their overall output[2] and career trajectories.[3] Combining quantitative approaches with more nuanced,

---

[1] Aaron Kozbelt, 'Longitudinal hit ratios of classical composers: reconciling "Darwinian" and expertise acquisition perspectives on lifespan creativity', *Psychology of Aesthetics, Creativity, and the Arts*, 2/4 (2008), 221–35. Dean Keith Simonton, 'Creative productivity, age, and stress: a biographical time-series analysis of 10 classical composers', *Journal of Personality and Social Psychology*, 35/11 (1977), 791–804.

[2] Aaron Kozbelt, 'Performance time productivity and versatility estimates for 102 classical composers', *Psychology of Music*, 37/1 (2009), 25–46.

[3] Aaron Kozbelt, 'Factors affecting aesthetic success and improvement in creativity: a case study of the musical genres of Mozart', *Psychology of Music*, 33/3 (2005), 235–55. Kozbelt, 'Longitudinal hit ratios'. Simonton, 'Creative productivity, age, and stress'. Dean

qualitative investigations of composers' creative processes can yield a rich and rigorous descriptive account of musical creativity. Arguably, such a confluence can even form the basis of a relatively unified general theory of creativity, spanning multiple levels of analysis, methodologies and domains.[4] In this chapter, I sketch such a preliminary synthesis, linking quantitatively documented variability in composers' career trajectories with aspects of their working methods, evaluative processes and judgement criteria.

Throughout the chapter, I frequently use value-laden terminology, referring to the 'greatest' composers or 'eminent' composers and 'masterworks' in music history. While some may question this practice, quantitative assessments of the relative impact of notable creators and notable compositions on music history show large individual differences and extremely high internal consistency across measures, amply justifying such language.[5] I have sought to use value-laden terms only when the conclusions are supported by strong quantitative evidence. I begin with a consideration of how creativity unfolds over the lifespan, since this topic rests on the most secure empirical and quantitative foundation.

Lifespan Creativity and Composers' Career Trajectories

Nomothetic Models of Lifespan Creativity

Psychologists have developed two major perspectives on lifespan creativity. Both are *nomothetic*, seeking unitary, overarching explanations that emphasise the overall trend of the data, rather than variability within the data. One may be termed the expertise acquisition view,[6] and the other, the blind variation and selective retention (BVSR) view.[7] The two theories make radically different assumptions about the fundamental nature of creativity and quite divergent predictions about how creativity unfolds throughout creators' lives, with important implications

---

Keith Simonton, 'Emergence and realization of genius: the lives and works of 120 classical composers', *Journal of Personality and Social Psychology*, 61/5 (1991), 829–40.

[4]   David W. Galenson, *Painting Outside the Lines: Patterns of Creativity in Modern Art* (Cambridge, MA, 2001). David W. Galenson, *Old Masters and Young Geniuses: The Two Life Cycles of Artistic Creativity* (Princeton, NJ, 2006).

[5]   Charles Murray, *Human Accomplishment* (New York, 2003).

[6]   K. Anders Ericsson, 'Creative expertise as superior reproducible performance: innovative and flexible aspects of expert performance', *Psychological Inquiry*, 10/4 (1999), 329–33. John R. Hayes, 'Cognitive processes in creativity', in John A. Glover, Royce R. Roning, and Cecil R. Reynolds (eds), *Handbook of Creativity* (New York, 1989), 202–19. Robert W. Weisberg, *Creativity: Understanding Innovation in Problem Solving, Science, Invention, and the Arts* (Hoboken, NJ, 2006).

[7]   Dean Keith Simonton, 'Creative productivity: a predictive and explanatory model of career landmarks and trajectories', *Psychological Review*, 104/1 (1997), 66–89.

for the extent to which creativity can be controlled. Briefly, the expertise view emphasises that creators accumulate a vast amount of domain-specific knowledge and use it in the mostly rational problem solving processes that largely constitute creativity; this view is thus optimistic about creative control and longitudinal improvement. In contrast, the BVSR perspective emphasises an inherent major role of chance and serendipity in the creative process – particularly for truly outstanding creative productions – and is more pessimistic about prospects for either controlling the creative process or improving with age.

Quantitative Studies of Composers' Career Landmarks

The most direct evidence bearing on these two views of lifespan creativity comes from empirical studies in which aspects of creators' output are operationalised through purely quantitative means, for example, by *career landmarks*, which provide a thumbnail sketch of creators' careers. In music, these include ages at which various composers began studying music, began composing, wrote their earliest acknowledged masterwork, wrote their greatest work, wrote their final masterwork and stopped composing altogether. When career landmarks are applied to a large sample of composers, some of the results support the expertise acquisition perspective – most notably, the finding that even very prodigious and eminent composers require at least a decade of intensive musical study before producing any original works of enduring value.[8] That is, if one tabulates the ages at which different composers began studying music and the ages at which they wrote their first acknowledged masterworks (operationalised by substantial numbers of recordings or expert ratings), in virtually every case at least 10 years elapsed. The few exceptions to the so-called 10-year rule – Paganini, Satie and Shostakovich – wrote their first masterwork in their eighth or ninth year of study. This acquired domain-specific knowledge provides a foundation for guiding the complex problem-solving and decision-making processes that are necessary for significant creative achievement.

However, expertise acquisition alone does not explain some other results. For instance, the very greatest composers began studying music earlier, starting writing music earlier, wrote their earliest masterwork earlier, and wrote their last masterpiece later than their less eminent counterparts.[9] This suggests that the dynamic of expertise acquisition and its translation into creative productivity is modulated in important ways by factors related to something like innate talent. Moreover, expertise is often theoretically construed as superior reproducible performance on closed-ended tasks, which may not apply to the more open-ended situations characteristic of real-world creativity.[10]

---

[8]   Hayes, 'Cognitive processes'. Simonton, 'Emergence and realization of genius'.

[9]   Simonton, 'Emergence and realization of genius'.

[10]   Dean Keith Simonton, 'Creative development as acquired expertise: theoretical issues and an empirical test', *Developmental Review*, 20/2 (2000), 283–318.

Findings on differential ages at career landmarks can be understood via a parsimonious mathematical model undergirding the BVSR account.[11] This model takes individual differences in creative potential as a starting point; over time, a creator expends this potential through creation and recoups a smaller amount through learning. These assumptions permit the modelling of lifespan creative productivity through a differential equation with four parameters: creative potential, career age, ideation rate and elaboration rate. Creative potential is essentially talent, which allows some individuals to more rapidly assimilate knowledge and use it productively; career age is the number of years a person has been involved in a domain such as music; ideation and elaboration rates refer to the relative amount of time it takes to generate novel ideas and to construct a creative product. This differential equation yields the typical inverted, backwards J-shaped trajectory for quantity of creative output found in many domains: productivity starts low, rapidly climbs, peaks (usually around age 40) and then gradually declines. Varying the four parameters of the equation modifies the shape of the trajectory; for instance, greater creative potential increases overall productivity and broadens the age span encompassing the career landmarks described above, although with no change of predicted age for the creation of best work, all of which is consistent with empirical findings.[12]

Quantity vs Quality Career Trajectories

A key tenet of the BVSR model is that quality emerges from quantity, and that the two should thus be positively correlated – a claim that has been empirically corroborated.[13] This relation applies to creators' overall output as a predictor of eminence, as well as within different periods of their careers; that is, at the point in their careers when creators are the most prolific, they are most likely to produce their best work, as well as to produce the greatest amount of second-rate work. Consistent with this dynamic of quantity driving quality, similar career trajectories should thus be obtained when applied to all works, irrespective of quality, or only to a creator's most noteworthy productions.

To what extent is this actually the case? Rather than assessing productivity merely by total output, alternative measures can take the quality of different products into account, via recording counts, citations in music history books or expert ratings. Studies of the citation frequency of operas[14] and expert ratings of the differential aesthetic significance of masterworks across a variety of musical

---

[11]   Dean Keith Simonton, 'Creative productivity and age: a mathematical model based on a two-step cognitive process', *Developmental Review*, 4/1 (1984), 77–111.

[12]   Murray, *Human Accomplishment*. Simonton, 'Creative productivity: predictive and explanatory'.

[13]   Simonton, 'Creative productivity, age, and stress'. Simonton, 'Creative productivity: predictive and explanatory'.

[14]   Simonton, 'Creative development'.

genres[15] each showed a single-peaked age function for work quality that was similar to that for productivity: the quality of individual works starts low, increases and then declines somewhat later in composers' careers. This suggests some benefit of expertise, since on average composers improve for long stretches of their careers.

Similar results have been found for another way of assessing composers' career trajectories: hit ratios, or the proportion of masterwork-level music to total music written in different time intervals in composers' careers (rather like yearly batting averages in baseball). This measure assesses the ability of creators to learn to wisely invest their creative resources, a key issue in conceptualising the fundamental nature of creativity. In contrast to the expertise perspective, the BVSR view has explicitly posited an inability of creators to do so, in line with its tenet of 'constant-probability-of-success', by which hit ratio should show no relation to creator age. Some earlier research[16] showed empirical support for the BVSR position, but those studies arguably had some key methodological and statistical limitations – particularly in aggregating information across creators in a way that failed to properly account for the nested structure of the data. In the most extensive recent study addressing the question of composers' longitudinal hit ratios,[17] the complete outputs of 65 eminent composers (15,657 works) were tabulated and weighted by performance time; each work's masterpiece status was operationalised by three measures: expert ratings, citation in music history books and recording counts. Works were assigned to five-year age intervals, synchronised across composers by age at first masterwork, and hit ratios were calculated for each interval for each composer. Results showed that the overall hit ratio trajectory was a single-peaked function, with a maximum around age 50. This finding was quite robust, with age accounting for more variability in hit ratio than in overall productivity: 49.0 vs 34.4 per cent, respectively. Reliable age effects held even during composers' mature periods and even when composers' greatest masterworks themselves were removed from the dataset. This finding is highly inconsistent with the null relation between hit ratio and age posited by the BVSR perspective.

Just as intriguing as this overall relation between age and hit ratio – and even more important in the context of this chapter – is the observed variability in composers' career trajectories. Using multi-level statistical modelling, which overcomes the data nesting problems mentioned above, composer-level characteristics (such as birth year and eminence level) were used to attempt to explain the variability among composers in the overall regression terms – particularly in the slope, since that term indicates whether a given composer generally improves or declines with age. Several variables predicted individual differences in hit ratio trajectory slopes;

[15] Aaron Kozbelt, 'Age and aesthetic significance in classical music: a multi-level reanalysis of Halsey's (1976) Ratings', *Empirical Studies of the Arts*, 29/2 (2011), 129–48.

[16] Wayne Dennis, 'Creative productivity between the ages of 20 and 80 years', *Journal of Gerontology*, 21/1 (1966), 1–8. Simonton, 'Creative productivity, age, and stress'.

[17] Kozbelt, 'Longitudinal hit ratios'.

most notably, composers who wrote their best works later in their careers showed stronger agewise increases in hit ratio during their mature periods, even when those works were themselves removed from the dataset. Very similar results were found for expert ratings of masterworks, likewise using multi-level modelling.[18]

In addition, late-peaking composers evinced weaker relations between average annual output and hit ratio across age intervals.[19] This suggests that, for composers with later career peaks, quantity does not drive quality to the extent that it does for early-peaking composers – an important modulation of the BVSR view's claims. In other words, late-peaking composers appear to have developed a kind of wisdom that allows them to invest their creative resources more wisely, in contrast to the more hit-or-miss quality of early-peaking composers.

In sum, this set of results suggests that outstanding creative achievements are embedded in meaningful longer-scale spans of development, rather than being isolated events that appear merely as a function of quantity of production. Composers show strong and consistent individual differences in career trajectories: some continually improve, while others show either early peaks and lengthy declines or relatively flat trajectories. Such varied results are hard to reconcile with pure versions of the expertise or BVSR views. An alternative conceptualisation is to adopt a less nomothetic approach, in which inter-creator variability is organised by a typology, whereby different creators may be grouped into categories or along dimensions diagnostic of different career trajectories.

Understanding Variability in Career Trajectories: A Typological Approach

Numerous typologies have been proposed over the years, as one way of understanding the substantial variability among creators.[20] Here I focus on a typology devised by economist David Galenson, who has documented substantial individual variation in the career trajectories (especially career peaks) of creators in several artistic domains and related these differences to variation in working methods.[21] Galenson's typology divides creators into two basic categories. For one group, dubbed 'seekers' or 'experimentalists', creative behaviour is a struggle achieved through trial and error. This group tends to use perceptual criteria in evaluating their work and prioritise skill and the execution of ideas over the raw originality of ideas. Such creators see themselves as building on tradition and show great continuity over their careers, gradually developing their style in rather small increments. They often produce their best work late in their lives. For instance, Paul Cézanne produced his greatest paintings the year he died, aged

---

[18]   Kozbelt, 'Age and aesthetic significance'.

[19]   Kozbelt, 'Longitudinal hit ratios'.

[20]   Aaron Kozbelt, 'Gombrich, Galenson, and beyond: integrating case study and typological frameworks in the study of creative individuals', *Empirical Studies of the Arts*, 26/1 (2008), 51–68.

[21]   Galenson, *Painting Outside the Lines*. Galenson, *Old Masters and Young Geniuses*.

67, after decades of constant improvement. Moreover, the reputation of Cézanne (and other experimentalists) tends to rest on an overall body of work of relatively consistent quality, rather than on one or two singular achievements.

Members of the other category, termed 'finders' or 'conceptual innovators', show much more certainty during the creative process, often create an explicit initial plan while working and prioritise generating ideas over their elaboration, which can often be perfunctory. Finders often rebel against tradition, are more overtly concerned with originality, and show less longitudinal continuity than seekers, often changing styles abruptly. Their reputations typically rest on a small number of outstanding individual pieces, rather than on an overall body of work. Because major conceptual innovations overturn a domain's rules, a hard-won body of skills and knowledge is not absolutely necessary for finders, and they often produce their major contribution early, sometimes by their mid-twenties. In visual art, Pablo Picasso exemplifies this trend, having produced his most important work by age 30, after which the average quality and impact of his work declined steadily for 60 years.

Galenson's theory is controversial, with some scholars noting conceptual and methodological shortcomings or complications.[22] For instance, the truncated career trajectories of short-lived creators such as Schubert are hard to interpret; extremely eminent creators tend to show early first and late last hits, necessitating a closer look at the distribution of hits within that range to understand their trajectory. Prodigies may produce notable works early, but these must be contextualised through their later development; different metrics of career peaks may be more loosely associated among some kinds of creators than others, and so forth. Despite such caveats, Galenson's typology has considerable heuristic value and, at best, broad potential as a unified theory of creativity.[23] It provocatively engages the issue of inter-creator variability in ways that transcend both the expertise and BVSR frameworks, across multiple levels of analysis. Mindful of its limitations, I now apply aspects of the typology to classical composers, beginning with individual differences in career trajectories.

Classical composers' career trajectories often echo the extreme cases of Cézanne and Picasso noted by Galenson. Some improved continually throughout their long careers, by any metric. For instance, in hundreds of works spanning some 40 years, Haydn developed the basic forms of classical music, producing his finest symphonies, string quartets, piano sonatas and choral music in his

---

[22] Fabien Accominotti, 'Creativity from interaction: artistic movements and the creativity careers of modern painters', *Poetics*, 37/3 (2009), 267–94. Victor Ginsburgh and Sheila Weyers, 'Creation and life cycles of artists', *Journal of Cultural Economics*, 30/2 (2006), 91–107. Dean Keith Simonton, 'Creative life cycles in literature: poets versus novelists or conceptualists versus experimentalists?', *Psychology of Aesthetics, Creativity, and the Arts*, 1/3 (2007), 133–9.

[23] Aaron Kozbelt, 'Theories of creativity', in Mark A. Runco and Steven R. Pritzker (eds), *Encyclopedia of Creativity*, 2nd edn, 2 vols (San Diego, CA, 2011), vol. 2, 473–9.

sixties. Brahms showed similar progress across a wide variety of musical genres, continually improving the quality of his work until his death at age 63. Likewise, each of Verdi's operas incrementally builds on its predecessors, culminating with *Otello*, arguably 'the finest of all operas [by any composer]',[24] finished when Verdi was 74, and *Falstaff*, completed at the age of 80. Bartók demonstrated a similar incremental trend until, from his mid-fifties onward, he wrote nothing but masterworks for the last decade of his career. Besides these gradual ascents, other 'late bloomers' produced little notable music until remarkably late: Franck and Bruckner, although active composers from their teens onward, wrote almost no masterpieces before their fifties; Janáček's reputation, aside from his opera *Jenůfa*, rests almost entirely on the works composed after his mid-sixties.[25]

Other composers show career trajectories characteristic of conceptual innovators. Some produced their best-known work in a fairly narrow window early on – even when they remained productive for decades thereafter – and this work dominates their reputation. At the extreme is the phenomenon of 'one-hit wonders' in classical music – figures like Ponchielli, Boito, Weill or Halévy – who on average tended to write their best work at younger ages than did 'multi-hit' composers.[26] Among top-tier composers, Stravinsky is perhaps the clearest example of a conceptual innovator. Like his friend and near-exact contemporary Picasso, Stravinsky constantly sought novelty, changing styles abruptly and repeatedly throughout his 70-year career. Nonetheless, he remains most lauded for three ballets – *L'Oiseau de Feu*, *Petrouchka* and *Le Sacre du Printemps* – written by the age of 30, which far outstrip his other works in popularity. The tight concentration of Stravinsky's highest-impact works early in his long career is very characteristic of conceptual innovators, as articulated by Galenson. Similarly, Satie's *Gymnopédies* and *Gnossiennes* for piano greatly outdistance his other compositions in recording counts; significantly, they are among his earliest works, completed by his mid-twenties and preceded by only about 20 minutes of previously composed music. Schumann likewise wrote some of his most characteristic and oft-cited music in his early twenties, such as the *Papillons* (Op. 2), and produced almost three-quarters of his masterwork-level music between the ages of 24 and 33. Shostakovich's career peak is not concentrated like that of Stravinsky, Satie or Schumann, but the early arc of his career is typical of conceptual innovators: he finished his First Symphony, still one of his most discussed and recorded works, at the age of 19, only six years after he started to compose. His Fifth Symphony, often regarded as his greatest achievement, was written at the age of 30.[27]

---

[24]   Charles Osborne, *The Complete Operas of Verdi* (London, 1969), 429.

[25]   Data from Kozbelt, 'Longitudinal hit ratios'.

[26]   Aaron Kozbelt, 'One-hit wonders in classical music: evidence and (partial) explanations for an early career peak', *Creativity Research Journal*, 20/2 (2008), 179–95.

[27]   Data from Kozbelt, 'Longitudinal hit ratios'.

Not all composers can be as readily classified as the preceding examples, in line with some of the caveats mentioned above, for instance, the truncated careers of short-lived composers, the early achievements of musical prodigies, and the early first hits and late last hits typical of the career trajectories of very eminent composers.[28] For instance, the short lifespans of Mozart and Schubert (35 and 31, respectively) necessarily mean that these composers produced major creative work at a young age, which could lead one to classify them as conceptual innovators. However, both also showed profound and continual development, in line with Galenson's category of experimentalists, and neither showed any sign of burning out, both producing masterpieces until just a few weeks before their deaths. Had Mozart and Schubert lived longer, it is likely that they would have continued to produce musical masterpieces and to grow in significant ways. However, the ultimate arc of their career trajectories – had they lived another few decades – will obviously never be known, leaving their categorisation with respect to Galenson's typology unresolved. Moreover, some longer-lived figures show a curious mixture of characteristics of Galenson's two categories; for instance, Beethoven and Debussy each made major conceptual innovations by their early to mid-thirties (for example, the vastly increased scale of thematic development and expressive intensity of the 'Eroica' Symphony and the novel harmony and shimmering orchestration of *Prélude à l'Après-Midi d'un Faune*, respectively), which strongly influenced the course of music history. However, both also showed some prototypical seeker characteristics, including a creative process plagued with uncertainty and revision, and reliable improvements in hit ratio and masterwork quality during their maturities. Thus, while the present discussion of composers emphasises the extremes of Galenson's framework, the classifications should be regarded as tentative; future work should not only classify creators but also identify which aspects of the typology are most relevant to understanding differences in creators' career trajectories.[29]

Despite these caveats and the complexity of the issues, the observed contrast in the career trajectories of, say, Verdi compared with Stravinsky is not merely a convenient handpicked comparison but reflects broad, robust statistical relations. Such results reinforce the relevance of Galenson's typology to classical music. However, the typology's greatest value is not merely in establishing the substantial inter-creator variability in career trajectories, but in the links between career trajectories and the way in which individuals approach the task of creation – in other words, in the nature of the creative process. Galenson's framework suggests that the well-documented variability in creators' career paths should be linked to variation in their creative process in systematic ways.

---

[28]   Kozbelt, 'Longitudinal hit ratios'. Kozbelt, 'Age and aesthetic significance'.
[29]   Kozbelt, 'Longitudinal hit ratios'.

The Creative Process in Music

Speed of Composition

To initiate a discussion of the creative process, consider one of the most striking aspects of great composers: their ability to write music quickly. The sheer output of many composers is astonishing – Handel's complete works would take some 253 hours to perform; Schubert produced on average a minute of music every day for 20 years.[30] Such productivity can only arise through extreme *process fluency*, whereby a person engages in a relatively effortless production of a high-quality creative work.[31] Handel's *Messiah* was composed in 24 days; Mozart wrote his half-hour "Linz" Symphony (K. 425) in four days and his two-hour opera *La Clemenza di Tito* (K. 621), in 18 days; Schubert composed eight songs in a day on several occasions and wrote the eight-minute-long first movement of a string quartet (D. 112) in four and a half hours. Schoenberg's most popular work, the half-hour sextet *Verklärte Nacht* (Op. 4), was composed in three weeks, the complex monodrama *Erwartung* (Op. 17) in about two weeks, and his String Trio (Op. 45) in four weeks (at the age of 72).

In contrast, other composers routinely produced music more slowly. Some, like Wagner and Messiaen, required years for each of their major compositions, probably owing to the careful planning and preparation needed for works of such vast scale and intricacy. Others, like Chopin, Debussy, Ravel, Duparc, Webern and Duruflé, seem to have been temperamentally fastidious, taking extraordinary pains even with relatively brief works; as Debussy remarked, 'it sometimes takes me weeks to choose between two chords'.[32] Bruckner's productivity was hampered by a pervasive lack of confidence and a willingness to heed friends' advice, leading to protracted revisions and multiple versions of his symphonies. Beethoven's creative process was replete with false starts and revisions – major works such as the Fifth and Ninth Symphonies, *Fidelio*, the *Missa Solemnis* and the "Diabelli" Variations each evolved significantly over many years. Brahms, a ruthless self-critic, allegedly destroyed three times as much music as he eventually published, claiming that his three published string quartets were preceded by some 20 aborted efforts, and his First Symphony, conceived in his mid-twenties, took almost 20 years to bring to completion.

Inter-composer variation in composition speed has many possible explanations, which, in the BVSR model, are simply subsumed by the parameters of ideation and elaboration rates. Differential ideation and elaboration rates do account for observed inter-genre career landmark differences in classical music. For instance, composers write their first, best and last songs (a relatively easily

---

[30]   Kozbelt, 'Performance time productivity'.

[31]   David N. Perkins, *The Mind's Best Work* (Cambridge, MA, 1981), 164–77.

[32]   Leon Vallas, *Claude Debussy: His Life and Works*, trans. Marie O'Brien and Grace O'Brien (New York, 1973), 224.

conceived and elaborated genre) earlier than their corresponding landmarks for orchestral works (which, plausibly, have longer rates).[33] However, while conceptualising creative productivity in terms of ideation and elaboration rates may be descriptively useful for modelling longitudinal output, it typically underemphasises inter-creator differences and yields no details on the particulars of composers' creative processes – which Galenson's model suggests are critical for understanding variation in career trajectories. Moreover, emphasising ideation and elaboration rates and compositional speed *per se* may simply not be useful for determining the point in creators' careers when they produce their greatest work. For instance, among modern artists, extreme conceptual innovators include the fast-working Picasso and the often slow-working Duchamp, both of whom peaked in their twenties.[34]

Rather than emphasising the rates of ideation and elaboration, another tactic for understanding the basis of variability in composers' career trajectories is to distinguish their relative emphasis, combined with a more process-oriented perspective detailing how composers approach the task of composition, make decisions and evaluate works-in-progress. Galenson's theory suggests that composers who emphasise the generation of musical ideas and downplay their development should show characteristics of conceptual innovators, or finders. In contrast, composers whose creative process prioritises the development of musical themes (that is, the execution or elaboration of their ideas) should show characteristics of experimentalists, or seekers. To pursue this issue, I now examine how some eminent composers have approached the task of composition, and I make connections to their observed career trajectories, specifically, how composers elaborate their raw ideas into finished products, with a specific emphasis upon musical form and structure, evaluative processes, and creators' judgement criteria and compositional goals.

Structuring Behaviour via Traditional vs Novel Musical Forms

Writing an interesting piece of music is a hugely complex undertaking, involving many component processes. Consider composition from the perspective of a complex process of ill-defined problem-solving and decision-making: composers must engage in a large number of decisions. They must generate basic musical ideas (for instance, a melody, harmonic progression, rhythmic pattern, formal structure or timbral combination), evaluate them in terms of their goals and other aesthetic and pragmatic criteria, assemble the ideas into a coherent musical structure, consider issues of scoring and performability, work out voice-leading and counterpoint, control the pacing, dynamics and structure of the music, gauge its likely emotional impact, and so on, until the composition is deemed to be finished.

---

[33] Kozbelt, 'One-hit wonders'.

[34] Galenson, *Painting Outside the Lines*.

Depending on a composer's approach, this maze of decisions may be navigated with greater or lesser efficiency. In any case, in emphasising the gradual nature of elaborating musical ideas, the key point is that compositions do not write themselves. Composers need to organise and structure not only the music itself, but also their behaviour and creative process, to transform their ideas into some performable finished product.

How should a composer do this? Some may choose to rely on music tradition and their own earlier compositional experience as guides in developing their ideas. Historically, familiarity with and mastery of traditional musical forms (such as sonata allegro, rondo, ternary, and so on) were the cornerstones of training in composition, providing aspiring composers with schemas to be able to compose with some fluency. Schemas are mental structures used 'to perceive or act effectively by anticipating the organization of what the person apprehends or does, so the person needn't function as much from scratch'.[35] Schemas serve as means of structuring a creator's behaviour and decision-making throughout the creative process, facilitating the strategic deployment of domain-relevant knowledge and the dynamic evaluation and elaboration of creative ideas, in order to guide an emerging creative product to a (hopefully) successful outcome. Composers have long recognised the utility of such schemas. For example, as Aaron Copland noted, 'every well-trained composer has, as his stock in trade, certain normal structural moulds on which to lean for the basic framework of his compositions'.[36] Professional composers' schemas are rich and varied, applying to various musical forms and structures as well as rules for voice-leading, counterpoint, modulation, harmony and so forth, which constitute the symbol system of classical music at any point in time.

When composers know they are writing pieces in traditional forms, more or less following traditional musical procedures and language, this typically guides and constrains their creative process in ways that can promote process fluency. Not only do they have numerous completed examples from past works in that form, but their own previous experience in writing in that form gives them a dynamic sense of how the compositional process itself should unfold as a work progresses. With years of practice, the principles for writing in a form can become internalised and implicit, allowing composers to write with great speed. Many composers working in traditional forms could indeed produce music quickly if necessary, and much of the music of extremely prolific Baroque and Classical era composers – for example, Vivaldi, Handel, J.S. Bach, C.P.E. Bach, J.C. Bach, Boccherini, Haydn and Mozart – is in such traditional forms. Even in the wake of Beethoven, when thematic development became far more important than previously, figures like Schubert and Dvořák were still able to produce music in traditional forms quickly. Not coincidentally, most of these individuals, along with other relatively conservative composers like Mendelssohn, Brahms and Bruckner, tended to show

---

[35]   Perkins, *The Mind's Best Work*, 173.

[36]   Aaron Copland, *What to Listen for in Music* (New York, 1939), 31.

substantial longitudinal improvement in work quality and hit ratios, with their most acclaimed works often appearing near the ends of their careers.[37]

This capacity for longitudinal improvement among such composers may be attributable to several factors. One is their habit of more or less deliberately building on earlier works, in an attempt to learn from experience and improve the quality of their works over time. For such composers, 'improvement' is probably gauged largely in terms of the criterion of craftsmanship. Standards of craftsmanship are likely to function along the lines of the mainstream inherited principles and schemas, rather than a criterion like radical originality, which challenges and undermines the very tradition that they value. A related factor, alluded to earlier, is the focus by more traditionally minded composers on the *development* of ideas, rather than on their generation. This propensity is clearest in considering the growth of sonata form – the type of musical structure characteristic of classical symphonies and string quartets, for instance – in which the development of musical ideas is built into its very structure. Individual creators who are able to acquire skill and schemas in such potential-laden musical forms are likely to be able to continually improve, as the forms themselves offer extremely wide scope for rich development, both within individual works and in their cumulative longitudinal effect.

However, not every composer is content to follow or build on traditional ways of doing things. Many noteworthy composers have essentially rejected conventional forms and means of expression; in such cases, however, composers must find some other way of structuring their behaviour in order to actualise their compositions. Throughout music history, the invention of novel forms has been a hallmark of musical innovation – from Schumann's or Satie's non-traditional piano works to the tone poems of Liszt and Richard Strauss to Wagner's massive music dramas to Schoenberg's and Webern's atonal miniatures. Fundamental changes in music notation among twentieth-century composers, for instance in the works of Cage, Berio or Stockhausen, likewise reflect significant conceptual innovation. In many of these cases, the early peaks characteristic of conceptual innovators are evident.[38]

Since conceptual innovators often do not depend on standard schemas for composition, they often adopt fairly explicit and algorithmic methods of representing and organising their musical materials – since they still need to structure their behaviour and their creative product. Recent music history abounds in such instances: the tone row tables of Schoenberg and his followers; Boulez's total serialism of musical elements; Messiaen's use of permutations of rhythmic, timbral and harmonic elements; Xenakis's musical application of mathematical and statistical ideas, including probability, set theory and game theory; Cage's thorough-going use of chance elements, and so forth. While the latter's use of aleatoric modes of composition may seem anti-algorithmic, it shares with these

---

[37]   Data from Kozbelt, 'Longitudinal hit ratios'.

[38]   Kozbelt, 'Longitudinal hit ratios'.

other modernist approaches a minimising of the need for wilful intervention into the process of elaborating musical ideas. Such approaches stand in striking contrast to a related factor, alluded to earlier, the focus by more experimentalist or traditionally minded composers on the *development* of ideas.

Because conceptually oriented composers do not build on tradition or a foundation of acquired knowledge, when they strike out in novel directions, critical receptions of their efforts are intrinsically more hit or miss – a dynamic in line with the BVSR perspective. This haphazardness is compounded by the observation that finders' contributions depend more critically on the basic concept or idea, a particularly chance-intensive process,[39] instead of careful elaboration, which is perhaps more reliably guided.[40] The extreme certainty that is one of the most fundamental characteristics of conceptual innovators[41] may prevent them from even noticing learning opportunities during the process of elaboration, in contrast to their experimentalist peers, who deliberately seek improvement within tradition.

To some degree schemas play similar roles for both traditionally minded and iconoclastic composers, in organising creative thought and behaviour; the difference is that novel forms and musical styles require novel schemas, which may need to be adhered to fairly strictly, since otherwise the bases for making creative decisions and evaluating progress are unclear.

Self-evaluations of the Quality of Musical Ideas and Works

Relative to its importance, the topic of self-evaluation has received relatively little attention in the creativity literature. However, self-evaluation is itself another aspect amenable to empirical investigation and informs many basic questions on the nature of creativity, particularly the extent to which the creative process can be meaningfully controlled and, concomitantly, the extent to which creators can show longitudinal improvement. The extent to which creators can effectively judge their own ideas and works remains largely unanswered, and this aspect of artistic creativity has not been directly addressed by Galenson. Although some composers' self-critical comments are fairly well-known in the classical music literature, citing quotations haphazardly or in a handpicked way can lead to biased or misinformed conclusions. To more objectively assess this issue and its bearing on creativity more generally, qualitative data sources (either composers' autobiographical commentary or anecdotal evidence) must be rigorously and systematically examined.

In recent years, some progress on this topic has been made, chiefly in an archival study of Beethoven, a study that comprehensively collected and analysed

---

[39]   Dean Keith Simonton, *Origins of Genius: Darwinian Perspectives on Creativity* (New York, 1999).

[40]   Kozbelt, 'Longitudinal hit ratios'.

[41]   Galenson, *Old Masters and Young Geniuses*, 179.

his self-critical statements.[42] All of Beethoven's published letters and conversations were examined to identify instances where he commented on the quality of any of his works. Explicit self-criticisms of 70 compositions were found, spanning his whole career and most musical forms. Some self-assessments were very positive: Beethoven referred to his Ninth Symphony, Op. 125 as 'the grandest I have written'[43] and described his Piano Sonata No. 28, Op. 101 as 'difficult to perform ... [but] what is difficult, is also beautiful, good, great and so forth ... this is the most lavish praise'.[44] Other self-evaluations were less enthusiastic; for instance, he wrote that the three overtures [to *The Ruins of Athens*, Op. 113, *Zur Namensfeier overture*, Op. 115 and *King Stephen*, Op. 117] 'do not belong to my best and greatest works'.[45] In the empirical study Beethoven's assessments were then compared with each work's masterwork status according to three citation measures. On each measure, Beethoven's positive or negative evaluations were reliably associated with those of posterity, and the likelihood of assessments concordant with those of posterity strongly increased with age. His comments comparing several similar masterpieces were likewise largely consistent with expert ratings and recording counts, for instance in his preference of his late string quartets to his earlier efforts, or his Third and Fourth piano concertos to his First and Second. Finally, the study indicated that the ranking of works by listener-hours (number of complete recordings of a work multiplied by its performance duration) corresponded closely to Beethoven's intra-genre preferences – for instance, in his explicit superlative praise of his Third and Ninth symphonies, the two works that substantially outdistance all of his other pieces in listener hours. All told, this set of results suggests considerable self-critical acumen on Beethoven's part.

Like the qualitative studies of career landmarks and trajectories described above, the potential of undertaking quantitative study of composers' self-evaluations seems likely to yield insights and testable hypotheses on the nature of musical creativity. For instance, Beethoven's own largely ascending career trajectory, coupled with his astute self-criticality, suggests a relation between self-criticism and longitudinal improvement; in other words, composers who improved throughout their careers should be accurate self-critics. It is not difficult to see that being able to readily ascertain or forecast the quality of musical ideas and works-in-progress would be a tremendous benefit to a composer's creative process – and lead to longitudinal improvements in hit ratio and work quality.

To date, this case study of Beethoven[46] represents the only published systematic attempt to exhaustively quantify and examine this issue. However, preliminary analyses of at least one other composer, Haydn, show a similar

---

[42]   Aaron Kozbelt, 'A quantitative analysis of Beethoven as self-critic: implications for psychological theories of musical creativity', *Psychology of Music*, 35/1 (2007), 147–72.

[43]   Emily Anderson (ed.), *The Letters of Beethoven*, 3 vols (London, 1961), letter 1305.

[44]   Ibid., letter 749.

[45]   Ibid., letter 664.

[46]   Kozbelt, 'Beethoven as self-critic'.

trend. Across Haydn's assessments of more than 90 of his compositions derived from letters, biographies and accounts of conversations, a positive association is evident between Haydn's own self-criticisms and a composite citation measure representing posterity's assessments.[47] As noted earlier, Haydn's career trajectory showed continual improvement until his retirement in his early seventies, by any measure – hit ratio, critical assessment of his works, citation indices or recording counts. Thus, the preliminary findings for Haydn are consistent with the hypothesis outlined above.

Beyond the straightforward claim that composers who show substantial longitudinal improvement should be highly accurate self-critics, another possibility is that such composers are particularly *harsh* self-critics. As with accuracy, harshness and high standards would likewise be potentially useful as a means of self-improvement. Probably the most striking example of this phenomenon is that of Brahms, who, like Beethoven and Haydn, showed career-long improvement. Several anecdotes will suffice. Regarding his largely finished First Piano Concerto, Op. 15, probably the greatest masterwork of his early period, Brahms wrote to his friend, the violinist Joseph Joachim, 'I'm sending you the Finale to be rid of it at last. Will it satisfy you? I doubt that very much. The ending was actually becoming good, but now it doesn't seem so to me'.[48] Later in his career he agreed to perform his own G-major Violin Sonata, Op. 78 with Joachim, 'provided the violinist would first play Bach's sonata in the same key. When Joachim had finished, Brahms threw his own music to the floor, and cried: "After that, how could anyone play such stuff as this?"'.[49] Even the positive evaluations made by Brahms are tempered by considerable modesty, and his reverence for musical tradition is manifest.

As with career trajectories and choice of musical forms, these examples culled from largely experimentalist composers represent only one side of the story. If evaluative capacity has some relation to career trajectories and accompanies the creative process itself in systematic ways, then the other side of the relation should be that more conceptually oriented composers should show inaccurate or overconfident judgements. As noted before, this issue has yet to be explored in a thoroughly quantitative way; however, in browsing through the letters and statements of conceptually oriented composers such as Wagner, Liszt, Schoenberg and Stravinsky, this trend appears evident. It is often difficult to find negative or modest comments about their own works, and their positive assessments brim with confidence – a far cry from the modest self-deprecation of Brahms. For instance, Stravinsky wrote of his *Le Sacre du Printemps*, 'One must wait a long time before the public becomes accustomed to our language, but of the value of what we have

[47]   Aaron Kozbelt, unpublished data.

[48]   Styra Avins (ed.), *Johannes Brahms: Life and Letters*, trans. Josef Eisinger and Styra Avins (Oxford, 1997), 148.

[49]   Robert Haven Schauffler, *The Unknown Brahms: His Life, Character, and Works* (Westport, CT, 1972), 240.

done I am certain, and this gives me the strength for further work'.[50] Wagner, in a typically manic letter, raved of his *Tristan und Isolde*, 'Tristan is and remains a miracle to me! I find it more and more difficult to understand how I could have done such a thing: when I read through it again, my eyes and ears fell open with amazement!'[51] Schoenberg's positive appraisals extended even to minor, decades-old compositions. Consider this anecdote by a student of Schoenberg's shortly after his arrival in the United States:

> [Schoenberg]... had brought some of his earlier songs to show us ... As usual with him, he was overflowing with praise of his own efforts. True enough, he rather belittled one of the songs: "This one," he said, "I do not know so well – I wrote it one day very fast, because I had not enough music paper to finish my string quartet and I had to have something to do while I was waiting to get some!" But then he continued, to say that it was good too – "Of course!"[52]

Such quotations suggest that prototypical conceptual innovators are biased to judge their own works very favourably – again in line with Galenson's assertion that certainty and confidence during the creative process is perhaps their most telling characteristic. However, as noted above, a full quantitative exploration of this issue among either more conceptually oriented or experimentalist composers has yet to be undertaken, so it is not clear whether the hypotheses outlined in this section are correct or not – but they are testable in any case.

Confidence and Uncertainty Writ Larger

Differences in career trajectories, choice of musical forms and evaluative processes hardly exhausts the differences between Galenson's categories of experimentalists vs conceptual innovators, applied to composers. In passing, I here note some instances of how the issues of confidence vs uncertainty pertain to broader levels of composers' creativity – namely, how and when they attempt major works, and how they regard their prospects for posthumous fame. In line with the confident self-assurance of such conceptually oriented composers is their frequent audacity in attempting major works early in their career. Shostakovich's First Symphony has already been mentioned in this regard; similarly, the 19-year-old Wagner, within just three years of his first attempts at composition, produced the well-wrought Symphony in C, almost 40 minutes long. Stravinsky had written only a handful of works – none for orchestra –

---

[50] Vera Stravinsky and Robert Craft, *Stravinsky in Pictures and Documents* (New York, 1978), 102.

[51] Stewart Spencer and Barry Millington (trans. and ed.), *Selected Letters of Richard Wagner* (London, 1987), 499.

[52] Dika Newlin, *Schoenberg Remembered: Diaries and Recollections (1938–1976)* (New York, 1980), 62–3.

before plunging into his half-hour Symphony in E-flat, Op. 1 at the age of 23. The 25-year-old Schoenberg, likewise with virtually no experience of writing orchestral music, nonetheless undertook what would be his biggest work, the *Gurre-Lieder*, scored for a massive orchestra and chorus totalling some 400 performers. Contrast these examples with Brahms's career-long 'pattern of writing almost exclusively for musical combinations he [was] personally familiar with',[53] or Bruckner's persistence in taking lessons in counterpoint and other aspects of music composition until his late thirties.

The early success (or self-perceived success) of many conceptual innovators, combined with the confidence and audacity to make a major conceptual innovation in the first place, also contributes to making them more sure of their own accomplishments and place in history. In contrast, the slow ascent and sometime lack of confidence characteristic of seekers leads to the opposite effect. This disparity is nicely encapsulated by the following quote of Haydn, from a letter dated 10 August 1801: 'I have often doubted whether my name would survive me'.[54] This is an astonishing comment from a composer who had all but finished his life's work, which had in large measure propelled one of the most profound revolutions in music history. An eerily similar and equally staggering remark was made by Brahms, just three years before his death, in which he foresaw his stature as, 'the place I shall one day have in the history of music: the place that Cherubini once had and has today'.[55] Such understated self-appraisals could not be more different from a comment by Schoenberg in the late summer of 1921: 'Today I succeeded in something [the invention of the tone row] by which I will have assured the dominance of German music for the next century'.[56] Despite Schoenberg's secure place in music history, there would be little dispute that his claim was rather overconfident.

Perceptual vs Conceptual Judgement Criteria

Composers' evaluations of their individual ideas and works, as described above, are mainly assessments of the quality of a work, or how closely it measures up to the composer's goals. However, composers' particular goals and compositional concerns, and thus their judgement criteria for their ideas and works, vary a great deal. Beyond raw accuracy or confidence in making evaluations, Galenson construed the difference between conceptualists and experimentalists in terms of perceptual vs conceptual criteria. Among visual artists, for instance, perceptual criteria would be rooted in a viewer's experience of the lines, colours and forms

[53]   Avins, *Johannes Brahms*, 419.

[54]   Howard Chandler Robbins Landon, *The Collected Correspondence and London Notebooks of Joseph Haydn* (London, 1959), 189.

[55]   Schauffler, *The Unknown Brahms*, 249.

[56]   Egbert M. Ennulat (trans. and ed.), *Arnold Schoenberg Correspondence* (Metuchen, NJ, 1991), 2.

depicted in the work. In contrast, conceptual criteria are more rooted in viewers comprehending some particular idea on the part of the creator. In Galenson's view, these differential criteria are related to creators' career trajectories in that the perceptual criteria require more experience to implement well, while a clear-cut conceptual approach permits a straightforward check to determine if an artistic goal has been met. Along these lines, conceptually minded individuals can typically articulate their creative goals more explicitly than can experimentalists.

A similar difference in orientation exists among composers. Many late-peaking seekers do not articulate their compositional goals explicitly with clear-cut conceptual or theoretical criteria. Instead, they tend to rely on more perceptual criteria. This is often manifested by a refusal to slavishly follow the 'rules' if they lead to an undesirable sensory effect. For example, late in his life, Haydn remarked:

> In the heat of composition I never thought about [rules]. I wrote what seemed to me good and corrected it afterwards ... Several times I took the liberty of not offending the ear, of course, but of breaking the usual textbook rules, and wrote beneath these places the words *con licenza*. Some cried out, "A mistake!" and tried to prove it by citing Fux. I asked my critics whether they could prove by ear that it was a mistake? They had to answer No. My own ear ... hears no mistake in those places; on the contrary, I seem to hear something beautiful, so I begged leave to sin against the rules.[57]

Verdi echoed this attitude: 'I have never written music following fixed ideas ... I had no hesitation in writing three successive parallel fifths in a certain passage. And if I did commit this error in harmony ... it was because it was necessary for the effect I wished to produce'.[58]

Verdi regaled against other characteristics of conceptual innovation: originality for its own sake and the use of fixed aesthetic systems as an aid to composition, stating that:

> It is wrong simply to disregard the past, ignore the importance of tradition and deliberately do precisely the opposite of what has been done heretofore, simply to be modern at all costs ... Certainly one should explore new avenues, but not at the cost of substituting artificiality and mannerism for the spontaneity of true inspiration ... Art and systems of art ... are opposites; and those artists act wrongly who sacrifice imagination and invention to a preconceived system.[59]

---

[57]   Vernon Gotwals (trans. and ed.), *Haydn: Two Contemporary Portraits* (Madison, WI, 1968), 109.

[58]   Marcello Conati (ed.), *Encounters with Verdi*, trans. Richard Stokes (Ithaca, NY, 1984), 170.

[59]   Ibid., 283.

In a similar vein, Bartók spoke directly about his aversion to theory in composing:

> I never created new theories in advance, I hated such ideas ... [My] plans were
> concerned with the spirit of the new work and with technical problems ... all
> more or less instinctively felt, but I never was concerned with general theories
> to be applied to the works I was going to write ... even now I would prefer to try
> new ways and means instead of deducing theories.[60]

In contrast to experimentalists' statements, emphasising perceptual rather than
theoretical or conceptual criteria, more conceptually oriented composers tend
to show the opposite tendencies. For instance, more conceptually oriented
composers often have a very clear and explicit sense of what they are trying to
achieve when they create a piece of music. Indeed, Galenson's theory implies that
one would expect conceptual innovators to be better able than experimentalists to
articulate their compositional goals. An outstanding example is Wagner, arguably
the most ambitious conceptual innovator in music history, who wrote reams of
prose detailing his aesthetic theories, sometimes years in advance of instantiating
them in his musical compositions. Stravinsky clearly stated his own compositional
goals, which often varied from work to work, and his conceptualist orientation was
consistent throughout his career. As he noted, 'I attempt to erect certain kinds of
architectural constructions. My objective is form ... Nevertheless, I do not believe
in the triumph of forms ... ideas triumph, not forms'.[61] Similarly he stated that,
'when I compose, a great number of musical combinations occur to me. I have to
choose and to select. But what standards should I use? ... The result resembles a
predetermined physical or chemical experiment'.[62] Schoenberg likewise clearly
articulated his musical theories,[63] and declared that he was always occupied 'with
the desire to base the structure of my music *consciously* on a unifying idea',[64] and
his friend Webern similarly advised, 'Don't write music entirely by ear. Your ears
will always guide you aright, of course, but you must *know* why one progression
is good and another bad'.[65] Contrast the attitudes of Schoenberg and Webern with
those of Haydn and Verdi, cited above.

While conceptual innovations undoubtedly introduce novelty into the domain
of music, they can also outstrip the ability of audiences to appreciate such
innovations. Often this is a function of the great complexity or unfamiliarity of the

---

[60]   Halsey Stevens, *The Life and Music of Béla Bartók*, 3rd edn (New York, 1993),
225–6.

[61]   Stravinsky and Craft, *Stravinsky in Pictures*, 193.

[62]   Ibid., 196.

[63]   See, e.g., Arnold Schoenberg, *Style and Idea*, ed. Leonard Stein, trans. Leo Black
(Berkeley, CA., 1975), 207–8, 214–49.

[64]   Joseph Machlis, *Introduction to Contemporary Music*, 2nd edn (New York, 1979),
237.

[65]   Sam Morgenstern (ed.), *Composers on Music* (New York, 1956), 457.

music, which may require a score or specialised knowledge simply to make sense of it. In other cases, a composer may push the very boundaries of the auditory modality; a passage like the 'Epode' in Messiaen's *Chronochromie*, written for 18 solo string parts, each playing an independent fast-tempo birdsong, comes to mind.[66] In other cases, composers disregard traditional musical perceptual issues altogether, most famously in Cage's infamous *4:33*, which forces the audience to attend to its own ambient sounds during the performer's prolonged *tacet*.

The creator–audience dynamic in extreme conceptual innovation, in which novelty is prioritised over virtually every other quality, including basic perceptual and communicative capacities, can lead to an ever-increasing gulf between the creator and the audience. Some have provocatively argued that this dynamic inexorably proceeds to the point where the insatiable quest for novelty ultimately makes art (and music) unintelligible, leading to their death.[67] An alternative view more optimistically appraises the evolution of the arts by de-emphasising novelty as the most important aspect of creativity, and placing more stress on the other criterion of creativity – that of value, or adaptive solutions to problems.[68] Galenson regarded both experimentalists and conceptual innovators as essential for the endeavour of art: conceptualists create new styles and forms while experimentalists develop such styles and forms into mature symbol systems.[69] Rather than attempting to resolve these complex issues here, perhaps it is enough to note that the critical evaluation of these issues in cultural values and aesthetics is a vital question, worthy of deep debate and exploration, but one that would take us too far afield from our main concern, namely, the nature of the process of musical composition, and how variability in this process – composers' working methods, evaluative processes and compositional concerns – is related to variability at other levels of analysis – the arc of composers' career trajectories.

Conclusion

The application of Galenson's creator typology to classical composers is relatively straightforward and can be subsumed into mainstream creativity theories in terms of a differential emphasis on ideation vs elaboration. The well-documented variability in composers' career trajectories appears to be related to qualitative differences in their approaches, methods and values in the process of creation – precisely the factors identified by Galenson as distinguishing his two groups. The

---

[66] Claude Samuel, *Conversations with Messiaen*, trans. Felix Aprahamian (London, 1976), 86–91.

[67] Colin Martindale, 'The evolution and end of art as Hegelian tragedy', *Empirical Studies of the Arts*, 27/2 (2009), 133–40.

[68] Aaron Kozbelt, 'The evolution of evolvability, applied to human creativity', *International Journal of Creativity and Problem Solving*, 19/1 (2009), 101–21.

[69] Galenson, *Old Masters and Young Geniuses*.

qualitative and quantitative approaches described here converge onto a unified theoretical account that relates individual differences at two very different levels of analysis: the nature of individuals' creative process and their lifespan creativity trajectories. Specifically, composers with ideation-intensive processes and more conceptual evaluation criteria are more likely to peak earlier in their careers, while those focusing on the elaboration of ideas and applying more perceptual criteria appear to have greater prospects for long-term improvement, even late into their lives. Such a conclusion, by which variability at multiple levels of analysis is parsimoniously related to a unified set of constructs, promises a richer understanding of the nature of creativity more generally.

The approach outlined in this chapter is not without its limitations, however. While some aspects of the argument, such as career trajectories, rest on a highly quantitative basis, other aspects, such as evaluative statements or compositional concerns made by composers, are more open to interpretation. Moreover, I have here relied extensively on quotations and empirical findings from a relatively small set of composers in order to illustrate the most salient points of my argument. Numerous others – Monteverdi, Gluck, Berlioz, Tchaikovsky, Mahler, Sibelius, Ives and many twentieth-century composers – have gone completely unmentioned, precluded by space limitations, but would likewise richly inform this discussion.

Despite such limitations, the approach advocated here has several advantages. Firstly, it proposes testable, falsifiable hypotheses that act to sharpen the empirical study of creativity. Secondly, it lays the groundwork for a relatively unified theory of artistic creativity, addressing questions and spanning levels of analysis that are rarely combined. Thirdly, the variability encompassed by Galenson's types provides an empirical and conceptual basis from which to launch a discussion of larger cultural issues in musical aesthetics revolving around the tension between the development of existing traditions and the freedom to break out of them. To some degree, this tension has – in multifarious ways – brought forth all of the masterpieces in the Western musical tradition, breaking new aesthetic ground and communicating something of lasting value to listeners, generation after generation.

References

Accominotti, Fabien, 'Creativity from interaction: artistic movements and the creativity careers of modern painters', *Poetics*, 37/3 (2009), 267–94.

Anderson, Emily (ed.), *The Letters of Beethoven*, 3 vols (London: Macmillan, 1961).

Avins, Styra (ed.), *Johannes Brahms: Life and Letters*, trans. Josef Eisinger and Styra Avins (Oxford: Oxford University Press, 1997).

Conati, Marcello (ed.), *Encounters with Verdi*, trans. Richard Stokes (Ithaca, NY: Cornell University Press, 1984).

Copland, Aaron, *What to Listen for in Music* (New York: McGraw-Hill, 1939).

Dennis, Wayne 'Creative productivity between the ages of 20 and 80 years', *Journal of Gerontology*, 21/1 (1966), 1–8.

Ennulat, Egbert M. (trans. and ed.), *Arnold Schoenberg Correspondence* (Metuchen, NJ: The Scarecrow Press, 1991).

Ericsson, K. Anders, 'Creative expertise as superior reproducible performance: innovative and flexible aspects of expert performance', *Psychological Inquiry*, 10/4 (1999), 329–33.

Galenson, David W., *Painting Outside the Lines: Patterns of Creativity in Modern Art* (Cambridge, MA: Harvard University Press, 2001).

Galenson, David W., *Old Masters and Young Geniuses: The Two Life Cycles of Artistic Creativity* (Princeton, NJ: Princeton University Press, 2006).

Ginsburgh, Victor and Sheila Weyers, 'Creation and life cycles of artists', *Journal of Cultural Economics*, 30/2 (2006), 91–107.

Gotwals, Vernon (trans. and ed.), *Haydn: Two Contemporary Portraits* (Madison, WI: University of Wisconsin Press, 1968).

Hayes, John R., 'Cognitive processes in creativity', in John A. Glover, Royce R. Roning and Cecil R. Reynolds (eds), *Handbook of Creativity* (New York: Plenum Press, 1989).

Kozbelt, Aaron, 'Factors affecting aesthetic success and improvement in creativity: a case study of the musical genres of Mozart', *Psychology of Music*, 33/3 (2005), 235–55.

Kozbelt, Aaron, 'A quantitative analysis of Beethoven as self-critic: implications for psychological theories of musical creativity', *Psychology of Music*, 35/1 (2007), 147–72.

Kozbelt, 'One-hit wonders in classical music: evidence and (partial) explanations for an early career peak', *Creativity Research Journal*, 20/2 (2008), 179–95.

Kozbelt, Aaron, 'Gombrich, Galenson, and beyond: integrating case study and typological frameworks in the study of creative individuals', *Empirical Studies of the Arts*, 26/1 (2008), 51–68.

Kozbelt, Aaron, 'Longitudinal hit ratios of classical composers: reconciling "Darwinian" and expertise acquisition perspectives on lifespan creativity', *Psychology of Aesthetics, Creativity, and the Arts*, 2/4 (2008), 221–35.

Kozbelt, Aaron, 'Performance time productivity and versatility estimates for 102 classical composers', *Psychology of Music*, 37/1 (2009), 25–46.

Kozbelt, Aaron, 'The evolution of evolvability, applied to human creativity', *International Journal of Creativity and Problem Solving*, 19/1 (2009), 101–21.

Kozbelt, Aaron, 'Theories of creativity', in Mark A. Runco & Steven R. Pritzker (eds), *Encyclopedia of Creativity*, 2nd edn, 2 vols (San Diego, CA: Academic Press, 2011).

Kozbelt, Aaron, 'Age and aesthetic significance in classical music: a multi-level reanalysis of Halsey's (1976) ratings', *Empirical Studies of the Arts*, 29/2 (2009), 129–48.

Machlis, Joseph, *Introduction to Contemporary Music*, 2nd edn (New York: Norton, 1979).

Martindale, Colin, 'The evolution and end of art as Hegelian tragedy', *Empirical Studies of the Arts*, 27/2 (2009), 133–40.

Morgenstern, Sam (ed.), *Composers on Music* (New York: Pantheon, 1956).

Murray, Charles, *Human Accomplishment* (New York: Basic Books, 2003).

Newlin, Dika, *Schoenberg Remembered: Diaries and Recollections (1938–1976).* (New York: Pendragon Press, 1980).

Osborne, Charles, *The Complete Operas of Verdi* (London: Indigo, 1969).

Perkins, David N., *The Mind's Best Work* (Cambridge, MA: Harvard University Press, 1981).

Robbins Landon, Howard Chandler, *The Collected Correspondence and London Notebooks of Joseph Haydn* (London: Barrie and Rockliff, 1959).

Samuel, Claude, *Conversations with Messiaen*, trans. Felix Aprahamian (London: Stainer and Bell, 1976).

Schauffler, Robert Haven, *The Unknown Brahms: His Life, Character, and Works* (Westport, CT: Greenwood Press Publishers, 1972).

Schoenberg, Arnold, *Style and Idea*, ed. Leonard Stein, trans. Leo Black (Berkeley, CA: University of California Press, 1975).

Simonton, Dean Keith, 'Creative productivity, age, and stress: a biographical time-series analysis of 10 classical composers'. *Journal of Personality and Social Psychology*, 35/11 (1977), 791–804.

Simonton, Dean Keith, 'Creative productivity and age: a mathematical model based on a two-step cognitive process', *Developmental Review*, 4/1 (1984), 77–111.

Simonton, Dean Keith, 'Emergence and realization of genius: the lives and works of 120 classical composers', *Journal of Personality and Social Psychology*, 61/5 (1991), 829–40.

Simonton, Dean Keith, 'Creative productivity: a predictive and explanatory model of career landmarks and trajectories', *Psychological Review*, 104/1 (1997), 66–89.

Simonton, Dean Keith, *Origins of Genius: Darwinian Perspectives on Creativity* (New York: Oxford University Press, 1999).

Simonton, Dean Keith, 'Creative development as acquired expertise: theoretical issues and an empirical test', *Developmental Review,* 20/2 (2000), 283–318.

Simonton, Dean Keith, 'Creative life cycles in literature: poets versus novelists or conceptualists versus experimentalists?', *Psychology of Aesthetics, Creativity, and the Arts*, 1/3 (2007), 133–9.

Spencer, Stewart and Barry Millington (trans. and ed.), *Selected Letters of Richard Wagner* (London: Dent, 1987).

Stevens, Halsey, *The Life and Music of Béla Bartók*, 3rd edn (New York: Oxford University Press, 1993).

Stravinsky, Vera and Robert Craft, *Stravinsky in Pictures and Documents* (New York: Simon and Schuster, 1978).

Vallas, Leon, *Claude Debussy: His Life and Works*, trans. Marie O'Brien and Grace O'Brien (New York: Dover, 1973).

Weisberg, Robert W., *Creativity: Understanding Innovation in Problem Solving, Science, Invention, and the Arts* (Hoboken, NJ: Wiley, 2006).

Chapter 3

Musical Imagery in the Creative Process

Freya Bailes and Laura Bishop

Introduction

We know that music a person has heard in the past can be retrieved from memory and mentally re-experienced with high precision and accuracy. Most people, including those without musical training, fall victim to 'earworms'[1] and can acknowledge the faithfulness with which these intrusive representations of familiar tunes replicate the original. Yet at the same time, as we re-present existing music in our mind's ear, the ability to imagine novel musical patterns is an important part of the creative process for skilled musicians. While there have been copious studies of creativity at large, and a substantial subset devoted to music, few have focused on the contribution of the conscious processes involved in imagining music. Our current understanding of the conscious, endogenous representation of music known as musical imagery is rudimentary, and a study of its relationship to imagination and creative musical practice has barely begun.

This chapter will examine musical imagery in its relationship to musical imagination. Imagination is defined as 'the faculty or action of producing mental images of what is not present', but also as 'creative mental ability'.[2] Imagination is a mysterious human capacity, seeming to defy our natural tendency to schematise and reaching beyond perceptual experience. The relationship between imagery or imaging (for example re-presenting a sequence of just-heard notes in the mind) and imagination or imagining (for example creating a new sequence of notes in the mind) has a long history of philosophical and literary study, yet cognitive science has neglected this relationship,[3] and psychological research has generally focused on visual imagination at the expense of other domains, including auditory. With respect to music, there are plenty of anecdotal accounts of 'hearing' new musical ideas in imagination,[4] but there has been very

---

[1]   C. Philip Beaman and Tim I. Williams, 'Earworms ('stuck song syndrome'): towards a natural history of intrusive thoughts', *British Journal of Psychology*, 101/4 (2009), 637–53.

[2]   *Collins New English Dictionary* (London, 1997).

[3]   Nigel J.T. Thomas, 'Are theories of imagery theories of imagination? An active perception approach to conscious mental content', *Cognitive Science*, 23/2 (1997), 207–45.

[4]   Freya Bailes, 'Translating the musical image: case studies of expert musicians'. In:

little psychological research into musical imagination and creation. Mountain[5] addresses what she terms the 'myths and realities' of composers' use of mental imagery, but does not go much beyond a review of famous examples of composers describing their inner hearing of musical ideas. Such a reliance on self-report limits our understanding of the experience of musical imagery in compositional activity to a handful of articulate composers who have been willing to translate a non-verbal process into a verbal description.[6]

To begin to redress this balance, we will provide an overview of the creative functions of musical imagery, with a particular focus on the musical imagery of composers. Different orders of imaging as they relate to composition are then described. We will ask how it is that musical imagery can at once liberate and constrain, and how models of 'imagination imagery' (that is, mental imagery characterised by an element of novelty, see Khatena[7]) translate to the case of musical composition. Our general propensity to imag(in)e music will be explored, and an account will be provided of a recent experience sampling survey, which found that respondents with no musical training imagine original compositions in the course of everyday life.

The Creative Functions of Musical Imagery

Musical imagery is reportedly used in a variety of creative contexts, with the most obvious being composition. Many composers, including famous examples such as Beethoven, Schumann and Mozart, are said to have composed using their inner hearing, or mental music.[8] One composer (G.N.) interviewed in depth by the first author about his experiences with mental imagery[9] made a distinction between imagining music, which involves the development of novel musical materials, as occurs in composition, and imaging music, which is a way of contemplating given musical material. Bennett[10] approached the study of musical creation by

---

A. Chan and A. Noble (eds), *Sounds in Translation: Intersections of Music, Technology and Society* (Canberra, 2009), 41–59.

[5] Rosemary Mountain, 'Composers and imagery: myths and realities'. In: Rolf Inge Godøy and Harald Jørgensen (eds), *Musical Imagery* (Lisse, 2001), 271–88.

[6] Martin L. Nass, 'The development of creative imagination in composers', *International Review of Psycho-Analysis*, 11 (1984), 481–91, Bailes, 'Translating the Musical Image'.

[7] Joe Khatena, *Imagery and Creative Imagination* (Buffalo, NY, 1984).

[8] Marie Agnew, 'The auditory imagery of great composers', *Psychological Monographs*, 31 (1922), 279–87.

[9] Freya Bailes, 'Musical imagery: hearing and imagining music', PhD dissertation (University of Sheffield, 2002), Bailes, 'Translating the musical image'.

[10] Stan Bennett, 'The process of musical creation: interviews with eight composers', *Journal of Research in Music Education*, 24/1 (1976), 3–13.

conducting semi-structured interviews with eight professional composers, and as a result formulated a model of the process that starts with a 'germinal idea'. While this germinal idea need not take the form of conscious inner hearing, it is frequently described in these terms. Mountain[11] makes the important point that music is written to serve a range of functions, and that 'the intentions and objectives will necessarily condition the process and consequently the specific use of imagery'. We will return to the specific uses of imagery in compositional process below.

Improvisation is sometimes used as a compositional tool,[12] and in itself is another creative process in which mental imagery may well play a role. Composers often report an initial approach to composition in which ideas are first mentally improvised, pending elaboration and refinement. Drawing a distinction between 'ordered thinkers' and 'chaotic thinkers', Finke[13] claims that the latter are particularly skilled improvisers owing to their ability to rapidly form remote and novel associations. Current research in our laboratory has investigated the physiological arousal associated with imagining improvisations, and has shown that such mental creation is associated with changes in arousal around points at which improvisers have been instructed to move from one improvisational idea to another.[14] Such an approach holds great potential to explore the attention and arousal associated with the generation of new musical ideas. For example, it might be possible to measure the physiological arousal of composers performing a composition task, to study its alignment with moments of inspiration and moments of conscious idea testing.

Musicians also report using imagery to inform expressive performance.[15] In an interview-based study of 26 professional brass musicians, all members of leading symphony orchestras, two themes arose: that imagery aids in developing an interpretation of music to be performed, and that it facilitates communicating this interpretation to an audience.[16] Imagery in the form of mental rehearsal enables

---

[11]   Mountain, 'Composers and imagery', 272.

[12]   Bennett, 'The process of musical creation'.

[13]   Ronald A. Finke, 'Imagery, creativity and emergent structure', *Consciousness and Cognition*, 5/3 (1996), 381–93.

[14]   Roger T. Dean and Freya Bailes, 'Using time series analysis to evaluate skin conductance during movement while performing, improvising and imagining music' (under review).

[15]   Helane S. Rosenberg, and William Trusheim, 'Creative transformations: how visual artists, musicians and dancers use mental imagery in their work'. In: Joseph E. Shorr (ed.), *Imagery: Current Perspectives* (New York, 1990), 55–7; and William H. Trusheim, 'Audiation and mental imagery: implications for artistic performance', *The Quarterly Journal of Music Teaching and Learning*, 2 (1991), 138–47.

[16]   Patricia Holmes, 'Imagination in practice: a study of the integrated roles of interpretation, imagery and technique in the learning and memorisation processes of two experienced solo performers', *British Journal of Music Education*, 22 (2005), 217–35.

the performer to experiment with alternative interpretations without the need to attend to technical demands[17] and without interference from auditory or motor feedback.[18] The renowned pianist Horowitz mentally rehearsed for this reason; having grown accustomed to the sound and touch of his own piano, he wished to avoid disrupting his performance plans by introducing feedback from a different instrument.[19] Used concurrently with musical performance, imagery provides information about how notes should sound and feel.[20] The mental representation guiding expressive performance contains not only information about which notes to play when,[21] but also information about how those notes should be played.[22] Our recent findings add to a growing body of research suggesting that expressive timing, dynamics and articulation are components of a conscious, guiding, online image. Just as during composition or improvisation, then, it seems that a function of imagery in the context of performance is to mediate exploration of musical ideas without the effects of externalising them. In each case, musicians begin with an idea or structure and are able to manipulate it into a new form with a freedom that surpasses what would have been possible had they been tied to the constraints of music production and perception.

How Composers use Imagery

For Saxton,[23] composing 'traces a path from the intangible imagination to the tangible reality of a created work'. Musical imagery can be used in a variety of ways at all stages along this path. Leman[24] reminds us that, unlike actual sound, we are relatively free in our minds to image sound when we like. Imagining music allows us to rehearse new combinations of sounds without an instrument, a strategy espoused by Schumann, who is reported to have said, 'When you

---

[17] Ibid.

[18] Rosenberg and Trusheim, 'Creative transformations'.

[19] Harold C. Schonberg, *Horowitz: His Life and Music* (London, 1992).

[20] Peter Pfordresher, 'Coordination of perception and action in music performance', *Advances in Cognitive Psychology*, 2/2–3 (2006), 183–98.

[21] Ibid.

[22] Bruno Repp, 'Effects of auditory feedback deprivation on expressive piano performance', *Music Perception*, 16/4 (1999), 409–38; Clemens Wöllner, and Aaron Williamon, 'An exploratory study of the role of performance feedback and musical imagery in piano playing', *Research Studies in Music Education*, 29/1 (2007), 39–54.

[23] Robert Saxton, 'The process of composition from detection to confection'. In: Wyndham Thomas (ed.), *Composition, Performance, Reception: Studies in the Creative Process in Music* (Aldershot, 1998), 6.

[24] Marc Leman, 'Modeling musical imagery'. In: Rolf Inge Godøy and Harald Jørgensen (eds), *Musical Imagery* (Lisse, 2001), 57–76.

begin to compose, do it all with your brain. Do not try the piece at the instrument until it is finished'.[25] Berlioz is said to have described the piano as the 'grave of original thought',[26] and a composer interviewed by Bennett explained that 'the piano is too limiting'.[27]

Some composers, in contrast, lack confidence in their ability to compose away from an instrument. They cite the kinaesthetic dimension of physical production as essential to their composing, presumably because of the sensory reinforcement that this affords.[28] Furthermore, shifting from imagined sound to physical production, and vice versa, is inevitably a process of translation. A qualitative mismatch between the musical imagery and its performance is likely, whether a result of the inability to evoke a veridical sound in mind or the inability to match a desired sound through production.[29] Some composers find that 'real' sound is a more efficient means of developing an idea than imagined sound;[30] for instance, G.N. feels that timbral acuity is lacking in the mental imagery of his compositions, in comparison to the vivid quality of their actual musical realisation.[31]

Regarding the choice between hearing or imaging music, Schumann is said to have described inner musical hearing as the 'finer spirit'.[32] A conflict is therefore apparent between the need to ground compositions in a sounded reality and the desire to dissociate them from the limitations of the physical world. The ways in which composers use imagery may vary between individuals, depending on their capacity to imagine music or preferred composition style, but further discussion with composers as well as empirical study is needed to explore these possibilities.

Lessons from Visual Imagery in Creativity

Studies of the role of mental imagery in musical creativity share with studies in visual creativity their origin in anecdote; however, vision researchers have made considerable progress towards assembling empirical evidence in support of such anecdotes.[33] Moreover, they have produced ostensibly general models of imagery in creativity which, despite having a distinctly visual bias, may inform our understanding of musical imagery and the creative process. Obvious differences between visual and auditory imagery concern the primarily spatial extent of the

25 Agnew, 'The auditory imagery of great composers', 282.
26 Ibid.
27 Bennett, 'The process of musical creation', 8.
28 Nass, 'The development of creative imagination in composers'.
29 Bailes, 'Translating the Musical Image'.
30 Bailes, 'Musical imagery' and 'Translating the musical image'.
31 Bailes, 'Musical imagery'.
32 Agnew, 'The auditory imagery of great composers'.
33 Finke, 'Imagery, creativity and emergent structure'.

former and the temporal extent of the latter. However, visual imagery research is often concerned with transformation through time (for example, requiring the mental rotation of imagined objects), and has shifted away from the notion of a static entity in the mind. Finke's 'Geneplore Model' of creative thinking and imagination deserves special mention for its incorporation of mental representations or imagery. The model is simple, and proposes two phases: (1) the generative phase, in which mental representations are created; and (2) the exploratory phase, in which interpretations of the representation are explored.[34] While actual sounds are often played in generative and exploratory phases of musical creation, it is conceivable that mental imagery also has a role in each phase, and as we shall see, composers frequently describe the generative and exploratory functions of imagery.

Concerned with modelling the development of creativity, Ainsworth-Land identified four stages of growth: (1) the most primitive ability to elaborate; (2) a replicative stage in which form but not function is modified (for example improving through modification); (3) a mutualistic stage of high-level combinations, such as metaphors; and (4) transformation or invention, in which structure is destroyed and reintegrated.[35] Mental imagery was incorporated into Ainsworth-Land's 'Stage Development Model'[36] as outlined in Table 3.1.

These orders are not tied to specific periods of a child or adult's development; rather, they potentially operate at all stages of life, as appropriate to the creative activity in hand. According to Ainsworth-Land,[37] very few processes or creative products belong to one order alone, and progress from one to another is dependent on a 'high degree of intense personal involvement with and commitment to the

Table 3.1   Orders of imagery in the 'Stage Development Model' of creativity

Order	Imaging
First	Spontaneous, concrete, direct representation, realistic
Second	Comfortable, predictable, awareness of ability to manipulate and control, analogical, comparative
Third	Abstract, symbolic, superimposing, metaphorical, controlled and spontaneous
Fourth	Renunciation of control, chaotic, psychedelic, illuminating, receptivity to unconscious material

Source: Ainsworth-Land (1982).

---

[34] Ibid.

[35] Khatena, Imagery and Creative Imagination.

[36] Vaune Ainsworth-Land, 'Imagery and creativity: an integrating perspective', *The Journal of Creative Behavior*, 16/1 (1982), 5–28.

[37] Ibid.

problem'.[38] We can use this Stage Development Model as a broad framework to describe various uses of musical imagery in composition, skipping the first order since this signifies the most basic re-presentation of sensory information.

Second-order Imaging

Imagery and creativity of the second order are goal-directed and involve a conscious manipulation of given material. Ainsworth-Land writes that 'it is the intent – improving, strengthening, extending, modifying – that is more significant than imaginal content'.[39] Creative imaging at this level therefore retains key properties of the original 'product'. Generating and mentally rehearsing a personal interpretation in music performance is an obvious example of second-order imaging, but various aspects of compositional process also align with this level. For example, G.N. explained that he might imagine extensions to (or elaborations of) what it is possible to produce on the piano.[40] The compositional process for G.N. is about making more of his musical 'inner hearing', for a richer product.

At times, musical imagery can serve as a mental playback of ideas that have been created during composition. Retra[41] conducted a study of composers, asking them to provide a verbal commentary in a compositional task during which they had no access to an instrument, and thus no means to 'hear back' their work other than mentally. Her analysis revealed that composers experience holding a conscious musical image in mind at moments of decision-making. Her findings seem to provide empirical support for Penrose,[42] who argued that conscious processes such as mental imagery enter the creative process at a stage of eliminating ideas.

Third-order Imaging

Third-order creativity necessitates a renunciation of familiar patterns, and a susceptibility to thinking and imaging in a new way. As in second-order imaging, the process of creation is intentional and goal-directed, yet it is combined with the ability to spontaneously 'receive' unconscious material. This seems to describe very well most compositional experiences with musical imagery. The combination of old and new implied by the third order is encapsulated by the words of composer Henry Cowell:

---

[38]   Ibid., 11.

[39]   Ainsworth-Land, 'Imagery and creativity', at 14.

[40]   Bailes, 'Musical imagery' and 'Translating the musical image'.

[41]   José Retra, 'An investigation into the musical imagery of contemporary composers', MA dissertation (University of Sheffield, 1999).

[42]   Roger Penrose, *The Emperor's New Mind: Concerning Computers, Minds and the Laws of Physics* (Oxford, 1999).

> Every conceivable tone-quality and beauty of nuance, every harmony and disharmony, or any number of simultaneous melodies can be heard at will by the trained composer; he can hear not only the sound of any instrument or combination of instruments, but also an almost infinite number of sounds which cannot as yet be produced on any instrument.[43]

He describes the composer's mind as 'the most perfect instrument in the world'[44] since it is both veridical in its representation of existing sound, and supposedly limitless in its capacity to 'hear' the new. While very few composers would describe their auditory imagery as perfect, and compositional capacity is to some extent limited by social, environmental, and cognitive constraints, Cowell's statement communicates an optimistic belief that the compositional mind is liberated from the constraints of more earthly instruments. Ainsworth-Land explains that 'third-order creativity and imaging require a change of perception. One needs to look through and into ideas, objects, functions, in order to break up one's perceptual set' and 'push against the limits of normal perception'.[45]

Fourth-order Imaging

Fourth-order imaging is characterised by spontaneity, and in that sense shares properties with first-order musical imagery. Where it differs is in the level of creativity represented, with fourth-order imaging akin to what is often dubbed 'inspiration'. Inspiration in composition is frequently equated with musical imagery; 'the myths that surround the one have confused investigation of the other'.[46] One of these myths is that inspiration takes the form of a complete and pure auditory image, to be translated in a sequential manner from the mind to paper. In reality, Mountain's evidence suggests that composers are more likely to have been mentally working on music for a while, perhaps progressing through lower orders of the Stage Development Model, modifying and developing an image rather than transcribing one in virgin form. The alternation between unconscious and conscious thought seems to be at the root of many misconceptions regarding the role of inspiration and the role of assimilation. While inspiration may strike as a seemingly complete idea, it is likely to be based on the unconscious amalgamation of assimilated musical experience. Thus inspiration and assimilation are likely to be part of the same experience.[47] Agnew describes the process as the 'conscious maturing of thought, through mental saturation with sound images'.[48] While

---

[43]   Henry Cowell, 'The process of musical creation', *American Journal of Psychology*, 37/2 (1926), 233–6, at 234.

[44]   Ibid.

[45]   Ainsworth-Land, 'Imagery and creativity', 22.

[46]   Mountain, 'Composers and imagery', 273.

[47]   Bailes, 'Musical imagery'.

[48]   Agnew, 'The auditory imagery of great composers', 287.

we have defined musical imagery to be the conscious experience of the qualia of music, it is inevitably underpinned by unconscious processes.[49] For Cowell, inspiration in the form of musical imagery was a feature of his early experiences with composition, and he describes a conscious effort to learn to control these experiences in order to imagine novel material at will.[50]

G.N. also described his compositional imagery as being controlled, and steered by his volition.[51] Yet at the same time he placed great faith in his unconscious musical processing, for example, trusting in his ability to solve a musical problem by sleeping on it. Stockhausen reports the unconscious resolution of a compositional problem overnight:

> I remember that very often when I'd worked until late at night, I gave up; the brain continued working on the problem during my sleep, and I knew the solution next morning.[52]

Bennett[53] also reported that composers frequently rely on a night's sleep to resolve the equivalent of writer's block. Removing a problem from conscious awareness is known as 'incubation' (see for example Finke[54] with respect to the role of incubation in creativity). It seems that composers may derive as much from the decline of irrelevant mental activity and consequent streamlining of thought as from unconscious processing *per se*. G.N. explains:

> In fact I really don't see any great divide between the conscious and the subconscious. I used to feel very puritanical about music that I'd worked on, as opposed to music that I hadn't worked on; you know valuing the one and not the other. But as the pieces recede from you in time, you can't remember which bits you worked on, and which bits didn't present any problems at all.[55]

Musical Imagery: Limitations and Liberations

A sticker on the door of a university music department instructs, 'feed your aural imagination: go to a live concert today'. We readily accept that our imaginations must be stimulated, in music as in the other creative arts. Exposure to musical ideas, be they pitch systems such as tonality, rhythms, timbral depth or formal

---

[49]   Finke, 'Imagery, creativity and emergent structure'.

[50]   Cowell, 'The process of musical creation'.

[51]   Bailes, 'Musical imagery'.

[52]   Stockhausen, cited on p. 52 of Jonathan Cott, *Stockhausen: Conversations with the Composer* (London, 1974).

[53]   Bennett, 'The process of musical creation'.

[54]   Finke, 'Imagery, creativity and emergent structure'.

[55]   Bailes, 'Musical imagery', 205.

concepts, allows us to adopt their properties and imagine them in a novel way. It hardly seems possible to invent a musical idea without prior exposure to these systems and concepts. The paradox then is that, the greater the exposure to existing musical ideas, through listening and imaging, the greater the likelihood of assimilating them wholesale, or incorporating them as part of a schematic representation of musical experience. This is not imagination, but rather the regurgitation of pre-existing musical thought. So what is the role, if any, of musical imagery in creation?

Leman makes the important observation that imagery is 'free because it is not driven by the outer environment, constrained because it is (i) embedded in a space that was first moulded by the outer environment, and (ii) subject to autonomous processing'.[56] So how does this interplay of constraint and freedom translate to musical composition? The raw materials of heard and imaged sound are largely shaped by environmental factors. In order to imagine new sound, manipulations of this mental source material are required. In the realm of visual creativity, work has demonstrated that imagination is indeed structured by prior knowledge. For example, elements from familiar visual scenes make an appearance in new designs.[57] Some degree of structural connectedness, most evident in the generative phase of the Geneplore Model, is necessary in order to avoid chaos, but this must be balanced out by imaginative divergence, which may be maximal during the exploratory phase.[58]

A potentially unavoidable link between imagery and bodily experience may help explain the contribution of perception to musical imagination. Cognitive science has long held that we are shaped by our experiences of the world around us. There are good adaptive explanations for this predisposition, since as a consequence we are ready to encounter and respond appropriately to those events that are statistically most likely to occur. The very notion of a mental representation runs counter to ecological accounts of psychology, which favour an understanding of imagery associated with action.[59] Musical imagery is argued to arise as the embodiment of plans necessary to actively anticipate environmental information.[60] Accordingly, our bodily experience and cognition are inseparable, and, in spite of the accounts of the composers above who describe drawing on imagery to escape physical limitations, it might be that we find it difficult to

---

[56]   Leman, 'Modeling musical imagery', 67.

[57]   Finke, 'Imagery, creativity and emergent structure'.

[58]   Ibid.

[59]   Kieron Philip O'Connor and Frederick Aardema, 'The imagination: cognitive, pre-cognitive, and meta-cognitive aspects', *Consciousness and Cognition*, 14/2 (2005), 233–56.

[60]   Ulric Neisser, *Cognition and Reality: Principles and Implications of Cognitive Psychology* (San Fransisco, CA, 1976).

imagine properties in the absence of their physical and motoric realisation.[61] Nass[62] describes a psychoanalytic view of the development of creative imagination in composers, and in doing so underscores his belief that composers are particular in their retention of sensorimotor styles and a close proximity to bodily processes, 'In early development, existence is experienced as action and action is the very essence of early perception'.[63]

The literature on the impact of imagined sound on the detection of a sound stimulus suggests that imagery might inhibit perception.[64] Perhaps it does not pay to be too involved in an imagined sound world, if this reduces sensitivity to a perception of 'real' sound. Yet hyperacuity to sensory stimuli has been described as a characteristic of composers.[65] Perhaps such perceptual sensitivity is sufficient to override any dangers associated with absorption in the imaginary, or perhaps it goes some way to explain the substance of the musical image. Greater acuity of perception means that more detailed information is available to be stored in memory, and then later retrieved and mentally re-presented. Musical imagery is a multimodal phenomenon, with the potential to include interactions of visual, kinaesthetic and haptic dimensions of imaged sound. Harvey cites Brian Ferneyhough writing on the subject of his compositional experiences, where the compositional idea is far from being a purely auditory one:

> The first sensation, the experience which begins to persuade me that I am actually going to write a piece, is very often a cross between a tactile, a visual, and an aural one. That is, I tend to perceive a mass, almost a tangible sculptural or sculpted mass, in some sort of imagined space, which is made up of these various elements.[66]

Musical Imagery as a Creative Tool

If environmental regularities shape our mental imagery, can we imagine beyond our perceptual experience? Khatena writes:

---

[61] See recent work on action-perception networks, such as Peter E. Keller, Simone Dalla Bella and Iring Koch, 'Auditory imagery shapes movement timing and kinematics: evidence from a musical task'. *Journal of Experimental Psychology: Human Perception and Performance*, 36/2 (2010), 508–13.

[62] Nass, 'The development of creative imagination in composers'.

[63] Ibid., 482.

[64] Timothy L. Hubbard, 'Auditory imagery: empirical findings', *Psychological Bulletin*, 136/2 (2010), 302–29.

[65] Nass, 'The development of creative imagination in composers'.

[66] Ferneyhough, quoted by Jonathan Harvey, *Music and Inspiration* (London, 1999), 30.

Images are representations of objects and events of the external world, and because of the mediating filtering system of past experiences, selectivity of aspects of sensory input determines their individual nature. These differ from one person to the next even though the original stimuli were the same.[67]

Here, Khatena's emphasis on 'selectivity of aspects of sensory input' highlights that perception in itself is personal and in important respects creative. Saxton articulates the intricate negotiation of perception, imagery and imagination involved in composition, saying that 'For a composer, there exists continual two-way osmosis between the material itself and applied methods of treating the "received" musical ideas'.[68] Perception or imagery may furnish these received ideas, while imagination works to develop them to present them in a new form.[69] Nass argues that the process of re-presentation, with an always fresh perspective, is 'the true mark of the creator'.[70]

One creative use of imagery, extensively studied in the domain of vision, is what can be called combinatorial play.[71] This involves the mental synthesis of different elements in order to create a new idea. Mental synthesis experiments have required that participants imagine various objects (dubbed 'preinventive forms'), and then form an original combination in mind. The results suggest that the very process of exploring the initial preinventive forms can lead to sudden insights of the form of the new combined object.[72] In order to translate the use of combinatorial play from vision to audition, it might help to reconceptualise combinations as operations that are more temporal than spatial. Future research could explore to what extent composers employ such a mental tool, as a window onto a third-order imaging technique that can be readily applied to the teaching of composition.

The process of testing new compositional ideas in imagination is resource intensive. Perhaps the constraints of working memory, which mediates the storage and processing of musical information, limits our ability to synthesise musical ideas in imagination. Halford, Wilson and Phillips[73] argue that processing capacity in cognition is restricted by relational complexity, which refers to the number of relations between elements or features of a stimulus or environment. Creative people are thought to have a greater capacity for processing relations between ideas. For example, Dailey and colleagues found that individuals scoring highly

---

[67]   Ibid., 11.

[68]   Saxton, 'The process of composition from detection to confection', 6

[69]   Bailes, 'Musical imagery', 228.

[70]   Nass, 'The development of creative imagination in composers', 488.

[71]   Finke, 'Imagery, creativity and emergent structure'.

[72]   Ibid., 385.

[73]   Graeme S. Halford, William H. Wilson and Steven Phillips, 'Processing capacity defined by relational complexity: implications for comparative, developmental, and cognitive psychology', *Behavioral and Brain Sciences*, 21 (1998), 803–65.

on the 'Remote Associates Test',[74] which was used to assess creative potential, made stronger associations between synaesthetic components and emotional terms than those with a lower score. Since word associations are held to be responsible for triggering the imagining of words and songs,[75] it could be that such creative individuals are similarly primed to imagine more music in the course of their everyday life.

Bailes[76] describes the case study of a composer, G.N., with a particular emphasis on his use of imagery before, during and after creating new musical work. G.N. reported relying on musical imagery in order to attain a mental flexibility, and thus to retain conceptual freshness. Indeed, he expressed that musical imagery 'might also help break free from learned material through its inadequacies as an exact mental representation of given music'[77] and, 'if it's a playback mechanism you can't be certain that every time it's the same'.[78] While G.N. described familiarity with music as a prerequisite to imagery, over-familiarity might stifle fresh development. Imagery as an imaginative tool may be characterised by its transience. As we will elaborate in the following section, some have argued that dynamic change is a fundamental aspect of the imaginative process, with fluidity a primary property.[79]

Imaginative Models

In this chapter we consider imagination to be the inventive manipulation of musical imagery, which shares many of the constraining properties of perception. In other words, the raw materials of both heard and imagined sound are largely shaped by environmental factors, as outlined above. Our accumulated knowledge forms a probability map or mental schema, which Bregman[80] describes as a highly potentiated internal state, ready to be activated. Theories converge to suggest that our schemata drive active perceptions of our environment, and a 'Perceptual Activity Theory'[81] extends the principle to imagery and imagination. Amalgamating ideas from Neisser and ecological psychology, Perceptual Activity

---

[74]   A. Dailey, Colin Martindale and J. Borkum, 'Creativity, synaesthesia, and physiognomic perception', *Creativity Research Journal*, 10/1 (1997), 1–8.

[75]   Lia Kvavilashvili and George Mandler, 'Out of one's mind: a study of involuntary semantic memories', *Cognitive Psychology*, 48, (2004), 47–94.

[76]   Bailes, 'Translating the musical image'.

[77]   Ibid., 48.

[78]   Bailes, 'Musical imagery', 201.

[79]   O'Connor and Aardema, 'The imagination'.

[80]   Albert S. Bregman, 'Auditory scene analysis: hearing in complex environments'. In: Stephen McAdams and Emmanuel Bigand (eds), *Thinking in Sound: The Cognitive Psychology of Human Audition* (Oxford, 1993), 10–36.

[81]   Thomas, 'Are theories of imagery theories of imagination?'

theory posits that mental imagery is the active updating of our schemata 'that specify how to direct our attention most effectively in particular situations: how to efficiently examine and explore, and thus interpret'.[82] According to Perceptual Activity Theory, 'imagery is experienced when a schema that is not directly relevant to the exploration of the current environment is allowed at least partial control of the exploratory apparatus'.[83] A wealth of neuroimaging data now exists to support auditory imagery as covert perceptual processes.[84] It is also noteworthy that motor imagery has been conceived as covert action, with Berthoz describing it as 'only the manifestation of the normal internal simulation which accompanies planning and execution of movements'.[85]

Thomas describes visual imagination as our potential to *see as*, and imagination involves *seeing as*, or interpreting, in a new way. It allows us to change perspective, and visual researchers have studied this experimentally by examining our propensity to alter the way in which we perceive ambiguous stimuli.[86] Applied to audition, auditory imagination is our potential to *hear as*. This is precisely what Schumann is reported to have done when hearing piano music as an orchestra in his mind's ear.[87] He was also described as experiencing different imaginative versions of one same piece of music. Dubiel believes that 'we cannot draw a boundary between "hearing what's there" and "imagining something", because hearing sound as music always involves imagination'.[88] In other words, we always interpret and 'hear as' when attending to sound, be that externally (perception) or internally (imagery) derived. With respect to visual imagination, O'Connor and Aardema cite Mark Twain saying, 'You can't depend on your eyes if your imagination is out of focus'.[89] Perhaps we should be equally wary of depending on our ears in such a case.

---

[82]   Ibid., 218.

[83]   Ibid., 218.

[84]   Andrea R. Halpern, Robert J. Zatorre, Marc Bouffard and Jennifer A. Johnson, 'Behavioral and neural correlates of perceived and imagined musical timbre', *Neuropsychologia*, 42 (2004), 1281–92; Sybille C. Herholz, Claudia Lappe, Arne Knief and Christo Pantev, 'Neural basis of music imagery and the effect of musical expertise', *European Journal of Neuroscience*, 28/11 (2008), 2352–60; Robert J. Zatorre, 'Brain imaging studies of musical perception and musical imagery', *Journal of New Music Research*, 28/3 (1999), 229–36.

[85]   Alain Berthoz, 'The role of inhibition in the hierarchical gating of executed and imagined movements', *Cognitive Brain Research*, 3 (1996), 101–13, at 110.

[86]   Finke, 'Imagery, creativity and emergent structure'.

[87]   Agnew, 'The auditory imagery of great composers'.

[88]   Joseph Dubiel, 'Composer, theorist, composer/theorist'. In: Nicholas Cook and Mark Everist (eds), *Rethinking Music* (Oxford, 1999), 262–83, at 264.

[89]   O'Connor and Aardema, 'The imagination', 233.

In his review of empirical findings in auditory imagery research, Hubbard[90] outlines an apparent conflict in studies that demonstrate either interference or facilitation of actual perception from auditory imagery.[91] The difference appears to lie in the nature of experimental tasks that require participants to either detect an auditory signal when imaging sound or make a judgement about a perceived stimulus in the context of auditory imagery. Auditory imagery interferes in the former condition, but facilitates performance in the latter. Such experimental tasks have the potential to inform us of the extent to which perception and imagery compete or concur, and thus reveal much about our imaginative potential. Outside of the research context, composers report being able to 'hear as', or superimpose a mental image on their perception of, for example, the piano.

> Images of musical sound – or of anything – are something more than convenient, disposable tools for the imagination and the memory: they are the mind's only contact with the reality they represent.[92]

Images, rather than being a mere by-product of cognition, are a conscious interpretation of our environment. Rowell's statement is comparable to the views of Dubiel,[93] whereby perception and imagery are so intertwined as to be conceptually inseparable. Schemata based on past experience mediate perception, so that each perceptual act is a process of extracting meaningful information from the perceptual event. The musicians featured in Bailes[94] describe imagery comprising features that correlated directly with those features they found interesting and meaningful in perception. This is consistent with evidence from a composer who describes musical imagery as an ability to attend to sounds in imagination, much as a listener attends in perception.[95]

While imagery, perception and imagination might be inextricably intertwined, we nevertheless experience variations in the dominance of each. O'Connor and Aardema[96] provide a compelling explanatory framework, albeit tailored to visual imagination in which they argue that intention and level of absorption are able

---

[90] Hubbard, 'Auditory imagery'.

[91] Robert G. Crowder and Mark A. Pitt, 'Research on memory/imagery for musical timbre'. In: Daniel Reisberg (ed.), *Auditory Imagery* (Hillsdale, NJ, 1992), 29–44; Martha J. Farah and Albert F. Smith, 'Perceptual interference and facilitation with auditory imagery', *Perception and Psychophysics*, 33/5 (1983), 475–8; Timothy L. Hubbard, and Keiko Stoeckig, 'Musical imagery: generation of tones and chords', *Journal of Experimental Psychology: Learning, Memory, and Cognition*, 14 (1988), 656–67.

[92] Lewis Rowell, 'The musical imagery of India'. In: Rolf Inge Godøy and Harald Jørgensen (eds), *Musical Imagery* (Lisse, 2001), 289–302.

[93] Dubiel, 'Composer, theorist, composer/theorist'.

[94] Bailes, 'Translating the musical image'.

[95] Ibid.

[96] O'Connor and Aardema, 'The imagination'.

to account for these apparently distinct phenomena. This is important when explaining the ability of composers to simultaneously perceive their surroundings, imagine musical content and explore imaginative perspectives. Their absorption or otherwise in their musical imagery, combined with the presence or absence of competing demands on their attentional resources, surely modulates their experience of this imagery–perception–imagination relationship. These differing forms of conscious experience lead O'Connor and Aardema to devise a 'Possibilistic Model of Consciousness'. Their underlying premise is that we live in a world of possibilities, and the content of our conscious awareness represents the most focused possibility: 'Imagination is the active exploration of this latent possible space in the same way that perception is the active exploration of the visible space'[97] … 'thus imagination can operate both inward and outward, but is ever present within all mental experience, regardless whether its causal history lies in the outside world or the one within'.[98] When musical imagery occurs in the context of imaginative exploration of a possibility space, it is easy to see how it is essentially dynamic, since the creative imperative necessitates the potentially never-ending search for alternative possibilities, not currently in conscious focus. 'The space between the seen and unseen becomes a possibility space of what is about to be',[99] which might just as easily concern a space between 'the heard and unheard'. From a psychoanalytic stance, Nass[100] describes composition as serving the development of a sense of reality, and as a form of reality testing. Exploration of this 'reality' or possibility space might comprise convergence or divergence, mutation or hybridisation.[101]

Propensity to Imag(in)e

According to the Possibilistic Model, intentional space between an individual and their world does not simply exist, it needs to be 'filled up creatively'.[102] Applied to the act of musical composition, this suggests a scenario in which we creatively explore musical possibilities, and in cases in which music is not physically present in our environment, we may imaginatively fill the void by immersion in our world of possibilities through musical imagery. The filling of such a musical void can occur unintentionally, as in the phenomenon of an earworm or the occurrence of a moment of inspiration, or it could be the intentional dedication of conscious thought to composition. As argued by O'Connor and Aardema, 'a gradient of

---

[97]   Ibid., 242.
[98]   Ibid., 243.
[99]   O'Connor and Aardema, 'The imagination', 254.
[100] Nass, 'The development of creative imagination in composers'.
[101] Khatena, *Imagery and Creative Imagination*.
[102] O'Connor and Aardema, 'The imagination', 244.

absorption covarying with degrees of possibility accommodates smoothly our sporadic changes in consciousness whilst maintaining our sense of reality'.[103]

In a recent study, Bailes[104] sought to examine the prevalence and nature of 'everyday' musical imagery in university music students. Using an experience sampling method in which participants were contacted by mobile phone at quasi-random times of the day, she found that very few everyday episodes of musical imagery reported by these students, including composition students, were considered to be of original music. The separate case study of the composer G.N. also addressed his experiences of everyday 'tune on the brain' occurrences, finding that these were common, passive memory images of heard music, and quite distinct in character from his compositional imagery, to which he would deliberately devote his time.[105] Results from these two studies seem to suggest that intentional compositional imagery is quite distinct from the more common 'earworm' experience of having previously heard music running round the head. This is perhaps not surprising insofar as both professional and student composers have been trained to consider musical creation as a deliberate activity, in many ways removed from daily life. Moreover, composers might well disregard or downplay musical imagery experienced outside of composition time as 'merely' variations of existing music, or as empty ideas not worthy of development.

In recent work, the first author has extended her study of everyday musical imagery to the wider population. Forty-seven participants from western Sydney received a text message at six quasi-random times of the day, for a period of seven days, prompting them to fill out an experience sampling form to describe their current musical experiences, 'real' or imagined. The experience sampling form combined closed and open questions to elicit information about who participants were with, what they were engaged in doing, and how they felt, particularly during episodes of musical imagery. Space was provided for participants to name the music in their mind, describe its genre or state that the music was their own composition. Eight respondents (four men and four women) reported imagining their own compositions for a median of 21 per cent of episodes. None of the eight respondents had musical training, and their Ollen Musical Sophistication Index[106] range was from 42 to 248, where a score under 500 represents the likelihood that an expert would classify the individual as 'less musically sophisticated'. The imaginative properties of earworm experience serve as a reminder of our creative potential manifest in everyday life, providing empirical support for an inclusive philosophy of creativity in pedagogy.

---

[103]   Ibid., 245.

[104]   Freya Bailes, 'The prevalence and nature of imagined music in the everyday lives of music students', *Psychology of Music*, 35/4 (2007), 555–70.

[105]   Bailes, 'Musical imagery'.

[106]   Joy Ollen, 'A criterion-related validity test of selected indicators of musical sophistication using expert ratings', PhD dissertation (Ohio State University, 2006).

Composers often describe using musical imagery as a form of memory representation, to retain their compositional ideas in mind (e.g. G.N.[107]). Mozart is notoriously said to have had an exceptional memory for music, with an alleged ability to inwardly hear his completed works as a whole.[108] Even in earlier compositional stages, Mozart described retaining pleasing ideas in memory, even humming them.[109] In this case, composition and everyday imaging surely overlapped. Others, such as Berlioz, who dreamed of musical ideas, would need to rely on good memory skills to recall them by day.[110] Many factors are known to impact on memory, including arousal at the time of encoding a stimulus or, in this case, idea in the form of a musical image. Bennett[111] speculates on the possible implications of arousal impairing short-term recall but enhancing long-term recall for composers. Perhaps only a select few ideas make it into compositional development, and these may well relate to the emotional state of the composer at the time of imaging. Some circumstances are more conducive to an absorption in our inner world than others, and the conditions in which famous composers choose to work or are inspired are often reported. For example, Nass[112] thought it important to note that two composers from his study developed compositional ideas while on bicycle rides. Bennett[113] describes one composer going for a walk to relieve a sort of musical writer's block. Mozart too is said to have been inspired while travelling, either by carriage or walking, when alone and 'of good cheer', after eating or when unable to sleep at night.[114] The contemporary composer John Tavener talks of 'doing other things – buying fish, choosing wine, driving the car, going for a walk … all during this time the notes and patterns of notes are beginning to form in my head … it's been simmering, as it were, rather like wine when it's fermenting'.[115] Bennett found that most of the classical composers of his study worked with 'feelings of tranquility, security, and relaxation'.[116]

Anecdotal accounts frequently describe the constant or persistent musical imagery of composers. For example, Wagner is said to have 'suffered' from persistent replays of operas he conducted. Agnew[117] reports that Tchaikovsky was tormented by persistent music in his mind during early childhood, to the extent

[107]   Bailes, 'Musical imagery'.
[108]   Agnew, 'The auditory imagery of great composers'.
[109]   Ibid.
[110]   Ibid.
[111]   Bennett, 'The process of musical creation'.
[112]   Nass, 'The development of creative imagination in composers'.
[113]   Bennett, 'The process of musical creation'.
[114]   Khatena, *Imagery and Creative Imagination*.
[115]   John Tavener, *The Music of Silence: A Composer's Testament* (London, 1999), 144.
[116]   Bennett, 'The process of musical creation', 3.
[117]   Agnew, 'The auditory imagery of great composers'.

that it prevented him from sleeping. We do not know whether this mental music was novel or a repetition of music he had heard. He also spoke of having particular fragments stuck on a 'mental replay' all day long.[118] Nass[119] tells of an individual who since childhood had experienced constant musical imagery that he did not recognise, and so attributed to his own invention. Cowell describes a process of explicitly rehearsing others' compositions in his 'mind's ear', as an apparently successful strategy to develop his 'sound-mind'.

> No sooner did I begin this self-training than I had at times curious experiences
> of having glorious sounds leap unexpectedly into my mind – original melodies
> and complete harmonies such as I could not conjure forth at will, and exalted
> qualities of tone such as I had never heard nor before imagined.[120]

Research into interoception,[121] the subconscious awareness of bodily response, suggests that this can have significant consequences on psychological state. For instance, it seems that our perceptions are subconsciously tuned to our own biological rhythms such as heartbeat. Recent research[122] has found a positive relationship between scores on a measure of so-called transliminality and self-reported incidence of having a 'tune on the brain'. A high transliminality score is taken to indicate a greater propensity for material to pass in and out of conscious awareness. This area has yet to be fully explored and understood, but it seems likely that a lower transliminal threshold might bring interoceptive processes into conscious awareness, and thus trigger musical imagery. Nass[123] relates the metaphor used by a composer from his study of detecting a ripple on the surface of a psychic pool, while Bennett[124] writes of subconscious musical material breaking through to consciousness, and being seized by an attentive, conscious mind.

Summarising work on interior monologue, or 'thinking aloud' by Hogenraad and Orianne, Hubbard[125] connects their findings of a 60–90 minute periodicity in the strength of reported incidents with the periodicity of REM sleep, suggesting that mental imagery strength operates on such a circadian cycle. The idea is intriguing, but remains to be investigated both theoretically and experimentally by future work.

---

[118] Ibid.

[119] Nass, 'The development of creative imagination in composers'.

[120] Cowell, 'The process of musical creation', 235.

[121] For example Y. Kadota, G. Cooper, A.R. Burton, J. Lemon, U. Schall and A. Lloyd, 'Autonomic hyper-vigilance in post-infective fatigue syndrome', *Biological Psychology*, 85/1 (2010), 97–103.

[122] M. Wammes and Imants Baruss, 'Characteristics of spontaneous musical imagery', *Journal of Consciousness Studies*, 16/1 (2009), 37–61.

[123] Nass, 'The development of creative imagination in composers'.

[124] Bennett, 'The process of musical creation'.

[125] Hubbard, 'Auditory imagery'.

Musical Dreams

There are many reports of imaginative imagery during dreams (for example Kekulé famously dreamed of the benzene ring, while Bennett[126] and Massey[127] review musical examples), and this is another area in need of systematic exploration. Berlioz is an example of a composer who often claimed to dream of his themes.[128] On numerous occasions he describes writing down those he could remember on waking. It is surely hard to disentangle what might genuinely be experienced during sleep from imagery experienced on waking, known as hypnopompic imagery. An exceptional memory is undoubtedly necessary to recall the details of such a musical dream, and Massey[129] would argue that the task is made easier by what he sees as the musical dream's resilience to distortion (unlike language and visual imagery). His assertion is based on a combination of autobiographical introspection with respect to his own dreams, anecdotal accounts from others, and an interpretation of the neuroscientific literature in which right hemisphere dominance is associated with a certain integrity of musical content. According to Massey,[130] music has a structural coherence that lends it an inner propulsion, and makes it susceptible to retaining its form both during and after a dream. From a cognitive perspective, structural cogency does facilitate the chunking of elements in memory. Another aspect of Massey's review of the historical study of musical dreams, and among the more interesting observations, is a link between the frequency of musical dreams and musical training, even though 'non-musicians' have reported the phenomenon. Massey writes that, for many cultures, music is believed to be communicated from another world through the medium of dreams, and thus dreaming is essential for invention.[131] However, not all musical dreams comprise original material, and sometimes composers dream of extracts of their already composed music. Massey[132] describes such an instance for Wagner. Such accounts demand study of the prevalence and nature of imagery occurring during sleep as well as the mechanisms that would enable such a process to take place.

---

[126]   Bennett, 'The process of musical creation'.

[127]   Irving J. Massey, 'The musical dream revisited: music and language in dreams', *Psychology of Aesthetics, Creativity, and the Arts*, S/1 (2006), 42–50.

[128]   Agnew, 'The auditory imagery of great composers'.

[129]   Massey, 'The musical dream revisited'.

[130]   Ibid.

[131]   Ibid.

[132]   Ibid.

Conclusions

A number of important questions remain unanswered. Are composers better able to 'hear as' than non-composers?[133] Do composers with a particularly faithful episodic memory for the music they have heard differ from those who more readily assimilate their memory within a schematic representation? Do composers who do not retrieve the music of others in their mind's ear tend towards greater novelty? Alternatively, does the ability to recreate a veridical memory image furnish a qualitative richness from which to generate new ideas, which is otherwise lacking for the composer with a less precise recall, and who may draw on schematic cliché? When experiencing musical imagery in everyday life[134] are composers, whatever their style and experience, discernibly more imaginative (incorporating more novel elements) than their non-composer musician counterparts? Both the Stage Development Model and the Possibilistic Model predict that commitment to and absorption in creative processes are associated with higher levels of creative achievement, suggesting that dedicated composers would indeed experience more imaginative imagery than those lacking in compositional motivation.

This chapter has reviewed our current knowledge of the role and use of musical imagery in the creative process, with a particular focus on composition. We have described some of the ways in which composers draw on musical imagery, and identified orders of compositional imagery that seem to align with Ainsworth-Land's Stage Development Model of imagery in creativity.[135] A particular challenge for future research in this area will be to use the rich anecdotal reports of imagery use in composition, many of which have been cited here, as a starting block for studies with the capacity to pinpoint the underlying cognitive mechanisms involved. Since imagery is at once referred to by musicians as being a means to free thought, while at the same time constrained by our cognitive make-up, a model is required that will allow for this juxtaposition of old and new. Both the Perceptual Activity Theory[136] and the Possibilistic Model[137] are compelling frameworks for the dynamic exploration of our sensory world that seem to reconcile this paradox. Moreover, they have the power to relate intentional imaging, as is often used in composition, to unintentional, everyday imaging, as occurs when we have a 'tune on the brain'. The imaginative properties of earworm experience serve as a reminder of our creative potential manifest in everyday life, providing empirical support for an inclusive philosophy of creativity in the act of musical composition.

---

[133] Thomas, 'Are theories of imagery theories of imagination?'

[134] Freya Bailes, 'The use of experience-sampling methods to monitor musical imagery in everyday life', *Musicae Scientiae*, 10/2 (2006), 173–90; Bailes, 'The prevalence and nature of imagined music'.

[135] Ainsworth-Land, 'Imagery and creativity'.

[136] Thomas, 'Are theories of imagery theories of imagination?'

[137] O'Connor and Aardema, 'The imagination'.

References

Agnew, Marie, 'The auditory imagery of great composers', *Psychological Monographs*, 31 (1922), 279–87.

Ainsworth-Land, Vaune, 'Imagery and creativity: an integrating perspective', *The Journal of Creative Behavior*, 16/1 (1982), 5–28.

Bailes, Freya, 'Musical imagery: hearing and imagining music', PhD dissertation (University of Sheffield, 2002).

Bailes, Freya, 'The use of experience-sampling methods to monitor musical imagery in everyday life', *Musicae Scientiae*, 10/2 (2006), 173–90.

Bailes, Freya, 'The prevalence and nature of imagined music in the everyday lives of music students', *Psychology of Music*, 35/4 (2007), 555–70.

Bailes, Freya, 'Translating the musical image: case studies of expert musicians'. In: A. Chan and A. Noble (eds), *Sounds in Translation: Intersections of Music, Technology and Society* (Canberra: ANU E-Press, 2009), 41–59.

Beaman, C. Philip and Tim I. Williams, 'Earworms ('stuck song syndrome'), towards a natural history of intrusive thoughts', *British Journal of Psychology*, 101/4 (2009), 637–53.

Bennett, Stan, 'The process of musical creation: Interviews with eight composers', *Journal of Research in Music Education*, 24/1 (1976), 3–13.

Berthoz, Alain, 'The role of inhibition in the hierarchical gating of executed and imagined movements', *Cognitive Brain Research*, 3 (1996), 101–13.

Bregman, Albert S., 'Auditory scene analysis: hearing in complex environments'. In: Stephen McAdams and Emmanuel Bigand (eds), *Thinking in Sound: The Cognitive Psychology of Human Audition* (Oxford: Clarendon Press, 1993), 10–36.

Collins New English Dictionary (London: HarperCollins, 1997).

Cott, Jonathan, *Stockhausen: Conversations with the Composer* (London, 1974), 52.

Cowell, Henry, 'The process of musical creation'. *American Journal of Psychology*, 37/2 (1926), 233–6.

Crowder, Robert G. and Mark A. Pitt, 'Research on memory/imagery for musical timbre'. In: Daniel Reisberg (ed.), *Auditory Imagery* (Hillsdale, NJ: Lawrence Erlbaum Associates, 1992), 29–44.

Dailey, A., Colin Martindale and J. Borkum, 'Creativity, synaesthesia, and physiognomic perception', *Creativity Research Journal*, 10/1 (1997), 1–8.

Dean, Roger T. and Freya Bailes, 'Using time series analysis to evaluate skin conductance during movement while performing, improvising and imagining music' (under review).

Dubiel, Joseph, 'Composer, theorist, composer/theorist'. In: Nicholas Cook and Mark Everist (eds), *Rethinking Music* (Oxford: Oxford University Press, 1999), 262–83.

Farah, Martha J. and Albert F. Smith, 'Perceptual interference and facilitation with auditory imagery', *Perception and Psychophysics*, 33/5 (1983), 475–8.

Finke, Ronald A., 'Imagery, creativity and emergent structure', *Consciousness and Cognition*, 5/3 (1996), 381–93.

Halford, Graeme S., William H. Wilson and Steven Phillips, 'Processing capacity defined by relational complexity: implications for comparative, developmental, and cognitive psychology', *Behavioral and Brain Sciences*, 21 (1998), 803–65.

Halpern, Andrea R., Robert J. Zatorre, Marc Bouffard and Jennifer A. Johnson, 'Behavioral and neural correlates of perceived and imagined musical timbre', *Neuropsychologia*, 42 (2004), 1281–92.

Harvey, Jonathan, *Music and Inspiration* (London: Faber and Faber, 1999), 30.

Herholz, Sybille C., Claudia Lappe, Arne Knief and Christo Pantev, 'Neural basis of music imagery and the effect of musical expertise', *European Journal of Neuroscience*, 28/11 (2008), 2352–60.

Holmes, Patricia, 'Imagination in practice: a study of the integrated roles of interpretation, imagery and technique in the learning and memorisation processes of two experienced solo performers', *British Journal of Music Education*, 22 (2005), 217–35.

Hubbard, Timothy L., 'Auditory imagery: empirical findings', *Psychological Bulletin*, 136/2 (2010), 302–29.

Hubbard, Timothy L. and Keiko Stoeckig, 'Musical imagery: generation of tones and chords', *Journal of Experimental Psychology: Learning, Memory, and Cognition*, 14 (1988), 656–67.

Kadota, Y., G. Cooper, A.R. Burton, J. Lemon, U. Schall and A. Lloyd, 'Autonomic hyper-vigilance in post-infective fatigue syndrome', *Biological Psychology*, 85/1 (2010), 97–103.

Keller, Peter E., Simone Dalla Bella and Iring Koch, 'Auditory imagery shapes movement timing and kinematics: evidence from a musical task'. *Journal of Experimental Psychology: Human Perception and Performance*, 36/2 (2010), 508–13.

Khatena, Joe, *Imagery and Creative Imagination* (Buffalo, NY: Bearley, 1984).

Kvavilashvili, Lia and George Mandler, 'Out of one's mind: a study of involuntary semantic memories', *Cognitive Psychology*, 48 (2004), 47–94.

Leman, Marc, 'Modeling musical imagery'. In: Rolf Inge Godøy and Harald Jørgensen (eds), *Musical Imagery* (Lisse: Swets & Zeitlinger, 2001), 57–76.

Massey, Irving J., 'The musical dream revisited: music and language in dreams', *Psychology of Aesthetics, Creativity, and the Arts*, S/1, (2006), 42–50.

Mednick, S.A. and M.T. Mednick, *Remote Associates Test, College, Adult, Form 1 and Examiner's Manual, Remote Associates Test, College and Adult Forms 1 and 2* (Boston, MA: Houghton Mifflin, 1967).

Mountain, Rosemary, 'Composers and imagery: myths and realities'. In: Rolf Inge Godøy and Harald Jørgensen (eds), *Musical Imagery* (Lisse: Swets & Zeitlinger, 2001), 271–88.

Nass, Martin L., 'The development of creative imagination in composers', *International Review of Psycho-Analysis*, 11 (1984), 481–91.

Neisser, Ulric, *Cognition and Reality: Principles and Implications of Cognitive Psychology* (San Francisco: W.H. Freeman, 1976).

O'Connor, Kieron Philip and Frederick Aardema, 'The imagination: cognitive, pre-cognitive, and meta-cognitive aspects', *Consciousness and Cognition*, 14/2 (2005), 233–56.

Ollen, Joy, 'A criterion-related validity test of selected indicators of musical sophistication using expert ratings', PhD dissertation (Ohio State University, 2006).

Penrose, Roger, *The Emperor's New Mind: Concerning Computers, Minds and the Laws of Physics* (Oxford: Oxford University Press, 1999).

Pfordresher, Peter, 'Coordination of perception and action in music performance', *Advances in Cognitive Psychology*, 2/2–3 (2006), 183–98.

Repp, Bruno, 'Effects of auditory feedback deprivation on expressive piano performance', *Music Perception*, 16/4 (1999), 409–38.

Retra, José, 'An investigation into the musical imagery of contemporary composers', MA dissertation (University of Sheffield, 1999).

Rosenberg, Helane S. and William Trusheim, 'Creative transformations: How visual artists, musicians and dancers use mental imagery in their work'. In: Joseph E. Shorr (ed.), *Imagery: Current Perspectives* (New York: Plenum, 1990), 55–7.

Rowell, Lewis, 'The musical imagery of India'. In: Rolf Inge Godøy and Harald Jørgensen (eds), *Musical Imagery* (Lisse: Swets & Zeitlinger, 2001), 289–302.

Saxton, Robert, 'The process of composition from detection to confection'. In: Wyndham Thomas (ed.), *Composition, Performance, Reception: Studies in the Creative Process in Music* (Aldershot: Ashgate, 1998), 6.

Schoenberg, Harold, *Horowitz: His Life and Music* (London: Simon & Schuster, 1992).

Smith, J. David, Daniel Reisberg and Meg Wilson, 'Subvocalization and auditory imagery: interactions between the inner ear and inner voice'. In: Daniel Reisberg (ed.), *Auditory Imagery* (Hillsdale, NJ: Lawrence Erlbaum, 1992), 95–117.

Tavener, John *The Music of Silence: a Composer's Testament* (London: Faber & Faber, 1999).

Thomas, Nigel J.T., 'Are theories of imagery theories of imagination? An active perception approach to conscious mental content', *Cognitive Science*, 23/2 (1997), 207–45.

Trusheim, William H., 'Audiation and mental imagery: implications for artistic performance', *The Quarterly Journal of Music Teaching and Learning*, 2 (1991), 138–47.

Wammes, M. and Imants Baruss, 'Characteristics of spontaneous musical imagery', *Journal of Consciousness Studies*, 16/1 (2009), 37–61.

Wöllner, Clemens and Aaron Williamon, 'An exploratory study of the role of performance feedback and musical imagery in piano playing', *Research Studies in Music Education*, 29/1 (2007), 39–54.

Zatorre, Robert J., 'Brain imaging studies of musical perception and musical imagery', *Journal of New Music Research*, 28/3 (1999), 229–36.

Chapter 4

Meaningful Engagement
with Music Composition

Andrew R. Brown and Steve Dillon

Introduction

Musical value cannot be experienced without direct knowledge of music, and engagement with the interactive elements of materials, expressive character and structure. Through these channels something is communicated, something is transmitted, some residue of 'meaning' is left with us. When a work of art stirs us it is more than simply sensory stimulation or some kind of emotional indulgence. We are gaining knowledge and expanding our experience ... contributing to knowledge of ourselves and of the world.[1]

In this chapter we explore and identify the relationships between the act of music composition and the concept of meaningful engagement. We examine the act of composition as a set of situated behaviours and actions people do in private and public contexts that are motivated by the pleasures and satisfaction of making music.

The notion of meaningful engagement is presented as a conceptual tool that can be applied to categorise and examine creative practices such as music composition. We suggest that creative acts can be considered in two complimentary dimensions: (1) types of actions and the extent of engagement with music through them; and (2) contexts for action and the opportunities for meaning they provide. Through these lenses the experience of meaningful engagement involves an immersion in a creative process that enables a composer to connect with his or her intuitive experience, or 'acquaintance knowledge',[2] of music. This occurs as a result of an increased sensitivity and awareness of musical materials. Furthermore, it acknowledges that creating music can facilitate an understanding of structural relations, the potential for expressive development and relationships with others. In our previous research we have identified different modes of engagement with composition and how these can be conducted in three different contexts of meaning. In this chapter we are

---

[1]   Keith Swanwick, *Musical Knowledge: Intuition, Analysis, and Musical Education* (London, 1994), 4.

[2]   Ibid., 46.

particularly concerned with composing as a creative activity and in exploring how people engage meaningfully with it. Throughout the chapter we will draw on examples from our studies of compositional activities by experienced composers, highlighting various creative approaches and forms of expertise.

Background

Our notion of meaningful engagement relates to a way of behaving or acting that embodies what Martin Heidegger calls an 'involvement' in events that is based on 'being-in-the-world'.[3] From this perspective an involved person has an intuitive, rather than intellectual, connection with their world, not unlike the sportsperson who is involved in their game by being 'in the zone'. This involvement reflects a philosophical emphasis, in Heidegger and other phenomenologists, on human participation in the world and in the generation of knowledge and meaning. Heidegger was reacting against a tradition of objectifying the world as a place that exists independently of human interpretation or manipulation awaiting observation and discovery. In its place he proposed that people are located in the world as an active part of it and that understanding and meaning emerge from interaction with the world. The relevance of Heidegger's phenomenological approach to music-making was underscored by his particular concern with artistic activities, most notably poetry, as providing a particular kind of disposition. Heidegger suggested that effective art-making requires a different level of involvement than habitual or superficial technical work, and articulated this as a bringing together of *techne* and *poiésis*.[4]

John Dewey's discussion of creative expression outlined in *Art as Experience* draws a direct connection between technical and artistic music activities in relation to music. 'The abiding struggle of art is thus to convert materials that are stammering or dumb in ordinary experience into eloquent media'.[5] Our work shares with Heidegger and Dewey a conviction that the arts provide unique opportunities for deep engagement, and access to meaning that is significant for the individual artist, their audience and communities.

The nature and value of meaningful engagement in this sense can be found in psychologist Mihaly Csikszentmihalyi's research with artistic practices in developing his theory of optimal experience, or 'flow':[6]

> From their accounts of what it felt like to do what they were doing, I developed a theory of optimal experience based on the concept of flow – the state in which

---

[3]   Martin Heidegger, *The Question Concerning Technology and Other Essays* (New York, 1977).

[4]   Heidegger, *The Question Concerning Technology*, 34.

[5]   John Dewey, *Art as Experience* (New York, 1934), 229.

[6]   Mihaly Csikszentmihalyi, *Flow: The Psychology of Happiness* (London, 1992).

people are so involved in an activity that nothing else seems to matter; the experience itself is so enjoyable that people will do it even at great cost, for the sheer sake of doing it.[7]

Csikszentmihalyi's studies present evidence that optimal experience is a present and desirable state for composers.[8] Csikszentmihalyi's presentation of an interview he conducted with an unnamed leading composer of American music in the 1970s articulates this idea of flow:

> You are in an ecstatic state to such a point that you feel as though you almost don't exist. I have experienced this time and again. My hand seems devoid of myself, and I have nothing to do with what is happening. I just sit there watching it in a state of awe and wonderment. And [the music] just flows out of itself.[9]

The notion of meaningful engagement relates to experiences like this and outlines the range of actions and contexts in which they may arise. It builds on the insights of Heidegger, Dewey and Csikszentmihalyi and examines the idea of creative involvement and treats phenomena from the perspectives of behaviours and contexts.

Thus, to illustrate aspects of meaningful engagement with music composition, we will draw on our observations of creative processes and interviews with five experienced composers, from a detailed study presented in detail elsewhere.[10] The musical genres and compositional techniques employed by these composers were diverse; however, they did share a passion and capacity for making music that we identify as a meaningful engagement with composition. This approach we argue is of value because it provides an understanding of the act of composition, as an expressive and experiential practice. Through an appreciation of how composers engage with music-making and derive meaning, we can identify what composers do and what they might experience. Further, by reflecting on meaningful engagement with music composition, we can perhaps gain insights into human creativity more broadly. In the next section we will introduce the notion of meaningful engagement in more detail, before applying it to the process of music composition.

---

[7]   Csikszentmihalyi, *Flow*, 4.

[8]   Csikszentmihalyi, *Flow*, 108–13.

[9]   Mihaly Csikszentmihalyi, *Mihaly Csikszentmihalyi on flow*. Podcast retrieved from http://www.ted.com/talks/mihaly_csikszentmihalyi_on_flow.html on 2 September 2011 (Online, 2004).

[10]   Andrew R. Brown, 'Music composition and the computer: An examination of the work practices of five experienced composers', PhD thesis (Brisbane, 2003).

The Meaningful Engagement Matrix

By combining our reflections on literature in psychology and philosophy with studies of music-making in many contexts,[11] we have identified different modes of engagement with creative activities and explored how these are undertaken in three different contexts of meaning. There are five modes of engagement and three contexts of meaning that we define here. These are drawn together to form the meaningful engagement matrix (MEM), shown in Figure 4.1. This configuration of meaning and engagement seeks to provide a descriptive taxonomy of creative actions situated within personal, social and cultural contexts. The order of the modes and contexts does not imply a particular hierarchy, rather individuals can shift between modes and contexts during a single creative activity.

The five modes of compositional engagement are:

1. *Attending* – the composer can act as an audience to their own or others' work, in the presence of a performance, recording or simply imagining the work. While attending, the composer stands apart from the compositional process such that the composing medium, tool, score or performer is objectified. A composer may use this mode to evaluate the completeness of a work or to attempt to dispassionately assess the development of their work.
2. *Evaluating* – this mode of engagement is one where a composer examines works or materials in an analytical or judgemental way. As an evaluator, a composer may judge draft material for possible inclusion in a composition, look for links and connections that assist structural organisation, or look to see how multiple works can make up a program, album or oeuvre.
3. *Directing* – crafting a composition has much to do with articulating a musical statement through controlling and moulding musical materials. When engaged in the mode of directing, a composer may consciously manipulate musical materials to shape them into a desirable form or instruct others or some automated process to achieve their desired outcome. This mode of engagement is the one most commonly understood as compositional activity since it involves the deliberate manipulation of musical representations.
4. *Exploring* – in the explorer mode of engagement, a composer is involved in an open-ended experimentation with musical materials. Exploring

---

[11]   Brown, 'Music composition and the computer'. Steven C. Dillon, 'The student as maker: An examination of the meaning of music to students in a school and the ways in which we give access to meaningful music education', PhD thesis (Melbourne, 2001). Steven C. Dillon, *Music, Meaning and Transformation: Meaningful Music Making for Life* (Cambridge, 2007). Steven C. Dillon, 'Examining meaningful engagement: musicology and virtual music making environments'. In: Elizabeth Mackinlay, Brydie-Leigh Bartleet and K. Barney (eds), *Musical Islands: Exploring Connections between Music, Place and Research* (Newcastle upon Tyne, 2009), 297–310.

may involve a process of seeking materials or organisational patterns for inclusion in a composition. Unlike the mode of directing, which is often associated with the pursuit of a clear goal, exploration is typically part of a process of clarifying a loosely formed conception within partially defined boundaries

5. *Embodying* – at times compositional activity might be best characterised as improvisatory or intuitive. The embodied mode of engagement acknowledges such moments. Often in this mode, the composer is comfortable to fall back on learned patterns and habits as an improvising performer might do. Unlike performance, however, embodiment in composing need not be a real-time activity and so feedback processes may well be deferred.

We also suggest that any engaged composer operates in three contexts that provide for a range of meaningful experiences:

1. *Personal context* – the personal context consists of a composer's own reflections on their activities. A sense of satisfaction and pleasure can arise from personal interactions with musical materials and processes, from the skilful use of techniques and processes, or from a sensitive appreciation of the individual characteristics of sounds and sound structures. More broadly, Csikszentmihalyi suggests that 'as long as [an activity] provides clear objectives, clear rules for action, and a way to concentrate and become involved, any goal can serve to give meaning to a person's life'.[12]

2. *Social context* – social contexts can provide opportunities for meaning that result from interaction with others framed by musical practices. This may include developing meaningful relationships with others through synergistic and cooperative interaction. Meaningful relationships with others can be enhanced by the ineffable qualities of musical interaction.[13] Within the act of composing or creative production, value can arise in the transaction between creator and performers where the expressive qualities of the composition are realised or extended by the musicians. Similar capacities for a social context to enhanced achievement and extend opportunities for meaningfulness have been described by Lev Vygotsky as a zone of proximal development[14] and by Edwin Hutchins as distributed cognition.[15]

---

[12] Csikszentmihalyi, *Flow*, 215.

[13] Steve C. Dillon and Andrew R. Brown, 'The educational affordances of generative media in arts education'. In: *Proceedings of the International Association for Technology, Education and Development: INTED 2010* (Valencia, 2010), 5311–20.

[14] Lev Vygotsky, *Mind in Society: Development of Higher Psychological Processes* (Cambridge, MA, 1978).

[15] Edwin Hutchins, *Cognition in the Wild* (Cambridge, MA, 1995).

3. *Cultural context* – positive feedback in cultural contexts includes any form of public acknowledgement that the community values a composer's music-making abilities and/or outputs. These abilities may include the re-creation of traditional forms, or innovative techniques that extend the expressive qualities of the form and contributes to cultural evolution. Meaning in cultural contexts may be activated by feedback from critical experts and peers, the public or the wider musical world. It may take the form of audience applause at a concert, sales of recorded media, or critical musicological analysis of the work by academics.

These aspects of meaningful engagement are not an exhaustive list of compositional states, nor are they mutually exclusive. However, by describing compositional activity in this way we hope that the compositional process might become less mysterious and more available to debate and understanding. These proposed aspects of meaningful engagement can be depicted as a matrix to allow for the intersection of modes of engagement and contexts for meaning, as shown in Figure 4.1.

The cells in the matrix are locations where modes of engagement and contexts of meaning interact. For example, the exploring + personal cell may describe the early stages of a new work where ideas and materials are experimented with, while the exploring + cultural cell may describe the deliberate seeking of concert experiences of novel works as inspiration, or the limited public presentation of a draft work to gauge audience reaction. The cells formed by the aspects of meaningful engagement in the matrix are states with blurred boundaries, and a particular compositional activity or experience may well show characteristics of two or more cells.

The unfolding of a particular compositional activity may mean that the composer oscillates between aspects of meaningful engagement (at times frequently) such that he or she may even be in a state of multi-modal engagement, and meaning can arise in different contexts from the one activity. However, our observations suggest that composers and activities seem to have a tendency

	Attending	Evaluating	Directing	Exploring	Embodying
Personal					
Social					
Cultural					

Figure 4.1   The meaningful engagement matrix (MEM)

towards particular areas in the MEM. For example, the exploring + personal cell is characteristic of the early stages of development and illustrative of composers who use improvisation as a generative process, while the attending + social cell is characteristic of being present at public performances of completed works and is more prominent in composers who seek such feedback and regularly redraft work in light of those experiences. Being aware of gravitation to a particular cell and of one's dominant location on the MEM can expose opportunities for new compositional experiences and practices.

Applying the MEM

The meaningful engagement matrix has the capacity to act as a tool for categorising and examining compositional practice. For example, compositional approaches and equipment may privilege certain behaviours and we have observed that composers can form habits that gravitate towards particular cells in the MEM. While a composer may have a tendency to engage in some modes and contexts more often than others, our observations suggest that experienced composers undertake activities in most cells of the matrix at some stage. Therefore, we propose that a rich musical experience involves activities across a broad range of cells in the matrix, whilst a heavy concentration of activities in just a few cells potentially limits expressive musical opportunities.

The selection of technological tools used in composition is another influencing factor in directing activities to discrete locations on the MEM. A compositional tool can operate to either encourage or limit a composer's particular actions and experiences.[16] Any emphasis on composition as an active interaction with tools, such as notation systems, acoustic instruments or computers, refers to Heidegger's thinking, which underscores the importance of the creative arts in helping to understand human relationships with technology: 'Because the essence of technology is nothing technological, essential reflection upon technology and decisive confrontation with it must happen in a realm that is, on the one hand, akin to the essence of technology and, on the other, fundamentally different from it. Such a realm is art.'[17] Where a compositional activity appears on the MEM it can be attributed to either of two perspectives: the composer's approach and practices, or the design and use of compositional tools and techniques.

---

[16]   Malcolm McCullough, *Abstracting Craft: The Practiced Digital Hand* (Cambridge, MA, 1996).

[17]   Heidegger, *The Question Concerning Technology*, 35.

Compositional Acts through the Lens of Meaningful Engagement

In this section we draw examples from a study of the practices of a group of five prominent composers: Steve Reich, David Hirschfelder, David Cope, Brigitte Robindoré and Paul Lansky, chosen for their varying compositional practices and musical styles. As these composers were experienced and well respected by their peers, their activities could be regarded as indicative of experienced compositional practice. Over a period of 12 months the progress of projects was monitored by examining the development of materials and score, observing and recording video recordings of the composer's working environment and semi-structured interviews on topics relating to their work habits, motivations, tools, inspirations and experiences. Selections from these data pertinent to the notion of meaningful engagement form the focus of this chapter, while a fuller description and analysis of their practices is available elsewhere.[18] In the remainder of this section we present elaborations and illustrations that relate to these composers' modes of engagement and contexts of meaning.

Mode of Engagement: Attending

An example of the 'attending' mode of engagement was evident in David Hirschfelder's practice, and was a perspective he fostered. In his interviews he described making an effort to regularly distance himself from the compositional process in order to reflect on progress, a task he admitted did not come easily to him. As a film composer, pressing deadlines regularly challenged him, and so learning to form a habit of shifting attention was a way of increasing efficiency in his workflow. He commented on how he shifted between moments of directing and embodying, and between those of attending and reflecting:

> It's subjectivity and then objectivity. It's being subjective so you are the product and you are that gut reaction, then it's being able to step right outside of that as a listener and being totally objective and saying "How's that working?" Because, if you stay subjective and too married to an idea it sometimes makes it difficult to move on. It's necessary to move on because I believe there are two forms of music, finished and unfinished, and that's all. You can always say music is unfinished, but too many people sign off on things too early because they remain subjectively attached. I speak completely from experience. I'm guilty of that sin, and probably will be again. That's why I like to have the time to listen to things after I've let it go. I think I can give myself credit for being able to detach myself a lot earlier than I could when I was younger. When I was younger it would take

---

[18]   Brown, 'Music composition and the computer'.

me weeks or months to get unattached to an idea and see it as others see it ... I think I can literally detach in about half an hour now.[19]

While attending to his work to review it, Hirschfelder was able to suppress his ownership of it, in order to hear the resulting music directly or immediately as others would. Similarly Paul Lansky said that, 'as you work on the piece you're listening to it day in and day out, and you've got to make it sound continuously good. If it starts to sound crummy then you're not paying attention'.[20]

The skills of attending can be applied beyond one's own act of composition. Composers, as a rule, regularly listen to music of others, either from recordings or at concerts; indeed they usually seek out such opportunities as well as being engaged in discussions, debates and collaborations with performers, conductors, film directors, recording engineers and others about how music sounds and should be interpreted. These activities show that the social and cultural aspects of attending are vital aspects of the lives of the composer's we interviewed.

Mode of Engagement: Directing

All composers 'direct' their work to varying degrees and the composers we examined reflected this diversity in their balance of experimenting and steering. Steve Reich provided a clear example of how the directing and exploring compositional modes are differentiated when making a distinction between the 'inspiration' and 'execution' aspects of composing. Reich estimated that the balance between work at or away from the computer was divided about 'sixty/forty with the computer getting sixty percent'.[21] This was further underscored in his practice by the use of different tools for each stage. Reich generally used an acoustic instrument, often the piano, or at times the tape recorder or sampler, for the generation and selection of ideas and materials such as motifs and chord progressions. After this phase, his sketched material was transferred to the computer for elaboration and development. As he stated, most of his time was spent in the development and arranging stage at the computer; activities that align with the directing + personal cell of the MEM.

Reich reinforced the directorial nature of his compositional approach with statements about his deliberate control over the process and the role of technology as an enabling tool: 'Without the possibility of sampling I wouldn't have done

---

[19] David Hirschfelder, Personal interview with Andrew R. Brown (Melbourne, 22 December 1997).

[20] Paul Lansky, Telephone interview with Andrew R. Brown (Princeton, 28 October 1997).

[21] Steve Reich, Personal interview with Andrew R. Brown (New York, 19 January 1998).

Different Trains,[22] and without doing *Different Trains* and the possibility of sampling I wouldn't have thought of any solution to music theatre that *I* would have been interested in'.[23] He described how, during the composition of *Hindenburg*,[24] the computer's ability to manipulate the pitch of samples enabled him to shape the recorded material to his musical ends. The software provided independent control over the speed and pitch of recorded voice samples, a capability unavailable for his previous works, including *Different Trains*. When Reich talks about his change of attitude from accepting samples as they were to a more deliberate manipulation of audio samples through pitch shifting, his comments underscore the conscious decision-making that characterises the 'directing' aspect of meaningful engagement.

> [For *Hindenburg*] I wanted to be able to structure the piece harmonically the way I would structure a piece which was not using samples, where the harmony would be worked out independently from the sampled material. I wanted to set up a tempo and get a head of steam going rhythmically the way I did with my other pieces. So, I've decided that in this piece I will change, drastically if need be, any of the sampled material to fit the music. I start off in three flats, and if Herb Morris [whose voice is sampled] is not in three flats (and he's not) then I'm going to make him in three flats. When I want to stretch his voice out then I just stretch it out. So the whole aesthetic is different, and the whole technical means of working is better – it harkens back to the way I was writing before I was working with samples. It's like having your cake and eating it.[25]

What seems important in the directing mode of engagement is that composers have a musical goal in mind and resources are directed towards achieving that. This assumes, of course, that a goal has been established. Creative processes may be described as being in two stages: the design of the broad outline and the execution of the detail. Sloboda suggests a two-stage process of composition.[26] In the first 'inspiration' stage, a skeletal idea or plan emerges, while in the second 'execution' stage ideas and plans become clearer through elaboration. He argues that the processes of planning and detailed filling-in could inform each other and need not operate as either a linear top-down or bottom-up progression.

[22]   Steve Reich, *Different Trains*, for string quartet and tape in three movements (1988).
[23]   Steve Reich, Telephone interview with Andrew R. Brown (Vermont, 11 November 1997).
[24]   Steve Reich and Beryl Korot, *Hindenberg*, Act 1 of the video opera *Three Tails* (New York, 2002).
[25]   Reich, Personal interview.
[26]   John Sloboda, *The Musical Mind: The Cognitive Psychology of Music* (Oxford, 1985). John Sloboda, *Exploring the Musical Mind: Cognition, Emotion, Ability, Function* (Oxford, 2005).

I shall be highlighting two facets of the psychological activities involved. One is the persistent occurrence of superordinate structures or plans which seem to guide and determine the detailed note-by-note working out. The other is the degree to which these plans can, particularly in composition, be rather provisional. They can, for instance, be changed in the light of the way a particular passage "turns out" … The art of composition lies, in part, in choosing extensions of initial thematic ideas that honour superordinate constraints, often to be formalized in terms of hierarchical structures governing sections or movements.[27]

The 'directing' aspect of meaningful engagement involves the deliberate application of skills and techniques towards a goal, even if it is somewhat unclear. When engaged in this way, we suggest, a composer's relationship with the medium and representation systems is characterised by a seeking of control over such systems in order to articulate a vision. When directing, the skills and experience of the composer are applied towards musical expression through the manipulation of the musical resources available.

This approach may extend beyond the writing of music to include its subsequent production, performance, recording and distribution. For Reich, paying attention to the social and cultural aspects of having his music realised and well accepted involved a similar 'directing' approach. In terms of the MEM, the organising of performers and rehearsals falls into the direct + social cell and making decisions about commissions, performances, recording and distribution involves curatorial skills that exemplify the directing + cultural cell.

Mode of Engagement: Embodying

The 'embodying' mode of engagement reflects moments of fluid interaction with composing often associated with an intimate relationship with compositional tools. This type of meaningful engagement can be seen in the compositional practice of Paul Lansky. He is now a composer of instrumental music, but at the time of interview Lansky was predominantly a computer musician whose compositional practice involved writing software code to realise his works. This is a situation that may not seem congenial to an embodied style of engagement. His relationship with composing using the computer is a result of many years of building, modifying and working with his own computer music software.[28] Lansky's compositional processes included significant computational processing that took minutes or sometime hours to complete; audio feedback, which is important for sustaining an embodied approach, was not immediate. Yet this did not limit his embodied engagement with the process, which to him was not unlike instrumental performance. Lansky said that he enjoyed the drawn-out process of constructing a compositional algorithm and waiting for the computer to respond with a result

---

[27] Sloboda, *The Musical Mind*, 103, 116–17.

[28] Paul Lansky, *Cmix* (Princeton, 1978).

as, 'It gives me a chance to think about what it is I've done. I'm not performing here, I'm sort of improvising in real-slow time'.[29] The intimate nature of the 'embody' mode of engagement develops alongside the composer's familiarity with the medium and with increasing compositional skills. For Lansky, familiarity and experience with the medium made the activity more playful and absorbing rather than predictable and routine. Composer David Cope also used computer-based compositional tools. His engagement in the compositional process was maintained despite the intrusion of computer programming and musical analysis into his compositional workflow.

Mode of Engagement: Exploring

Cope's style of composition is more interesting perhaps as an example of how composers value opportunities to 'explore'. For Cope, meaningful engagement occurs during the algorithmic music generation process, in which his computer programs yield music based on rules and processes constructed by him. He sees himself as a 'designer of works, not a builder of notes'.[30] The various iterations of algorithmic works are explorations of each musical space he demarcates. The algorithmic processes can take from a few seconds to a few minutes depending upon the complexity of computation and the amount of material to process. Meaningful engagement can be maintained despite these delays because of Cope's interest in the results of the processes, and the potential for surprise and delight as much as confusion and disappointment. Algorithmic experimentation and the computational skills this requires is Cope's method of exploring music spaces that are of interest to him.

> if I want to include programming as part of the compositional process … [then] I have been composing all along. Because I do program every day. It's not just a mental exercise; it's what I do. In other words, instead of having a martini at the end of the day – I don't drink at all – I simply work on code. It's therapeutic, healthy for me mentally, it helps clean me out.[31]

While Cope's explorations were often located in the spaces of musical and algorithmic structures, Brigitte Robindoré exhibits these characteristics in the timbrel space. Robindoré, is a Franco-American electroacoustic composer who spent considerable time in France studying and working with the tools and techniques developed by Iannis Xenakis. She worked in the 'explore' mode as she

---

[29]   Paul Lansky, Personal interview with Andrew R. Brown (Princeton Junction, 23 January 1998).

[30]   David Cope, Telephone interview with Andrew R. Brown (Santa Cruz, 14 October 1997).

[31]   David Cope, Telephone interview with Andrew R. Brown (Santa Cruz, 12 November 1997).

collected sound materials for *O'er the Sea*,[32] an electroacoustic work inspired by her connection with the great Finnish harpsichordist Jukka Tiensuuthat, which was started in Paris in the late 1990s and competed and first performed in Santa Barbara in 2001.[33] Her musical interest in that instrument became focused on its high noise (harmonically complex) content. In her pursuit of useful sounds Robindoré employed techniques both familiar and unfamiliar to her. The familiar techniques included sampling a great variety of conventional and creative harpsichord sounds and processing them using granular synthesis, frequency modulation synthesis and fragment looping with the UPIC system.[34] The less familiar techniques included a type of infrasonic modulation inherent to the UPIC system and synthesis via aliasing. The nature of exploring, even in familiar territories, means that the composer may often be confronted with the unfamiliar. Robindoré felt that the history of western instrumental and computer music provided minimal discussion on the purely noise content of sound. There was no vocabulary to draw on, no lexicon. She felt the creative descriptions seemed to stop with Luigi Russolo's futurist orchestra which he described in terms of 'whispers, roars, hissing, puffing, creaking, hoots'. She explained,

> It would be nice to have some words to analyse the sounds so you could say, "yes, this is what I'm hearing, it's a frequency band between 2K and 2.5K, it's stronger, its noise content is …". But what kind of noise contents are there?[35]

Because musical ideas are often loosely formed and move beyond previous experiences, composers often find it difficult to express verbally what they are looking for or what they have found; while the intention to explore may be conscious, the process of exploration is, to varying degrees, intuitive and ineffable. This was how Robindoré described her experience of finding suitable sounds to somehow match her metaphysical inquiry:

> There are times where I'm not quite grasping what the idea is that I need to be expressing, or that I feel. But, I have certain sounds which lead me to them, it's not always from the ideas. For example, in the tape piece … with harpsichord, there are sounds which I know I have to find, but I'm not sure yet of the metaphysical idea behind them. I can feel that it's coming.[36]

---

[32]   Brigitte Robindoré, *O'er The Sea*, electroacoustic composition (2001).

[33]   The newspaper *The Santa Barbara Independent*, reviewed the premier performance of *O'er The Sea* on 21 November 2001.

[34]   Gérard Marino, Marie-Hélèn Serra and Jean-Michel Raczinski, 'The new UPIC system: origins and innovations', *Perspectives of New Music*, 31/2 (1993), 258–69.

[35]   Brigitte Robindoré, Personal interview with Andrew R. Brown (Paris, 6 February 1998).

[36]   Robindoré, Personal interview.

The comments from our composers suggest that exploring can involve searching for appropriate material, treatments and structures within a loosely defined musical space. This search may involve solo activity and contemplation but can also involve collaboration, discussion, critique and other social activities,[37] drawing in the associated socio-cultural influences that may influence musical spaces and exploratory processes.

Exploration is often depicted in creativity research as a search for solutions, especially in the information-processing view of creativity.[38] Robindoré's search for appropriate timbre-materials can be seen in this light. Others suggest creativity is just as importantly a search for opportunities to elaborate or develop. Feldman et al. suggest that, 'Such processes as problem finding and problem formulation are as critical to creativity as problem solving'.[39] This is a view sympathetic with the characterisation of Cope's composing processes as the design of spaces of algorithmic exploration. Edward de Bono, in his book on creativity, also suggests that creativity is more concerned with finding alternative problem definitions than finding solutions. For de Bono, seeing a problem from a different perspective reframes the situation, thus increasing the solution space.[40] Similarly, Spinoza, Flores and Dreyfus identify that the disclosure of irregularities or the problematising of situations is more significant than solution-finding. Their work is based on Heidegger's ontological notion of 'worldhood' where a 'world' includes equipment, purposes and identity. 'These identities are the meaning or point of engaging in these activities'.[41]

In our studies we have seen that composers engaged in exploring musical possibilities often build a conceptual map of musical space and even, at times, build a model of this space on paper or in a computer music system. Cope or Lansky's algorithmic processes lend themselves directly to modelling and we can extend this view to MIDI sequencers or paper-based scores as models. For example, Reich explained how he used the computer to produce MIDI-based renderings of his compositions to assist him in composing and to enhance communication with performers.

---

[37]   Gerry Stahl, *Group Cognition: Computer Support for Building Collaborative Knowledge* (Cambridge, MA, 2004).

[38]   Allan Newell and Herbert Simon, *Human Problem Solving* (Englewood Cliffs, NJ, 1972).

[39]   David Feldman, Mihaly Csikszentmihalyi and Howard Gardner, *Changing the World: A Framework for the Study of Creativity* (London, 1994).

[40]   Edward De Bono, *Serious Creativity: Using the Power of Lateral Thinking to Create New Ideas* (London, 1992).

[41]   Charles Spinosa, Fernando Flores and Hubert Dreyfus, *Disclosing New Worlds: Entrepreneurship, Democratic Action, and the Cultivation of Solidarity* (Cambridge, MA, 1997), 17.

It's very much like an architect, who makes drawings and then he makes a marque, a model. It's almost exactly like an architect's model. You can call the client in and have them take a look at it, and you can alter it. I send my MIDI mock-ups to conductors with the score.[42]

As Reich indicates, a model can capture and store musical ideas, which can then be viewed from many perspectives, reflected upon and developed further. The model, and the medium used to construct it, act as a cognitive amplifier for the composer by externalising thought and allowing the exploitation of the cultural knowledge inherent in the representation system. By solidifying concepts in models, the medium frees the composer's mind for new thoughts and enables exploration and experimentation. They can act as objects for contemplation or social and cultural interactions. When models are rendered as public objects, such as audio mockups of compositions, they can facilitate peer and audience feedback in a public exploration. This process has been extended in recent times through internet distribution channels and a culture of public beta versions and multiple remixes.[43] These activities and experiences further define the characteristics of the explore + cultural and explore + social areas of the MEM.

Mode of Engagement: Evaluating

The practices of musical revision, including remixing, have been a part of composition for a long time. There is ample evidence that composers have revised and reissued their own works after reflection or receiving feedback, often publishing several versions over many years. Manuscript revision has been found in Beethoven's compositional work, as documented in research collected by William Kinderman.[44] It has also been commonplace for composers to take elements from other composers' works as the basis for new compositions. The analytical and reflective activities this involves align with the 'evaluating' mode of engagement.

Evaluation played its part within our case studies of composers. The analytical and algorithmic design processes employed by Cope and Lansky are examples of compositional acts sometimes requiring analysis of existing music or sonic objects for algorithmic description. This is evidenced in Lansky's algorithmic mimicry of jazz piano style in *Heavy Set* from the Album *Ride*.[45] Cope's Experiments in Musical Intelligence (EMI) system goes further to require the algorithmic description of the analytical process as well. Analytical

---

[42]   Reich, Personal interview.

[43]   Lawrence Lessig, *Remix: Making Art and Commerce Thrive in the Hybrid Economy* (New York. 2008).

[44]   William Kinderman (ed.), *Beethoven's Compositional Process* (Hillsdale, NJ, 1991).

[45]   Paul Lansky, *Ride* (New Rochelle, 2001).

and descriptive practices such as these characterise the evaluate + personal aspects of the MEM.

The evaluating mode of engagement is closely aligned with the mode of attending, especially where it relates to reflection and making judgements about composed material as it develops. Cope's evaluating role with the EMI system amounted to selection from various instances of completed algorithmic works. Over time he actively sought to embed himself in the role of evaluator during the algorithmic compositional processes and developed several software applications to support this, including CUE, Alice and more recently Emily Howell. These software tools are interacted with as algorithmic collaborators that make musical suggestions to stimulate him as a composer or to generate fragments of material that are selected and structured by the composer. The interest expressed by Cope in this algorithmic partnership is that the processes produce novel material, perhaps beyond what might otherwise be imagined by the composer, while maintaining aesthetic decision-making control. This direction of combining generative processes with evaluative judgments was also in response to a criticism Cope had of purely recombination techniques (including those of his own EMI software), that his familiarity with the material was so intimate that the sources of recombined suggestions were too easily identifiable, and therefore, added too little new information to his compositional process. These examples illustrate how a composer, acting within the evaluating mode, can act as a judge of the value of musical materials, whether their own or those of another, or even of a machine.

As this discussion illustrates, these composers act in a multitude of ways that we call modes of engagement, and they can do so in personal, social and cultural contexts. The way they approach their practice and combine these modes and contexts constitutes their 'working style'.[46] A composer's working style is often shifting and changing, and these changes may result in differences in productivity, satisfaction and musical results. We suggest that a productive working style is one that encourages meaningful engagements across the range depicted by the MEM. For the experienced composers we have interviewed, this working style is manifest in regularly occurring habits and capabilities that lead to meaningful engagement with composition. We refer to these as the 'attributes' of meaningful engagement.

Attributes of Meaningful Engagement with Music Composition

The attributes of meaningful engagement are those aspects of practice that lead to a satisfying involvement in the act of composition. These attributes have similarities to personal traits of creative individuals identified by psychologists,

---

[46]   Spinosa et al., *Disclosing New Worlds*, 19.

including Guilford, Gardner, Boden and Csikszentmihalyi.[47] Gardner suggested that such traits foster the development of musical talent in the early years of childhood, at about the same period when language development is most rapid and when people develop abilities in musical memory, pattern recognition and familiarity with symbol systems within the domain. We have noticed similar traits in our studies that have included children and adult musicians, but the attributes of meaningful engagement reflect our observations of experienced musicians and may be used as aspirational characteristics for younger or developing composers.

Whilst looking at personal attributes of behavioural characteristics, following Csikszentmihalyi's approach we de-emphasise issues of personality type and psychoneurological condition as important indicators of personal creativity. Instead we emphasise actions, skills and motivations and examine how these are applied in personal, social and cultural contexts. The attributes we identify relate to the act of composing rather than outcomes, and highlight how the composers perceive composing and their role as a composer in their community. Attributes are independent of particular tools or musical genre, but may indirectly contribute to the musical result by enhancing the compositional experience and process. We identify five such attributes:

- motivation;
- challenge;
- involvement;
- sensitivity;
- virtuosity.

Our research suggests that composers who are meaningfully engaged choose a sufficiently complex task (the attribute of challenge) that will maintain their interest (the attribute of motivation) through all the composition and production stages. By paying attention to the material (the attribute of involvement), they notice a great range of opportunities and are able to make effective choices between those possibilities (the attribute of sensitivity). Their skill in using the available tools and medium (the attribute of virtuosity) provides them with the capacity to realise any musical idea that emerges. These attributes will be discussed in turn.

---

[47] Joy Paul Guilford, 'Traits of creativity', in H.H. Anderson (ed.), *Creativity and its Cultivation* (London, 1959, 142–61, reprinted in P.E. Vernon (ed.), *Creativity* (New York, 1970), 167–88. Howard Gardner, *Creating Minds: An Anatomy of Creativity Seen Through the Lives of Freud, Einstein, Picasso, Stravinsky, Eliot, Graham and Ghandi* (New York, 1983). Margaret Boden, *The Creative Mind* (London, 1990). Mihalyi Csikszentmihalyi, *Creativity: Flow and the Psychology of Discovery and Invention* (New York, 1996).

Motivation

Sloboda observed that composers were intrinsically motivated by the exploration of relationships between musical events, and that this was a sustaining force for them:

> The consequent delight that any creative worker experiences in the sheer fecundity of his medium is, arguably, not simply a pleasant by-product of creative activity, but the essential source of motivation which keeps him involved with his own material through "blocks" and blind alleys in the creative process.[48]

There are many motivations to compose music. The personally engaged composer seems to be intrinsically motivated by the task of composing itself; external encouragement, from a wide variety of social sources, may add to the level of motivation. The sources of socio-cultural motivation usually relate to financial gain or recognition by peers and the community. A composer's compositional motivations can often be tied to other activities and life goals, including raising a family, obtaining or maintaining employment, and other forms of self-expression such as writing, computer programming or visual design practice. Cope explained that his motivations for writing the work *Transformations*[49] were multi-faceted and included the opportunity for performance by a university ensemble. He also had the opportunity to apply ideas he was developing when writing a book about algorithmic composition. Further motivations were his ongoing interest in computer-based musical intelligence and having a test vehicle for the development of the CUE software.

The evidence drawn from these analyses suggests that motivation is significant for understanding compositional expertise when the physical and socio-cultural context is altered. Examples of the influence of shifting contexts are presented by Reich's movement between New York and Vermont or Lansky's involvement with significant administrative responsibilities at work. Without fundamentally changing compositional activity, changes to the personal context, such as loss of motivation, can seriously alter or even derail the compositional processes. An interesting example of this was discussed by Cope, who attributes to composer's block the shifting of his attention from composing in a traditional way to developing the EMI system. In these situations musical goals that motivate composers can exist in hierarchies. For instance, a composition might constitute one aspect of a larger project, or a series of compositions might explore different perspectives of one musical idea, theme or technique. As examples of this, Reich's *Hindenburg* was part of *Three Tales*, and Robindoré's work *O'er the Sea part of a collection of works involving Harpsichord*. Composers may have overarching motivations that span many projects and often last for years, as well as ones that

---

[48]   Sloboda, *The Musical Mind*, 138.

[49]   David Cope, *Transformations* (unpublished composition).

relate to a single composition or a section of a work with a much shorter life span. Sometimes the very large-scale goals may not be immediately apparent, even to the composer, and emerge and evolve as connections between projects become evident. Cope spent 15 years working on automated analysis and composition generation with EMI before returning to his original goal of computer-assisted composition. He explains his primary motivation for developing compositional software; 'The basic force is that I envision myself, before I am dead, working comfortably [with a compositional music system], and I don't do that yet'.[50] In his work with the Emily Howell system in the early 2000s, Cope seems to have moved closer to this goal. Even short-term motivations may not be easily articulated. Often motivations are understood as feelings or gut reactions that are revealed and satisfied in the compositional activity they inspire. Even so, meaningful engagement in a compositional task is stimulated primarily by the composer's motivation. Experienced composers seem to be well aware of what stimulates their interest and seek opportunities that enable them to follow those interests, increasing the chances that they can be engaged in meaningful projects.

Challenge

The experienced composer seems to select tasks that challenge them in a variety of ways; the complexity of the task is an important consideration, as is the time available to complete it. For Lansky, as an example, the major challenge of *Things She Carried*[51] was to create a piece that sustained audience interest for over an hour. Challenging compositional projects, such as this, move composers into unfamiliar territory that might require writing for an unfamiliar medium, instrument or ensemble combination, or require the learning of new techniques and processes.

Psychological research indicates that such challenges are important because they stimulate the composer. For example, research by Csikszentmihalyi into optimal experience found that a task is more likely to induce flow if its complexity is sufficient to require the focusing of all of a person's energies and skills, but not so complex as to be frustratingly difficult. He found that people were happiest when undertaking an appropriately difficult challenge:

> The best moments usually occur when a person's body or mind is stretched to its limits in a voluntary effort to accomplish something difficult and worthwhile. Optimal experience is thus something we make happen.[52]

---

[50]   Cope, Personal interview.

[51]   Paul Lansky, *Things She Carried* (New Rochelle, 1997).

[52]   Csikszentmihalyi, *Creativity: Flow and the Psychology of Discovery and Invention*, 3.

Meaningful engagement, which might lead to flow, may well be maximised when challenge and skills are in productive tension, which is usually seen as an oscillation between developing skills and rising challenges. Experienced composers in this study demonstrated an ability to select appropriate challenges and to undertake ongoing skill development to meet new challenges. This trait that some people have to successfully manage skills and challenges is referred to by Csikszentmihalyi as an 'autotelic' personality, and appeared to be present in each of the experienced composers discussed in this chapter. Autotelic characteristics are internally driven, self-actuated behaviours that provide a sense of purpose and curiosity. For composers, it can manifest as an ability to identify appropriate tasks and contexts that provide interesting and stimulating work. Our observations indicate that experienced composers display this characteristic by repeatedly identifying opportunities or creating challenges within a task, whose success or failure relates to developing the skills required to meet them. While it is clear that some tasks are more complex than others, it may not always be easy to find an appropriately challenging compositional project. With commissions and other professional work, there can be many constraints on the required outcome. We suggest that being challenged is a state of mind, or in Heideggerian language, a 'way of being'. If a task was perceived as simple, the composers in our study would find some way of making it more complex in order to make it more interesting. If the task was very complex, they may structure it into more manageable chunks. This was demonstrated by Hirschfelder, who added complexity to a film music commission, *The Interview*, through extending his repertoire of melodic techniques.[53]

> For the first time in my life I've actually embraced serial techniques. I've written tone rows and, for parts of the film, I've taken what was a tonal melody and actually turned it into a tone row so that the shape's the same but it becomes atonal. I've started doing things like that and have had a lot more fun and I've now become a Schoenberg fan which I wasn't twenty years ago.[54]

We conclude that a compositional task is more likely to lead to meaningful engagement if it presents an appropriate challenge. This challenge unfolds within the mind of the composer and each task is open to an interpretation that identifies the opportunities for meaningful engagement that it presents.

Involvement

Meaningful engagement is more likely when a composer is deeply involved with their task, when they are focused on it and absorbed in all its aspects. Lansky

---

[53]   *The Interview*. A film directed by Craig Monahan (Australia, 1998).

[54]   Hirschfelder, Personal interview.

explains how computer programming became an integral part of his compositional work style.

> There was a certain point about 20 years ago when I was about to throw in the towel, and I said "if I'm going to do [computer music composition] I have to like all aspects of it". I developed a real love of working at a very low level with materials like that.[55]

To be meaningfully engaged means to be focused on the compositional task and, for a time, to ignore other considerations. This can be observed when composers concentrate intensely on their work and in their attention to detail in finalising a composition. We suggest that this involvement or focus results in a composer being more attentive to musical detail that enriches his or her experience and understanding of the work. This opens up opportunities for further elaboration and refinement. Lansky demonstrated this kind of focus on detail as a compositional technique to draw in the listener on repeated hearings of his recorded works. The details are generally fairly complex, as in pieces like Table's Clear about which he comments that 'In a way, the listener has to invent the music in his own head as he listens'.[56]

As well as attending to the detail of the composition, meaningfully engaged composers, perhaps counter-intuitively, appear aware of the context in which they work and how this affects the composition. This aspect of involvement includes an awareness of the broader cultural circumstances in which they are composing. While the commercial context was ever present in Hirschfelder's film scoring work, it was clear that, even in non-commissioned work, he was well aware of his context, aiming to create something that is not just self-indulgent but has meaning for someone else. Furthermore, he was conscious that there would be an audience that would perhaps enjoy experiencing it.[57] In this regard, an experienced composer may be likened to the master chess player who is aware of many possible next moves and can look forward several moves and consider the longer-term consequences of each option. Holding in mind a diverse range of possible compositional options and constraints represents a significant cognitive load, and is the reason why the attribute of involvement requires the full concentration of the composer.

These observations about the contextual awareness of experienced composers resonate with the ecological theory of interaction with the world that emphasises a direct or intuitive awareness of the world around us. At the core of this theory is J.J. Gibson's notion of *affordance*, where the physical environment presents opportunities for action as perceived by the person (or animal) interacting with

---

[55]   Lansky, Personal interview.

[56]   Paul Clark, *The Paul Lansky Interview* (electronicmusician.com, 1997).

[57]   Hirschfelder, Personal interview.

it.[58] This notion of affordances was taken up by the field of design and human–computer interaction. In this context design strategies can be determined through leveraging the perceived affordances of artefacts.[59] Involvement, as an attribute of meaningful engagement, has overtones of Gibson's ecological psychology, but substitutes awareness for the physical environment with awareness of the cultural context. This reinforces a view that music composition involves an intuitive, not simply a reflective, act of creativity. The ability to be involved may be developed through reflection, but can be considered to involve both a pre-conscious awareness and an active and participatory state. Thus, through 'involvement' of this kind a composer may be more fully attuned to all aspects of the compositional activity.

A similar state is described by Spinosa, Flores and Dreyfus, which they term 'intensified practical involvement'; they emphasise that involvement should be viewed as embodied and hermeneutic rather than as metaphysical:

> We should be aware of the Cartesian tendency to imagine the skill of noticing and holding on to disharmonies as primarily intellectual, as noticing a problem in one's life and stepping back to analyse it, to puzzle through it, in one's mind. Rather, the skill of uncovering the tension between standard, commonsense practices and what one actually does is a skill of intensified practical involvement.[60]

This description of 'intensified practical involvement' resonates with our observations that the attribute of involvement appears to allow composers to notice opportunities for compositional action. Involvement, as a focusing on the task, seems to be assisted by particular compositional habits. Experienced composers we observed often had a ritual of composing that set the conditions that enabled them to give the task full attention. For example, composers may work in familiar settings, in a studio that is free from distractions, with equipment that is constantly set up and operational, including comfortable seating and subdued lighting, in a work space that is maintained at a comfortable temperature and is visually pleasant.

In summary, being involved with a compositional task, a composer is focused upon his or her goal but aware of external influences. A composer can perceive the requirements of a composition in great detail and is mindful of many possible directions in which it could develop. In short, meaningfully engaged composers are involved in what they do by being focused and aware.

---

[58]   James J. Gibson, *The Ecological Approach to Visual Perception* (Boston, MA, 1979).

[59]   Donald Norman, *The Invisible Computer: Why Good Products can Fail, the Personal Computer is so Complex, and Information Appliances are the Solution* (Cambridge, MA, 1988).

[60]   Spinosa et al., *Disclosing New Worlds*, 23.

Sensitivity

As we have indicated, involvement can lead to a heightened ability to assess what changes to make and opportunities for new additions. This kind of sensitivity to conditions can be considered independently and goes beyond simply 'noticing' to include the ability to make judgements about which actions to take. We have observed that a composer who is meaningfully engaged is in a state that enhances the use of skills and understandings to develop the composition further. For example, deciding which actions to take requires an acute awareness of the composition's current state. This may be in addition to being aware of the detail and possibilities that come from involvement. These two attributes of involvement and sensitivity are related and cooperative. We suggest that having a heightened and multi-faceted sensitivity to the compositional materials and processes can be productive for the composer. Spinosa, Flores and Dreyfus suggest that, 'Skilled practitioners respond appropriately to small perturbations that rule-followers miss'.[61]

Perkins further defines this idea when he suggests that creative processes are more about selection than problem solving.[62] Stimulation of creativity through improvisation and exploration, and linking seemingly unrelated ideas is a way of embodying and extending our understanding of creative possibilities. De Bono describes how lateral thinking can be used to generate ideas and involves a process of 'harvesting' in order to select from those ideas.[63] Daniel Dennet's pseudo-Darwinian depiction of the creative process highlights the idea that 'The exploitation of accidents is the key to creativity, whether what is being made is a new genome, a new behaviour, or a new melody'.[64] The experienced composers we studied consistently demonstrated the ability to exploit or ignore accidents. We suggest that this quality of informed aesthetic choice is due to the heightened sensitivity to the creative materials.

During the compositional process, the appropriate selection of themes, materials and transformations, requires sensitivity to the significant aspects of the ongoing and emerging composition and, according to Varela and his co-authors, it is through these choices that we both articulate and create meaning. In focusing on awareness and sensitivity, the essence of intelligence 'shifts from being the capacity to solve a problem to the capacity to enter into a shared world of significance'.[65]

---

[61]   Ibid., 179.

[62]   David Perkins, *The Mind's Best Work* (Cambridge, MA, 1981).

[63]   De Bono, *Serious Creativity*.

[64]   Daniel Dennett, 'Collision detection, muselot, and scribbles: some reflections on creativity'. In: David Cope (ed.), *Virtual Music: Computer Synthesis of Musical Style* (Cambridge, MA, 2001), 288.

[65]   Francisco Varela, Evan Thompson and Eleanor Rosch, *The Embodied Mind: Cognitive Science and Human Experience* (Cambridge, MA, 1991), 207.

There is a similarity between such embodied sensitivity and Polanyi's[66] notions of tacit knowledge, which emphasises an intuitive understanding built up through experience. Intuitive knowledge is often associated with unconscious thought. Sloboda acknowledges that a distinction between the conscious and unconscious aspects of composition is 'irrelevant' and that a complete compositional theory needs to take account of both.[67] Polanyi's definition of tacit knowledge is not centred upon the unconscious or habitual, but arises through active and skilful action.

> I regard knowing as an active comprehension of the things known, an action that requires skill. Skilful knowing and doing are performed by subordinating a set of particulars, as clues or tools, to the changing of a skilful achievement, whether practical or theoretical. We may then be said to become "subsidiarily aware" of these particulars within our "focal awareness" of the coherent entity that we achieve. Clues and tools are things used as such and not observed in themselves.[68]

Therefore it appears that changes in awareness that arise from sensitivity are at the heart of creative practice. Musical decisions about selection and choice are enabled by sensitivity and linked with aesthetic experience. They seem to go beyond simple decisions about preference.[69] Sensitivity allows for making judgements and choices about how the composition can best proceed. Sensitivity includes the ability to assess the developing composition, including the appropriateness of musical materials, the effectiveness of structure and the degree of completeness. Sensitivity also includes the ability to select from the opportunities afforded by available techniques and tools and to prioritise appropriately any external demands. This kind of heightened sensitivity to musical materials is evident in the practice of experienced composers who see the potential for development and transformation of that material that others might not.

Sensitivity involves interpretation and the making of meaning and this implies self-awareness and the ability to perceive the effect music may have on others. Experienced composers in our studies trusted their own judgement with regard to the quality of their work. Paul Lansky articulated this when asked how he judged his own work. He replied, 'I listen to it'.[70] This ability is developed through repeated experience and awareness of the social context that determines what musical expressions will be valued or considered creative.[71] A sensitive

---

[66]   Michael Polanyi, *Personal Knowledge: Towards a Post-critical Philosophy* (Chicago, IL, 1958).

[67]   Sloboda, *The Musical Mind*, 119.

[68]   Polanyi, *Personal Knowledge*, vii.

[69]   Howard Gruber, 'Aspects of scientific discovery: aesthetics and cognition'. In: John Brockman (ed.), *Creativity* (New York, 1993), 48–74.

[70]   Lansky, Personal interview.

[71]   Feldman et al., *Changing the World*.

composer knows what he or she likes and does not like, and is aware of how to act in response to their perceptions about the current state of the composition and its context. In interpreting cultural values, an experienced composer is able to locate opportunities for the performance and distribution of their work and constructs opportunities for compositional action. William Clancey describes the ability to 'read' culture and to interpret context in his writings on situated cognition where he argues that interpretive awareness is an

> active construction ("bringing forth") of functionally relevant features (called affordances by J.J. Gibson). The process is not that of "grasping (pre-existing) features" but of making distinctions.[72]

Experienced composers who demonstrate analytical critique in the way they develop strategies for making decisions about the next compositional step are deliberate about improving those strategies to become more effective composers.

Sensitivity leads to action through decision-making. In this regard the attribute of sensitivity is related to intuition, aesthetic judgement, or 'gut' reaction. However, our observations reveal that a sensitive composer relies on both aesthetic and intuitive awareness, even while taking account of the pragmatic and technical considerations. In Hirschfelder's words, compositional decisions involve 'a gut reaction, coming from a heart, speaking to other people's hearts'.[73] Nicholas Cook suggests that experienced composers are more effective than inexperienced because 'they generally have a distinct idea of what they are looking for'.[74] Our notion of sensitivity further acknowledges the idea that compositional goals can be unclear while the sensitivity of the experienced composer enables distinctions about the most effective possibilities that will move the composition forward. The lack of definition of a compositional endpoint requires composers to be sensitive about closure and a recognition that no further action is required. Sensitive composers have the ability not to be overwhelmed by the possibilities arising from involvement with the material. Rather, they can discern possibilities, and select materials for development that align with their musical aims and match the possibilities afforded by their contexts.

In summary, sensitive composers are creative and discerning about the details and development of their compositions. As a result, they become empowered to act creatively and productively within the compositional process. This assists in making the task personally meaningful and leads to the work becoming socially and culturally relevant.

---

[72]   William J. Clancey, *Situated Cognition: Human Knowledge and Computer Representations* (Cambridge, 1997), 86.

[73]   Hirschfelder, Personal interview.

[74]   Nicholas Cook, *Music, Imagination and Culture* (Oxford, 1990), 197.

Virtuosity

A productive flow of compositional activities was characteristic of the composers in our studies. This requires familiarity with techniques and processes and is developed through experience, expressed in the composer's skills of imagination, analysis, compositional technique, tool usage and knowledge of context. Hirschfelder's ability to manage multiple tasks from sequencing to scoring and recording under the high-pressure timelines of commercial film production illustrates this familiarity. Lansky and Cope's low-level programming coding fluency also displayed these qualities.

The implications for an instrumental composer include the responsibility to know the capabilities and idiosyncrasies of the instruments. Similarly for composers working with mixed media or theatre, the knowledge demands extend to visual integrations, staging considerations and the like. The development of virtuosity results from repeated practice and years of experience. While such virtuosity is well acknowledged for instrumental performers, it is as true for our case study composers. Varela, Thompson and Rosch suggest that:

> As one practices, the connection between intention and act becomes closer, until eventually the feeling of difference between them is almost entirely gone. One achieves a certain condition that phenomenologically feels neither purely mental nor purely physical; it is, rather, a specific kind of mind–body unity.[75]

Composers' virtuosity in this study extends beyond technical and notational dexterity to include their understanding and capacity for imaginative action. A virtuosic composer appears to develop a repertoire of possible actions and skills to execute fluidly with the tools at hand. There is, however, an important distinction between the understanding of techniques and the ability to predict the musical results of the use of those techniques. To some degree, experience with compositional techniques results in the ability to predict the musical results of their application. Indeed, we expect that this ability to project consequences plays a significant part in the effectiveness of virtuosity not just to get a task done but to get the right task done.

However, there is an argument that creative decisions are required despite knowing only partially, or broadly, what the results of particular actions will be. The notion of creativity as novelty assumes that a composer will explore some previously unexplored musical territory. Sloboda recognised that a composer's familiarity with techniques and tools engendered a positive trust in them as a medium of expression:

> I suspect that an important component of compositional skill is a degree of "trust" in one's medium – a certainty that the habitual process of generation

---

75   Varela et al., *The Embodied Mind*, 29.

will yield material which is richer than one first sees, and which, even if initially unsatisfactory, usually contains within it discoverable properties which can be used to profit. This trust is partly engendered by the sheer fact of previously solved problems; but it also has something to do with increasing awareness of the richness of a medium such as the tonal system.[76]

A composers' virtuosity manifests as a practical understanding that goes beyond knowledge about the techniques or medium themselves to include the knowledge of how to utilise these skilfully as craftsmanship.

Virtuosity extends beyond techniques and tools to include an understanding and management of the compositional context, which includes previously composed music, the availability of resources including time, equipment and personnel, and considerations relating to the presentation and distribution of the work. Familiarity with such contextual aspects is built up, like other aspects of virtuosity, through experience.

In summary, virtuosity includes an intimate understanding of the compositional process and skill with available technologies that can enable a composer to operate productively. This may provide personal satisfaction, lead to respect from the community, and enable a continuity of workflow that is an important attribute of meaningful engagement.

Conclusion

In this chapter we have presented the concept of meaningful engagement and shown how it can illuminate our understanding of the act of music composition. We have described how composers may construct meaning through a variety of engagements with music-making in personal and socio-cultural contexts, and have illustrated these points with examples from experienced composers. Our observations are that experienced composers are meaningfully engaged in the act of composition. We agree with Sloboda that a composer's 'engagement with music can be seen as important and purposeful work'.[77]

We have outlined aspects of meaningful engagement in two dimensions: modes of engagement and contexts for meaning. Modes of engagement relate to different types of compositional activity – attending, evaluating, directing, exploring and embodying. These activities can be situated in personal, social or cultural contexts that provide descriptive feedback that adds to the meaningfulness of compositional activities. These dimensions are depicted as a meaningful engagement matrix where each mode and context combination occupies a cell in the matrix. The MEM provides a way of visualising the breadth of compositional activities. Our experience suggests that a composer's working style often emphasises activities

---

[76] Sloboda, *The Musical Mind*, 138.
[77] Sloboda, *Exploring the Musical Mind*, 201.

in particular areas of the MEM, and that compositional work frequently oscillates between cells and can move around the matrix over time or during different stages of the creative process. We have observed that over time experienced composers are active over most of the MEM and, as such, the MEM has analytical utility in highlighting types of compositional activity that may be dominant or ignored.

We have provided descriptions of how five experienced composers manifested aspects of meaningful engagement, and have described characteristics common to them as 'attributes' of meaningful engagement: motivation, challenge, involvement, sensitivity and virtuosity. Managing motivation and appropriate challenges appears to be critical to meaningful engagement. Through sensitivity to the materials, expressive desires and context, experienced composers are able to shape and direct compositional outcomes. They display virtuosity with particular compositional techniques and tools to realise these outcomes.

Through our study of the way composers compose, we see them involved in purposeful situated behaviours, motivated by the pleasures and satisfaction of making music – in other words, meaningful engagement.

References

Boden, Margaret, *The Creative Mind* (London, Cardinal, 1990).

Brown, Andrew R., 'Music Composition and the Computer: An examination of the work practices of five experienced composers', PhD thesis (The University of Queensland, Brisbane, 2003).

Clancey, William J., *Situated Cognition: Human knowledge and Computer Representations* (Cambridge: Cambridge University Press, 1997).

Clark, Paul, *The Paul Lansky Interview* (electronicmusician.com, 1997, accessed September 2011), http://www.electronicmusic.com/features/interview/paul lansky.html.

Cook, Nicholas, *Music, Imagination and Culture* (Oxford: Oxford University Press, 1990).

Cope, David, Telephone interview with Andrew R. Brown (Santa Cruz, 14 October 1997).

Cope, David, Telephone interview with Andrew R. Brown (Santa Cruz, 12 November 1997).

Cope, David, *Transformations* (unpublished composition).

Csikszentmihalyi, Mihalyi, 'Society, culture, and person: a systems view of creativity'. In: Robert. J. Sternberg (ed.), *The Nature of Creativity* (New York: Cambridge University Press, 1988), 325–39.

Csikszentmihalyi, Mihaly, *Flow: The Psychology of Happiness* (London: Rider Books, 1992).

Csikszentmihalyi, Mihaly, *Creativity: Flow and the Psychology of Discovery and Invention* (New York: HarperCollins, 1996).

Csikszentmihalyi, Mihaly, *Mihaly Csikszentmihalyi on flow*. Podcast retrieved from http://www.ted.com/talks/mihaly_csikszentmihalyi_on_flow.html on 2 September 2011 (Online, TED Talks, 2004).

De Bono, Edward, *Serious Creativity: Using the Power of Lateral Thinking to Create New Ideas* (London: HarperCollins, 1992).

Dennett, Daniel, 'Collision detection, muselot, and scribbles: some reflections on creativity'. In: David Cope (ed.) *Virtual Music: Computer Synthesis of Musical Style* (Cambridge, MA: MIT Press, 2001), 283–91.

Dewey, John, *Art as Experience* (New York, Putmans, 1934).

Dillon, Steven C., 'The student as maker: an examination of the meaning of music to students in a school and the ways in which we give access to meaningful music education', PhD thesis (La Trobe University, Melbourne, 2001).

Dillon, Steven C., *Music, Meaning and Transformation: Meaningful Music Making for Life* (Cambridge: Cambridge Scholars Publishing, 2007).

Dillon, Steven C., 'Examining meaningful engagement: musicology and virtual music making environments'. In: Elizabeth Mackinlay, Brydie-Leigh Bartleet and K. Barney (eds), *Musical Islands: Exploring Connections between Music, Place and Research*. (Newcastle upon Tyne: Cambridge Scholars, 2009), 297–310.

Dillon, Steve C. and Andrew R. Brown, 'The educational affordances of generative media in arts education'. In: *Proceedings of the International Association for Technology, Education and Development: INTED 2010* (Valencia, Spain, 2010), 5311–20.

Dillon, Steve C. and Andrew R. Brown. 'Access to meaningful relationships through virtual instruments and ensembles'. In: *International Society for Music Education (ISME) 2010 Seminar of the Commission for Community Music Activity CMA X11* (Open University of China, Hangzhou, 2010).

Feldman, David, Mihaly Csikszentmihalyi and Howard Gardner, *Changing the World: A Framework for the Study of Creativity* (London: Praeger, 1994).

Forman, Miloš (director), *Amadeus* (Los Angeles, CA: Warner Brothers Pictures, 1984).

Gardner, Howard, *Creating Minds: An Anatomy of Creativity Seen Through the Lives of Freud, Einstein, Picasso, Stravinsky, Eliot, Graham and Ghandi* (New York: Basic Books, 1983).

Gibson, James J., *The Ecological Approach to Visual Perception* (Boston, MA: Houghton Mifflin, 1979).

Gruber, Howard. 'Aspects of scientific discovery: aesthetics and cognition'. In: John Brockman (ed.), *Creativity* (New York: Touchstone, 1993), 48–74.

Guilford, Joy Paul, 'Traits of creativity'. In: H.H. Anderson (ed.), *Creativity and its Cultivation* (London: Harper, 1959), 142–61. [Reprinted in P.E. Vernon (ed.), *Creativity* (New York: Penguin Books, 1970), 167–88.]

Heidegger, Martin, *The Question Concerning Technology and Other Essays* (New York: Harper & Row, 1977).

Hirschfelder, David, Personal interview with Andrew R. Brown (Melbourne, 22 December 1997).

Hutchins, Edwin, *Cognition in the Wild* (Cambridge, MA: MIT Press, 1994).

Kinderman, William (ed.), *Beethoven's Compositional Process* (Hillsdale, NJ: Pendragon Press, 1991).

Lansky, Paul, *Cmix* (Princeton, NJ: Princeton University, 1978).

Lansky, Paul, *Things She Carried* (New Rochelle: Bridge Records, 1997).

Lansky, Paul, Telephone interview with Andrew R. Brown (Princeton, 28 October 1997).

Lansky, Paul, Personal interview with Andrew R. Brown (Princeton Junction, 23 January 1998).

Lansky, Paul, *Ride* (New Rochelle: Bridge Records, 2001).

Lessig, Lawrence. *Remix: Making Art and Commerce Thrive in the Hybrid Economy* (New York: Penguin, 2008).

Marino, Gérard and Marie-Hélèn Serra and Jean-Michel Raczinski, 'The new UPIC system: origins and innovations', *Perspectives of New Music*, 31/2 (1993), 258–69.

McCullough, Malcolm, *Abstracting Craft: The Practiced Digital Hand* (Cambridge, MA: MIT Press, 1996).

Monahan, Craig (director), *The Interview* (Australia: Pointbank Pictures, 1998).

Newell, Allan and Herbert Simon, *Human Problem Solving* (Englewood Cliffs, NJ: Prentice-Hall, 1972).

Norman, Donald. *The Invisible Computer: Why Good Products can Fail, the Personal Computer is so Complex, and Information Appliances are the Solution* (Cambridge, MA: MIT Press, 1988).

Perkins, David, *The Mind's Best Work* (Cambridge, MA: Harvard University Press, 1981).

Polanyi, Michael, *Personal Knowledge: Towards a Post-critical Philosophy* (Chicago, IL: University of Chicago Press, 1958).

Reich, Steve, *Different Trains*, for string quartet and tape in three movements (1988).

Reich, Steve, Telephone interview with Andrew R. Brown (Vermont 11 November 1997).

Reich, Steve, Personal interview with Andrew R. Brown (New York, 19 January 1998).

Reich, Steve and Beryl Korot, *Hindenberg*, Act 1 of the video opera *Three Tales* (New York, 2002).

Robindoré, Brigitte, Personal interview with Andrew R. Brown (Paris, 6 February 1998).

Brigitte Robindoré, *O'er The Sea*, electroacoustic composition (2001).

Sloboda, John, *The Musical Mind: The Cognitive Psychology of Music* (Oxford: Clarendon Press, 1985).

Sloboda, John, *Exploring the Musical Mind: Cognition, Emotion, Ability, Function* (Oxford: Oxford University Press, 2005).

Spinosa, Charles, Fernando Flores and Hubert Dreyfus. *Disclosing New Worlds: Entrepreneurship, Democratic Action, and the Cultivation of Solidarity* (Cambridge, MA: MIT Press, 1997).

Stahl, Gerry, *Group Cognition: Computer Support for Building Collaborative Knowledge* (Cambridge, MA: MIT Press, 2004).

Swanwick, Keith, *Musical Knowledge: Intuition, Analysis, and Musical Education* (London: Routledge, 1994).

Varela, Francisco, Evan Thompson and Eleanor Rosch, *The Embodied Mind: Cognitive Science and Human Experience* (Cambridge, MA: MIT Press, 1991).

Vygotsky, Lev, *Mind in Society: Development of Higher Psychological Processes* (Cambridge, MA: Harvard University Press, 1978).

Chapter 5
The Practice of Diverse Compositional Creativities

Pamela Burnard

This chapter argues that there is no single creativity for all musics and that different contexts give rise to different types of music creativities and involve practices as diverse as the musics themselves. In exploring three different compositional practices, I distinguish between various meanings of musical creativity, as they have been mythologised over time and have grown in the breadth of their application and reference in contemporary practice. The compositional practices featured include those of a turntablist (DJ) composer whose practice calls into question conventional understandings of the interplay between innovative sampling, audiences and constructed socio-spatial principles; a contemporary classical composer whose compositional creativity is guided by principles of genre mastery and artistic originality; and an audio designer and game music composer who works in the videogame industry, where priority is given to team collaboration and developing complex user-interface technology. The chapter concludes with an argument for expanding current understandings of musical creativities, widening and accommodating diverse compositional practices in the context of music education, and in terms of radically rethinking professional music training.

In many ways, this chapter is the outcome of my attempts to value all students' compositional practices and to raise some of the professional issues that musicians and music educators are confronted with. These are largely concerned with the interpretation and assessment of compositional practices, and the forms of practice and representation that gain success in the context of public funding and examination systems. Another starting point for this chapter relates to what I want to say about myths that limit how we think about musical creativity. Myths, or the stories we tell ourselves concerning how things came to be and therefore how they are, are derived from assumptions whose function, according to Small[1] 'is to provide present-day people with models and paradigms for values and behaviour' that supposedly reflect the past practices of the 'great composers'. What these myths are, who makes them and how they are retold, shall be discussed next.

---

[1]   Christopher Small, *Musicking: The Meanings of Performing and Listening* (Hanover, NH, 1998), 89.

Myths and Myth-making

Myths have always been a way for people to explain their societies, their belief systems, the lives they live and, in the case of music, the lives of the artists we elevate to the status of heroes and celebrities. Myths are of great significance to those in the music industry and music education. Professional musicians position themselves within the creative and cultural industries and locate their practices guided by the relationships and dynamics between: artists, writers and producers; those who market, deliver and distribute music, such as managers, record companies and publishers; the funders, consumers and audiences of music, who ultimately pay for it all; and, of course, those of us who work in education, whose perceptions and assessments of musical creativity exemplify its complexity. Myth-making and myth-telling are deeply embedded in accounts and representations of composers and their compositional practice.

Consider, for example, Brian Wilson and his exaltation of Beethoven in the following quote:

> You wonder if some god said, "I'll create a being whose work will mean so much to so many people, a being whose work will enrich people, put sun in their lives, show them a way to express themselves, to understand themselves, to find their place in the world. And yet I'll make him suffer terribly. I'll remove him from his own gifts and I'll make the world he improved a foreboding cell for him".[2]

Myth has it that Beethoven, the Romantic hero, made no less than twelve versions of the C Sharp Minor Quartet, Op. 131. He was also known to improvise for half an hour on any theme – even for pieces supposedly notated in a final form.

The power of personal myth-making can be seen in statements by or about artists, in the cultivation of public opinion. Wolfgang Amadeus Mozart was claimed to say:

> Nor do I hear in my imagination the parts successively; I hear them all at once. What a delight this is! All this inventing, this producing, takes place in a pleasing, lively dream ... When I am, as it were, completely myself, entirely alone, and of good cheer say, travelling in a carriage, or walking after a good meal, or during the night when I cannot sleep; it is often on such occasions that my ideas flow best and most abundantly. When and how they come, I know not; nor can I force them ... The committing to paper is done quickly enough, for

---

[2]   See Carys Wyn Jones, *The Rock Canon: Canonical Values in the Reception of Rock Albums* (Aldershot, 2008), 40.

everything is already finished; and it rarely differs on paper from what it was in my imagination.[3]

Unlike Beethoven, who was portrayed as never ceasing to improvise upon his notated work, Mozart was thought to make few changes to his completed compositions. Even reputable dictionaries and theorists furnish us with conceptions of composing based on the mythical idea of these 'imagined wholes'. In fact, Mozart extemporised the majority of his compositions and also made preliminary sketches of his major works. His compositional practice was improvisational in nature. We are told that he commented on the 'wearisome' nature of the 'labour' of composition.[4] The myth that, for a piece of music or the 'work' to first come into being, it must first be imagined is perpetuated by Langer, who stated:

> The first stage is the process of conception that takes place entirely within the composer's mind (no matter what outside stimuli may start or support it), and issues in a more or less sudden recognition of the total form to be achieved. (p. 121)[5]

However, a distinction between improvisation and composition can be made on a technological and temporal basis but also as historical constructions. Improvisation occurs in the present time, the here and now, whereas a composition occurs over time, if not in the rethinking of ideas at least in the time required to notate the piece. Or does it? Contemporary accounts of compositional practices and phases of work by composers such as Stockhausen, Ligeti, Xenakis and Berio emphasise a wealth of possible vocabularies and categorisations of practices.[6] How composers coordinate their efforts, how they think, how they start and, of course, how they finish their compositions – in performance, in musical association with ensembles, or in the immediacy of performance creativity – show that compositional practices are multiply mediated, fluid and ever changing. The analysis of compositional practices challenges the telling of myths associated with compositional practices, which are narrowly construed as imagined sounds or carefully notated fixed manuscripts, and refocuses on what is essentially a test procedure involving immediate sound feedback from a set

---

[3]   Mozart, cited in Brewster Ghiselin (ed.), *The Creative Process: A Symposium* (Berkeley, CA, 1952), 34.

[4]   Robert W. Weisberg, *Creativity: Beyond the Myth of Genius* (Oxford, 1993).

[5]   Susanne K. Langer, *Feeling and Form: A Theory of Art Developed from Philosophy in a New Key* (London, 1953).

[6]   Ann McCutchan, *The Music That Sings: Composers Speak about the Creative Process* (Oxford 1999). Simon Emmerson, 'Composing strategies and pedagogy', *Contemporary Music Review*, 3 (1989), 133–44.

of 'action repertoires', which then forms the basis for documenting, developing and discovering ideas.

Digital technologies have had a considerable impact on redefining compositional practices with new approaches to and ways of viewing what composing is, new ways of conceiving of the changing practices and new forms of composition that provide the basis of its production and reproduction, whether supported through elite or religious patronage, market exchange, or public and subsidised cultural institutions.

Accounts by Goehr[7] remind us of the dangers and inappropriateness of accepting any single theory of the nature of compositional practice. The trend amongst contemporary composers is to cast doubts on the compositional mechanism of the commissioning, promotion and publication of musical works that has been with us since the late classical era. They claim that the 'masterwork syndrome' or 'the work concept', which centred on the belief that musical works were fixed and transcended any particular performance, is archaic and discriminates against true experimentation. Emmerson is critical of western musical practice because composers were: (i) allowed the creation of just one version of each composed piece; (ii) denied revisions of works judged in final form on the basis of a 'once and for all'; and (iii) in the control of and responsive to power brokers in the arts as defined by the critics (p. 143).

A number of familiar examples will illustrate my point further. Firstly, there are the dominant western music ontologies as indicated by Goehr and then examined by DeNora[8] in her account of the construction of Beethoven's genius. She unpacks the mythologising of the 'great composers' and the privilege afforded to the residual model of a single heroic individual composer-genius who must create perfectly formed, self-contained works; composing 'finished' pieces, *works* or art *objects* that have the privilege of sourcing the location of musical creativity and meaning in the musical score rather than in its performance. Secondly, there is the historical conception of musical creativity, which is rooted in notions of divine creators and mythic moments of creation. From the perspective of contemporary music, the multitude of ways and radically changing forms that characterise contemporary compositional practice call for a radically revised conception of a multiplicity of musical creativities. Combined with this is a romantic, idealistic view of the primacy of composition and its associated hierarchy of 'masterworks' that were thought of as being perfectly formed, finished and 'untouchable', which came to emerge as 'facts' of music history, while, all the time, Mozart, the epitome of the 'great genius', employed a range of different practices, rather than just one. Thirdly, the collaborative forms of musical authorship, as indicated by Wolff[9] on

---

[7]   Lydia Goehr, *The Imaginary Museum of Musical Worlds: An Essay in the Philosophy of Music* (Oxford, 1992).

[8]   Tia DeNora, *Beethoven and the Construction of Genius* (Berkeley, CA, 1995) and *Music in Everyday Life* (Cambridge, 2000).

[9]   Janet Wolff, *The Social Production of Art* (London, 1993).

the social production of art, Becker[10] on collective art worlds and Cook[11] on art-music models in collective improvisational performance, afford and emphasise a radically different constellation of improvised musics and technological mediation, where practices of re-composition, remixing and new forms of live, improvised musics are made. Having explored some of the myths and assumptions underpinning the portrayal of compositional creativity I will now introduce three composers who articulate some of the principles and norms implicit in real-world contemporary practices.

A Methodology for Articulating Real-world Practices of Diverse Compositional Creativities

The socio-personal perspectives as espoused by social psychologist Amabile[12] suggest that a social and distributed nature of creativity arises in ways in which a number of components converge. These include social environment, task motivation, intrinsic and extrinsic rewards, domain-relevant skills (music aptitude, experience) and creativity-relevant skills (fluency, flexibility, originality). Here, Amabile directs our attention to the *social dimensions* of creativity and human beings' abilities, as social creatures, to act as independent social agents who profoundly affect each other as they interact and coordinate actions around individual and socially agreed-upon goals. This is immensely helpful in considering how compositional creativities are constituted in moments of practice. It is always 'of the moment', brought out when a set of dispositions meets a particular problem, choice or context. All cultural production constructs and engages relations not only between persons, but also between persons and things, and it does so across both space and time. Thus, compositional practices not only manifest themselves in attitudes, approaches and values set within the composer's world (i.e. the cultural field), but are also shaped by the material and cultural conditions of existence in which they are placed from the beginning (the real-world context).

Bourdieu's account of the cultural field and the role of cultural intermediaries[13] argues that individuals are socialised in diverse ways, and that this socialisation provides children, and later adults, with a sense of what is comfortable or what is natural in terms of the 'taking in' of rules, values and dispositions as 'the *habitus*', which he defines as 'the durably installed generative principle of regulated

[10]   Howard Becker, *Art Worlds* (Berkeley, CA, 1984).

[11]   Nicholas Cook, *Music: A Very Short Introduction* (Oxford, 1998).

[12]   Teresa M. Amabile, *Creativity in Context: Update to the Social Psychology of Creativity* (New York, 1996).

[13]   See Pierre Bourdieu, *The Field of Cultural Production: Essays on Art and Literature* (Oxford, 1993).

improvisations ... [which produces] practices'.[14] These background experiences also shape the amounts and forms of resources (*capitals*) that individuals inherit and draw upon, accumulate and are imbued with as they confront various institutional arrangements (*fields*) in the social world. Composers are always attuned to, and work within and across fields (for example, being affiliated to a particular contemporary chamber ensemble, orchestra, institution, academy, venue or record label) and are attuned to the dynamics of the fields within areas of the creative and cultural industries. Bourdieu describes a *field* as consisting of a 'separate social universe having its own laws of functioning' (p. 162). A field is an area of production that is made up of specific forms of practice, methods and principles of evaluation of both practice and work produced in the field. Bourdieu's notion of 'habitus' concerns those particular dispositions and attitudes towards practice that a person acquires, unaware of their constitution according to particular rules, in the sense that such dispositions seem natural. These dispositions relate to modes of perception and thinking, and ways of evaluating one's own actions and those of others. What is implicit about the compositional habitus for a video game composer and a sound designer working for a gaming company is the specific conditions that a company sets up in terms of its structures and the perception it creates about roles played by the team and the practices in which they collaboratively engage.

In this chapter, three composers – a turntablist composer, a classical contemporary composer and a media composer – were selected from interviews with 20 composers aged between 22 and 62 years.[15] These composers were selected to demonstrate the explicit practices of three diverse cases. The composers featured in this chapter live and work in Europe, Australia and the USA. The criteria applied for selecting the composers featured in this chapter include: (i) being employed as professional composers; (ii) having their music performed regularly; and (iii) negotiating multiple selves that shift between composer, performer and musician.

The interviews employed semi-structured protocols based on the authors' previous work and the literature, as well as more open-ended questions to encourage descriptions and stories of the network of connections that bind composers together. This reveals how work is allocated among them, how they perceive their careers, how they define artistic success, and how they establish, or try to establish, vital connections with stakeholders/gatekeepers. It also shows how they experienced their schooling, the privilege of certain traditions, and their experience of a diversity of musical creativities. Following the interviews, the transcript material was reduced by eliminating the words of the interviewer and replacing these with italicised words that changed each question into a statement in order to preserve the meaning and flow of the exchanges while, at the same time, indicating that the composers' narratives came from the question posed by

---

[14]   Pierre Bourdieu, *Outline of a Theory of Practice* (Cambridge, 1977).

[15]   Pamela Burnard, *Musical Creativities in Practice* (Oxford, 2012).

the interviewer. Next, a structural approach was used to produce a shorter narrative account with sequential and non-repetitive language. These condensed narratives were then written in the third person to illustrate the presence of the researcher in the account. The narratives were examined further to elicit common and more conceptual themes across the narratives, using an adapted version of constant comparison inquiry.

Introducing DJ/Turntablist Simon Lewicki
aka DJ Groove Terminator (b. 1969)

DJs know how to deploy and create music to 'move' a crowd; the collective experience of space is as important as the mutual tuning-in and the construction of the 'we' of collective creativity. They know what the 'game' requires in that they know precisely how to guide the collective experience of club cultures. DJing is associated with a particular DJ's production style and acts, in a particular local club and music scene, at a particular point in time and place, and although the emphasis is often on their unique methods, technique and trendsetting (for example, the innovative remixing of records or mashups of digital data), the creativity of individual DJs tends to favour specific knowledge of musical styles or identifiable genres, as well as knowledge of the complexities of subgenres (with nearly 100 distinct subgenres within dance music). Techniques in mixing can be highly innovative and offer a sense of exclusivity, a different way of experiencing sound and a break with established methods, in order to situate each dance scene.

Simon was originally a hip hop DJ and was featured in the 2000 Australian edition of the Ministry of Sound's Club Nation series, as well as on several other Ministry of Sound compilations. While maintaining his career as an active recording artist, a producer of multi-platinum selling releases and DJ, he has also composed and produced TV and radio commercials. He currently lives in Los Angeles, where he DJs, produces and undertakes frequent tours as a guest international DJ at clubs in Europe, Australia and across the USA. From an early age, within his particular cultural setting and urban youth practices, he learned the production and practical operational knowledge required of a DJ. Simon's DJing was characteristically produced within a system of close-knit local networks, crossing over between radio techniques and pioneering club disco work, and using record mixtures and superimpositions of 'beats' or 'breakbeats',[16] and

---

[16]   David Toop (2004) explains 'drumbeats' eloquently as 'A conga or bongo solo, a timable break or simply the drummer hammering out the beat – these could be isolated by using two copies of the record on twin turntables and playing the one section over and over, flipping the needle back to the start of one while the other played through. The music made in this way came to be known as beats or break beats'; 'Uptown throwdown'. In M. Forman and M. Neil (eds), *That's the Joint! The Hip-Hop Studies Reader* (London: Routledge, 2004), 236.

'scratching',[17] as well as samples of rock music and funk with some MCing[18] over sets.[19] Simon has won awards, including Best National DJ. His song *Here Comes Another One* was the theme of the popular Australian (and worldwide) reality TV show 'The Block' and he is currently engaged in continent-hopping guest appearances. Simon makes it clear from the outset that he understands the importance of positioning himself and his resources within the field(s) in which he is operating and that what is required is an ability to manoeuvre and negotiate conditions and contexts 'of the moment':

> **Simon**: I grew up in Adelaide in Australia. My step-dad was the station manager and he put together the first community radio station in Adelaide. My mum used to do a show on Saturday afternoons, and so I'd go in with her, and sort of mess around in the record library and make myself tapes. And then someone offered to teach me to 'panel', which is to run the equipment in the studio … I'd also find ways to sneak into the studio during the graveyard shift and make these crazy mix tapes for myself all night, and then I started a high school radio programme, one day a week … Around the age of 17 or so I was at an age of going out quite a lot, and in the last two years of high school, I really got the bug for it, and I started DJing in nightclubs, even before I turned 17. I'd lie about my age to get in and stuff. And I pretty much got the bug very early on. So we're talking the mid to late 80s. So, I was there doing that for a while, and then at the first advent of the first wave of hip-hop culture and then with 'house music' coming in and everything, I kind of got swept up in that. There was three things basically you could do in the hip-hop culture, and that was dance or do graffiti, or DJ. And I was a terrible dancer; I was a very, very average artist. It was the music that really excited me, so I basically kind of fell into it that way. I was always making tapes for my friends. And it was sort of about sharing great music.

Simon was one of the first to pick up on break-beat music in Australia, synchronising beats with a particular sound, personal mystique and identity, and orchestrating a powerful interaction with the crowd. His DJ name 'Groove Terminator' is itself a 'brand', with celebrity status infusing all aspects of his work:

> **Simon**: I picked up very early on that there was a basic sort of rotating rule of three operating throughout the night. I learnt this by basically hanging around with other DJs, trying to pick up tips. The rule of three is play one they know, a new one, and something they love. But not necessarily in that order, but it's like that's the rule of three that you'd always go to as a working DJ going out doing

---

[17]   'Scratching' is a term coined to describe the practice of the real-time manipulation of 12-inch discs on adapted turntables (David Toop, 2004).

[18]   MCing (also known as rapping) refers to spoken or chanted rhyming lyrics.

[19]   Christopher Cox and Daniel Warner (eds), *Audio Culture: Readings in Modern Music* (London, 2009).

mobiles or weddings. It's a rule I apply doing really cool inner city clubs as well. When you're reading the crowd you can tell if you've got tracks or songs that are playing with a lot of energy you're just going to wear the crowd out instantly. You want to keep them there for hours, but also, at the same time, if you're like the resident at the club, as opposed to the guest DJ, which is the culture of DJing now, sort of the resident, you need to be able to work the bar as well. So you need to get people worked up, and get them sweaty for a couple of songs, they need to go off and drink, and spend some money behind the bar, and then you need to get them to come back and dance on.

The emphasis for Simon is on branding. The logic of DJ practice is imminent in the building of an identity, a celebrity DJ status and a certain DJ style for each scene, club and circuit. DJ success depends on independent control over technique and style, but, perhaps, most of all, on a whole lifestyle and individualism that matches perfectly with the art of the club scene.

> **Simon**: Preparing for a gig sees me thinking about the music. You spend a lot of time in the first fifteen years going into record stores several times a week to shop for imports. These days it's so easy to jump online and get trawling through online stores. I get sent most of the music I play these days. But you have to spend a lot of time listening to a lot of music … Thinking about a specific gig, you do a lot more preparation, thinking about the type of club, the space, the place and that sort of thing. You think about if you want to keep it cooler, or keep it a bit more commercial, or what sort of vibe you want to produce. Then I think about the tracks and sets, the first song and option four or five other tracks. You think about potential goalposts or points in the set you'll move between; where you can transition from point to point, and where you can change in direction and can move around. The points are flexible. You need to be able to move those, because the crowd may react differently to what you expect. So you need to be able to change the mood up quite quickly without it becoming a train wreck. When I'm DJing I always tend to think of working out how I can blend a song into another song and what new music I can create out of blending these two seemingly disparate bits of music together. That's what I enjoy most, the mixing of tracks.

Technology is a huge catalyst for creative choices. It enables the DJ to alter, adapt, deconstruct, innovate and use record mixing in different ways to move different crowds.

> **Simon**: I make my own sound and create my own sort of vibe and that's what I look for and what keeps me excited. It is all also about using technology, showing your dextrous abilities and your technical prowess in deconstructing and reconstructing the songs. You've got to have the tools available and you've got to know your genres in order to repackage a genre that you may want to

bring back. It's also about self-marketing. As a DJ, you see yourself as a creator, a creative individual. I don't think I've created a genre yet but I've made some massive discoveries with mixing genres that really grabbed me and crowds I've played for. And being at the top of the game and one of the biggest in the world, means you're seen as a celebrity and getting Grammy nominations as part of the mainstream community as a whole.

For Simon, DJing seems to depend on intuition and game-sense as much as on his mastery of explicit procedures. DJs implicitly agree to be ruled by the conventions of their field and immediately set up personal relations with the game, as well as with other DJs and the 'rules' of the game, which concern the creative sense of audience interaction and the innovative practices of re-composition. This creative menu can include dub, toasting, scratching, reworking musical materials and blending the contents of separate vinyl records in order to create something new or to cover, rework or transform the original in subsequent mashups.

Establishing DJ status and mystique binds the DJ to the crowd. This process is one of the strategies DJs adopt over time to position themselves with an eye to which clubs, gigs and crowds will be chosen and played to at the pinnacle of their career. The DJ's relationship with the dance crowd is crucially important. Ultimately, both the DJ and the crowd need to grasp each other's intentions, the former through the performance, and the latter through dancing. This demonstrates aspects of social, distributed and relayed creativity in terms of originality and the value accorded to the interactional qualities of DJ, dance crowd, sound systems and the myriad social forms embodying the music as it is repeatedly relayed and transformed across time, space, gesture, dance, bodies and place.

We can observe the compositional creativity of the DJ as giving form and meaning to the creativity sparked by a kind of fictive, parallel universe within a club scene. This compositional creativity incorporates the setting up of playlists on a computer, sequencing, beat-matching, mixing and remixing sounds and songs for a live audience, and generating the 'buzz' or energy that results from the interaction of tracks. The various aspects of creativity a DJ portrays appear to be fluid and constantly changing from one situation to the next. At the same time, they are embedded in clear-cut social and cultural contexts, with values ascribed to distinctive subgenres, usually specified by a short generic list (for example, 'techno-hardcore-alternative-trance', 'ragga-hip-hop-jungle' or 'funky-soulful-house'). Sounds are remixed live with other sounds and break-beats are mixed with other recorded sound material. There is a fusion of *re- and de-composition*[20] where raw musical material is broken up and ideas are recycled and remixed. For the DJ, compositional creativities embody the physical expression of a collective experience.

---

[20]   Arnold Berleant, 'Musical de-composition'. In P. Alperson (ed.), *What is Music: An Introduction to the Philosophy of Music* (Pennsylvania, PA, 1987).

Introducing Contemporary Classical Composer Liza Lim[21] **(b. 1966)**

Australian composer Liza Lim is a Professor of Composition and the Director of CeReNeM (www.cerenem.org) at the Centre for Research in New Music at the University of Huddersfield, UK. She was appointed in 2008, having worked as a freelance composer for 20 years. Liza's research and composition work has been focused on the area of intercultural exchange, looking particularly at Chinese and Australian indigenous art, aesthetics and ritual culture. Her early work examines the role of ambivalence, particularly in diasporic cultural conditions, as a space for the transformation of cultural knowledge, and this is allied with her strong interest in the politics of translation and other kinds of transactions in cultural meaning. Her compositional work in the area of narrative multiplicity is informed by analyses of Chinese poetry, calligraphic structure and the many traditions of folk stories. Liza's collaborations with Chinese, Japanese and Korean musicians inform her interest in kinaesthetic approaches to performance, whereby the physicality of gesture is interrogated as the basis for formulating new approaches to instrumental technique and listening. Liza, as with the other composers interviewed in this sample, was self-directed towards composing, and from her early adolescent years, spent a good deal of time and energy exploring the experience of composing:

> **Liza**: I have been writing music since I was at high school. I have thought of myself as a composer since I was about 11 years of age. I'm now 43, so that's over 30 years of work. I would say that the kind of exposure I had at school, particularly to contemporary music and the notion of making your own music through improvisation and composition, was the formative thing which turned me into a composer.

A strong home influence with parental encouragement and a nurturing school environment were key elements in preparing Liza for a male-dominated musical world.[22] Liza is a composer who has developed a strong reputation and some of her earliest formative experiences came from being part of a community that encouraged this sort of attitude and creative disposition in music. At the age of 11, Liza was encouraged by her teachers at an independent/private school in Melbourne to turn from piano and violin studies to composition:

---

[21] For Liza's background and works, see: http://www.ricordi.co.uk/composers/index-liza.php and http://www.ricordi.de/lim-liza.0.html?&L=1.

[22] See Lucy Green, *How Popular Musicians Learn: A Way Ahead for Music Education* (Aldershot, 2001) for a discussion of gendered approaches to student composers, and Jann Pasler, *Writing Through Music: Essays on Music, Culture and Politics* (Oxford, 2008) for interesting discussions about the challenges for women in developing careers as composers.

> **Liza**: My first instrument was piano and then I started learning violin around that time. I wasn't particularly clued into music as a child at primary school. It was the impact of going to a particular high school that I think kind of really switched on something inside of me ... I owe everything to them ... Perhaps unusually I began composing with a graphic score and experimenting with sounds rather than traditional notation. But I would say it was a little bit later that I had more of a sense of trying to create my own language and developing my own voice.

In their early years, teachers and peer musicians have a major impact on young people in terms of developing their musical identities and identifications as composers. Such influences form part of the social context in which they are situated, such as family, bands and school. Liza's teachers, peers and the school community encouraged her ('everything I wrote got played') and made composing seem not a peculiar thing to do. Being recognised as a composer came without any direct pressure. Liza was accepted and widely acclaimed as a young and gifted composer during her formative school years, when she found her self-identity, reputation and distinctive voice as a composer of new works:

> **Liza**: At the heart of my work has been much collaboration with many musicians. And they have certainly been, I would say, also, the formative kind of impulse for a lot of my work ... fellow students, all the way along. In fact I still work with someone I went to school with, the singer Deborah Kayser who was in my last opera *The Navigator* (2008). So very long-term collaborative relationships with key performers are what I would say has really characterised my work as a composer ... I had the most fantastic sort of level of support from people around me. Everything I wrote got played. I mean some of the early works I wrote were for the school orchestra where there was a sense of "give it a go".

It is evident in the composer's life world that music reinforces social relations and, in particular, social and personal networks. Liza's compositional practice bears the stamp of the history, culture(s) and social interactions within the communities of which this artist is a member.

One of Liza's important communities is ELISION, a contemporary music ensemble that creates opportunities for experimentation:

> **Liza**: Working with ELISION[23] offers me all types of opportunities for just sort of plunging in and trialling and testing ideas, and that's why I said that the contact with performers was absolutely critical, because for me the creative

---

[23]   The ELISION Ensemble is a chamber ensemble specialising in contemporary classical music, concentrating on the creation and presentation of new works. The ensemble comprises a core of around 20 virtuoso musicians from Australia and around the world (www.elision.org.au).

laboratory is crucial for finding out what works and what doesn't work, in a very concrete sense ... And it's not just the technical, but it's the interpersonal level as well that's really important here. In a sense, much of the work I do is a customisation of sound that derives from these contacts with performers. These are the idiosyncratic aspects rather than anything else. I've always tried to characterise the work I do in terms of trying to move further and further away from any sort of generic sense of what is happening, towards an evermore specific and finely tuned sense of the particular: this moment, this sound in this way, this type of energy in relation to the performer.

The dualism of her individual and inward, and socially constituted and outward practices, is shown in her discussion of individual and social dimensions, which are defined by the intent of her composing.

Liza: Another aspect of the way I'm in dialogue with a wider context is the way my compositional work often focuses on aspects of intercultural exchange looking particularly at Chinese and at Australian Indigenous art, aesthetics and ritual culture. This hasn't been an abstract study but very much something arising from interactions with different kinds of performers and artists from various traditions. ... I did study with a number of different composers in Australia and abroad. I went through my undergraduate training as a classical performer. It was a bit later that I was part of a composition course. I was often just sort of left to my own devices as well. So I would say that the contact with composers was a different kind of input from the other kinds of experiences I was having with performers. ... While the contact with performers was absolutely critical, I did study with two teachers who emphasised musical craftsmanship. One was the Australian-Italian composer Riccardo Formosa, who took a very artisanal approach to composition with a sense of the hand-crafting of every sound and with things like orchestration ... sound for me is also key ... Looking for different solutions for how a sound can transform, listening for what happens when you push the sound in a certain way, being very specific in terms of its qualities and knowing certain things about the boundaries of where things start to morph, so that I can actually compose with these different degrees of transformation ... This close connection to the morphology of sound has been honed by the experience of writing pieces which are for a specific situation with performers ... There are particular performers that really inspire me and so a work is made in close collaboration with the performers and they form part of the interaction.

Central to Liza's experience of 'individual creativity' is the assumption that there is not merely an accidental, but an essential relationship between the work and its written and aural manifestations. The work is not static but is essentially historical and social in nature; as she puts it, 'the performers form part of the interaction' with its generative origins. These meanings live on, and are renewed, in each new performance; and, as in creative collaborations (or collaborative creativity), this process is profoundly affected by the nature of the social and cultural relationships between artists.

> **Liza**: I have an on-going concern or interest in Aboriginal aesthetics ... since 2004 I've experimented with different ways of realising these ideas. I've a collection of works where what I'm looking to create in these works are qualities of sound which are highly mobile, and quite three-dimensional. So if you imagine a point on a surface, you can move that in any direction, and then drop below the surface, that is, the sound can be understood in a spatial way, the sound can take on different qualities of density and opacity. The types of vocabularies I might use to describe what I'm doing with the sound or how it develops come from meteorology – weather patterns and dynamical systems. And so that connects with a particular aesthetic world, which prompts me to look for new techniques to realise these structures.

Creativity is also bound up with the re-opening and re-creation of cultural source material, in improvisatory inclusions, and in the physicality of performance – another type of creativity wherein language, gesture and bodily significations are condensed in the musical performance.

> **Liza**: There are some major effects of socialisation from which you get so many messages; you can lose contact with your own specific individual creativity ... there's even more pressure now with new media and technologies which is about moving away from the highly individual, with an overriding message about conforming to a utilitarian, economically driven view of things ... society is a very big teacher ... but in a way, I think that individual expression in all areas of composition even if it only holds a very tiny place in the bigger picture has value by virtue of offering a different kind of message about what the nature of exchange might be ...
>
> I'm receiving impressions all the time, for instance from different parts of the world when I travel, my interactions with people and situations and then there are impressions from specifically musical situations as well. I build up a very aural–tactile–formal sensorium of impressions and somehow I do think my work arises from this 'lived experience' – sometimes in quite concrete ways, at other times in very unforeseen and abstracted ways where it would be difficult to trace the sources.
>
> Some of the work I've done with performers, and particularly with Asian, for instance, Japanese, Korean and Chinese performers, has focussed on particular modes of performance practice where this sense of the kinaesthetic touch is an intimate part of the musical meaning of the work. And so in those kinds of projects I'm connecting very directly with that specifically musical-aesthetic kind of information.

Liza describes her practice ('regular time I spend at the desk') as involving both the self and social worlds. Here, compositional creativity is a dialectic involving an act (writing 'at the desk') of individual expression (that 'can hold a tiny place') in relation to a complex set of musical–structural–cultural properties. While it potentially involves a complex set of intentions, these are supplemented by actual performances and the development of performance traditions. Thus, we can say that seeing how music comes to offer particular things means seeing how it constitutes aspects of the social world. Yet, what counts as creativity differs, depending on the context, which creates different possibilities.

> **Liza**: There are certain things I might write for specialist contemporary music solo performers that I feel are not possible in the same way with an orchestra. Over time, I've shifted from thinking about these differences as constrictions in a negative way to becoming very interested in the creative possibilities offered by more bounded situations.
>
> I'm hardly ever concerned about what the audience will think because if you start worrying about whether people are gonna like you, I think that's the end of you as an artist. To shoot for artistic originality is to feel complete fearlessness, you've just got to want it so much that you're going to do it no matter what anyone thinks or says or does ... It's not really about the mastery of the materials. One is trying to go beyond the pre-existing forms of "language". And when I say "a language", I include the most experimental work as well as the more traditional mainstream kind of approach to making music.

There are at least two ways of characterising Lisa's compositional creativity. First, as '*artistic originality*', that is, when works have a stock of possibilities that originate as the unique artistic intent of the composer – unique in the form of site-specific practices that require 'fearlessness' (risk-taking, individual independence). Second, creating a work, the primordial value of which is genre 'mastery', is constituted by and depends on that which has gone before in pre-existing forms of language, including experimental and traditional forms of music-making.

> **Liza**: I begin from a place where I think I'm offering something that is very finely focused and individualised. For me, that's my job. An important aspect of the point of art seems to me that it can hold a multitude or perhaps infinite number of possible meanings and experiences for people. So for me, I'm not saying I want people to feel a certain kind of way, but really what I would like is to offer something that opens out towards a sense of many possible meanings.
>
> This plays into the social context of music, where there are certain kinds of occasions and situations where people's expectations are for entertainment or for something which is going to positively reinforce their sense of importance and status ... then there's the opening night, which is always the invited

audience of very important people with expectations of a certain kind of glamour. Unfortunately, this aspect of social reception can often get confused in discussions about accessibility ... I'm more interested in an audience that's incredibly engaged, that has this language for engaging with a whole range of works ... Most people like what they already know, that's a kind of conservatism, rather than necessarily going out and seeking experiences that are completely new.

Liza's compositional creativity is defined by the interaction between developing inwardly directed practices that constitute the 'self', which as ascribed by intention, individual vocabularies, musical languages, original voice – individual creativity – and outwardly directed social modes of creativity. As such, these paths take shape in the creative laboratory that Liza participates in when working with ELISION in developing new performance techniques, mixed media or cross-arts, and in forms of indigenous cultural and intercultural aesthetics that manifest in the compositional and improvisatory modalities found in performance. For Liza, the ranges of ways in which the self and social realms enable multiple creativities are always in motion.

Introducing Audio Designer Kenneth Young (b. 1980)

This section explores the compositional creativities of a media composer and audio designer who brings together the ideas of teams and coordinates the integration of these ideas into a unique product in the video game industry.

The creation of video games is not only a cultural and sociological process; it is also a newly economic one because of the rapid increase in the popularity of the medium in the last decade. In the USA alone, the video games industry generated $40 billion in revenue in 2010 and it is arguably one of the most significant sources of entertainment today. Video games also comprise a voracious market for new music. Video games provide interaction with, and information for, the player, whose experience is strikingly similar to that of playing music; each requires a high level of control over some physical instrument (such as a joystick), involving recognition of where one is at each moment, and relying on a combination of learned patterns and contextually appropriate improvisation.

Audio designers, who produce the game music and soundtracks for such interactive applications, work with all aspects of games audio, including the programming, application and production stages. They make innovative use of existing technologies, develop new ones and use online audio tools to use and write music to express intense emotion, evoke a sense of drama and communicate a story.

Game music is often dubbed 'adaptive' music because it is designed to depend on the player's or character's actions; such audio interactivity[24] endows on-screen characters with emotions, adding depth of sentiment to the playing experience.[25] Sound design is used to create and add to the tensions of the game-playing experience in a console game, and can be a key component for orienting prospective attention. For example, in the game *Mr. Sinister*,[26] which features a character called Mario, the music changes when he jumps to the next level, but its happy, friendly style remains the same.

The third composer to be discussed, sound designer Kenneth Young, was born in Edinburgh, Scotland, and lives in London, where he works as the lead audio designer at Media Molecule.[27] At the time of writing, he is responsible for the audio experience in the games they make, most recently the PlayStation 3 title *LittleBigPlanet* and its sequel. A strong sense of personal efficacy has had consequences for his career in terms of his personal history stresses, the importance of his education and his desire to successfully establish a career in the gaming world. The following account gives a clear sense that Kenneth has an appetite and disposition for questioning the known, for experimenting and pondering over questions and possibilities, and has the social resilience that is required of creative people, especially in the games industry:

Kenneth: Well, my family is musical; my dad was a very keen semi-professional musician when he was younger and still loves to play. And my mum is from a musical family – her brother is a professional musician. I played the violin from the age of six or seven and had lessons practically every week until I was about twenty-one. And then, when I finished high school, I knew that I was really into music, but I also knew that I didn't want to do performance. Because, well … I was good and people seemed to enjoy my playing but, I'm not sure, I haven't quite worked out why yet. I don't know; I'd hate to blame my parents and say it

---

24   For more discussion of sites and works involving interactive audio for the web, see http://www.vispo.com/misc/ia.htm.

25   Nick Collins and Julio d'Escrivan (eds), *The Cambridge Companion to Electronic Music* (Cambridge, 2007), 38–54.

26   Mister Sinister is a fictional character that appears in comic books published by Marvel Comics. The character first appeared in Uncanny X-Men #221 (September 1987) and was created by writer Chris Claremont and artist Marc Silvestri (see http://en.wikipedia.org/wiki/Mister_Sinister and http://www.giantbomb.com/mr-sinister/94-7151)/.

27   Media Molecule is a British videogame developer based in Surrey. The studio's first game was the PlayStation 3 title *LittleBigPlanet*. *LittleBigPlanet*'s best selling point became its set of level-creation tools, and the ability to publish that content on the Internet. Media Molecule won the Studio of the Year award at the Spike Videogame Awards 2008. The game also won numerous game of the year awards leading to a 'Game Of The Year Edition' a year later. Their next project is *LittleBigPlanet2* (see http://en.wikipedia.org/wiki/Media_Molecule).

was purely parental pressure. Maybe I was just rebelling and doing the opposite of what they wanted, that might be one aspect of it. But I think also I just didn't get a lot out of it.

Choices and decisions made at school level came into play again at the level of higher education, where, in a straightforward sense, he positioned himself and made choices that were located within an established matrix of influences:

> **Kenneth**: It was around 2001/2002 that I'd been thinking about and looking at obvious applications such as post-production work, film work, TV and broadcasting. But that just seemed ... I think the world of films certainly was very attractive to me, but I was clever enough to know that I had little chance of getting to work on, you know, the kind of films that I enjoyed at the time that, actually, in the UK that kind of work is less prevalent. And, you know, starting that gig you've got to work in Soho on a less than minimum wage whilst living in London! And it just didn't look very attractive, whereas in the games industry you're actually a full-time employee and you've got this salary coming in every month. And I obviously really enjoy games as well. I knew that I wasn't particularly employable when I finished my undergraduate degree. I didn't have any experience of sound to picture, which, even though interactive audio doesn't work in exactly the same way as linear media, is still the bedrock where a lot of the theory and technique is based. And so that's why I did the Masters degree down in Bournemouth in Sound Design. I basically spent that year just learning about all that side of things, as well as investing most of my free time finding out as much as I could about interactive audio, the collaborative process of making games, researching the games industry itself to see where all the companies are around the UK, who was making what, and getting my finger on the pulse of the job market. And I was lucky enough to get a job with Sony's London game development studio pretty much straight out of that Masters degree. And that was a junior position, which essentially means you do lots of menial tasks ... I suppose it was an apprenticeship.

Kenneth's choices and his decision to pursue sound design, and acquire expertise and experience in designing innovative products within the collective enterprise of an organisation, demanded a certain disposition (habitus), entrepreneurial thinking[28] and a determined trajectory that together enabled his induction as an apprentice into the collaborative communities and competitive field of digital media. He soon learned how teams create a novel emergent product, how to be

---

[28] The essence of entrepreneurial thinking, according to Volkman et al. (2010) is, amongst other traits, hopeful thinking. It is action-oriented and team-oriented, and sees the potential feasibility of an opportunity. Christine Volkman, Kim Oliver Tokarski and Marc Grunhagan, *Entrepreneurship: Concepts for the Creation and Growth of New Ventures* (Berlin, 2010).

responsive to a changing environment, how group creativity works, and how to successfully tap into and contribute to team collaboration in a company, wherein teams rely on diverse skills and expertise throughout a project cycle.

Kenneth makes the point that, through the mechanisms of apprenticeship, he learned the attitudes and values of this young and emerging field. The complexity of collective creativities makes high demands:

> **Kenneth**: My job title is "audio designer". The reason I'm an "audio" designer is because I'm in charge of both sound and music. There are a lot of people in my industry that are called "sound designers", and they're primarily responsible for sound effects editing, dialogue editing and their implementation. But my remit, partly because I work in a small company, is that I'm in charge of all the audio; everything you might hear is my responsibility. So, my role is to make sure that the game sounds good and supports and enhances the player experience.

Environment is often cited as a component that is a very influential factor for successful innovation and its subsequent realisation and acceptance in the market. For Kenneth, meeting the needs and demands of consumers means creating new and innovative ways of using both 'sound' and 'music' to enhance the experience of video games.

Investing in breakthrough technology allows organisations to orient themselves to creating open, dialogical teams for anticipating/developing new musical responses and solutions from sound designers and composers. What Kenneth implies and acknowledges is the value-status or accrual of cultural capital from identified features, be they new renderings of musical combinations, remixed existing compositions, sampling and sequencing, or new forms that defy old compositional practices as licensed by the gaming field. We glimpse these various dimensions as Kenneth draws attention to the value of generative techniques in both video and audio, and highlights the key message of the recognition received from those in the field who reconfigure and innovate mappings between sound and vision:

> **Kenneth**: The games industry kind of cannibalises itself, and if one product is particularly successful then that can often set a benchmark … a benchmark which everyone else will either just emulate, or maybe try and improve on a little bit. So if that kind of benchmark product doesn't have anything particularly interesting going on with the audio, then it can be quite hard to actually persuade the powers that be to spend the time and resources required to develop new software to allow you to do things which will hopefully set the new or next benchmark that everyone else is going to aim for.

Importantly, the development of breakthrough techniques in the gaming field helps to constitute the field of power as a meaningful market in which it is worth investing one's energy. It is regarded as cultural capital: recognition of the legitimacy of a creative idea that turns into an innovative practice – in this case, user-generated creativity. It defines a world endowed with value and status for the product and its developers. Enhanced capacity for recognising potentially creative opportunities and the interactive co-operation of the different participants working in all areas of the enterprise culture is an active process, constituted by the logic of the field, and the unwritten rules of the game:

> **Kenneth**: Some of the work that I did on my last project, *LittleBigPlanet*, was a bit different. One of the main features of the game was that, although it was a traditional product in the sense that you buy it and you get to play the game, it also featured a built-in editor which allowed the people who'd bought the game to create their own games and then upload them for other people, who had the game, to play. And so that required that I think about how to empower the player to add sound and music to their own creations. Now, as a professional game developer, I spend all my time adding sound and music to the games that I'm working on … But one of the wider reasons user-generated content is attractive to the industry as a whole is that there is serious interest in having consumers that buy our product, holding on to that product. So, it's the concept of trying to turn the product into a service, and that's obviously partly to do with monetising the use of the product beyond the initial purchase … But with *LittleBigPlanet* user-generated content is the game's *raison d'être*.

For Kenneth, the creativities that occur in complex collaborative and organisational settings such as this are defined in terms of the values of the company he works for. Media Molecule, which is collective in character, proclaims as its *raison d'être* that its workers and customers adopt collaborative strategies to interact together as teams, performing a range of creative tasks. The sound and musical tasks are specifically rendered by Kenneth but, as the music is bound up in the broader interplay of the sound and music's social, technological and temporal dimensions, the product is developed and produced collaboratively in a world endowed with cultural capital, in which it is worth investing one's energy:

> **Kenneth**: The reason we're so small is partly because the kind of games we choose to make facilitate that. You know, we're not making a game which has absolutely massive amounts of content, which is where the resource drain is. If you can imagine creating lots of different art, animation and models, essentially creating a whole world from scratch, you need a lot of people to do that. What we do is create a fair amount of assets, set the bar, and then give the assets and creative tools to our community, and they build the games for themselves. So we don't have that massive content creation bottleneck.

Innovation can be characterised by features that add something new, with the degree of novelty being important either for the collective enterprise itself, in terms of technology development, or in terms of application-specific aspects of the product. Then, of course, there is the added value and high importance of 'customer-centric thinking'.[29] There is a complex dynamic going on here. The evolution of sound design is associated with how innovators engage people in the community, and attempt to influence them in order to build a prototype/model that will influence their actions. What Kenneth describes are the mind-sets and actions used to gain acceptance and feedback on the company's products from outside and inside the organisation. There is also a kind of positioning of the product that is enabled by gaining a profound understanding of customers' requirements and the technological possibilities of the product. The creative problem-solving skills required to address these challenges requires strategies for the incorporation of user ideas and responses, and ways of facilitating creativity and feeding back on the problem-solving process.

> **Kenneth**: The feedback comes in different ways. Feedback comes in the form of ideas, suggestions, restrictions they find themselves frustrated [with] because the game isn't doing one of the things they want it to do. There's a few ways that we read or gather this information. We get valuable feedback via e-mails and Internet forums. Sometimes when you read what someone's frustrated with, they've got their own idea about why they're frustrated. And if you follow that feedback directly you're not necessarily going [to] solve their problem, because the consumer isn't necessarily aware of what it is that's annoying them about the product. It's a lot more valuable to us to observe them using it.

Clearly, one important challenge of audio design is how users respond to different ideas associated with uncertainty and risk. Observations of how users in the target market respond to and engage with product innovations, such as new or significantly improved aspects of the game and its communicative sounds and music, may be done in many different ways:

> **Kenneth**: There are a couple of ways that we use observation to help us improve a game; the first way we use observation is by conducting focus-testing during actual development. If you just watch someone you can see where they get stuck or frustrated straight away. This is important because it's really easy when you're making a game to make assumptions about what people's perception or experience of playing the game is going to be – in reality you're too close to the project to really have that fresh insight. But if someone's just got the product in front of them, then you're watching them and you thought you were communicating an idea effectively. But, all of a sudden, you can see that it just doesn't work and that you need to improve an aspect of your product. That's quite powerful, just watching what they create, seeing how fun it is to play the game and where it falls down, and how you can perhaps make it better. And then the second way we use observation is to actually release a finished game, and

---

[29]   Ibid.

use the experience of seeing millions of people use it to learn from it, and apply this knowledge in updates or even future products.

Clearly, in the video games environment there are opportunities and risks in the application of specific technologies, which audio designers such as Kenneth cannot normally influence. The organisation interacts with the external environment, and there are any number of forces operating on the company: budgets, investors, market forces, competitors, customers, local and global economies and the important challenge of anticipating what will happen in the future.

When asked to reflect on the interplay between sonic and musical creativities, and what typically happens with the introduction of new technologies, particularly with the integration of customer views and technological aspirations, Kenneth describes a further aspect – collective creativity – where the members of the collective compete with one another, with each person's collective contributions inspiring the others to raise the bar and think of new ideas. The compositional practice appears to involve a highly participatory process.

> **Kenneth**: Well, there's a million and one ways to think about these things. I mean, for me, I don't view the audio as a separate part of the product, or of the project. Yet, I think audio is often viewed that way. I think as a specialist it's really easy to subcategorise all the stuff that you're doing, and think of it separate to everything else. But I think the key to it being successful is making sure that you've got a really clear idea of what it is you're trying to do. Not in terms of the audio, but in terms of what is the overall work you're creating or contributing towards. And so, for me, I take a lot of inspiration from the art direction.

Clearly, the organisation Kenneth works for is a collective enterprise, and as players in the company acquire more capital, so they become more valued. However, capital also exists in ever-changing configurations in relation to the field that generates it, and the values of the gaming industry are constantly being renegotiated in implicit and explicit ways. In fact, consumers also know that collaborators participate in the process and practice of legitimising a product, particularly in the ways that audio interactivity works, blending innovation in design and execution throughout the project's life cycle:

> **Kenneth**: The issue of who is responsible for defining how music is used in our work is important. Music is something which many people are really passionate about, even if they don't actually have much knowledge of it other than as a consumer. And I think that's where a lot of uses of music show themselves to be a bit weak. You quite often have someone who's quite senior on a project who's really into consuming music, and, precisely because they're in a senior position, they're able to dictate how music should and could be used in the project they're

working on. And that can be awkward for the audio personnel, who you would hope would have more of an idea of how to use music.

And so, for me, when I say I take my direction for the music from the art direction, I think that's a sensible way to do it, and ensures that rather than fighting against what you're perceiving when you're playing the game, that the music is actually a part of the experience, it enhances it. I don't think that's necessarily the way everyone does it, because the use of music in games is often quite naïve. We talk about wall-to-wall use of music, or wallpaper music. Unlike in a film where the music would be scoring the emotions in the scene or trying to heighten the drama in some way, for the most part during the "gameplay" (where you're controlling a character or doing something), there's not generally any story involved there irrespective of whether it's a narrative game, so you don't have the same emotions that you would have in a film. You know, you're not dealing with sadness, you're maybe dealing with frustration, or you're dealing with the joy that someone gets out of completing a task … In a film the creator dictates the experience and says "this is how it is and you can take it or leave it. You can enjoy it or you can leave the cinema". But in a game, because the audience is a part of the experience, because they are participating in it, they're controlling a character, or they are moving something about on screen. It's a lot harder to know what they are feeling, because their experience is less dictated, it's dictated in part by the players themselves.

The limitations and successes of game sound and music can be identified by means of road testing. Such games appear to be characterised by degrees of artistic freedom and commercial constraints that may or may not balance out, given that to produce a cultural artefact for the market requires intervention, guidance, collaboration and consumer feedback. There is a reliance on the institutional networks that have been set in place, along with a need to accumulate capital acquired through being in a central position in the field in which creativities are realised. All of this relates to how the company positions itself within the field.

Kenneth: It is collaborative, I can't just dictate what the music is going to do without listening to anyone else's input, that would just cause frustration and make everyone unhappy. So I've developed processes which I think give me what I want and what I think is best for the project, whilst also giving the team the ability to have some input into the decisions that I'm making … The process I've developed is that if anyone's got suggestions for a piece of music, I will always take that and consider whether it's suitable for the project or not. The way I like to think of individual pieces or sections of music is in terms of their role within the project – where is it used, how is it used, what are its requirements. Once I've identified this, I call it a "slot" – this is also an important part of the budgeting and scheduling process. And so I will come up with two or three choices for that particular slot – what I've done is selected three bits of music which I think will work and, although I've got my favourite, I know that if the team picks my plan B or plan C, it's still going to work. So, I can hand that choice over to the team and say "Okay, guys, which of these do people generally like the best, and more importantly why?" I'm not particularly interested in people saying "I like that piece of music". I'm a lot more interested in people saying "I like this piece of music and I think it works because blah, blah, blah", because that lets me know if the music is working in the game rather than if they simply like the music in and of itself.

It is worth emphasising at this point that, in reference to the issue of selecting licensed music, there are indeed royalty-free soundtracks and entertainment-industry-driven software that allow the building of musical arrangements and make use of pre-recorded audio files called 'loops' and 'one-shots'. Loops contain rhythmic patterns that sound designers can extend to fill any amount of time, while one-shots contain sound effects and other non-repeating sounds. Combining and arranging sound effects and other non-repeating audio, when creatively re-using the music of the past and sound sources of the present, is part of standard digital music tools and applications such as Pro Tools, Logic and Ableton.

The interplay of capital, new digital technologies and the voracious market for new games is vital to the collective enterprise. The social value and status assigned to these capital-bearing products of entertainment and art are grounded in the use and re-use of existing materials and this goes hand-in-hand with the construction of specific principles of perception and appreciation of the social world (with assets in the educational market). All of this represents a highly significant shift in how gaming is evolving and targeting its players with new music and methods of musical interactivity.

Concluding Thoughts

The narrative analysis of the composers' interviews reveals a fusion or interaction between developing inwardly directed practices, which constitute the 'self' within a compositional act. This is defined by intention, self-expression, individuality and outwardly directed social practices such as those particular dispositions and attitudes that relate to social modes of perception, thinking and ways of composing.

However, in exploring the range of ways in which the sociality of their own creativity is constructed through these narratives, it is important to revisit each composer separately and view how their multi-layered personas are both enabled and understood in terms of the self and the social realms that foster their creativity, as shown in Figure 5.1.

These composers' accounts of their compositional creativity provide evidence of a multiplicity of issues and values. The nature of the activity is characterised by the complementarity and interplay of multiple types of creativity (individual

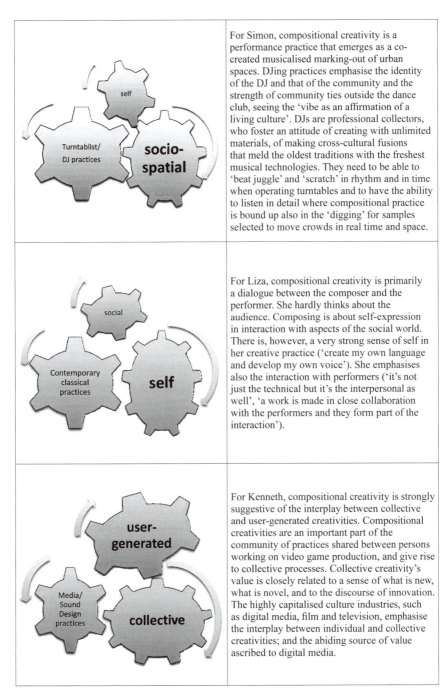

For Simon, compositional creativity is a performance practice that emerges as a co-created musicalised marking-out of urban spaces. DJing practices emphasise the identity of the DJ and that of the community and the strength of community ties outside the dance club, seeing the 'vibe as an affirmation of a living culture'. DJs are professional collectors, who foster an attitude of creating with unlimited materials, of making cross-cultural fusions that meld the oldest traditions with the freshest musical technologies. They need to be able to 'beat juggle' and 'scratch' in rhythm and in time when operating turntables and to have the ability to listen in detail where compositional practice is bound up also in the 'digging' for samples selected to move crowds in real time and space.

For Liza, compositional creativity is primarily a dialogue between the composer and the performer. She hardly thinks about the audience. Composing is about self-expression in interaction with aspects of the social world. There is, however, a very strong sense of self in her creative practice ('create my own language and develop my own voice'). She emphasises also the interaction with performers ('it's not just the technical but it's the interpersonal as well', 'a work is made in close collaboration with the performers and they form part of the interaction').

For Kenneth, compositional creativity is strongly suggestive of the interplay between collective and user-generated creativities. Compositional creativities are an important part of the community of practices shared between persons working on video game production, and give rise to collective processes. Collective creativity's value is closely related to a sense of what is new, what is novel, and to the discourse of innovation. The highly capitalised culture industries, such as digital media, film and television, emphasise the interplay between individual and collective creativities; and the abiding source of value ascribed to digital media.

Figure 5.1   The self and the social realms that foster each composer's creativity

and social, collaborative and collective). Composers also use technology as a mediating tool for rethinking compositional practices.

We see individual (or self) and social (collective and audience-generated) creativities favour close relationships between musicians and instruments, composers and scores, artists and audiences in ways that embody myriad compositional creativities. The capacity of musicians to coordinate and sustain their diverse creative activities, whether self- or corporately employed, or affiliated with universities or other organisations, depends on their ability to achieve a sustainable compositional practice. The reality of musicians' practices is related to their potential roles within and outside of the cultural or creative industries. It is related to the musical networks in which they move, their awareness as cultural entrepreneurs of the need to continually review and develop their career goals and skills, and their alliances with particular fields of musical production (for example, the classical, folk, jazz, popular music, digital media or games industries).

New industries overlap the music industry. The effect of this is to change how artists and audiences, DJs and crowds, audio designers and consumers think about musical creativities, and how they cultivate distinguishing features based on 'in group' identification and interaction. Think, for example, of the DJ – producer and remixer, re-user, decomposer, sound organiser, 'scratcher' and sharer of music in digital formats – and consider the many ways in which existing music is recycled, remixed and repackaged. Here, in the midst of existing hierarchical social relations, the DJ imports ready-made material as a common and well-established practice.

Different techniques of compositional creativity involve unwritten rules of the game, but generate practices and attribute meanings in accordance with the values of the field. Developing new understandings, new practices, new pedagogies and new access to purposeful activity inspired by contemporary fields of music requires a shift from past curricula focused on the narrowly specialised 'subject' of music, to an orientation that champions contemporary practice. This will have a profound effect on our students as well as teachers, and will cause the nature of compositional creativities themselves to move into the spotlight and become subject to change. The challenge and goal for all music educators is to make compositional activities more relevant, in ways that give students faith in their own means of expression and the ability to distinguish between different kinds of music creativities that have the potential to be recognised and valued as real-world practice.

References

Amabile, Teresa M., *Creativity in Context: Update to the Social Psychology of Creativity* (New York: Springer, 1996).
Becker, Howard, *Art Worlds* (Berkeley, CA: University of California Press, 1984).

Berleant, Arnold, 'Musical de-composition'. In: P. Alperson (ed.), *What is Music: An Introduction to the Philosophy of Music* (Pennsylvania, PA: The Pennsylvania State University Press, 1987).

Bourdieu, Pierre, *Outline of a Theory of Practice* (Cambridge, Cambridge University Press, 1977).

Bourdieu, Pierre, *The Logic of Practice*, trans. R. Nice (Oxford: Polity Press, 1990 [1980]).

Bourdieu, Pierre, *The Field of Cultural Production: Essays on Art and Literature* (Oxford: Polity Press, 1993).

Burnard, Pamela, *Musical Creativities in Practice* (Oxford: Oxford University Press, 2012).

Collins, Nick and Julio d'Escrivan (eds), *The Cambridge Companion to Electronic Music* (Cambridge: Cambridge University Press, 2007), 38–54.

Cook, Nicholas, *Music: A Very Short Introduction* (Oxford: Oxford University Press, 1998).

Cox, Christoph and Daniel Warner (eds) *Audio Culture: Readings in Modern Music* (London: Continuum, 2009).

De Nora, Tia, *Beethoven and the Construction of Genius* (Berkeley, CA: University of California Press, 1995).

De Nora, Tia, *Music in Everyday Life* (Cambridge : Cambridge University Press, 2000).

Emmerson, Simon, 'Composing strategies and pedagogy', *Contemporary Music Review*, 3 (1989), 133–44.

Ghiselin, Brewster, *The Creative Process: A Symposium* (Berkeley, CA: University of California Press, 1952).

Goehr, Lydia, *The Imaginary Museum of Musical Worlds: An Essay in the Philosophy of Music* (Oxford: Clarendon Press, 1992).

Green, Lucy, *How Popular Musicians Learn: A Way Ahead for Music Education* (Aldershot: Ashgate, 2001).

Jones, Carys Wyn, *The Rock Canon: Canonical Values in the Reception of Rock Albums* (Aldershot: Ashgate, 2008).

Langer, Susanne K., *Feeling and Form: A Theory of Art Developed from Philosophy in a New Key* (London: Macmillan, 1953).

McCutchan, Ann, *The Music That Sings: Composers Speak about the Creative Process* (Oxford: Oxford University Press, 1999).

Pasler, Jann, *Writing Through Music: Essays on Music, Culture and Politics* (Oxford: Oxford University Press, 2008).

Small, Christopher, *Musicking: The Meanings of Performing and Listening* (Hanover, NH: Wesleyan University Press, 1998), 89.

Toop, David, 'Uptown throwdown'. In: M. Forman and M. Neil (eds), *That's the Joint! The Hip-Hop Studies Reader* (London: Routledge, 2004).

Volkman, Christine, Kim Oliver Tokarski and Marc Grunhagan, *Entrepreneurship: Concepts for the Creation and Growth of New Ventures* (Berlin: Gabler Verlag, 2010).

Weisberg, Robert W., *Creativity: Genius and Other Myths* (Oxford: Freeman, 1993).

Wolff, Janet, *The Social Production of Art*, 2nd edn (London: Macmillan Press, 1993).

Chapter 6

Constraint, Collaboration and Creativity in Popular Songwriting Teams

Joe Bennett

Popular music has at its economic, musical and cultural centre a single item of intellectual property – the pop song. Over many decades of consumption, popular song has established a set of musical and literary constraints within which creativity operates. These constraints are arrived at by economic and democratic means, being rooted in the quasi-evolutionary process of natural selection engendered by commercial markets, most easily demonstrable through 'the charts'. In popular music, as in any art form, new artists can and do challenge established creative constraints, but what is perhaps remarkable about western popular song is how little the core structural characteristics of mainstream songs have deviated from some of the norms established in the early to mid twentieth century, despite the rapid technological, cultural and social change that drives the popular music industry.

The process of creating popular song differs significantly from that for the majority of instrumental art music in two important respects: firstly, it is a partly literary act, songs having lyrics; secondly, it is extremely common for the composition to be co-written. Historically, around half of US and UK 'hits' are written by collaborative teams, most commonly comprising two individuals.[1] At the time of writing (late 2010), current industry practice in the UK is for the majority of pop singles to be written collaboratively, with very few contemporaneous top 10 hits being written by individuals.[2] This chapter focuses on the collaborative processes used by songwriting teams within the constraints of song form, and particularly on the 'negotiated creativity' that is, I contend, a prerequisite for the successful function of most songwriting teams.

Before we address the central question of *how* songs are written collaboratively, we must identify the nature of the created object itself, and ask at a musically specific level 'what is a song?' Defining the term appears simple enough: Chambers[3] defines 'song' as 'a set of words, short poem, etc to

---

[1] Terry F. Pettijohn II and Shujaat F. Ahmed, 'Songwriting; loafing or creative collaboration?: A comparison of individual and team written billboard hits in the USA', *Journal of Articles in Support of the Null Hypothesis*, 7/1 (2010), 2.

[2] PRS for Music, Database search results, http://www.prsformusic.co.uk (2010).

[3] Chambers, *Chambers 21st Century Dictionary* (London, 1996), http://www.chambersharrap.co.uk/chambers/features/chref/chref.py/main?query=song&title=21st.

be sung, usually with accompanying music'. However, even if we accept the broad classification that the word means simply 'that which is sung' (excluding the small but significant number of instrumental hits that Anglo-American popular music has produced since the 1950s), we need to locate the studied object among many sub-genres, including hymn, lieder, opera, pop song, folk song and children's songs.

This chapter focuses on the Anglo-American commercial mainstream popular song since the 1950s, and more specifically on the 'single', that is, a musical/ literary work intended to be appreciated[4] in isolation, not as part of a long-duration listener experience such as a musical theatre show, opera or concept album. There are several reasons for this choice. Firstly, selecting songs intended for commercial consumption increases the likelihood that the composer/s will be trying actively to engage the listener, so creative decisions will share this common incentive.[5] This contrasts with more 'pure' artistic self-expression in (typically amateur) songwriting, where creative goals may be conflicting, highly personal or nebulous. Secondly, commercial popular song, despite its cultural ubiquity, has had little study applied to the process of its creation. Previous research studies[6] have focused on instrumental composition rather than exclusively on songwriting, often in an educational setting, where participants are, by definition, amateur composers. These individuals may therefore have a different set of creative imperatives and constraints from songwriters who are incentivised to create a 'hit', or at least a song that will appeal to a significant numbers of listeners. Thirdly, commercial popular song has an attendant measure of its effectiveness in the form of popular music charts. Originally these were calculated through sales of sheet music, then subsequently by physical sales of singles, and now by downloads or online streams; the music 'chart' is a powerful metric when defining trends in song, covering as it does some 80 or more years of Anglo-American hits. Apart from (helpfully) ranking the most successful songs in order of listener popularity, the practice of using charts as a metric for what constitutes song norms may mediate some of the inevitable subjectivity of musical taste among individuals regarding what makes a 'good song'. Fourthly, songwriters by definition need to write lyrics; in copyright terms, a lyric is usually considered to be a literary work representing 50 per cent of the song. On a pragmatic level, studying the process of collaborative lyric-writing provides text-

---

    [4]   Given that singles are usually intended for purchase, perhaps 'consumed' would be a better word.

    [5]   Greg Clydesdale, 'Creativity and competition: The Beatles', *Creativity Research Journal*, 18/2 (April 2006), 129.

    [6]   John Kratus, 'A time analysis of the compositional processes used by children ages 7 to 11', *Journal of Research in Music Education*, 37/1 (1989), 5. Pamela Burnard and Betty Anne Younker, 'Mapping pathways: Fostering creativity in composition', *Music Education Research*, 4/2 (2002), 245–61. Jeanne Bamberger, 'The development of intuitive musical understanding: A natural experiment', *Psychology of Music*, 31/1 (January 2003), 7–36.

based observational data that are considerably easier to track than the complex music-only decision-making pathways identified by Burnard and Younker.[7]

I contend that the popular song is defined – artistically and musically – by the market forces that perpetuate its survival. This is not commercial cynicism, but rather an extension of the Darwinian model applied by Csikszentmihalyi[8] to all forms of creativity. In Csikszentmihalyi's 'systems model', a creator creates new work that is validated by a 'field' of experts. If validated, it goes on to join the 'domain' of prior works, which in turn will influence existing and future creators. This definition of creativity (that a work must not only be original but also must be an influence on other creators) has rather a high threshold, much higher perhaps than the simple musical/literary uniqueness required to define a popular song as 'original' in copyright terms. Boden distinguishes between creativity that is original to its creator and creativity that is globally original:

> [We should] make a distinction between "psychological" creativity and "historical" creativity (P-creativity and H-creativity, for short). P-creativity involves coming up with a surprising, valuable idea that's new to the person who comes up with it. It doesn't matter how many people have had that idea before. But if a new idea is H-creative, that means that (so far as we know) no one else has had it before: it has arisen for the first time in human history. Clearly, H-creativity is a special case of P-creativity. [...] But for someone who is trying to understand the *psychology* of creativity, it's P-creativity that's crucial. Never mind who thought of the idea first: how did *that* person manage to come up with it, given that *they* had never thought of it before?[9]

If we apply Csikszentmihalyi's definition more loosely, and allow for the 'domain' of work to include all popular music that is released,[10] then all original songs are creative (and in Boden's terms, arguably always H-creative). Thus, case studies do not necessarily need to beget hits in order to provide useful information about

---

[7]   Considering that several of Burnard and Younker's observational subjects were songwriters, it is notable that their research does not substantially address lyric creation. This may be due to the authors' stated intent to study 'composers', but it does perhaps demonstrate that lyric writing is considered by some to be an insignificant part of the songwriter's creative process, despite its apparent equal value to the composition (at least in copyright terms).

[8]   Mihalyi Csikszentmihalyi, 'Society, culture, and person: A systems view of creativity'. In: *The Nature of Creativity: Contemporary Psychological Perspectives* (Cambridge, 1988), 325–39.

[9]   Margaret Boden, *The Creative Mind: Myths and Mechanisms*, 2nd edn (Abingdon Routledge, 2004), 2.

[10]   By 'released' I mean that someone has spent time and money on preparing the song for consumption, typically through recording and distributing it, implicitly on the basis of a (usually economic) return. This usefully filters out beginner songwriters who may not have achieved sufficient skills or experience to provide helpful interview or study subjects.

collaborative songwriting as long as any work/process being studied is undertaken by experienced songwriters who understand 'song craft'.

To illustrate the evolution of creative constraints (within which both H- and P-creativity can exist), let us analyse the time-duration of hit single recordings, and compare track length over several decades, using the top 10 best-selling singles in the UK from the five decades from 1960 to 2000.[11] The longest duration of these is Bryan Adams's *Everything I Do (I Do For You)*, at 6 minutes and 33 seconds (6:33); the shortest is The Beatles' *Can't Buy Me Love* at 2:13. The mean average track length per decade varies from 2:43 (1960s) to 4:07 (1990s). Interestingly, after the 1960s the figures for track length show insignificant variation over many years. The mean average track lengths per decade are 2:43 (1960s), 4:03 (1970s), 4:04 (1980s), 4:07 (1990s) and 3:49 (2000s) – with a standard deviation of only 0:51 for the whole sample set over 50 years. Given the large amount of popular music that is produced, the large number of consumers and the market forces at play, we can infer that song duration is a market-defined norm, and that substantially longer or shorter songs did not 'survive' in their environment – that is, the centre of the commercial mainstream. The requisite economy of communication thus becomes part of the songwriter's skillset: 'we must accomplish our aims and tell our entire story *in a time frame of about three minutes* (plus or minus). Every word, every note must count'.[12]

Duration is just one example of a constraint, and I choose it for illustration because, being low-bandwidth numeric data, it is a simple parameter to measure. To take lyric themes as another example, 80 per cent of the hits cited above deal with lyrics related to romantic love – this is something of a truism in popular music and a statistic that does not vary significantly by decade if other similar metrics are used (for example, the Billboard hot 100 chart). Listed below are typical constraints relating to form, key, literary elements, tempo, time signature and melodic pitch range,[13] most of which show very little overall variation in their prevalence in UK/US chart hits of the last 50 years.[14]

- first-person sympathetic protagonist/s, portrayed implicitly by the singer;
- repeating titular choruses (where the song is in chorus form), usually containing the melodic pitch peak of the song, summarizing the overall meaning of the lyric;

[11]   Joe Bennett, 'How long, how long must we sing this song?', *Joe Bennett music blog*, 2011, http://joebennett.net/2011/05/03/how-long-how-long-must-we-sing-this-song/.

[12]   Jimmy Webb, *Tunesmith: Inside the Art of Songwriting* (London, 1999), 37.

[13]   Joe Bennett, 'Collaborative songwriting – the ontology of negotiated creativity in popular music studio practice', *Journal of the Art of Record Production 2010*, 5 (July 2011), http://tinyurl.com/jarp-bennett-2011.

[14]   Shaun Ellis and Tom Engelhardt, 'Visualizing a hit – InfoVis final project', *Can Visualizing 50 Years' Worth of Hit U.S. Pop Song Characteristics Help us Discover Trends Worthy of Further Investigation?* 2010, http://sites.google.com/site/visualizingahit/home.

- rhyme – usually at the end of lyric phrases;
- one, two or three human characters (or a collective 'we');
- an instrumental introduction of less than 20 seconds;
- inclusion of the title in the lyric;
- sung between a two-octave range from bottom C to top C (C2–C4), focusing heavily on the single octave A2–A3;
- thematic lyric content relating to (usually romantic) human relationships;
- use of underlying 4-, 8- and 16-bar phrases, with occasional additions or subtractions;
- based on verse/chorus form or AABA form;
- 4/4 time;
- one diatonic or modal key;
- between two and four minutes in length.

Over decades, many songs will have been written that fall outside these norms, for example, longer than five minutes, or dealing with non-romantic subject matter, but these songs are statistically less likely to be mainstream hits. It therefore follows that experienced songwriters will be familiar with these constraints even if they choose occasionally to break some of them according to artistic impulse. Returning briefly to our simple example of track duration, we can infer that songwriters, at least those hoping for a mainstream hit, can reasonably be expected to work within the creative constraint that song recordings should be longer than two minutes and shorter than five. Even specialist/niche genres of popular music (club/dance music, folk-pop, metal, hip-hop) show a general statistical tendency to adhere to the majority of the norms listed above, with genre-defined deviations from mainstream characteristics. For example, metal is less likely than mainstream pop to deal with themes of romantic love; hip-hop is likely to use simpler chord progressions than metal; folk-pop is likely to contain more heavily developed lyrics than club/dance music; prog-rock is more likely to challenge mainstream norms of tempi or time signature than pop.

To frame this in evolutionary terms, popular song is in a constant state of mutation, with songs representing unique individuals who are 'born' with identifiable genetic characteristics (for example, form, tempo, lyric theme, harmonic rhythm, bar count, duration, melody) 'inherited' from the domain of existing successful/influential songs. Genres could be identified as 'species', which have evolved to suit their fan-base 'environment'. Characteristics of individual songs will vary, and are required to do so to avoid accusations of plagiarism, but they do not deviate so substantially that individuals cannot survive in their environment (or rather, if they do this, they 'die' in commercial terms). So, again using track duration as our illustrative example, a popular song lasting for 30 seconds, or even 30 minutes, would be very unlikely to be purchased by the public in large enough quantities to survive and therefore 'reproduce' by affecting the domain of existing work.

However, it is also reasonable to assume that songwriting is experiencing constant experimentation, and we can easily locate successful examples of occasional challenges to one or more norms. I use song duration as an example of a constraint with occasional deviations; Webb[15] applies similar logic to song form:

> If you can't say what you need or want to say with a verse/chorus/verse/bridge and *another* chorus, perhaps you should admit to yourself that you are working on an *experimental* song. [This] is a song wherein a writer has deliberately set out to "break the form".

Acknowledging that such songs are the exception rather than the rule, Webb concludes that (as he argues, 'evolved') conservatism is inherent in song form, at least for the moment:

> The traditional boundaries of the American song create a kind of benign tyranny […]. Perhaps [someone someday will] set popular songs free from what remains of formal restraint. There is no sign of such an annihilator on the horizon.

It appears, then, that only a small number of song innovations are strong enough to enter, and fewer still to dominate, the domain. Thus, market forces in the form of massed listener preferences over 'generations' of purchasing/chart/airplay cycles will 'naturally select' the characteristics that are most likely to ensure survival. Csikszentmihalyi's Individual-Field-Domain paradigm describes a constant cycle of creation, selection and, implicitly, rejection.

As the generations pass, some of the mutations in individual songs can self-propagate; examples include tempo variation (early 1990s dance music is generally faster than mid 1970s disco) and the increased use of 'four-chord loops' in the song accompaniment (measurably more common in top 10 hits in the 2000s than in any previous decade).[16] Sometimes an environmental change combined with a particularly successful mutation begets a dramatic shift in the dominant species; the most obvious example in popular song's evolution is the relatively sudden shift from AABA or 32-bar form (the form itself famously derided by Adorno)[17] in the early part of the twentieth century to chorus-form songs being dominant from the late 1950s onwards. Adorno's excoriating critique of popular music made the error of analysing one form (popular song) based on the analytical criteria of another (instrumental western art music), thus equating the simplicity of the former (in harmonic and structural terms) with banality. Not all critical writers have made the same mistake; William Mann's equally intellectualised

---

[15]   Webb, *Tunesmith*, 122–3.

[16]   Bennett, 'Collaborative songwriting'.

[17]   Theodore W. Adorno, 'On popular music', *Studies in Philosophy and Social Science*, IX (1941), 17–48, http://www.icce.rug.nl/~soundscapes/DATABASES/SWA/On _popular_music_1.shtml.

analysis of the early work of The Beatles[18] is cheerfully flattering as it analyses the harmonic and timbral aspects of the songs by judging them by the criteria of other popular music of the era.

Popular music being a market-driven art form, arguably existing within a complex and evolving 'youth culture', it may be impossible to identify accurately the manifold external environmental changes that may cause these changes in song form, but the changes themselves are easily statistically observable over time if a relatively robust metric is used. In searching for such drivers of change, we could speculate that the move toward chorus-based songs (from AABA form) is a result of a more assertive self-defining youth culture demanding greater musical immediacy (socio-cultural), or a result of consumer empowerment of a new postwar generation (socio-economic), or even as the result of the increased availability of legal and illegal stimulants such as amphetamine and caffeine (pharmacological). The approach taken here is to avoid such speculation and observe only the measurable musicological characteristics – and to identify these as creative constraints upon the songwriting team.

I reiterate here that this chapter focuses unashamedly on songs, and song characteristics, that have been defined by the popular mainstream. This is only one environment of many in popular music, and our mainstream has many tributaries. If market forces, in the form of single or download purchases, are a significant driver of song form evolution in chart hits, different factors may cause changes in other forms of popular music. For example, Noys[19] takes the aforementioned pharmacological approach, suggesting that particular recreational drugs drove tempo changes in dance music during the early 1990s:

> As [techno] arrived in Britain (1987–88) it began to be speeded up by those working in this idiom from around 120 BPM to around 150 BPM.[20] In fact at the time there were references to "speed house", describing the use of the drug meta-amphetamine to enjoy this music. Therefore, Hardcore Dance originated in a matrix which was not purely to do with the widespread availability of Ecstasy or "E" (an hallucinogenic known medically as MDMA) but also speed (the drug) and the desire for speed.[21]

Although Noys's implication (that drug choice affected tempo in an evolving new sub-form) is inevitably more speculative than mine, it is also difficult to

---

[18] William Mann, '*The Times*: What songs The Beatles sang by William Mann', *The Times*, 27 December 1963, http://www.beatlesbible.com/1963/12/27/the-times-what-songs-the-beatles-sang-by-william-mann/.

[19] Benjamin Noys, 'Into the "jungle"', *Popular Music*, 14/3 (1995), 322.

[20] BPM = beats per minute. In classical terms the (usually) crotchet pulse of the music's tempo. The term BPM is the preferred language in popular music composition and production circles.

[21] Here, Noys uses the term 'matrix' in the same way that I use the term 'environment'.

refute. Certainly it is measurably true that house music of the late 1980s had a higher average tempo than mainstream pop of the same era, and that many of the consumers of the music were drug users.

Even if one accepts the contention that song form is defined by constraint, constraints themselves are not necessarily a restriction on creativity, as Amabile[22] acknowledges; 'People will be more creative if you give them freedom to decide how to climb a particular mountain. You needn't let them choose which mountain to climb. In fact, clearly specified goals often enhance people's creativity'. To quote one professional songwriter I interviewed, his creativity operates clearly within the constraints of song form, rather than necessarily challenging the form itself:

> [as a songwriter] you're like a monkey in a zoo that's never known anything else – you just accept your territory. The box is kind of a given really: it's what you do in the box that is exciting.[23]

The need to create unique song ideas within the constraints of popular song 'norms' is an ever-present creative challenge for any songwriter. Deviate too far from the norms and the risk of the song 'failing' rises; stay too closely within them and the song may exhibit cliché – or even plagiarism – and fail anyway.[24] The popular music listener demands a limited bandwidth of novelty.

Why Collaboration?

Perhaps surprisingly, given the cultural significance ascribed to *individual* songwriters in the media, songwriting *teams* are responsible for an approximately equally large number of (number 1) hits in the UK/US charts of the last 50 years or so. Pettijohn and Ahmed ask – but perhaps fail to answer – the following questions in their statistical study of chart hits 1955–2009:

> Do groups, with their shared areas of expertise, create better songs than individuals working alone? Do songwriting individuals have to compromise their visions when working in groups, thereby producing a lower quality song?[25]

Pettijohn and Ahmed's statistical findings show that songwriting teams were responsible for approximately as many number one Billboard chart hits as

---

[22] Teresa M. Amabile, 'How to kill creativity', *Harvard Business Review*, 76/5 (1998), 81.

[23] Jez Ashurst, 'On collaborative songwriting', interview by Joe Bennett, audio, 2010.

[24] Marade et al. define this as 'risk'; Angelo A. Marade, Jeffrey A. Gibbons and Thomas M. Brinthaupt, 'The role of risk-taking in songwriting success', *The Journal of Creative Behavior*, 41/2 (2007), 125–49.

[25] Pettijohn and Ahmed, 'Songwriting; loafing or creative collaboration?'

individual songwriters, and that a two-person songwriting team is the most common group size. Beyond this, their inferences are speculative and perhaps a little specious, in that the research does not acknowledge the unknowable number of *unsuccessful* songs that contribute to the successful – and therefore measurable – division of number ones between collaborators and individuals.[26]

Thus, their conclusions regarding 'social loafing' (described as 'the likelihood of individuals contributing less when working on a task as part of a group than when working on a task alone')[27] are to be treated with caution: songs that are anything less than market-ready are unlikely to be successful anyway, and given the highly competitive nature of songwriting and the number of songs competing for dominance, any hypothetical loafer may not be part of a hit-creating team in the first place owing to the prior intervention of music industry 'gatekeepers' such as record labels and publishers. In the words of one songwriter:

> [as a professional] everyone you write with is talented. It goes without saying. I've never been in a room with a collaborator who's been signed [by a publishing company or record label] and thought "Hold on – how the hell did you get where you are?" They've all got something to bring to the table.[28]

If we compare Pettijohn and Ahmed's findings with quantitative evidence of publication, it appears that discussion of the songwriting act, arguably under-developed though it is in academe and in the media, disproportionately favours interest in individual songwriters rather than teams. Zollo[29] provides the largest single collection of interviews with world-famous songwriters, undertaken over more than 10 years. Of the 62 interviews in the collection, only two are with collaborative teams, and a further eight are with individuals who are known or partly known for collaboration. However, my main reason for undertaking research into collaborative songwriting as opposed to individual songwriting is a pragmatic one of observational methodology – it is easier to observe collaborative teams at work because the requisite need to communicate and negotiate creative ideas makes them manifest and more overtly observable. We cannot know the internal workings of an individual songwriter's mind (or that of any composer) without intervening, almost certainly destructively, in their working methods. Sloboda[30]

---

[26]   This unknown and forever lost 'cutting room floor' material is essential to the operation of Csikszentmihalyi's Systems Model and to the evolutionary process it implies, but it is in the nature of evolution that it only preserves examples of *successful* reproduction – unsuccessful individuals are lost to history. As the British author Douglas Adams once famously summarised the evolutionary process – 'that which survives, survives'.

[27]   Pettijohn and Ahmed, 'Songwriting loafing or creative collaboration?', 2.

[28]   Ashurst, 'On collaborative songwriting'.

[29]   Paul Zollo, *Songwriters on Songwriting* (Boston, MA, 1997).

[30]   John Sloboda, *The Musical Mind: The Cognitive Psychology of Music* (Oxford: Clarendon Press, 1985), 102–3.

identifies four possible methods by which we may understand the psychology of solo composition: examination of historical repertoire; interview with the composer; real-time observation; and analysis of improvisation. He discounts the first two categories as being too distant from the compositional act and subject to distortion; the fourth is a particular subset of performance that does not directly relate to a less instantaneous musical activity such as songwriting and is arguably not 'composition' in its truest sense. So we are left, in Sloboda's view, with real-time observation as the only way of studying the act of composition, by solo composers, at least:

> The only thing which [sic] gives a chance of working is to have a living composer speaking all his or her thoughts out loud to an observer or a tape-recorder while engaged in composition.[31]

Collins[32] takes this approach using verbal protocol methodologies, triangulating real-time reporting from the composer with computer 'save as' files and interview-based verification sessions. The results provide what he describes modestly as 'moments of insight [into] aspects of creative problem-solving'. Collins acknowledges the limitations of this method but attempts to circumvent some of them with the data-driven approach of using iterative 'save as' files from computer sequencer software. This does provide a usefully different evidence base for triangulation purposes, but may generate its own attendant problem of encouraging the researcher to focus on arguably non-compositional processes. Many of the comments made by Collins's subject (and the data generated by the MIDI files) suggest that the methodology has shifted the focus of study onto *arrangement* rather than *composition*. The dividing line between these two practices in instrumental art-music is far from clear, of course, particularly when composing for a large ensemble such as an orchestra.[33] Happily, for songwriters, the song and the arrangement/recording (or at least the final manifestation of it) are often isolated from each other; this is helped in part by the legalities and economics of music publishing, in which the song and its recording are separate copyrights in most western countries. That said, the phenomenon of the performance being easier to observe and analyse than the song is not unknown to songwriters, or to teachers of songwriting such as myself.[34]

---

[31]   John Sloboda, 'Do psychologists have anything useful to say about composition?' In: *Third European Conference of Music Analysis*, Montpellier, 1995, 6.

[32]   David Collins, 'Real-time tracking of the creative music composition process', *Digital Creativity*, 18/4 (December 2007), 239–56.

[33]   Or, in the case of Collins's observed composer, a software-based virtual orchestra on a computer workstation.

[34]   Joe Bennett, 'Performance and songwriting: The picture and the frame', UK Songwriting Festival website, 2009, http://www.uksongwritingfestival.com/2009/01/22/performance-and-songwriting-the-picture-and-the-frame/.

Observing Collaboration

So, having identified the nature of the object to be studied (song as opposed to recording), the musical genre in question (commercial mainstream popular song) and the type of compositional practice to be observed (collaborative songwriting), then the final remaining question is one of methodology. What approaches can provide the most meaningful and authentic evidence of the compositional processes used by collaborating songwriters?

Related to Sloboda's dismissal of three of his four possible approaches to understanding composition, I have identified elsewhere the difficulties of using interviews with songwriter-artists as the exclusive evidence base for studies of their creative process:

> mysteriousness [...] is a cultural asset i.e. it is desirable for some songwriters, particularly singer-songwriters, to shroud their craft in romance and mystery. The majority of interviews with songwriters obviously feature those who are also artists, who will have an artistic persona to sell, and therefore a motive for concealing more mundane, contrived or even random aspects of the composition process that may be perceived by fans as unromantic. Many contemporary artists, even (current UK) singer-songwriters like Katie Melua, James Morrison, Lily Allen, James Blunt and Newton Faulkner, actually use backroom co-writers, but are incentivised to obfuscate their collaborative processes because of the need to sell the authenticity of the song – and therefore their own credibility as "songwriters".[35]

One other difficulty with Collins's verbal protocol methodology is that it is necessarily interventionist, requiring the composer to pause during composition in order to communicate the research evidence. Not only does this disrupt the compositional act, it can also make the composer ever more aware of the research process and thus contributes to the 'observation effect' (of participants altering their behaviour owing to the knowledge that they are being observed). This presupposes that a songwriter has agreed to be observed in the first place. Some songwriters I initially approached for potential interview were reluctant to take part, citing busy schedules, fear of some form of 'industrial espionage' and sometimes, even in the case of very successful songwriters, a remarkable degree of self-doubt that their collaborative processes would stand up to scrutiny by industry peers. There is no precedent among songwriters (or in the field of psychology research) for thorough real-time observation of the songwriting process.[36] Compounding these problems

---

[35]   Bennett, 'Collaborative songwriting', 11.

[36]   Here, I must acknowledge the detailed work of Jeanne Bamberger, whose experiments have included amateur songwriters. This work did undertake real-time observation and used a laboratory-based methodology that successfully isolated melodic selection from the rest of the creative process, albeit by substantially reducing the creative

was the fact that, in the highly competitive and economically driven environment of the music industry, there was no incentive for these busy songwriters to participate in unpaid academic research.

The US/UK music industry famously runs on informal 'networking' relationships,[37] and it was becoming increasingly clear in my early discussions with songwriters that they liked to work with individuals who were known to them, or recommended through existing industry contacts. Therefore it became necessary to build working relationships with a number of experienced collaborative songwriters, and then to use an observational process that would generate 'real' and useful original songs that would be as resistant as possible to the observation effect.

Therefore my evidence base for the study of collaborative songwriting processes uses three sources. Firstly, I act as co-researcher,[38] writing songs with many different collaborators, recording the process in real time, and interviewing the co-writer immediately retrospectively about our shared experience of the process. Secondly, I draw upon a large number of previously published interviews with successful songwriters, together with the limited (and certainly edited) footage of successful songwriters at work,[39] balancing these artefacts' arguable status as primary sources with the risk of participants and mediators romanticizing the creative process. Thirdly, I have referenced the manifold 'how-to' songwriting texts, most of which include at least a section on co-writing.[40]

Professional Collaboration

All commercial songwriting is an economically and creatively speculative activity. The songwriter cannot know during the creative process whether the song will be successful, and even successful songwriters may create many 'duds'; not every creative idea will work every time. Ashurst asserts that he and other successful pop songwriters are highly experimental in this context, actively seeking new and innovative ideas rather than working from formulae:

---

choices available to the composer. Jeanne Bamberger, 'The development of intuitive musical understanding: A natural experiment', *Psychology of Music*, 31/1 (2003), 7–36.

[37]   Keith R. Negus, 'The discovery and development of recording artists in the popular music industry' (Polytechnic of the South Bank, 1992), 99.

[38]   The term was used in this context by Sam Hayden and Luke Windsor, 'Collaboration and the composer: case studies from the end of the 20th century', *Tempo*, 61/240 (April 2007), 32, http://www.journals.cambridge.org/abstract_S0040298207000113.

[39]   For example, Linda Brusasco (director), 'Secrets of the pop song – "ballad"' (BBC2, July 2011).

[40]   Chris Bradford and British Academy of Composers and Songwriters, *Heart & Soul: Revealing the Craft of Songwriting* (London, 2005). Walter Carter, *Writing Together: The Songwriter's Guide to Collaboration* (London, 1990). Jason Blume, *6 Steps to Songwriting Success: The Comprehensive Guide to Writing and Marketing Hit Songs* (New York, 1999).

[commercially successful co-writers] are really free to experiment and try stuff out; they're excitable about an idea that is just fresh, and who knows whether it's going to work or not? They don't say "These chords work. This melody works. I'm in this box and this is my world." [...] You'd expect them to say "This formula has worked for me before", but it's just the opposite.[41]

Given the lack of guarantees of successful outcomes, the only incentive a professional songwriter has for undertaking any new collaboration is a belief, based on the other collaborator's track record or musical/literary skills, that the finished song will stand a chance of being commercially or artistically successful.

All of the songwriters cited in this chapter are professionals; I use the term literally, meaning individuals who have earned money from their songs (through the Performing Right Society[42] or other royalty collection agency income). This is partly because commercial success (or at least industry engagement) is a reliable metric for measuring whether the listening public has engaged with a songwriter's work, helping to put aside subjective debates of the artistic merits of one songwriter's work over another's. However, even more importantly, amateur songwriters[43] appear to exhibit different creative practices from professionals. This contention is the result of observations undertaken throughout my own teaching of amateur songwriters at various levels of UK education over a 20-year period, from adult beginners and young children through to aspirant professionals studying undergraduate and postgraduate programmes. The motivation for some amateurs to write songs does not necessarily require any consideration of the listener's experience – and frequently, in beginner songwriters, does not include it. A common example is the challenge of autobiographical authenticity in a lyric;[44] amateur songwriters will often prioritise this over literary issues of universality, word economy and syllabic rhythm. This may be due to the influence of media; artist-songwriters frequently focus on issues of emotional authenticity or biography (as opposed to more craft-based issues such as syllable-count, drafting and editing, imagery and metaphor, and so on) when discussing their songwriting in mainstream press interviews. Zollo's work[45] is a notable exception – among a small number of others[46] – because, owing to the

---

[41]   Ashurst, 'On collaborative songwriting'.

[42]   Performing Right Society, 'Performing Right Society (UK) – about', PRS For Music website, 2011, https://www.prsformusic.com/aboutus/pages/default.aspx.

[43]   Similarly, I use the term amateur in a literal rather than pejorative sense.

[44]   A phrase I use frequently when teaching students about this balance is that 'human relationships are more complex than songs'. This is intended to help learners to engage with two of the fundamental principles of lyric writing – clarity and word economy.

[45]   Zollo, *Songwriters on Songwriting*.

[46]   Webb, *Tunesmith*. John Braheny, *The Craft and Business of Songwriting: A Practical Guide to Creating and Marketing Artistically and Commercially Successful Songs*, 3rd edn (Cincinnati, OH, 2006).

intended audience,[47] his interview subjects are encouraged to focus on the craft of songwriting and thus concern themselves less with romanticising their own creative processes.

Additionally, there are many musical and lyric-writing traits that are common in beginner/student songwriters but appear less often in successful songs. These practices include: composing phrases that begin on the second beat of the bar and/or on the fifth note of the scale; avoiding melodic anacruses;[48] over-using the 3:3:2 rhythm in accompaniments or melodies;[49] over-reliance on unchanging chord loops; limited use of imagery; and lack of repetition in choruses. These characteristics have been observed in my own teaching of several hundred music student songwriters in the UK, and it appears that such habits can become 'unlearned' over time as more songs are written; it would be interesting to discover whether these compositional habits are particular to UK beginner songwriters or universal (and common in beginner songwriters from wider cultural circles). As one songwriting teacher I interviewed suggested, beginners are often more eager than professionals to challenge the constraints of form:

> A lot of [student] writers are really desperate to rebuild the whole house whereas an experienced songwriter is happy with the house – they just want to decorate it in a new way.[50]

Professional songwriters, as we have seen, are often difficult to contact and are certainly fewer in number than amateur or aspirant songwriters, or musicians in full-time education. The reluctance of busy creative professionals to participate in academic studies is well documented, most clearly perhaps by Csikszentmihalyi in his study of 91 'exceptional individuals'. Below is the response from the secretary of composer George Ligeti to Csikszentmihalyi's request for an interview:

> [Mr Ligeti] is creative and, because of this, totally overworked. Therefore, the very reason you wish to study his creative process is also the reason why he

---

[47]   The interviews in *Songwriters on Songwriting* were originally published in *SongTalk*, the journal of the National Academy of Songwriters – so the intended audience would have been almost exclusively other songwriters rather than more general music consumers.

[48]   Anacrusis – a musical phrase that begins before the first beat of the bar. In songwriting circles it is more often referred to as a 'pickup bar' (UK) or 'pickup measure' (USA).

[49]   To be fair to student songwriters, the 3:3:2 rhythm (dotted crotchet; dotted crotchet; crotchet, or put another way, a downbeat, a 'pushed quaver' before the third beat, and the fourth beat) is extremely common in popular music – see Don Traut, '"Simply irresistible": Recurring Accent Patterns as Hooks in Mainstream 1980s Music', *Popular Music*, 24/1 (January 2005), 60, http://www.journals.cambridge.org/abstract_S0261143004000303.

[50]   Ashurst, 'On collaborative songwriting'.

(unfortunately) does not have time to help you in this study. He … is trying desperately to finish a Violin Concerto.[51]

Another of Csikszentmihalyi's potential interviewees responded,

> I have admired you and your work for many years, and I have learned much from it. But, my dear Professor Csikszentmihalyi … I hope you will not think me presumptuous or rude if I say that one of the secrets of productivity (in which I believe whereas I do not believe in creativity) is … NOT doing anything that helps the work of other people but to spend all one's time on the work the Good Lord has fitted one to do, and to do well.[52]

It is perhaps because of the elusiveness of creative professionals, and the lack of incentive for them to participate in creativity-based studies, that so many previous studies into composers have focused on music students or children, and are thus found in educational psychology literature rather than in the work of popular musicologists. Hayden and Windsor,[53] Burnard and Younker[54] and Kratus[55] all use children or student composers as their research subjects. Even studies that may appear to use professional composers have different criteria for defining their subjects in this way; Devries[56] studies a songwriting partnership that has not yet been successful; Roe[57] deals with professional composers but specifically for solo bass clarinet; Nash[58] sets clear parameters for 'successful composers', although his observations did not extend to the creative act itself.[59] To summarise the selection problem – professional composers are more authentic but more elusive and less likely to co-operate; amateur and student composers are more accessible,

---

[51] Mihaly Csikszentmihalyi, *Creativity: Flow and the Psychology of Discovery and Invention* (New York, 1996), 14.

[52] Ibid.

[53] Hayden and Windsor, 'Collaboration and the composer'.

[54] Pamela Burnard and Betty Anne Younker, 'Problem-solving and creativity: Insights from students' individual composing pathways', *International Journal of Music Education*, 22/1 (April 2004), 59–76, http://ijm.sagepub.com/cgi/doi/10.1177/0255761404042375.

[55] John Kratus, 'A time analysis'.

[56] Peter DeVries, 'The rise and fall of a songwriting partnership', *The Qualitative Report*, 10/1 (2005), 39–54.

[57] Paul Roe, 'A phenomenology of collaboration in contemporary composition and performance' (PhD Thesis, York, 2007).

[58] Dennison Nash, 'Challenge and response in the American composer's career', *The Journal of Aesthetics and Art Criticism*, 14/1 (September 1955), 116–22, http://www.jstor.org/stable/426646.

[59] Nash concerns himself with the personality types of composers rather than their processes, and he uses 'techniques of interview, schedule, and Rorschach's Test' to ascertain these.

but potential studies may not illuminate the processes by which effective – and affective – music is composed.

The Co-writing Process

Collaborators, indeed all songwriters, consistently state that there are no rules for the songwriting process. Even songwriters who work in well-defined genres warn against using systems for composing. Notwithstanding, there are some creative practices that could be considered, if not ubiquitous, then at least commonly understood by a large number of experienced co-writers. Many of these are not necessarily exclusive to co-writing, and are also used by solo songwriters.

Writing from the title outwards is a common technique for addressing the creative challenge of framing the main lyric theme. Lydon[60] summarises this practice thus: 'Many old pros advise beginners, 'Find your title first'. These few words are the core of a lyric, the seed from which the lyric grows.'

Co-writing sessions, notably in Nashville, may begin with each collaborator bringing a small number of titles to use as stimulus material.[61] The title can suggest a core meaning and may also enable discussion about rhymes, placement of 'hooks',[62] lyric scansion or even melodic shape. This simple technique deals effectively with one of the creative challenges reported by amateur songwriters: that is, the tendency to postpone the process of identifying the literary theme of the lyric in favour of easier and more immediate processes such as providing chordal accompaniment.

> [guitarists who are new to songwriting] often try writing songs 'in the right order', strumming the intro chords and then hoping lyric inspiration will strike in the fifth or ninth bar of music. This seems perfectly logical as a method for writing a song, but in practice it is often just a delaying tactic, putting off until later the dreaded moment where you're going to decide what you want to say.[63]

I will restate at this point that the title-first technique is just one example – albeit a popular one – of a process used by co-writers to kick-start their creative processes. It is not a template for writing a song, nor is it in use by all songwriters. However, its function in the creative process demonstrates an important point – that *something* has to come first; I refer to this as the 'initial stimulus'. In the case

---

[60]   Michael Lydon, *Songwriting Success: How to Write Songs for Fun and (Maybe) Profit* (New York, 2004).

[61]   Andy West, Personal communication with ex-Nashville songwriter Andy West, interview by Joe Bennett, 2005.

[62]   A memorable part of the song; a hook may be a title, sonic motif, lyric line, audio sample or melodic element, and is almost always repeated more than once.

[63]   Joe Bennett, 'Song meaning … it makes me wonder', *Total Guitar Magazine* (July 2011), 30.

of music-first approaches to songwriting, a typical initial stimulus could be a chord sequence, melodic phrase, audio sample or drum loop; in lyric-first approaches it is commonly the title, but may be any short lyric phrase or even a visual image.[64] The source of these fragments may be internally generated by one of the songwriters through 'play' – typically improvising on an instrument – or may be chosen by the songwriter from an external source, such as a sample library or even from an existing song. The initial stimulus may be chosen/created in advance of, or at the start of, the collaborative meeting. It can then be submitted for evaluation by the collaborative team. Evaluation of a stimulus most commonly occurs in songwriting teams whose creative process is genuinely collaborative (where ideas are discussed, adapted and negotiated) as opposed to demarcated (where ideas are handed from one co-writer to another in tag-team fashion).

Although all songs necessarily start with some form of stimulus, this is not to say that stimuli only occur at the start of the creative process. On the contrary, they must recur throughout because collaborators continually generate and evaluate new ideas. Thus, the following discussion of the songwriting team's processing of stimuli, which I shall call 'stimulus evaluation', applies recurrently and sometimes concurrently throughout the song's creation, and is applied to every creative idea that is proposed during the co-writing session.

During the evaluation stage of a stimulus it can be processed in four ways by the writing team; approval, veto, negotiation or adaptation. Approval allows the idea to take its place in the song, a process that usually requires consensus from the songwriting team. A co-writer may challenge another writer's stimulus, leading to veto (rejecting the stimulus), negotiation (arguing a case for accepting the stimulus) or adaptation (changing the stimulus until vetoed or approved). A stimulus is the beginning of a creative idea's pathway through the songwriting team's filter; consensus represents a successful end to its journey.

I contend that six (non-linear and interacting) processes are at play in a co-writing environment – stimulus, approval, adaptation, negotiation, veto and consensus. One writer will provide stimulus material and the other writer will approve, adapt or veto the idea (approval can obviously lead to consensus – I include both because there may be situations with more than two co-writers where one individual approves an idea but another provides veto or adaptation). If an idea is vetoed in its entirety the provider of the stimulus will either accept this or enter negotiation to defend or further adapt it. Consensus permits an idea to survive and – temporarily or permanently – take its place in the song (collaborative songwriters frequently report agreement that 'we'll fix that bit later' – for example, in the use of a dummy lyric that will later be replaced).[65]

Stimulus evaluation is a workable description of the processes that are used to generate the song in draft form, but rarely does a song arrive fully

---

[64] Boo Hewerdine, 'Boo Hewerdine – reflections on a collaborative songwriting process', interview by Joe Bennett, March 2011.

[65] Bennett, 'Collaborative songwriting'.

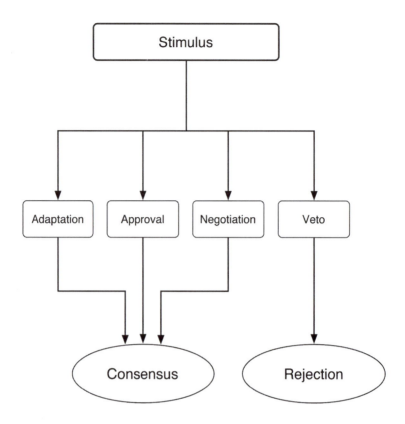

Figure 6.1   'Stimulus evaluation' model for collaborative songwriting

Note: This diagram represents the process by which a single creative stimulus (that is, a suggestion by an individual, or an external stimulus such as an audio sample) is evaluated by the songwriting team. Once a stimulus has been approved and the team has provided consensus, the creative idea takes its place in the song, although it may be adapted or replaced later if the team approves better stimuli.

formed in its first draft – many collaborative teams report extensive additional adaptation and negotiation even of ideas that are initially approved. Thus, the evaluative model moves from a micro to a macro function; the draft song itself, or temporarily approved 'placeholder' sections of it, can become the stimulus, and the partnership then evaluates these. I refer to this process – of replacing any temporarily approved stimuli with permanent equivalents – as the editing stage. The partnership becomes its own audience, listening to the song and deciding which elements 'work' and which need further adaptation, negotiation or veto. Or put another way, a stimulus can experience multiple adaptations throughout the songwriting process.

When the song is completed to the satisfaction of the co-writing team, sometimes in a single session, sometimes over several sessions, many partnerships will take the opportunity to reflect on the potentially finished song.[66] Sometimes this generates an additional process that is often described industrially as rewriting. Carter[67] identifies three situations in which this can occur – when the co-writers agree that a rewrite is needed; when they disagree whether a rewrite is needed; or when an external party (publisher, artist or producer) requires a rewrite. The solutions to these challenges may include additional rewriting activities by the partnership, lone work on the song by partnership members, or drafting in additional individuals in order to get the song finished. This latter approach, of cheerful promiscuity, is more likely among professional 'jobbing' songwriters who write songs for others to perform; it is less apparent or even non-existent among the many celebrated 'loyal' collaborative partnerships, particularly those where the artist is involved or part-involved (for example, Lennon/McCartney, Difford/Tilbrook or John/Taupin).

The difference to a partnership that loyalty can make demonstrates another important point about the way collaborative songwriting groups work – they are quasi-social. The relationship is dominated, necessarily, by the requirement to complete a specific task, but conversational negotiation usually occurs throughout the shared creative process, and prior learning (i.e. 'musical influences') plays an important role in the compatibility of individuals. So the group dynamic cannot easily be summarised by simplistic group-performance management theory such as Tuckman's often-challenged sequential 'Forming–Storming–Norming–Performing' approach,[68] especially when taking into account that the songwriters may or may not have co-written together before. Songwriter Boo Hewerdine reflects further upon the social aspects of the co-writing process, implying that a shared understanding of the social dynamic is an important prerequisite for productive activity:

> I love to talk [with the collaborator] before we start. And you process that information and you go into a very slight, trancelike state, and off you go. You're processing the information that you've heard and you're trying to channel it into something. You go into a little dream. [Collaborators] have to be comfortable enough to do that, and for it not to be at all an awkward social thing.[69]

Ashurst sees the social interaction as an integral part of getting the creative process started, particularly with new collaborators:

---

[66]   Two-day co-writes are not uncommon, where co-writers 'sleep on it' and may undertake 'homework' to generate additional stimuli for the following day.

[67]   Carter, *Writing Together*, 88.

[68]   Bruce Tuckman, 'Developmental sequence in small groups', *Psychological Bulletin*, 63/6 (1965), 384–99.

[69]   Hewerdine, 'Reflections on a collaborative songwriting process'.

[We often start with] a cup of tea and some biscuits! This can take an hour, or two hours, especially if we've got a two day co-write, just to get the lay of the land. Most of the time you want to ease into it a little bit and just have a chat. One reason that I think people want to write with me is that I'm nice to be in a room with for two days![70]

The working relationship can also be mediated by environment, particularly in cases where additional music-making hardware and software tools are available. Technology-rich environments such as recording studios can provide two new opportunities for the partnership – namely, rapid recording of ideas and additional stimuli. As we have seen, a stimulus can be musicological, such as a riff, melody or chord pattern, or literary, such as a title, rhyme or phrase, but it can also be sonic – a drum loop, audio sample, synthesiser sound or guitar effects preset. Indeed, songwriters working in production-heavy genres such as hip-hop or contemporary pop often report using 'production' ideas as a stimulus. Studio environments, encouraging as they do the recording of ideas as they arrive, can blur the line between songwriter, artist and producer, and indeed many songwriters use these multiple labels to define their practice.

Models of Collaboration

I have written elsewhere about seven possible working models for songwriting collaboration,[71] using the terms Nashville, Svengali, Demarcation, Jamming, Top-line writing, Asynchronicity and Factory. The terms are not mutually exclusive and frequently overlap in practice. Nashville co-writing is perhaps the most popularly understood model of 'writing a song together', because it involves (usually two) simultaneous co-writers, often with guitar or piano, collaborating in a technology-light pen-and-paper environment, and applying stimulus evaluation in real time through face to face conversation. Svengali writing involves the artist collaborating with a more experienced professional non-artist songwriter, where the latter party provides 'craft' to help to realise the artist's creative vision, and often includes some elements of demarcation. Demarcation represents a situation where the co-writers need not meet to collaborate – the baton is handed from one co-writer to the other linearly: a common example would be where a lyricist hands their lyrics to a composer for 'setting' or vice versa. The Jamming model is where musicians create live stimuli, typically through improvisation of accompaniment, enabling other writers – usually the singer – to improvise melody and lyric atop. Top-line writing is a form of demarcation where a complete or almost-complete backing track is supplied to a singer/writer who will create melody and lyric in response to its stimulus. Asynchronicity, where co-writers work separately but without assigning roles, is essentially the demarcation model in fragmented form:

---

[70]   Ashurst, 'On collaborative songwriting'.
[71]   Bennett, 'Collaborative songwriting', 6.

The co-writers work separately and iteratively, but do not necessarily define clear or exclusive creative roles. An example would be if two songwriter-producers worked separately on a multi-track audio file, passing it backwards and forwards (typically online) and making iterative changes in one or more cycles. The demarcation model is usually implemented asynchronously, but asynchronous writing need not be demarcated (by activity or creative contribution).[72]

The 'Factory' is a physical location where songwriters collaborate using one or more of the other models, and often incorporating other parts of the song production process, including recording, publishing, A&R,[73] marketing and administration. It has a long and dignified history, from Tin Pan Alley in the late nineteenth and early twentieth century through the Brill Building in the 1950s and 1960s through to the Xenomania building in the early twenty-first century,[74] and can produce a large number of 'hits' owing to its work ethic and quality-control systems, perhaps providing a competitive advantage in our evolutionary ecosystem of song survival. Xenomania, like Motown before it, unashamedly describes itself as a 'hit factory', with co-writing processes that include stimulus (and song) evaluation by committee.[75]

Models have a relationship to genre. Production-based genres such as hip-hop or contemporary pop will often favour technology-heavy models such as Top-line writing or Asynchronicity. Conversely, genres where the song is more easily transferable between performers (often 'traditional' song types that rely more on melody, lyric and harmony than production specifics) may more commonly use the Nashville model. The Demarcated model, famously divided between composer and lyricist in many partnerships, can also be used by necessity, owing to geographical distance or timescale. Sometimes it is only needed for parts of the process – for example, rewrites or last-minute edits.

Testing the Models

One of the USA's most successful twentieth century songwriting partnerships is that of Burt Bacharach and Hal David. Bacharach wrote the music and David the lyrics; their respective roles were fully demarcated in this respect and I use them to illustrate my 'Demarcated' model. The much-asked journalist's question of whether music or lyrics comes first in the songwriting process is answered by David:

---

[72]   Ibid., 7.

[73]   Artist and Repertoire – the process of discovering new talent.

[74]   Brian Higgins, 'Brian Higgins interview – *The Telegraph* (August 2009)', August 2009, http://xenomania.freehostia.com/press/brian_telegraph_aug09.html.

[75]   Linda Brusasco (director), 'Secrets of the pop song – "breakthrough single"' (BBC2, July 2011).

> [Burt] would give me melodies from time to time – I would give him lyrics. Very
> often we sat in a room and banged out a song together, back and forth, back and
> forth. Sometimes […] I'd be working at home on some melody he gave me, and
> he'd work separately on a lyric I may have given him.[76]

Here we see very clearly delineated stimuli: lyric and music are separate, and one
is written (individually) in response to the other. In this version of the Demarcated
model, opportunities for co-writers' evaluation of the stimuli are limited because
the collaborators may work separately from each other, but there were some
notable examples of Bacharach and David using successful negotiation in the
creation of a hit, as the former recalls:

> When I'm working on [melodies], I'm making up words. And the words might
> make no sense. With "Raindrops" as an example, I just kept hearing that phrase,
> "raindrops keep falling on my head." Hal tried to change it, and go to another
> lyric idea, but that was a very good one. I will sing whatever phrase it is that I'm
> hearing with the music.[77]

This requirement to make melodic lines 'sing well' is much reported by songwriting
teams; words and music must work together because in performance they are never
heard in isolation from one another. Bacharach's anecdote shows a stimulus (the
titular melody and lyric phrase from 'Raindrops') being initially vetoed by his co-
writer, but being defended by its creator by negotiation – in this case becoming an
unassailable example of Boden's 'H-creativity' (i.e. 'Raindrops' has since become
a well-known classic). Often a lyric that sings well may be literarily banal or even
nonsensical, or conversely a powerful lyric may have the wrong syllable count
to scan well with the composed melody; these tensions are frequently part of the
negotiation and adaptation process for co-writers.

I will now highlight a detailed example from my own co-researcher work,[78]
using primarily the Nashville model. In 2010 I undertook a co-writing session with
published songwriter Chris Turpin. This represented a three-hour co-write studio
session (including the recording of a 'guide vocal') and immediately afterwards a
retrospective discussion between us, which was transcribed to create a permanent
contemporaneous record of our thoughts on the song's creation at the time. He

---

[76]   Zollo, *Songwriters on Songwriting*, 210–11.

[77]   Ibid., 206–7.

[78]   I stress here that this example is not an attempt to define any template for writing a
song – all songwriters agree that methods can vary across individuals, genres, environments
or simply whim. Rather, I use this particular co-writing session as a framework for the
discussion of the way in which stimuli are processed and to provide examples of adaptation,
approval, negotiation and veto.

had, at the behest of his publisher,[79] undertaken several recent collaborations with other published writers, and on arrival at my studio was extremely comfortable and workmanlike in his preparedness to start co-writing. After the aforementioned tea and biscuits we began our co-writing session.

We began by looking for initial stimuli. I had (and constantly keep) a long list of potential titles; Chris had written a list of images and ideas in his songwriting notebook, of which a very small excerpt appears below. So for this session we had each independently decided to use as initial stimuli literary, rather than musical, material.

> Gold in the dirt. Born in the shadows of the corn. Whispers of home, hiss out the passing car tyres. Dirty nails and dry tears. Pick the love she need out the dirt. Shine like crushed tin, stars cut the black out of tonight, and I'm wild in her. Window lets the night into the car. Road. Numb in the dull spill of car radios, lights below like candles on a birthday cake. We're sweet on the night. Drinking in the air off the lake. Halfway to the bridge fell we're sleeping in Mexican skies, we shift the heart of this city.[80]

For my part, I had provided my title list (of around 200 possible titles) and we negotiated a shortlist of four; 'Open Doors', 'Hard to Find', 'Shallow Breathing' and 'Silver Strings'. This moment (around 10 minutes into the co-write session) represented the first example of stimulus evaluation, as it was the first time that any stimulus material had been presented for processing; in this case, stimuli were provided simultaneously by both co-writers. We both agreed that the title 'Silver Strings' and several lyric lines including 'Gold in the Dirt' would remain for the moment, and then, without discussion, we both picked up acoustic guitars and began strumming chords and singing these lines. Chris played a one-bar fingerstyle chord riff in an open tuning, providing basic accompaniment over which we could sing these phrases. The riff was implicitly approved by me (in that I did not attempt to veto or discuss it); my decision was born in part by a desire not to hold up the early musical composition process by editing ideas that may yet develop.

---

[79] It is common practice for UK music publishers to 'pair up' their songwriters in this way with co-writers on the same – or other – publishing rosters. This generates creative opportunities for the writer, and new Intellectual Property for both publisher and songwriter.

[80] Chris Turpin, 'Preparatory notes for songwriting session – extracts from songwriter's notebook' (unpublished, September 2010). It is perhaps obvious from this text that Chris has a creative interest in Americana-inspired imagery. He is an extremely proficient Delta-blues style guitarist: his own vocal performance style and his commercial releases have very clear blues-rock influences.

To cross-reference my description above with the experience of my co-writer, I include below Chris's own summary of the start of our collaborative session.[81]

> We both looked at each other and said "Have you got any ideas?" Joe mentioned he had a few titles knocking around and I said "I've got some notes that I've scribbled down [in idle moments]; we can draw these if we need images and … 'smells' and 'tastes'." And we sat down and we picked up two guitars. I immediately, because of the tuning of the guitar, starting playing a lick[82] that I've played in sound check a couple of times. And thought "Ooh maybe we could use this, why the heck not." And Joe agreed that it was a decent enough lick and we could use it. So then we sat down and he handed over a list of titles. I picked out three that were interesting, to my eyes, that evoked something or could evoke something that would be quite interesting and fitted in with the chords. We grabbed the lyrics, [chose]six lines that we thought were interesting images, and started to marry them together.[83]

We spent some time (another 10 minutes or so) simply improvising vocally around these lyric ideas over a one-chord accompaniment. This period of 'play' began to create fragments of usable melody and lyric; at this point explicit use of veto was unnecessary, because approval was used positively – either one of the co-writers would interject with 'I like that' if the other created a particularly pleasing or effective phrase. In this way, some poorer ideas (those that were tried and ignored by both parties) were vetoed by the partnership implicitly and rapidly without any verbal discussion. One of us acted as scribe and noted down lyric fragments as they were approved, and at this point more rhymes, lyric images, melodic phrases and rhythmic scansions began to emerge. It is worth stating here that treble clef music notation was not used at any point in the process; its presence seems to be rare in co-writing sessions. I am personally able to read clef-based music notation but many of the experienced songwriters with whom I have co-written cannot. 'Chord sheets' – lyrics with guitar chords written above each line – are, in my experience, a more common way of notating the song than music staves. Melody is more often committed to memory or to a recording device than to the written page. There are exceptions to this practice – Bacharach[84] uses clef-based notation

---

[81]   Although the accounts mostly concur, the co-writer's summary describes the events in a slightly different order from my own account (which was based on an audio recording I made of the co-writing session), demonstrating a minor but unavoidable problem with retrospective interviews – they rely on memory.

[82]   A short musical guitar phrase – in this case, a looped one-bar minor chord played fingerstyle with melodic embellishments.

[83]   Chris Turpin, 'Chris Turpin and Joe Bennett discuss a songwriting collaboration', interview by Joe Bennett, October 2010.

[84]   Zollo, *Songwriters on Songwriting*.

extensively to keep a note of new melodies – but music staves do not appear to be common in co-writing sessions.

Frequently, every five minutes or so, there would be a lull in our semi-improvisational activities and we might stop to discuss the lyric, particularly from a conceptual point of view. We asked questions of each other to try to clarify the thematic 'lyric framework'.[85] Who was our protagonist? What was his relationship to the titular 'Silver Strings'? Where was he in space and time during the song's narrative? What could he literally see in his physical environment and what metaphorical images could he 'see' in his emotional one?[86] We did not allow our lack of immediate answers to all these questions to hinder the creative process elsewhere: if we failed to agree these elements we would work on another element of the song – rhymes or chord progressions, perhaps – and see if changes in these areas gave us a different perspective on the thematic questions.

Rarely in the co-writing session was any new stimulus vetoed entirely negatively; at most, an idea that did not appeal to the other co-writer was met with courteous phrases such as 'it's not quite right for this section – how about this?' or 'I wonder if we can try a variation on that?', or, more often, with the other writer suggesting an adaptation of the stimulus. In this way, an atmosphere of mutual supportiveness was quickly established, and new stimuli were continually and efficiently generated, adapted, vetoed, approved or negotiated. It was implicitly understood (and in my experience this is always the case) that all 'approved' ideas could be changed later, as they frequently were later in the process, but the partnership's willingness to approve ideas – even temporarily – enabled a skeleton version of the song to be rapidly constructed, and we had created three and a half minutes of performable music and lyrics within the first hour of the session.

From this point onward we began improving and replacing existing elements of the song. Individual lyric phrases were discussed in the broader context of the song's story, and the lyric framework became clearer. 'Placeholder' melodic phrases were improved upon and syllable counts edited. The listener experience came more into focus; discussion points included 'would people find it boring to have a double verse here?', 'is the title line's melody strong enough to make everyone sing it at a live show?' and 'are we making it clear why the character's leaving town?' Lyric imagery was adapted and improved, with some discussion regarding the relative merits of particular metaphors and similes, and occasional consultation of an online rhyming dictionary. Completely new stimuli became less frequent at this stage, with most of the work focusing on the adaptation of the existing song. Occasionally the partnership would temporarily separate, on one or other partner's suggestion, to allow each co-writer to work independently for a

---

[85]   By this I mean the thematic content of the lyric – the 'story' or concept that drives the song. See Sheila Davis, *Successful Lyric Writing* (1988), 17.

[86]   Turpin stated, in the interview that followed the co-write, that consensus regarding matters of theme, character and narrative is very important to him. Many other songwriters state similar concerns regarding clarity of lyric theme and the believability of characters.

few minutes (Chris worked on edits to the chord changes and phrase lengths in the chorus while I wrote an additional final verse to the same rhythmic scansion that we had previously agreed); these individually created elements were then brought back to the partnership a few minutes later for evaluation.

Although our process most closely followed what I have described as the 'Nashville model' of co-writers working simultaneously and face-to-face, our environment for this particular co-write was technologically mediated; we had available a music computer with drum samples and the ability to record live guitars and vocals as needed. As the song began to take shape, some ideas (for example, the fingerstyle riff, the underlying chord progression for each section, and the chorus in its entirety) seemed to be achieving agreed permanence, so they were laid down 'on tape'. This had the effect of pushing the co-writers towards working on not-yet-fixed stimuli, such as, in this case, the verse lyrics. It also, owing to the fact that we were recording live instruments, committed us to a working tempo, at least for the 'demo' recording we intended to complete by the end of the session. To this end, a simple one-bar bass drum and hi-hat pattern was established on the computer, to provide more idiomatic (and hopefully inspiring) timekeeping than a metronome click.

By around two hours into the session, the boundaries between 'writing a song' and 'producing a demo' were becoming blurred. Lyrics were still being refined and melodies slightly edited, but as guitars and vocals were laid down it was clear that the partnership was starting to commit to chord progressions, melody and lyrics. Owing to the way music computers allow non-linear editing (even of completed audio takes), song form remains adaptable throughout the recording process; choruses, verses or even single beats can be moved, added or removed at any point. Thus, sections were moved around and auditioned through playbacks several times, with extensive negotiation regarding the listener's aural journey through the song's structure. Editing song form is of course equally easy – perhaps easier – when no recording has taken place, so this option (of making last-minute changes to the song's section-by-section structure) is by no means confined to technologically mediated songwriting environments.

It is unknown whether my own 'lab-based' co-write as described above will lead to an audience engaging with the song. Indeed, it is probable that the song will never be commercially released; Marade et al. state the unfortunate truism that 'failure and rejection are highly likely across every aspect of the songwriting process'.[87] However, owing to the co-researcher role and the extensive data collected, this observed co-write does provide us with a level of depth that is perhaps unattainable from existing hits, because any analysis of their creation would be necessarily retrospective.

For my final example, I shall discuss a collaboration demonstrating the substantial overlap that can occur between the process models, featuring two of the UK's most celebrated contemporary songwriting collaborators – Guy Chambers

---

[87]   Marade et al., 'The role of risk-taking in songwriting success', 128.

and Mark Ronson.[88] There are very few available recordings of real-time co-writing sessions, apart from my own primary research, against which to test process models, but the 2011 BBC TV mini-series *Secrets of the Pop Song*[89] provides a rare opportunity. Chambers and Ronson are filmed co-writing a song for – and with – new artist Tawiah, and although less than 10 minutes' worth of songwriting footage is shown (edited from a two-day co-writing session), there are many useful insights into process. The co-writers mainly use the Nashville model, in that they co-write together live in the room using guitars and voice, but include elements of the Svengali, Top-line and Demarcated models. The artist is the least experienced collaborator (Svengali model) and writes most of the lyric and melody (Top-line writing); Tawiah and Ronson are seen undertaking independent work on the lyric and backing track, respectively, and Ronson and Chambers are known for writing music rather than lyrics (Demarcated). Because the song is intended to be a pop single, the environment and process are both technology-rich (notwithstanding a brief acoustic guitar session in the park!), with a Pro Tools[90] operator on hand during the writing process. Detailed production work (e.g. Ronson supervising the recording of live drums) is undertaken even before the song is finished, blurring, as in my co-researcher example, the distinction between 'song' and 'track'.

All three co-writers provide stimuli throughout, including audio samples, chord sequences, lyric fragments and guitar riffs, and these are seen to be evaluated by the group. Veto, where used, is dealt with courteously and professionally (quasi-social), and frequently becomes adaptation. So we can infer from this example that the models can overlap substantially and that co-writing teams may select them opportunistically and instinctively as the song develops. With this overlap in mind, perhaps 'technique' might be a better term than 'model'.

It appears, then, that the stimulus evaluation framework may maintain its integrity when tested against interviews with successful co-writers, songwriting literature, my own co-researcher sessions, and broadcast footage of songwriters at work. The 'models' (Nashville, Svengali, Demarcation, Jamming, Top-line writing, Asynchronicity and Factory) overlap heavily in many situations, but appear to be experientially understood as working methods by a large proportion of active songwriters.

Conclusion

The qualitative evidence – of observed sessions combined with songwriter interviews – suggests that popular song is a tightly constrained form, and that

---

[88] Both well-known for their collaborations with, among others, Robbie Williams and Amy Winehouse, respectively.

[89] Brusasco, 'Breakthrough single'

[90] Pro Tools – one of the 'music industry standard' software applications for digital audio recording.

experienced co-writers are comfortable with this notion. The quantitative evidence – statistical norms in Anglo-American mainstream hits over many decades – suggests that the constraints themselves may have evolved through the application of Csikszentmihalyi's 'Systems Model' in the form of the free market of song consumers. In copyright/legal terms, all new songs, however (un)successful, are examples of Boden's 'H-creative' process. In cultural terms only 'hit' songs[91] can be considered in this way.

In my 'stimulus processing' theory I have posited a model by which the negotiation between co-writers may occur. There are opportunities here for further research, particularly into the quasi-social nature of the co-writers' relationship and how it affects decision-making. Csikszentmihalyi uses the term 'Flow'[92] to describe a trance-like state where creative individuals lose track of time and become more productive because they are 'in the zone'. We can speculate that the co-writing process helps individuals to achieve this state through a mutually supportive but workmanlike creative environment. Certainly my own experience as a songwriter, composer and teacher suggests that co-writing provides productivity advantages over solo songwriting for some individuals.

The collaborative songwriting process seems, to the casual observer, to contain many contradictions. It is highly professional and businesslike, but also social and informal. It has a significant economic imperative, and yet may not generate income. It creates a unique artistic object but stays within a constrained and evolved form. The song and the recording are different objects in law, but are often merged in creative practice. A co-written song may be first-person confessional, but is not necessarily autobiographical. Collaborative songwriters understand, manage and embrace these tensions, which have defined songwriting practice for more than a century. In the context of popular song creation, the co-writing partnership survives because, like any evolved organism, it inherits characteristics from previous generations whilst adapting continually to its environment.

References

Adorno, Theodore W., 'On popular music', *Studies in Philosophy and Social Science*, IX (1941), 17–48.

Amabile, Teresa M., 'How to kill creativity', *Harvard Business Review*, 76/5 (1998), 76–87.

Bamberger, Jeanne, 'The development of intuitive musical understanding: A natural experiment', *Psychology of Music*, 31/1 (2003), 7–36.

Bennett, Joe, 'Performance and songwriting: The picture and the frame', UK Songwriting Festival website, 22 January 2009, http://www.uksong

---

[91]   Not necessarily 'chart' hits – I use the term here more broadly to mean 'having engaged a large number of listeners'.

[92]   Csikszentmihalyi, *Creativity: Flow*.

writingfestival.com/2009/01/22/performance-and-songwriting-the-picture-and-the-frame/.

Bennett, Joe, 'Collaborative songwriting – the ontology of negotiated creativity in popular music studio practice', *Journal of the Art of Record Production 2010*, 5 (2011), http://arpjournal.com/875/collaborative-songwriting-%E2%80%93-the-ontology-of-negotiated-creativity-in-popular-music-studio-practice/ or http://tiny url.com/jarp-bennett-2011.

Bennett, Joe, 'How long, how long must we sing this song?', *Joe Bennett music blog*, 2011, http://joebennett.net/2011/05/03/how-long-how-long-must-we-sing-this-song/.

Bennett, Joe, 'Song meaning … it makes me wonder', *Total Guitar Magazine* (July 2011), 30.

Blume, Jason, *6 Steps to Songwriting Success: The Comprehensive Guide to Writing and Marketing Hit Songs* (New York: Billboard Books, 1999).

Boden, Margaret, *The Creative Mind: Myths and Mechanisms*, 2nd edn (Abingdon: Routledge, 2004).

Bradford, Chris and British Academy of Composers and Songwriters. *Heart & Soul: Revealing the Craft of Songwriting* (London: Sanctuary in Association with the British Academy of Composers and Songwriters, 2005).

Braheny, John, *The Craft and Business of Songwriting: A Practical Guide to Creating and Marketing Artistically and Commercially Successful Songs*, 3rd edn (Cincinnati, OH: Writer's Digest Books, 2006).

Brusasco, Linda (director), 'Secrets of the pop song – "ballad"', BBC2, July 2011.

Brusasco, Linda (director), 'Secrets of the pop song – "breakthrough single"', BBC2, July 2011.

Burnard, Pamela and Betty Anne Younker, 'Problem-solving and creativity: Insights from students' individual composing pathways', *International Journal of Music Education*, 22/1 (2004), 59–76.

Burnard, Pamela and Betty Anne Younker, 'Mapping pathways: Fostering creativity in composition', *Music Education Research*, 4/2 (2002), 245–61.

Carter, Walter, *Writing Together: The Songwriter's Guide to Collaboration* (London: Omnibus, 1990).

Chambers. 'Chambers Free English Dictionary', *Chambers 21st Century Dictionary* (Chambers, 1996), http://www.chambersharrap.co.uk/chambers/features/chref/chref.py/main?query=song&title=21st.

Clydesdale, Greg, 'Creativity and competition: The Beatles', *Creativity Research Journal*, 18/2 (2006), 129–39.

Collins, David, 'Real-time tracking of the creative music composition process', *Digital Creativity*, 18/4 (2007), 239–56.

Csikszentmihalyi, Mihaly, *Creativity: Flow and the Psychology of Discovery and Invention* (New York: HarperCollins, 1996).

Csikszentmihalyi, Mihaly, 'Society, culture, and person: A systems view of creativity'. In: Robert Sternberg (ed.), *The Nature of Creativity: Contemporary*

Psychological Perspectives (New York: Cambridge University Press, 1988), 325–39.

Davis, Sheila, *Successful Lyric Writing* (Writer's Digest Books, 1988).

DeVries, Peter, 'The rise and fall of a songwriting partnership', *The Qualitative Report*, 10/1 (2005), 39–54.

Ellis, Shaun and Tom Engelhardt, 'Visualizing a hit – InfoVis final project', *Can Visualizing 50-Years' Worth of Hit U.S. Pop Song Characteristics Help us Discover Trends Worthy of Further Investigation?* 2010, http://sites.google.com/site/visualizingahit/home.

Hayden, Sam and Luke Windsor, 'Collaboration and the composer: Case studies from the end of the 20th century', *Tempo*, 61/240 (2007), 28.

Higgins, Brian, 'Brian Higgins interview – *The Telegraph* (August 2009)', August 2009, http://xenomania.freehostia.com/press/brian_telegraph_aug09.html

Kratus, John, 'A time analysis of the compositional processes used by children ages 7 to 11', *Journal of Research in Music Education*, 37/1 (1989), 5.

Lydon, Michael, *Songwriting Success: How to Write Songs for Fun and (Maybe) Profit* (New York: Routledge, 2004).

Mann, William, 'The Times: What songs The Beatles sang by William Mann | The Beatles Bible', *The Times*, 27 December 1963, http://www.beatlesbible.com/1963/12/27/the-times-what-songs-the-beatles-sang-by-william-mann/.

Marade, Angelo, J.A. Gibbons and Thomas M. Brinthaupt, 'The role of risk-taking in songwriting success', *The Journal of Creative Behavior*, 41/2 (2007), 125–49.

Nash, Dennison, 'Challenge and response in the American composer's career', *The Journal of Aesthetics and Art Criticism*, 14/1 (September 1955), 116–22.

Negus, Keith R., 'The discovery and development of recording artists in the popular music industry' (Polytechnic of the South Bank, 1992).

Noys, Benjamin, 'Into the "jungle"', *Popular Music*, 14/3 (1995), 321–32.

Pettijohn II, Terry F. and Shujaat F. Ahmed, 'Songwriting; loafing or creative collaboration?: A comparison of individual and team written Billboard hits in the USA', *Journal of Articles in Support of the Null Hypothesis*, 7/1 (2010), 2.

PRS for Music, 'Performing Right Society (UK) – about', 2011, http://www.prsformusic.com/aboutus/pages/default.aspx.

PRS for Music, *PRS For Music (UK Collection Society) Database Search Results*. Performing Right Society, 2010. Available to members via www.prsformusic.com (as at October 2010).

Roe, Paul, 'A phenomenology of collaboration in contemporary composition and performance', PhD thesis (York, 2007; British Library).

Sloboda, John, 'Do psychologists have anything useful to say about composition?' In: *Proceedings of the Third European Conference of Music Analysis*, Montpellier, 1995.

Sloboda, John, *The Musical Mind: The Cognitive Psychology of Music* (Oxford: Clarendon Press, 1985).

Traut, Don, '"Simply irresistible": Recurring accent patterns as hooks in mainstream 1980s music', *Popular Music*, 24/1 (2005), 57–77.

Tuckman, Bruce, 'Developmental sequence in small groups', *Psychological Bulletin*, 63/6 (1965), 384–99.

Webb, Jimmy, *Tunesmith: Inside the Art of Songwriting* (London: Hyperion Books, 1999).

Zollo, Paul, *Songwriters on Songwriting* (Boston, MA: Da Capo Press, 1997).

Chapter 7

The Influence of the Extra-musical on the Composing Process

Shira Lee Katz

Copland[1] wrote that many composers believe that the meaning of music is the music itself and nothing more. Yet what if, instead of analysing composers' scores in an attempt to *find* meaning, we attempted to see what material or mental models were important to composers as they set out to write? This chapter analyses the writing process of three contemporary composers whose creative work is heavily influenced by content outside of the musical domain. In this context, the term 'creative' is a synthesis of Csikszentmihalyi's,[2] Gardner's[3] and Perkins's[4] characterisation of creativity, expressed in individuals who have forged new territory in a particular domain and have demonstrated tenacity in exploring the questions and problems of this area from different vantage points.

Knowledge about the creative process has increased dramatically over the last century, with a burgeoning literature on creativity together with a growing amount of research on the composing process. Despite this, there is still a gap in understanding the prototypical ways in which musical compositions come to fruition. What role do extra-musical factors play? Are composers even aware of the factors that influence their work? If composers do employ extra-musical influences as they compose, what is the role of this material in their work? In other words, there has been little investigation around the factors that inspire music composers when they write or about how initial ideas are synthesised as compositions develop.

In a research study, 24 interviews were conducted with composers, three of whom are the subjects of this chapter since they draw heavily from content domains outside of music. This chapter explores how non-music domains (for example, landscape architecture, poetry) influence the musical structure of these composers' output, within sections or movements, and with two of these three

---

[1]   Copland, Aaron, Richard Kostelanetz and Steven Silverstein, *Aaron Copland: A Reader: Selected Writings 1923–1972* (New York: Routledge, 2004).

[2]   Mihaly Csikszentmihalyi, *Creativity: Flow and the Psychology of Discovery and Invention* (New York, 1996).

[3]   Howard Gardner, *Creating Minds* (New York, 1993).

[4]   David Perkins, *The Mind's Best Work* (Cambridge, 1981).

composers the more granular elements, such as instrumentation and chord choice, the smaller musical details.

For the three composers discussed in this paper, the extra-musical influences on their work are ones they have been familiar with and have valued for many years. In addition, they are characterised by a strong element of modularity, since they are already divided into discrete sections (such as architectural structures); each extra-musical influence has a unique character or physicality such that they may provide a useful 'frame' as the composers organise inchoate masses of musical materials.

In addition to making an argument about the way composers map non-music models onto their music, this chapter also makes claims more broadly about models of the creative process, in particular, stage theory. Stage theory[5] is a widely accepted model of the creative process that hinges on the idea that the creative process is propelled forward in large part during what is known as the 'illumination stage', after 'preparation' and 'incubation' stages, and is characterised by rapid insight and even abandon. In light of the findings from these three composers, it is argued in this chapter that the illumination stage may more aptly be described as a period when the creator incorporates models from his or her past as opposed to making wholly new insights.

Instantaneous Creation or Involved Process?

There are three key questions about the creative process which contextualise the discussion in this chapter. Firstly, to what extent does a creator revise and revisit during the act of creation; secondly, what prominent theories of the creative process describe the stages of creative development; and thirdly, what is the role of metaphor, lateral thinking and constraint in creative synthesis?

The first question is essentially concerned with whether groundbreaking works come about quickly, as if in a split second, or whether the ideas and impulses that feed these creations unfold over time. The Ancient Greeks believed that creativity was a gift of the Muses[6] – that God was whispering into the ears of creators as if giving breath to their creations. Despite some lingering notions of the mystical surrounding the act of creation, there is far more agreement now that 'logic, method, and techniques' underlie the creative process.[7] Gruber and Davis,[8] in their

---

[5]   Wallas, Graham, *The Art of Thought* (London, 1926).

[6]   Dean Keith Simonton, 'Creativity as a constrained stochastic process'. In: R.J. Sternberg, E.L. Grigorenko and J.L. Singer (eds), *Creativity: From Potential to Realization.* (Washington, DC, 2004), 83–101.

[7]   Simonton, *Creativity*, 83–101.

[8]   Howard E. Gruber and Sara N. Davis, 'Inching our way up Mount Olympus: The evolving-systems approach to creative thinking'. In: R.J. Sternberg (ed.), *The Nature of Creativity* (New York, 1988), 243–69.

case studies reviewing doctoral dissertations over a period of 20 years, argued that what had been thought of as creative breakthroughs could actually be seen in the earlier work or ideas of these creators.

While there now appears to be much agreement that the creative process happens to some degree over a period time, there are differing ideas about the way in which it unfolds. Wallas,[9] in his stage theory, identifies four stages of the creative process based on creators' autobiographical accounts: preparation, incubation, illumination and verification. Simply put, preparation is the period when a creator assesses the creative arc or problem to be solved. Incubation occurs when the creator takes a mental break from the problem at hand. Illumination is sometimes referred to as the 'flash of insight' when there are signs that a solution is imminent, and verification is the stage of further refinement and conclusion. While many studies are still premised on Wallas's original stage theory, there are a number of theories that have since emerged to challenge his model. For example, Ghiselin[10] argues that there is no such clear distinction between the stages. Cawelti, Rappaport and Wood[11] postulate that many of the processes that are supposedly unique to each stage actually take place to some extent during all stages.

It is without question that composers work idiosyncratically, and that no one model can capture the full range of experience. For instance, in contrast to Beethoven, whose work was characterised by continuous and painstaking reworking, composers such as Mozart and Schubert seemed to write music, particularly the main themes and their subsequent development, 'with great ease and rapidity'.[12] Highlighting a dichotomy similar to that of Beethoven and Mozart/ Schubert, research by Galenson[13] argues for a model in which creative works can be made either expeditiously or over long periods of time. Galenson examined the careers of pre-eminent visual artists, plotting their age against their productivity, and determining at what point during their lifespan they were most productive. Galenson identifies two major types of creators: Experimental Innovators and Conceptual Innovators. The work of Experimental Innovators evolves gradually over time and involves constant revision, while Conceptual Innovators' work is characterised by efficiency and decisiveness, demonstrated most commonly earlier in their career.[14] Galenson's theory may provide two modes of working, but Wallas's is probably more useful for examining how works are created from start to finish.

---

[9] Wallas, *The Art of Thought*.

[10] Ghiselin, Brewster, *The Creative Process: A Symposium*, 2nd edn (Berkeley, CA: University of California Press, 1980).

[11] Scott Cawelti, Allen Rappaport and Bill Wood. 'Modeling artistic creativity: an empirical study', *Journal of Creative Behavior*, 2(26) (1992), 83–94.

[12] Howard Gardner, *Art, Mind, and Brain* (New York, 1982), 359.

[13] David W. Galenson, 'The two life cycles of human creativity', National Bureau of Economic Research Report (2003), Research summary, http://www.nber.org/reporter/fall03/galenson.html.

[14] For more detail, see Chapter 2 by Aaron Kozbelt.

The discussion presented thus far centres on whether the creative process happens precipitously or extends over time, and also how different phases of the creative process are characterised. Some researchers have considered the influence of initial inspirational factors on the whole of the creative process. For example. Beardsley[15] offers a dichotomous framing of initial inspiration, encapsulated in his 'Propulsive' and 'Finalistic' theories. According to Propulsive theory the first stage of the creative process dominates (or has the most influence) over the rest. In Finalistic theory, the creator defines his or her end point and then allows the preceding steps of creating to be driven by this aim.

Similar in conclusion to Beardsley's Propulsive theory, Csikszentmihalyi and Getzels[16] point to the importance of the initial conceptualisation of works of art in a study focusing on fine art students training at top art schools in the USA. The artists were asked to make still-life drawings. The authors found that much of the experimentation that students did before committing to a direction was a good indication of the ultimate novelty of students' artwork, more so than continuous reworking that might take place over a longer period of time. In a three-year case study of a single composer, Collins[17] found that what they wrote during the beginning stages of composing highly influenced the work's ultimate development. Collins collected the composer's scores at different stages of the writing process and interviewed the composer several times to chart progress over time.

Metaphor, Association and Constraint

In addition to investigating how compositions unfold over time, it is also important to understand more about the mental models that creators employ since many draw from concepts and material that are not obviously related to the musical material themselves. In fact, some composers draw from extra-musical domains as sources of inspiration for their pieces[18] by using metaphor to connect information within and between domains. Gruber and Davis describe metaphor as a synthesising agent – helping to express the relationship between two different realms.[19] They argue that metaphors are not simply a linguistic

[15]   Monroe C. Beardsley, 'On the creation of art', *The Journal of Aesthetics and Art Criticism*, 23/3 (1965), 291–304.

[16]   Mihaly Csikszentmihalyi and Jacob W. Getzels, 'Discovery-oriented behavior and the originality of creative products: A study with artists', *Journal of Personality and Social Psychology*, 19/1 (1971), 47–52.

[17]   David Collins, 'A synthesis model of thinking in music composition', *Psychology of Music*, 32/2 (2003), 193–216.

[18]   Louise Duchesneau, *The Voice of the Muse: A Study of the Role of Inspiration in Musical Composition* (New York, 1986).

[19]   In Andrew Ortony, *Metaphor and Thought* (Cambridge, 1979).

phenomenon, but are a conduit for connecting and mapping concepts onto one another in which an aspect of the initial domain is preserved when considered in the context of the target domain.

De Bono[20] also discusses a way of thinking that highlights making connections across domains as opposed to thinking within one domain. De Bono refers to this as 'lateral thinking', problem solving with information that is not overtly related to the initial problem or solution.

Metaphor and association, in making a bridge between seemingly disparate information, can help creators define what is and is not important. It is shorthand of sorts, and is perhaps a way of making the creative process more economical. In 1988, Calvino[21] spoke of six themes he believed would eventually be considered common to the great works of literature as we approached the year 2000: lightness, quickness, exactitude, visibility, multiplicity and consistency. Calvino's conceptualisation of 'quickness' in particular relates to the desire for efficiency. He argues that one of the most salient characteristics of folk tales is their economy of expression: folk tales move along efficiently against time as the protagonist swiftly defeats the villain or neatly identifies a 'moral lesson'. Calvino's prediction is relevant to this discussion of metaphor and lateral thinking, as it underscores the importance of efficiently zeroing in on what is most important in a creative setting. Schoenberg[22] explains too how he actively thinks about economy and efficiency in his own writing; in what is now referred to as 12-tone music, he saw himself efficiently imposing constraints on his process. He explains:

> These forms became possible because of a limitation I had been unconsciously imposing on myself from the very outset – limitation to short pieces, something which at the time I explained in my own mind as a reaction against the "extended" style. (262)

Upon reflection, Schoenberg realised that he was trying to create the building blocks of a style and had to identify the most essential features of this form before it could be extended. He describes this impulse or decision as a 'question of economy'.[23]

In sum, claims about inspiration have historically hinged on the question of whether creations evolve gradually or instantaneously. As I have already pointed out, psychologists have come to believe that this activity is best characterised as a 'drawn-out' process. Furthermore, from Wallas's stage theory to research from

---

[20]   Edward De Bono, *Lateral Thinking*. (New York, 1970).

[21]   Italo Calvino, *Six Memos for the Next Millennium* (Cambridge, MA, 1988).

[22]   Arnold Schoenberg, 'Opinion or insight?' In: L. Stein (ed.), *Style and Idea* (Berkeley, CA, 1975), 258–64.

[23]   Ibid., 262–3.

Beardsley,[24] Getzels and Csikszentmihalyi, and others, a convincing case could be made about the worthwhileness of examining the weight and nature of various phases in the process. This chapter argues that some composers reach to non-music domains for 'inspiration', and evaluating the role of key drivers such as metaphor and association in the process could provide additional insight into the creative process.

Composers Discuss their Process

At this point we can explore the role of non-musical mental models in the unfolding composing process in the work of three composers: Michael Gandolfi, Shulamit Ran and Ken Ueno. Michael Gandolfi is a Massachusetts-born male composer and currently Professor of Composition at the New England Conservatory of Music. Gandolfi's *Impressions from The Garden of Cosmic Speculation*[25] forms the major part of this exploration. Shulamit Ran, an Israeli-born female composer, is Professor of Composition at the University of Chicago and received a Pulitzer Prize for music in 1991. Her composition *O The Chimneys*[26] is the key part of discussion. Finally, we center in on composer Ken Ueno's *Kaze-no-Oka*[27] in the process of evaluating other influences on creative musical output. Ueno is a Japanese-American composer and Associate Professor at the University of California, Berkeley. He has won both the Rome and Berlin Prizes.

Gandolfi, Ran, and Ueno are part of a sample of some 24 composers varying in age, level of professional development and genre. They were selected not only because their work was considered to be novel, according to peers, but also because they were able to fluently talk about their writing process in interview settings.[28] Extensive research on the composers' backgrounds, written works and audio-recordings was conducted in advance, and composers were asked to select for discussion two pieces that they particularly liked from their own repertoire. Interview questions focused on the factors influencing them as they wrote these and they were encouraged to 'free-associate' as they talked through their process of writing each piece. They were asked to describe how these associations and ideas related to specific points in the music, and to discuss how they made their decisions. They were also asked to discuss how they incorporated inspirational sources or ideas into the piece and summarise what they considered to be their general process for creating a new piece.

[24]   Beardsley, 'On the creation of art'.

[25]   Michael Gandolfi, *Impressions from the Garden of Cosmic Speculation* (Cambridge, 2004).

[26]   Shulamit Ran, *O the Chimneys* (New York, 1973).

[27]   Ken Ueno, *Kaze-no-Oka* (Cambridge, 2005).

[28]   Irving Seidman, *Interviewing as Qualitative Research* (New York, 1988).

Interviews were transcribed verbatim and analysed using a form of grounded theory,[29] by which themes emerged inductively from the raw data[30] This approach was both 'emic' and 'etic'; conclusions were drawn about the factors that influenced composers both by trying to understand their mindsets and by inferring about some aspects of their process divorced of the language and conceptualisation that they put forth directly. Transcripts were coded and analysed based on guidelines by Boyatzis.

After determining the similarities and differences in the chronology of the writing process for each of the three composers, each step was coded, often both in extra-musical and musical terms if the composer described the relationship as such. This first wave of codes was quite broad, encompassing large groups of information that informed some of the overarching findings that emerged. A second wave of analysis was then conducted in order to understand some of the finer-grained distinctions. For instance, a broader finding was that composers drew from extra-musical domains that were associated with the macro-musical (large scale) structure of the pieces. In order to understand more about the nature of these extra-musical domains, however, these passages had to be recoded to determine the nature of these domains (for example, related to architecture, visual art). In sum, two waves of coding were conducted: one for macro-level themes and one for micro-level ones.

Inspiration from Outside of Music

Although no single prototype could represent all three composers' trajectories from the birth to the synthesis of their ideas, as stated previously, this group of three composers seemed to draw heavily from non-musical content domains to which each composer had been attracted long before they began composing. The representations that these composers envision within these extra-musical content domains help provide an overarching roadmap for their pieces, usually influencing the form of the piece as a whole. The specific model that the composer chooses from this content domain often has an element of modularity built in as well, meaning that the composer has conceptualised this domain with clearly demarcated physical or conceptual compartments within that translate into the different movements or sections of the piece. After determining the form of the piece, the composers' associations from this non-music model then inform the more specific elements of the piece, such as chord choice or rhythm, but particularly the instrumentation of each movement or segment. This prototype certainly cannot characterise all

---

[29] Anselm L. Strauss and Juliet M. Corbin. *Basics of Qualitative Research* (Newbury Park, CA, 1990).

[30] Richard E. Boyatzis, *Transforming Qualitative Information: Thematic Analysis and Code Development* (San Francisco, CA, 1988).

composers, but it does provide a foundation for identifying variations on this process or other prototypes.

Non-musical Models that Dictate Form

To illustrate key characteristics of this prototype, composers' general descriptions of how they developed their initial ideas or creative 'spark' are integrated with a more specific investigation of the process undertaken in writing their music. Gandolfi's piece, *Impressions from The Garden of Cosmic Speculation*, is an orchestral piece inspired by a sprawling garden designed by Scottish architect and critic, Charles Jencks. The garden merges fundamental principles of modern physics (such as quantum mechanics, super-string theory and complexity theory) with nature. The landscape of Jencks's garden 'bring[s] out the basic elements of nature that recent science has found to underlie the cosmos'.[31] The piece has four parts: 'Introduction: Zeroroom', 'Soliton Waves', 'Interlude: The Snail and the Poetics of Going Slow' and 'The Nonsense'. Gandolfi's piece is tied together at a conceptual level by the overarching physics and architectural principles of the garden, where each part of the garden is designed with a distinct character and aesthetic.

Like Gandolfi, Ran developed the main idea for her piece through extra-musical means. Ran describes how she was in New York City when she came across a book of poetry by Nelly Sachs[32] – the basis for *O The Chimneys*. Sachs's writing is concerned with the Holocaust, a subject about which Ran says she had always known she would write music. The first poem that Ran encountered in the book happened to be the poem, 'A dead child speaks', which became the first poem of *O The Chimneys*. In interview, Ran says she was deeply moved by the poetry and spent a large amount of time reading every poem in the book, deciding which ones she would use for her piece and how to shape them into a larger totality: 'That was the first really important decision in the case of this piece'. On the whole, Ran indicates that she did adhere to the architectural plan that she had intended for the piece, with each movement of the piece corresponding to a different poem from Sachs's collection: 'A dead child speaks', 'Already embraced by the arms of heavenly solace', 'Fleeing', 'Someone comes' and 'Hell is naked' (from *Glowing Enigmas II*). In a similar way to the compartmentalisation that Gandolfi observed in Jencks's garden, Ran's poems also provide a series of demarcations. All of Sachs's poems are concerned with the Holocaust, but each one provides a different perspective on this horrific event. For example, the first and second poems deal with similar subject matter, but told from the point of view of child and mother, respectively. In her interview Ran articulates that she knew it was going to be a

---

[31]   Charles Jencks, *The Garden of Cosmic Speculation* (London, 2003).

[32]   Nelly Sachs, *O the Chimneys; Selected Poems, Including the Verse Play, Eli*, transl. from the German by Michael Hamburger et al. (New York, 1967).

relatively large-scale piece that was going to be profoundly tragic and dark, but she also felt that it needed to have a measure of contrast, the unrelenting intensity of the subject matter notwithstanding.

The succession and ordering of the pieces was also very important to Ran as she wrote. The pairing of the first and second poems Ran thinks of as a sort of single unit, where the first flows directly into the second. She views this unit as 'the one heavy pillar point of the piece'. Ran contrasts the beginning and end anchor points with the two middle poems with a juxtaposition of two moods. She insists that the poems conjured powerful images conveyed in her music with a distinct 'architecture'.

Similar to Gandolfi, Ueno's conceptualisation of his piece, *Kaze-no-Oka*, stemmed from the domain of architecture. When commissioned to write it, Ueno offered that the task was very difficult since it was expected to be both a commemorative memorial piece in honour of the renowned Japanese composer, Toru Takemitsu, and a lively, upbeat concert opener. Ueno says that, prior to the composition, he had come across a structure of the architect, Maki, who had built a beautiful complex of three buildings meant to serve as a crematorium. The character of these buildings was 'totally in sync with the memorial character [of the piece]'. Embodied in the structures, says Ueno, was an irresolvable tension between multiplicities: 'The buildings can be seen as separate as well as belonging to the same complex; they are individual and together at the same time'. These buildings were situated on ancient burial mounds, and the name of the complex, Kaze-no-Oka, resonated poetically with the incorporation of the Japanese instruments biwa and shakuhachi, as well as the juxtaposition of these ancient Japanese instruments with the new – the 'modern' orchestra.

Unlike Gandolfi and Ran's pieces, Ueno's is not separated into movements. Instead, the overarching ideas encapsulated in the three buildings influenced the overall structure of his piece. Ueno points out that, while each building had a different structure, the whole musical piece still had to work as a unit. The structure of the buildings, says Ueno, maps out onto the piece (except for the cadenza); Ueno decided to make the cadenza a piece complete in itself, so that it could be extracted as a separate work for chamber orchestra. Much as he described the crematorium buildings, Ueno describes the piece as a singular form, which at the same time embodies a multiplicity. While the piece was a memorial, he still had to begin it 'with a character that foreshadowed the energy to come'.

How Associations Influence the Micro-musical Landscape

After determining the overall structure of their work, the composers' associations from the main content domain then informed the more specific elements of a given movement, such as chord choice, rhythmic figures and instrumentation. While the structure of *Impressions from the The Garden of Cosmic Speculation* is influenced by the principles and physical layout of the garden, Gandolfi says that each movement is distinct and has a unique colour. 'The Zeroroom', the title of the formal entranceway to the garden, provided inspiration for the first movement. Of the structure of 'The Zeroroom', Gandolfi describes a 'fanciful, surreal cloakroom flanked by an orderly procession of tennis racquets that appear to be traveling through the wall in a "quantum dance," and large photographs that progress from our place in the universe, galaxy, solar system, planet, to the precise position of the garden in the north of Scotland'. Gandolfi's music in 'The Zeroroom' mirrors the progression from the macro view of space to the myopic view of the yew tree in the garden. Gandolfi says he represents the cosmic vision of space in the opening with a delicate chord played by just the strings, which 'represents this kind of mystery'. As the piece progresses, the music becomes more present – with syncopated percussion and distinct repetition and more marked notes in the brass. The instruments continue to layer until they are undeniably insistent.

The second movement, 'Soliton Waves', is a depiction of soliton waves (waves that interact with other waves, pass through them, and then exit with no memory of the passage), which are omnipresent in the garden, the fence-work, the stonework and the shapes of the earth. Gandolfi decided to represent these waves in the piece through the staging of the strings, so that the melody is passed from the low to high strings and the choice notes of the basic chords change minimally as they are passed through the strings while the basic chords stay constant.

The following movement, 'Interlude: The Snail and the Poetics of Going Slow', refers to a mound of green grass that does a spiral turn in the earth of Jenck's garden. Gandolfi described the movement as going very slowly and it 'kind of turns – just like the snail mound'. The beginning mirrors his own feelings towards the piece, as he was trying to feel his way into the piece and 'respond to this big, pyramid-like object', hopefully creating a more emotional connection to it. His unfamiliarity is represented by the strings, which figuratively grunt at each other at the piece's outset, but develop a more harmonious dialogue as the piece progresses. The discordance at the beginning is achieved through a metaphorical dialogue between the families of strings.

The final movement, 'The Nonsense', Gandolfi says, started as 'one of these out-of-the-ether kind of ideas' – a pure gut response to the Nonsense building in the garden. The garden's Nonsense building was designed as an architectural model by James Stirling at the Neue Staatsgalerie in Stuttgart. Gandolfi suggests that he connected immediately with the building as a postmodern/modernist building structure in which there are 'beams that block your view at the top of the stairs and a stairway that leads nowhere'. In the same way that Gandolfi perceived that it was exciting for Stirling to construct 'The Nonsense', he wanted his movement to be energetic. The first thing that struck him about the music was that there was 'something kinda goofy about it … and fun'.

Similar to the pattern arising with Gandolfi's work, where the architectural structure of Jenck's garden informed at both a macro and micro level, Ran indicates that all of her musical choices in *O The Chimneys* were natural outgrowths of the topic of the Holocaust. In the first poem by Sachs, 'A dead child speaks',

Ran points out that she wanted to preserve the experience she had when she first read the poem; her choice to encapsulate forward momentum in this movement is brought to being in large part through the rush of the spoken voice of the mezzo soprano, accompanied by a cymbal following an intense instrumental opening of the ensemble of five instruments and the voice that subsequently disintegrates into shriek. The second movement, based on Sachs's poem, 'Already embraced by the arm of heavenly solace', is 'the same horrible tale [of the first poem] told from the point of view of the mother', says Ran, which is why she envisioned the first and second together as an anchor for the piece. For the third poem, the first of the inner two movements, Ran used 'a preponderance of lower sounds', achieved in this case with the combination of piano, bass clarinet, cello and timpani: 'those very same instruments in other music, in other music of mine, can be screaming out loud too, so the intimacy really is a matter of using them in a particular way'. Ran achieves much of the intensity and horror of the Holocaust through stark contrasts that range from haunting soft whispers to the shrillest, piercing highs.

Of the last movement of the piece, which is based on Sachs's poem, 'Hell is naked' (from *Glowing Enigmas II*), Ran exclaims, 'All hell breaks loose! ... a powerful, powerful poem'. Everything that was held back in the third and fourth poems is now realised in this last poem, says Ran. When she finished scoring this movement, she says she realised that it required a dynamic intensity extrapolating beyond the sound that the instruments could produce. In order to realise the more powerful sound that she now heard even after the last notes of the piece, Ran added recorded tape at the end to both literally and figuratively extend beyond the sound that the instruments could produce.

In a manner reminiscent of Ran and Gandolfi, many of the smaller elements that Ueno describes in *Kaze-no-Oka* centre on associations with the architectural burial grounds on which the piece is based, conveyed in large part through instrumentation. *Kaze-no-Oka* translates into, 'Wind over the hill'. Ueno wanted to show the contrast between the wind and the hill (or the earth) by emphasising the juxtaposition of the airy woodwinds and the earthy strings. He felt that this stark contrast efficiently encapsulated many of the contradictory factors that he had to 'solve' in the piece. Ueno felt that it was also important to convey the notion of loss through the dramaturgy. He says:

> My experience has been that when you lose someone, you go through different stages of disbelief. One of those stages is that you are waiting for that person to come back. Eventually, by letting go, it is possible to arrive at a beatific transcendence. Then you realize that as long as there is a memory, then that person ... those sounds ... are always with you.

Loss, in one sense, is conveyed through the piece's structure, says Ueno. The orchestra bows out before the cadenza and does not re-enter as one might expect. Ueno explains that a western audience is used to hearing a recapitulation, or the re-entry of the theme. While he knew that most people's references were concerti by western composers such as Beethoven and Mozart – those pieces that 'are always referencing the past' – he wanted the structure of his piece to 'mirror the psychological effect ... the temporality of loss'. Thus, Ueno says, 'At a certain point they [the orchestra] can't come back'; instead, the audience hears scratch tones, pizzicatos, Bartók pizzicatos (the plucking of the strings so hard that they hit the fingerboard), the biwa scrapings and the breath of the shakuhachi.

While a set of architectural buildings was of great inspiration to Ueno, he states that his greatest extra-musical influence is the playwright, Samuel Beckett, whose work relates to concepts of musical structure and temporality. Ueno references the play, *Catastrophe*, in which the main character stays virtually silent with a downward gaze until the very end of the play, when he finally looks up. Ueno compares the end of *Kaze-no-Oka* with the main character's actions in *Catastrophe*: here is one breath (of silence) in the piece, which is supposed to signify a return of sorts, as with Beckett's character. Selecting to highlight the absence of sound (or a breath of silence), as opposed to the grand re-entry of the theme, allows Ueno to pay homage to Japanese culture and the strong value it places on silence. The piece in fact ends with the quote, 'Keep Silence' from Takemitsu's piece, *November Steps*; it acts as an homage to Takemitsu (representing one of Takemitsu's most important musical understandings, and the silence since his passing).

What to Make of these Extra-musical Influences?

This chapter centres on a group of three composers who, in the act of musical composition, draw heavily from extra-musical ideas and concepts to dictate the form of their pieces. Gandolfi draws on Jencks's garden, relating locations in the garden to movements of the piece. Ran creates different movements of her piece from different poems on the same Holocaust theme, and Ueno translates the characteristics in different buildings of the memorial onto different parts of his piece. The frames in these extra-musical domains are often characterised by both an element of compartmentalisation and a sense of cohesion. For the smaller-scale aspects of the music (for example, instrumentation, rhythms, pitch choices), these composers drew on associations from the same extra-musical domain that informed the work's overall structure.

A crucial next step in more fully understanding what factors influence the composition process would be to identify other prototypical processes besides the one outlined in this chapter. Armed with information about these prototypical processes, one might better: (1) evaluate and compare existing theories of the creative process; (2) identify prototypical processes within the composition domain that could inform composers' processes; and (3) experiment with how these processes could inform musical pedagogy.

How might the prototype described in this chapter increase knowledge about the creative process more generally, though? For one, what might be needed to spur the creative process for some people is a powerful stimulus from outside of the 'home' domain in which a creator is working. For Gandolfi, the extra-musical content comprised the principles of physics conceptualised in a formal garden landscape. For Ran it was poetry inspired by the Holocaust. For Ueno it was a set of memorial structures. As with these three composers, the outside-domain content might already hold significant meaning for the creator. Thus there may be benefits for a creator who draws on content that is removed from the home domain. For one, a creator might feel freer to take risks if he or she were not directed into a known stereotypical musical pathway. In addition, the inspirational extra-musical framework that a creator looks for might also be non-musically structured, each with a different characteristic or character, such as was the case with the three composers discussed here. Finally, when establishing these frameworks, or starting-off points, it could be useful to actively draw on the concept of metaphor and lateral thinking, the rearrangement of information that is already available into new configurations.

And how might the findings have a bearing on existing models of the creative process? Let us avoid the discussion of whether these models click into place at the outset, middle or end of the process. Several key models of the creative process describe a phase of rumination or pre-work and also point to a stage of insight. The nature of this insight is often described as an increase of momentum that gives birth to new ideas. If the experiences of the three composers in this chapter represent some commentary upon the creative trajectory or direction of an unfolding musical composition, then it is important to consider that perhaps the most significant rumination or insight has been made *before* the composer actively works on their piece. It would be the formation of schema over time before the actual process of composition, then, that would be the key to insight. The transformational quality, in this case, would be the creator's ability to make connections between what has come before and what could be. In contrast to the current characterisation of the illumination stage, the work at this stage might actually be the sifting through existing extra-musical influences – albeit, unconsciously – and determining which ones provide the most useful frameworks for a new creation.

References

Babbitt, Milton, 'A life of learning'. Charles Homer Haskins Lecture from the American Council of Learned Societies (ACLS) (Washington, DC, 24 April 1991).

Barrett, Margaret, 'Creative collaboration: An eminence study of teaching and learning in music composition', *Psychology of Music*, 34 (2006), 195–218.

Beardsley, Monroe C., 'On the creation of art', *The Journal of Aesthetics and Art Criticism*, 23 (1965), 291–304.

Boyatzis, Richard E., *Transforming Qualitative Information: Thematic Analysis and Code Development* (San Francisco, CA: Sage, 1988).

Calvino, Italo, *Six Memos for the Next Millennium* (Cambridge, MA: Harvard University Press, 1988).

Cawelti, Scott, Allen Rappaport and Bill Wood. 'Modeling artistic creativity: An empirical study', *Journal of Creative Behavior*, 2(26) (1992), 83–94.

Collins, David, 'A synthesis model of thinking in music composition', *Psychology of Music*, 32/2 (2003), 193–216.

Copland, Aaron, Richard Kostelanetz and Steven Silverstein, *Aaron Copland: A Reader: Selected Writings 1923–1972* (New York: Routledge, 2004).

Csikszentmihalyi, Mihaly, *Creativity: Flow and the Psychology of Discovery and Invention* (New York: Harper Perennial, 1996).

Csikszentmihalyi, Mihaly and Jacob W. Getzels, 'Discovery-oriented behavior and the originality of creative products: A study with artists', *Journal of Personality and Social Psychology*, 19/1 (1971), 47–52.

De Bono, Edward, *Lateral Thinking* (New York: Harper & Row, 1970).

Dickinson, Peter (ed.), *Copland Connotations: Studies and Interviews* (Woodbridge: Boydell Press, 2002).

Duchesneau, Louise, *The Voice of the Muse: A Study of the Role of Inspiration in Musical Composition* (New York: Peter Lang, 1986).

Foss, Lukas with Leon Kirchner, 'Learning from performers', lecture series at Harvard University's Kirkland House (Cambridge, MA, 1985).

Galenson, David W., 'The two life cycles of human creativity', National Bureau of Economic Research Report (2003), Research summary, http://www.nber.org/reporter/fall03/ galenson.html.

Gandolfi, Michael, *Impressions from the Garden of Cosmic Speculation* (Cambridge: M51 Music, 2004).

Gardner, Howard, *Art, Mind, and Brain* (New York: Basic Books, 1982).

Gardner, Howard, *Creating Minds* (New York: Basic Books, 1993).

Ghiselin, Brewster, *The Creative Process: A Symposium*, 2nd edn (Berkeley, CA: University of California Press, 1980).

Gruber, Howard E. and Sara N. Davis, 'Inching our way up Mount Olympus: The evolving-systems approach to creative thinking'. In: R.J. Sternberg (ed.), *The Nature of Creativity* (New York: Cambridge University Press, 1988), 243–69.

Jencks, Charles, *The Garden of Cosmic Speculation* (London: Frances Lincoln, 2003).

Maxwell, Joseph A., *Qualitative Research Design: An Interactive Approach*, 2nd edn (Thousand Oaks, CA: Sage, 2005).

Ortony, Andrew, *Metaphor and Thought* (Cambridge: Cambridge University Press, 1979).

Patrick, Catherine, 'Creative thought in artists', *Journal of Psychology: Interdisciplinary and Applied*, 4 (1937), 35–73.

Perkins, David, *The Mind's Best Work* (Cambridge, MA: Harvard University Press, 1981).

Ran, Shulamit, *O the Chimneys* (New York: C. Fischer, 1973).

Sachs, Nelly, *O the Chimneys; Selected Poems, Including the Verse Play, Eli*, transl. from the German by Michael Hamburger et al. (New York: Farrar, Straus and Giroux, 1967).

Schoenberg, Arnold, 'Opinion or insight?' In: L. Stein (ed.), *Style and Idea* (Berkeley, CA: University of California Press, 1975), 258–64.

Seidman, Irving, *Interviewing as Qualitative Research*, 2nd edn (New York: Teachers College Press, 1988).

Simonton, Dean Keith, 'Creativity as a constrained stochastic process'. In: R.J. Sternberg, E.L. Grigorenko and J.L. Singer (eds), *Creativity: From Potential To realization* (Washington, DC: American Psychological Association, 2004), 83–101.

Strauss, Anselm L. and Juliet M. Corbin, *Basics of Qualitative Research* (Newbury Park, CA: Sage, 1990).

Ueno, Ken, *Kaze-no-Oka* (Cambridge: New Jack Modernism Music, 2005).

Wallas, G., *The Art of Thought* (London: Watts, 1926).

Audio Recordings

Gandolfi, Michael, *Design School* [CD] (Cambridge: M51 Music, 1995).

Gandolfi, Michael, *Impressions from the Garden of Cosmic Speculation* [CD] (Cambridge: M51 Music, 2006).

Ran, Shulamit, *O The Chimneys* [CD] 20th Century Voices in America (Englewood Cliffs, NJ: Vox Box, 1995).

Ueno, Ken, *Kaze-no-Oka* [CD] (Cambridge: New Jack Modernism Music, 2005).

Interviews

Gandolfi, Michael, 31 May 2006. Cambridge, MA.

Ueno, Ken, 26 June 2006. Cambridge, MA.

Ran, Shulamit, 5 June 2006. Chicago, IL.

Chapter 8

Improvisation as Real-time Composition

Simon Rose and Raymond MacDonald

Introduction

This chapter explores the process of improvisation in music, which we suggest represents real-time composition. Improvisation is found throughout different cultures and genres and, as Derek Bailey contends, 'Improvisation enjoys the curious distinction of being the most widely practiced of all musical activities and the least acknowledged and understood'.[1] As a rapidly expanding area of research, improvisation is attracting interest in diverse areas such as law, psychology, theatre, dance, business studies, new technology and education. As our understanding of improvisation in music develops there is a need to reassess how improvisation aligns with notions of musical creativity.

Part 1 of this chapter, 'The Development of Real-time Composition', explores the practice of improvisation in music, the background to real-time composition, and hegemonic power structures and musical improvisation. In Part 2, themes of improvisation are explored through original research based on interviews with ten highly experienced improvisers.[2] The chapter's exploration of improvisation as real-time composition acknowledges how understanding of composition and improvisation practice is simultaneously embedded in and constructed through education.

Part 1 – The Development of Real-time Composition

The Practice of Improvisation in Music

While there is no universally agreed definition of improvisation, most writers highlight the real-time development of musical ideas in performance and its ubiquitous presence within all forms of music-making.[3] The terms that have been coined which relate to such practice are wide and varied: free jazz, experimental

---

[1]   Derek Bailey, *Improvisation: Its Nature and Practice in Music* (London, 1992), ix.

[2]   Simon Rose, 'Free improvisation phenomenon: A site of developing knowledge', unpublished PhD thesis (Glasgow, 2011).

[3]   Bailey, *Improvisation*. MacDonald, Wilson and Miell (Glasgow 2011 forthcoming). B. Nettl and M. Russel (eds,) *In the Course of Performance* (Chicago, IL, 1998).

music, spontaneous music, chance, conduction, sound painting, jazz, jamming, non-idiomatic, open form improvisation, and others. Additionally there are many sub-genres within which some music is identified, such as reductionism, noise, electronic, onkyo, lower case, and so on. Most of these terms are relatively recent and, although we can delineate between them, they all rely upon the centrality of new musical material being generated in performance. Although there has been an exponential development of interest in improvisation, together with recent terms by which it is known, it is equally important to note that improvisation is an ancient musical practice; as Braxton[4] suggests, improvisatory music has always been around, it just has not been documented. Thinking of improvisation as solely 'jazz' can be grossly misleading. A 'stylised' form of jazz has become institutionally colonised and accepted as improvisation, and as a result the potential of improvisatory practice has become foreshortened for education. Accepted teaching practice of what has become widely understood as 'jazz' may obfuscate the much broader potential of improvisation. Specifically, jazz education traditionally focuses upon a narrow range of improvisational activities and musical conventions, however, if improvisation is viewed as a process rather than a genre, then significantly more musical practices, normally considered outside mainstream jazz, may be included. While it is only relatively recently that the act of improvisation has become thought of as a separate activity in music-making in western music, Bailey suggests[5] that improvisation has no need of making a case for itself – it remains an ever-present human activity.

In spite of greater understanding of the practice of improvisation, support for such improvisational activity within arts and education (from primary through to higher education) tends to be lacking and in the following two sections we explore the underlying reasons contributing to such continued marginalisation. In discussions of improvisation and composition, typically one is set against the other, creating an impression that the relationship between the two things is oppositional. As historical evidence for the mutual benefits of these currently separated activities abounds, such a separation seems to be acculturated rather than pragmatic. In the interviews (Part 2) improvisers make various references to their role as composers:

> I'm interested in being the performer as well as, if you like, the composer. And I do consider myself to be a composer it's just that most of my compositions are realised through comparatively spontaneous performance. (RJ, p. 6, l. 37)

Composition often infers *written* composition, and the presumption that the experience of sound can be faithfully and best represented by dots and lines on paper is left largely unchallenged. It is the tradition of written composition that tends to be regarded as the bedrock of 'serious music'. However, improvisation

---

[4]   Anthony Braxton, *Triaxium Writings* (Lebanon, NH, 1985).

[5]   Bailey, *Improvisation.*

and recording musical ideas by different means (for example, through the ever increasing variety of technological means) both contribute to the creative process of composition. It is the respective cultural connotations suggested by composition and improvisation that are often strongly evoked within this oppositional discourse. In the West, written composition is often aligned with 'high art' sensibilities and aspirations, and part of the defining of such an identity includes a distancing from improvisation. Paradoxically, classical music's estrangement from improvisation is relatively new, in terms of that music's history, and many of the most highly esteemed classical composers music were celebrated for their skill in improvisation.

A Background to Real-time Composition: Developments in Improvisation

There was a revolution in thinking about music, in some quarters, during the 1960s and 1970s, which coalesced around the practice that has become known as improvisation, or free improvisation. Musical activity overtly identified as improvisation (with some public profile) developed at that time simultaneously, in pockets, in parts of the developed world (for example, within Berlin, Amsterdam, London, Chicago, New York, San Francisco and Tokyo), although, as already mentioned, improvisation has always been present across musical cultures. An important swathe of activity occurred in the UK and the writings of notable musicians Derek Bailey, John Stevens and Cornelius Cardew stand out as important in revealing different aspects of these musical developments. Bailey's *Improvisation: its Nature and Practice in Music* (1992) surveys improvisation from a personal, musician's perspective. Bailey sets out to unpack the term and the activity of improvisation in an attempt at redefinition. Introducing the notions of idiomatic and non-idiomatic improvisation, in spite of the semantic shortcomings, has contributed greatly to the awareness of improvisation as a freestanding musical activity (or non-idiomatic).

An often cited text for teaching in relation to free improvisation, particularly for newcomers, is *Search and Reflect*. Here drummer John Stevens[6] collated exercises developed during his involvement with Community Music, London in the 1970s and 1980s. Stevens's influence upon the practice of free improvisation, including many of its major figures, is considerable.

Cornelius Cardew's influence is most noticeable through work with the group AMM (what these initials stands for remains a secret). AMM developed their 'laminal' improvisational approach to music-making, establishing a strong, lasting group identity through improvisation. Comparable contemporaries were the Italian Gruppo Di Improvvisazione Nuova Consonanza. Cardew's influence grew from work in composition and collaboration with Stockhausen. His political and philosophical commitments were realised in such work as the graphic score 'Treatise' (1963–1967), through which he radically realigned

---

6   John Stevens, *Search and Reflect* (London, 1985).

the composer/performer/improviser relationship. Such a graphic score can be viewed as an important stage in development, towards a fuller understanding of improvisation's potential in forming real-time composition: a turn from dependency upon the written score towards realisation of human potential for creating real-time composition by means of improvisation. Between the composer's notation and a shift towards the performer composing at the point of performance, through improvisation, 'Treatise' becomes a clear illustration of the theme of real-time composition. The performer is required to make decisions about every musical aspect of the performance, while the graphic shapes invite an openly subjective interpretation. There is no indication of the number of performers, instrumentation, and so on, and the piece was written and presented as free standing, without notes of guidance or instructions (a text reflecting on the piece was published some years later). While we identify Cardew as the composer, Treatise's realisation is, in practice, dealing explicitly with improvisation. Cardew's intention was very precisely aimed at drawing upon the responses of individuals and groups of musicians. The absence of explicit guidance regarding the musical content correlates directly to the notion of real-time composition through improvisation.

As mentioned previously, the processes of improvisation are broad and becoming increasingly acknowledged across human activity. While the focus of this chapter is with improvisation as real-time composition, we also acknowledge how improvisation extends across different spheres of human activity, in the process problematising academic disciplines;[7] as such it may be unhelpful to overly prescribe the activity of improvising. The extent of diversification in improvisation is indicated, to some extent, by the research range of Improvisation as Cultural and Social Practice (Canada), an ongoing project since 2004, through the universities of Guelph, British Columbia and McGill, drawing upon improvisation in music as a model while extending its research in improvisation across a number of fields. Research areas cover: improvisation, gender and the body; improvisation, law and justice; improvisation and pedagogy; improvisation and social aesthetics; improvisation and social policy; improvisation text and media; improvisation and transcultural understanding. Online publications reflecting these research areas include: George E. Lewis, Keith Sawyer, Sherry Tucker, Deborah Wong, Graham Lock, Pauline Oliveros, Ursel Schlicht and Roger Dean.[8]

The reasons why improvisation is gaining widespread attention at the present time are in themselves complex. 'Models' of improvisation are attracting interest across disciplines: psychology and business systems, information technology, music

---

[7]   Barry J. Kenny and Martin Gellrich, *The Science and Psychology of Music Performance: Creative Strategies for Teaching and Learning* (Oxford, 2002).

[8]   Online publication of www.improvcommunity.ca/about/research includes George E. Lewis (2008), Robert K Sawyer (2008), Sherry Tucker (2008), Deborah Wong (2006), Graham Lock (2008), Pauline Oliveros (2004), Ursel Schlicht (2008) and Roger Dean (2006).

therapy, as well as the more expected areas such as drama, dance and music.[9] At a broader level there seems to be a strong, multi-dimensional connection between the manner in which emergent technology is influencing our understanding of communication and relationships, and increased awareness of the utility of less fixed systems for effectively being in the world. New technologies encourage us to re-evaluate modes of functioning. The challenge to accepted, hierarchical models within media posed by new technology leads to an associated drift involving a more democratised engagement. In other words, new technology has encouraged us towards greater participation – rather than waiting to be told what to do, new technology creates the opportunity to act of our own volition, functioning with our own agendas and scripts in making sense of the plethora of information choices we now find available, with a new emphasis upon participation. While improvisation as real-time composition is, on the one hand, an ancient practice, contemporary real-time composition also reflects current themes of increased participation and an attendant diminished dependence upon formalised social structures.

Improvisation and Hegemonic Power Structures

As music does not exist in a socio-political vacuum, engagement with improvisation as real-time composition brings with it awareness of how improvisation in music functions within hegemonic power structures. The notion of democratised real-time composition, music created through participation, not reliant upon the wishes expressed in a written composition, may be a challenge to conventions associated with 'the composer' and the cultural capital associated with that term, it may also challenge the cultural dependency upon the notion of 'the score'. Improvisation may also form a challenge to the idea of ownership of music within the market, in terms of the need to identify the 'writer' within real-time composition practice. Music reflects society's political as well as cultural orientation and Attali[10] describes music importantly as a 'herald' of what occurs as societies develop. While comparisons between orchestral hierarchical structures and hegemonic power structures elsewhere, across society's institutions (such as army, education and health service), are easy to point out, and figures and movements in popular music can be readily cited as heralding, or reflecting, change (for example, Bob Dylan, Bob Marley, John Lennon and John Lydon), improvisation's relationship to politics is both profound and complex. Improvisation as a means of expression in contexts 'other' than where mainstream ideas and norms flourish forms strong connections to theories of 'subjugated knowledge', in other words understanding

---

[9] Sawyer, www.improvcommunity.ca/about/research. M.C. Boudrieu and David Robey, *Organization Science*, 16/1 (2005), 3–18. Claudio Ciborra, 'Improvisation and information technology in organizations', *ICIS 1996 Proceedings*, paper 26 (1996), http://aisel.aisnet.org/icis1996/26. Tony Wigram, *Improvisation: Methods and Techniques for Music Therapy Clinicians, Educators and Students* (London, 2007).

[10] Jacques Attali, *Noise: The Political Economy of Music* (Minneapolis, MN, 1985).

that abounds and at the same time is not recognised as part of 'legitimate' knowledge. At the same time the fluidity of improvisation, or 'the agility of the term' (SG), is enabling, lending itself to the need for human expression. Not dependent upon form, improvisation is able to create form, through, for example, intercultural activity.[11] As John Littweiler[12] suggests, the freedom in *free* jazz is the freedom to create form. The socio-political dynamics of the relationship between improvisation and composition are explored in George E. Lewis's *Improvised Music after 1950: Afrological and Eurological Perspectives* (1996):

> the AACM's revision of the relationship between composition and improvisation lies on an unstable fault line between the new black music and the new white music.[13]

The constructed cultural demarcation between improvisation and composition is discussed through accounts of Charlie Parker and John Cage as Lewis explores the manner in which the social and institutional positioning of improvisation and composition perpetuates inequality and prejudice. As Lewis puts it: 'New white music' has been historically assigned as 'serious', 'art', with 'new black music' situated as 'jazz'. This is echoed by Anthony Braxton's[14] reflections upon negative criticism of his citing European influences, such as Stockhausen, in his music, while it remains unquestioned that white musicians may be, for example, influenced by John Coltrane.

The 40-year history of Chicago's Association for the Advancement of Creative Musicians (AACM, with the motto 'great black music') provides an exemplar of commitment to collective, creative music practice. George E. Lewis[15] extensively documents this history of self-assertion in the face of oppression, as Muhal Richard Abrams explains:

> we intend to take over our own destinies, to be our own agents, to play our own music.

Improvisation's, or real-time composition's, capability and significant history of representing the 'other' voice, made most clear through the Afro-American music of the twentieth century, has contributed to its re-emergence as non-academic, remaining un-reliant, as it is, upon the academic preoccupation with and preference

---

[11]   Jason Stanyeck, 'Diasporic improvisation and the articulation of intercultural music', unpublished PhD dissertation (San Diego, CA, 2004).

[12]   John Litweiler, *Ornette Coleman: A Harmolodic Life* (New York, 1992).

[13]   George E. Lewis, 'Improvised music after 1950: Afrological and Eurological perspectives', *Black Music Research Journal*, 16/1 (1996), 91–122.

[14]   Graham Lock, *Forces in Motion* (New York, 1988), 119.

[15]   George E. Lewis, *A Power Stronger Than Itself: The AACM and American Experimental Music* (Chicago, 2008).

for text (texocentrism). As well as the all but forgotten forms of improvisation found in classical music, the practice of real-time composition can be found throughout different cultures: within court music, folk music, experimental music, rock music, jazz, old music and new music, as well as in the growing area of music specifically delineated as improvised music or free improvisation, in which musicians commit to a relatively open form of not predetermined musical performance.

In summary, in Part 1 we have discussed the practice of improvisation and its relationship with real-time composition. We have specifically outlined some developments in improvisational practice and have also discussed hegemonic power structures and improvisation. In the following section we further explore these issues by presenting some results of an interview study with eminent improvisers.

Part 2 – Describing the Process of Real-time Composition: Themes of Improvisation

To better understand what constitutes real-time composition, we have explored the development of improvisation in Part 1. Part 2 describes the process of real-time composition through analysis of interviews with experienced practitioners who utilise improvisation centrally in their work in music. Ten highly experienced improvisers in music, from Europe and North America, took part in semi-structured interviews and were asked the overarching question: what is improvisation for you? In this qualitative study, the primary interest was in where the interviewee's response would take the interview, while a series of supporting questions and prompts were also on hand. Agreed anonymity was the norm for the interviews. Interpretive Phenomenological Analysis[16] (IPA) was employed for its idiographic character, seeking depth in the interview process with emphasis upon the particular individual perspectives. Using a double hermeneutic involved a continuing process of going forwards and backwards between transcripts and analysis, through which superordinate themes were developed. The selected themes of improvisation are arranged as follows: the improviser as composer; embodied knowledge including kinaesthetic learning, listening, physical performance and improvisation; the relationship of improvisation to language; the development of learning in real-time composition. Within these selected themes, 'The Improviser as Composer' explores the ways in which improvisers regard their practice as composition. The encapsulating theme of 'Embodied Knowledge' explores the interviewees' reflections on the act of improvisation and their experiences of how improvisation in music becomes realised. The 'embodied knowledge' theme extends to explore listening, where the particular importance of listening for improvisation/real-time composition is discussed, and physical performance, where the nuanced notion

---

[16]   J.A. Smith, P. Flowers and M. Larkin, *Interpretive Phenomenological Analysis Theory, Method and Research* (London, 2009).

of the body in performance is explored. In 'The Relationship of Improvisation to Language', the proximity of the act of improvising in music to talk and our ability to explain improvising in music through words is discussed. 'The Development of Learning in Real-time Composition' discusses the inter-subjective nature of improvising in real-time composition and the development of learning through improvisation; we also discuss kinaesthetic learning as well as the creative, inclusive social potential of improvisation.

The following initials have been used to represent the ten interviewees and maintain anonymity: KM, RJ, RT, NJ, SG, LR, LM, UP, GB, NA.

The Improviser as Composer

Across the ten interviews with highly experienced improvisers, interviewees made reference to themselves as composers and the practice of improvisation as composition.

> They're effectively three mutual composers going out and creating their music which is a continually evolving body of music through the practice of improvisation. (RJ, p. 4, l. 1, on The Schlippenbach Trio – Alexander von Schlippenback, Paul Lovens, Evan Parker)

The idea of 'mutual composers' becomes important: improvisation is a challenge to the split between performer and composer roles, as separated activities, the fusing of these roles results in 'mutual composers', embodied in the act of improvisation. A characteristic of such real-time composition is that it is a continually 'evolving' music. The way in which individuals contribute their particular voice and musical choices, giving rise to the relationships within the group, and the way in which the music collectively develops at different times, is appropriately described as 'evolving'.

> There's often the claim with composers that we, and I include myself in that. (SG, p. 15, l. 30)

Interviewees' descriptions of themselves as composers were nuanced. Some referred to the act of improvisation as composition – improvising music being the same as real-time composition. The musical practice of others encompassed careers in which they were known, for example, for writing scores, while equally they pursued careers as improvisers. Between the open form of free improvisation and the written score that uses traditional notation, there were many variations of the predetermined score and non-predetermined music: some examples of this being 'Conduction' (Morris), instruction pieces (Stockhausen), game pieces (Zorn), and a range of graphic scores (Guy, Cardew, Braxton, Cage, Brown, Crumb and Feldman). In addition, pieces by composers such as John Coltrane, Charlie

Parker and Thelonious Monk provide vehicles for improvised compositions that retain difference at each performance.

Discussing particular contemporary variations on improvisation RJ reflects:

> they're actually making music in a way which is more akin to a composed process ... and they're aiming for a particular kind of music and they're filling in the details through improvisation. (RJ, p. 2, l. 15)

There is clearly a circularity within the composition/improvisation process. Musicians often refer to 'finding things' while improvising; these musical ideas then contribute to personal musical 'vocabulary', also described as 'ingredients' (RJ) or a 'grab-bag of ideas' (GB) and in turn become options in the compositional choices made during future improvisations. This also reiterates the evolving character of real-time composition.

> it's a very important thread throughout and I've always improvised. When I was composing music with conventional notation, if I got stuck I could improvise. So my composition teacher, Robert Erickson encouraged me to improvise and we were all encouraged by Robert Erickson to improvise. (SP, p. 1, l. 7)

In this description improvisation is employed as a specific device to aid the development of written composition within the bigger picture of improvisation. One interviewee fore-grounded a unified approach to composition and improvisation within their particular understanding:

> I think that I study composition and improvisation as a parallel because what I'm striving for is to be able to create spontaneous composition. And I think that this helps me know how composition works and then you can apply these principles during an improvisation ... if you look around at the great composers, I mean they all improvised. So I just feel it's important, for me, to study music as a whole. (LR, p. 1, l. 6)

While for LR 'spontaneous composition' is a goal, improvisation and composition are studied 'in parallel', suggesting equality and at the same time some distance.

Embodied Knowledge

The theme of embodied knowledge emerged in the interviews as being of particular significance for improvisation. The way in which musicians involve themselves in the act of creating real-time composition in the process of performance was understood as making clear connections to the concept of embodied knowledge. Interviewees cited the body and physical aspects of performance/composition of music in real time as important in a variety of ways.

The 'embodied knowledge' theme includes discussion of listening and physical performance and improvisation.

> The body knows what to do ... this is a very important aspect to improvisation ... allowing the body to lead. (UP, p. 5, l. 1)

> ... really essential, it's really important. It's what is. If you talk about being, it's right in there and having awareness upfront. (UP, p. 6, l. 10)

UP's 'the body knows' becomes a significant theme for interpreting improvisation. The 'body knows' and 'allowing the body to lead' are common precepts in dance and drama as well as elsewhere in physically located expressive arts. Why embodied knowledge is viewed particularly as a 'very important aspect for improvisation' in music improvisation is due to the challenge of creating music in the act of performance, leading to the need for greater insight regarding this process in order that practice may be effectively developed. Among experienced improvisers it is usual for there to be assumed understanding that *decisions about the music take place in the process of playing* in creating real-time composition. Equally, musicians who share no common spoken language may play together and produce music at a profound level through improvisation, demonstrating sophisticated, subtle understanding of the other's music. The music can thrive independently from verbal discussion. This is suggestive of how the music results from knowledge in the act of doing: music as an expression of embodied knowledge. The music is not usefully pre-described and, importantly, agency is with the individual's approach in the act of performance. Real-time composition leads to a particular focus on listening, through the embodied process of improvisation.

> As we sit here there's a lot of sound going on. It's about modes of attention. Inclusive attention and exclusive attention and being able to negotiate both at once. Your focal attention is only momentary, it's only brief but then it can be sequential. But the sequence of focused attention, we're getting waveforms but we're also getting packets ... You have a kind of smooth analogue way of processing and you have digital packets. But exclusive attention when you are trying to narrowly focus on some detail, to understand speech for example. Your attention is focussed on the speech, in order to detect it, understand it, interpret it, all of those things. But sometimes we are focusing in that way and also it can be expanded to include whatever else is happening around. (UP, p. 6, l. 36)

While there exists all kinds of accepted language for describing sound or playing, there seems to be a deficit of ways of expressing how we listen. Alluding to different kinds of listening, 'modes of attention', reaffirms a focus on the body's central importance for understanding improvisation and elucidating real-time composition. UP develops the theme of listening and response to include questions concerning consciousness.

> Creative consciousness – but it's not necessarily from the conscious mode that it comes … Different modes of consciousness: body consciousness is faster than thinking consciousness. (UP, p. 5, l. 19)

Here UP's description of 'body consciousness' reflects a common experience found in improvisation: for example, there may be a shared view of a piece of music's success and at the same time there is no conscious certainly about how the music has been created together. This may occur in groups that have been together over long periods, where the understanding between players exists at an intuitive, embodied level. UP's view is that, in participating in free improvisation, individuals and groups of players are able to act faster than the thought and to do so as part of a continuum; this can be understood in terms of embodied knowledge.

> The other bit of metaphor or idealism is what it felt like to be in a group where a sense of musical oneness which can go beyond music … a oneness was being created. So the feeling of being on a creative high and losing one's self in that creative process rather than intellectualizing or making it into an abstract where I'm saying to myself, "Oh this is going on now, I think I ought to do this." So it's stepping aside from that logico deductive space into more emotional fields I suppose. (KM, p. 3, l. 17)

KM describes the possibilities within the experience of playing as unifying of mind, body and group: as 'oneness', a 'stepping aside' from the dominance of cerebral rationality. What KM describes as 'oneness' draws attention to the significance of the body as the site of free improvisation where such unified experience takes place. Importantly for KM this is a group experience, suggesting inter-subjective, embodied experience encapsulated for KM by the term 'oneness'. The paradoxical use of the 'stepping aside' metaphor (when referring to 'oneness') is indicative of the challenge notions of the body or embodied knowledge may face. Although the mind/body split is often challenged in academic discussion, its legacy is widespread, for example throughout accepted academic approaches to learning. (In many ways such a mind/body split has itself become embodied, accepted unconsciously.) There is an uncertainty about what 'stepping aside' means, expressed through the idea of 'more emotional fields I suppose'. The 'I suppose' suggests a wariness about something other than that which may be cerebrally controlled (an idea found elsewhere in the interview). This is despite the reference to 'being on a creative high and losing one's self in that creative process'. It seems that there would be resistance to some of the developed notions of the body espoused by UP, such as: 'The body knows what to do … allowing the body to lead' (UP, p. 5, l. 1). Resistance to ideas associated with the body in learning are common, for example reflected in the hierarchy of relative importance placed on subjects in the National Curriculum in the UK: subjects with a cerebral emphasis are prioritised; those that involve the physical are often lower priority or optional. There are marked cultural differences between SP and KM and, given these differences, the point at which their respective positions overlap, 'oneness', becomes interesting. KM goes on to describe his experience of playing as unequivocally physical.

> Because I'm a wind player it's something that is going to be quite naturally centred in the diaphragm area. So there's going to be feeling coming from that centre of my body, there's sort of, of a grrrrr! (makes sound), that really gets me, and that's really what I want to do. (KM, p. 6, l. 27)

The overlapping of KM's and UP's descriptions suggests a meeting of the inter-subjective and embodied themes as an important characteristic of creating real-time composition. Understandings of the body in improvisation were also present in the transcripts at a pragmatic, workaday level in descriptions of performing.

> I normally bring a theatrical element to my playing, something a bit visual. I mean I don't overdo it but I mean I don't stand there like a statue and play and twenty minutes later step from the spot when I've finished. I don't play like that. I try to use the space. (NA, p. 5, l. 46)

For NA the music performance is also interpreted in physical as well as visual terms and the reference to 'a theatrical element' is unabashed in the communication of the performance. The activity of free improvisation for NA's individual approach, naturally extends towards a 'theatrical element' in which he tries to 'use the space' in performance. While UP's and NA's articulations of the free improvisation process are quite dissimilar, they nonetheless both make clear reference the body in the realisation of free improvisation, albeit from very different perspectives. UP's perspective is highly conceptualised and includes an openness to exploring different kinds of consciousness and perception, while NA's perspective directly reflects decisions regarding the development of pragmatic professional performance practice. Reference to the physical body and space was similarly present in RT's description of the process of developing as an improviser:

> People were laughing. And I don't remember what I was doing but I'm sure it wasn't Derek (Bailey) they were laughing at – but it was just what I was doing in my movement that cracked them up … When I discovered improvisation I also saw a retrospect of Buster Keaton. I was living in Montreal at the time. I went to see all of his films. I saw many short films – and I'm absolutely sure that he influenced me completely in the fact that I'm in front of people. It's kind of like a fake thing, it's pretentious and fake … from the beginning I was influenced by the theatre. (RT, p. 5, l. 5)

For RT improvisation is tied to expressing distinct individuality: 'that's who I am, what I am'. In the process assumptions about the nature of the performer/audience relationship are questioned, physically asserting individuality in performance through movement and voice and simultaneously through the physicality of his instrument (cello). Physicality for NA and RT is demonstrated in the use of movement, reflecting aspects of theatre and use of space apparent in their music performance. However, this is a quite different situating of the body from that of UP. The body for UP is implicitly and explicitly conceptually developed.

For NJ, performance practice with percussion is characterised by an unusual, knowing ambiguousness regarding the intrinsic physical aspect of performance with sound. Interrogating the sound leads to investigation of the source of the sound within the given space: enhancing the physical, visual act for an audience. The knowing physicality of NJ's performance creates a kind of *visual music*.

> NJ: A piano player has to stick to his instrument but my instrument is here, there and everywhere, more or less so I have to move a bit, and they say it is theatre but it is, I have nothing against it but … I do visual acts but for me it is also music. I have a rubber cymbal. And people hear a big cymbal in their heads, sometimes, and they see the cymbal. Not hearing, but they see the sound. I play with this seeing and hearing and turn it sometimes backwards round.

> SR: You play with the visual side which inevitably accompanies musical performance?

> NJ: Yes. Expectations or the visualization of musical sound. In some parts. (NJ, p. 8, l. 18)

The sometimes strange, comic effect of this additional level of communication is brought about through playing with audience expectations, leading to commonly asked questions: is it theatre or is it something else? While there is a knowing exploration of the physical aspect intrinsic to music involved in NJ's real-time composing, the 'visualisation of musical sound' does not exist in a cultural vacuum as NJ engages audience expectations. It can be noted that NJ is equally an established practitioner in a fine art context and that he does not necessarily separate out these activities. Although the rationale differs, there are nevertheless similarities with RT's reference to movement and doing 'strange things', together with his reference to the performer/audience relationship being 'fake, pretentious'. Both employ entirely coherent creative responses to the performing situation, created using free improvisation, as they experiment with physical, visual and movement elements in addition to their instrumentalist roles in the improvisation context creating real-time composition. For RT and NJ, real-time composition, expressed through embodied action, leads to 'extra musical' dimensions in performance.

The Relationship of Improvisation to Language

Participants' descriptions of the relationship between improvising in music and discussion of the music further expand the theme of the body through understandings of different kinds of knowledge. These descriptions are suggestive of approaches that may be adopted for the practice of forming real-time composition.

> working methods: first play, listen to it, then talk about it. Translating something that is embodiment, embodied sound making, then translate it into spoken word after the fact, which is really the right order. (UP, p. 2, l. 1)

UP's delineation of the relationship between music and talk becomes very significant in understanding the process of real-time composition. Making a clear separation between the two different activities SP reiterates embodied knowledge as the site of activity for improvisation. Introducing the term 'translate' suggests going from one spoken language to another, but clearly music and words are different phenomena. The verbal or textual response to sound or music, however articulate, is not the perceptual experience of music. Embodied sound first and spoken word second is a potent articulation regarding the theme of the body in improvisation.

> we discovered something very important … if we talked about improvisation before we did it, it usually fell flat, but if we sat down and improvised and then recorded it, and then talked, then it was interesting and we advanced our practise. … you're communicating with one another directly … spoken conversations don't have to happen before you play … the dialogue is in the sounds you're making. (UP, p. 1, l. 43)

> … we understand that we mustn't talk about it (before playing) … you're going to kill it if you do. (UP, p. 2, l. 15)

It is important for UP to lucidly articulate characteristics of the perceived relationship between talk and improvising and the way in which discussion may influence the creation of music. Discussion was seen as important for SG and was situated differently. In a number of ways the extract below holds a different emphasis of the place of discussion in relation to playing.

> an important part of the process – we had some extensive discussions … we'd play and then we'd talk about it and critique what we were doing … people would say things like 'I can't just stop what I'm doing and start talking' and I'd say well why not? You're already talking (laughs) … It's just that they had a self-conception of this is my playing and this, my other life. This is my heightened consciousness … awareness … and this is about my conscious life, and so to mix those up and break up that romantic conception of the improviser made it easier. (SG, p. 14, l. 9)

While emphasising the central importance of discussion for the process, SG concurs with UP's point: 'we'd play and we'd talk about it'. Where SG appears to differ is in encountering a reluctance to discuss after playing and his response being to 'break up that romantic conception of the improviser'. While it may be true that there exists a 'romantic conception of the improviser', music communicates in a different way than in words and the relationship between speaking and producing music can be overtly acknowledged (particularly with a view to providing other kinds of learning opportunities, where a student may excel in an area other than the spoken or the written). Successful articulation in one area may not be matched by successful articulation in the other and, as UP points out, however good the communication, talk first can 'kill it'. Discussion forms a central part of the process and can form a symbiotic relationship with the embodied process employed in free improvisation and the views of how this occurs differ for SG and UP.

> we're self teaching, we're learning from each other … We do an autodidact process, with the outcome of which – we don't even know (laughs). So we're teaching ourselves to do something that we don't really know what it is. We're just looking for an outcome and we'll know it when we see it, and that's a part of improvisation too. (SG, p. 14, l. 9)

The 'extensive discussions' in SG's extract are part of a method in the development of the process while working with an improvising orchestra. In the following extract SG stresses the need not to separate intuitive knowledge from other knowledge. Intuition is often regarded as something beyond discussion and sidelined, leading to the paradox of this being kept as a kind of subjugated knowledge. For SG there is also a clear connection between the situating of academic knowledge (legitimate) and intuitive knowledge (illegitimate) in relation to the cultural development of Afro-American music. SG emphasises not separating the processes involved in improvisation in musical activity from understandings of any other human activity:

> I spent the last 20 years stripping a lot of that out of my practice – the idea that there is some big difference in going on the stage and doing something … Increasingly I find the same structures are active all the time. And so I can learn just as much from that process of walking down the street as I can playing with some certified person or even a not so certified person or group of people. And that's what comes from paying attention. (SG, p. 2, l. 3)

SG makes an important point regarding the process of forming real-time composition through improvisation. He is reclaiming embodied knowledge, bodily activity, by diminishing the separation between the activities of talking and playing: acknowledging intuitive and cerebral understanding by bringing them together, as they are often found in everyday life. In the process of identifying embodied knowledge in free improvisation, drawing attention to it, we unwittingly artificially isolate it. For UP, improvisation is led by the 'body consciousness' and talk about improvisation before performing can 'kill it'. The view is informed by developed understandings of embodiment: re-situating and acknowledging intuitive/embodied knowledge by acknowledging a distinction between, for example, playing first and discussing afterwards. This practice has led to an expansion of diverse cross-cultural activity in which embodied knowledge is a corner stone. While these two compelling positions are different, they are both highly significant for understanding the importance of unified, intuitive, embodied activity in improvisation forming real-time composition.

One interview response became a play between what we presume to understand and do not understand in relation to the act of improvisation. The limitations of language are shown up, suggesting that for RT language is insufficient to describe what is taking place. The interviewee cited Buster Keaton and Samuel Becket as significantly influential at the formative stages of becoming an internationally acknowledged musician. Themes found in Becket's work (associated with Theatre of the Absurd) are reflected in the following extracts in which language is used while at the same time suggesting inadequacies in addressing fundamental understandings. Interestingly Keaton was a specialist in communication without words.

> it's ... like the theory of gravity, the gravita ... that we are here ... so, improvisation is up or down – in direction ... This is an example of improvisation – the moment surprises you, but at the point of deciding to go down or up can be very important in the whole spectrum of the thing – it's kind of like catching something that is in movement – for me this is what improvisation is, the moment of change can be totally important to what comes. (RT, p. 2, l. 21)

And

> I'll bring water into the discussion, because water is undividable, you can't divide water, water is one of the elements that you can't divide, alright air as well, these very important things that benefit us but are totally, these words, what is the word, water is of a consistency but it doesn't care about our practice of dividing. And I think something happens in music where the connection becomes one, then we're in the way of water and this would also be another way of saying its anti-gravitational in a certain way ... When we become one, we are flying together and I think, yes I think music has this we have made this language I think for some of these reasons – reasons to become one and to float I would say. (RT, p. 3, l. 18)

In these extracts the confusion of the mixed metaphors nevertheless draws attention to a serious idea. In general, assumptions concerning the nature of music and improvisation are on fundamentally uncertain footing. Grappling with articulating the phenomenon of free improvisation, RT switches frequently between imagery, the effect being to emphasise the way in which meaning here cannot be readily pinned down to a single idea, definition or analogy. This is reminiscent of SG's comment regarding the benefits of retaining an, 'agility in the term' improvisation. The last sentence is thematically potent for improvisation forming real-time composition. There are three strong ideas, conveyed through mixed metaphors. Firstly the idea of 'flying together' as 'one' is reminiscent of the experience explored by Csikszentmihayi,[17] described as 'flow' or reaching optimal experience. The theme of 'oneness' has occurred repeatedly in the interviews. Improvisation, described as 'this language', developed so that we 'become one and to float', brings together two of RT's themes. Improvisation as a 'made' language exists for a unique collective experience. Although we are examining improvisation through the medium of words, employing a double hermeneutic in analysis, it is essential to, at the same time, make acknowledgement that perceptual engagement in the improvisation process is not linguistic. RT's description of improvisation as language and the use of mixed metaphor effectively draw attention to this. Steve Paxton, known for his pioneering work in the development of Contact Improvisation Dance, has referred to improvisation as 'a word for something that can't keep a name'.[18] The practice of improvisation in music resists fixed models of thought, and categorisation as reducing aspects of the phenomena to single entities creates a misleading impression by devaluing the entirety of the experience. As improvisation exists in different ways, simultaneously, thinking about real-time composition in terms of *co-presence* relieves the tendency to overly 'pin down' and foreshorten understanding of the phenomenon. We acknowledge that several processes and interpretations are intrinsic to real-time composition.

The Development of Learning in Real-time Composition

The development of learning in real-time composition became a superordinate theme through interviewees' discussions of their practice in improvisation. Engagement with improvisation in music becomes a process of continuous learning, regardless of experience, but why should this be emphasised for improvisation in particular? Part of this may be explained by the non-predetermined character of free improvisation leading to a continuing, cycle of engagement with something not fixed and therefore it becomes inadequate to rely on a stock set of learnt materials and responses; if we do, we foreshorten the possibilities offered by the particular group situation. We need to 'pay attention', SG, to the shifting, emerging opportunities and develop how we contribute towards affecting this collective musical continuum. SG's view of improvisation was expressed as a 'socio-musical location' and the act of improvising in music a social exchange within a community: the act of real-time composition, improvisation, becomes a site of experience and learning about and for the collective. For SM, free

---

[17]   Mihaly Csikszentmihalyi, *Flow: The Psychology of Optimal Experience* (New York, 1991).

[18]   Actor: Steve Paxton: Contact Improv, http://www.theactingsite.com/steve-paxton-contact-improv/ (accessed 24 October 2011).

improvisation's openness to different backgrounds and forms makes way for the inclusion of all, and the celebration of difference. This characteristic of learning in improvisation also relates to the passion and commitment found among these improvisers for their chosen activity of making music in real time. High motivation, evident across the interviews, was focussed in the act of developing playing, creating real-time composition: this led to a continuum of learning. LR, now in his seventies, described in detail how for him musical improvisation is continuous learning.

> what I've done, and continue to do, is try to improve, all the time, so that I'm able to speak in any kind of situation … because it's also a thinker's game. So you want to be able to have the long range thinking. (LR, p. 6, l. 27)

> I call it a socio-musical location. (SG, p. 19, l. 32)

The 'socio-musical location' term allows us to map improvisation onto fresh and varied situations. For contemporary applications of improvisation in education, the potential of the 'socio-musical location' idea offers a basis for interpreting the potential of improvisation. However, what are the implications of the idea?

> there are bigger fish to fry in improvisation than aesthetics. (SG, p. 8, l. 40)

These larger issues are to do with questions of community, the quality of communication and personal development. Situating free improvisation as firmly environmental, '*creating*' and '*interacting*', allows for the inclusion of possibilities beyond aesthetic parameters.

> what you're hearing is the flow of intelligence and thinking … in these improvised music things, you're always hearing the intelligence and the intension regardless of what they're doing, you're always hearing it, but I sort of wanted to hear a lot of different variations for that. (SG, p. 12, l. 20)

With free improvisation, forming real-time composition, as a setting of communicative exchange through music, the experiential understanding developed in the group leads to personal development. The '*variations for that*' is an idea of self-determined social orchestration; developing the expressive possibilities that individuals and combinations are capable of.

> nobody felt the need to chime in or add a little bit of adornment and all those things you know, people didn't do that and so as a result you could hear that, it opened up the space, you could hear people play. Everybody likes the idea that they were being listened to and some people felt they were being listened to for the first time since they'd been in the group, that people were listening to them in a new way. (SG, p. 11, l. 24)

SG's perspective of the way in which the large group of musicians co-exist in the improvisation setting can be seen as providing a metaphor for successful learning: 'being listened to for the first time,' and being listened to in a new way.

LM's descriptions of participation and organising of improvisation emphasised personal themes of diversity and inclusion, as well as the interdisciplinary, and these are potent ideas for developing education.

> I come from jazz but also soul, blues and also cabaret, theatre and you know we have both learnt the new language of the more abstract free improvisation but also can integrate the different roots and histories, our own personal musical histories as well, so I do feel it is a beautiful contradiction you embrace what's gone before and replace it. (LM, p. 5, l. 18)

Aligning different personal and collective experience forms a source of creativity and it is clear from the interview that this view applies to those regardless of previous musical orientation or cultural background. With a willingness to engage and the development of trust, recognition of differences occurs at a musical and social level that can be understood as a process of growth. 'A beautiful contradiction' suggests a utopian idealising of free improvisation; however, grounded values within the description are revealed by a firm connection to socio-political commitment:

> Everyone's creative – no negotiation. (SM, p. 10, l. 3)

This succinct belief demonstrates understanding of the potential of improvisation for education as the form's openness offers the possibility of realising aims of inclusivity.

> you become virtuosic in different ways but there is such a thing that I really love which I call social virtuosity, it's a collective virtuosity which is multi ... you know, not streamed. And again John (John Stevens) was a master of that. Mixed ability virtuosity. That has its own particular power. There is something phenomenal about a group of different experiences, making really strong performance in music. (LM, p. 10, l. 14)

Improvisation is envisaged as providing the circumstances to explore 'social virtuosity'. This can be seen as an extension to the previously discussed 'socio-musical location'. When, for example, aligned with a detailed conceptualisation of the potential of listening, we can understand ways in which social and musical virtuosity may become educationally explored through improvisation/real-time composition.

An ongoing, much discussed theme among improvisers is that of the possibilities and limits of improvising in the large ensemble. There is a tension between the relative freedom of small group and solo settings and the demands of large group improvising. Within the former there is clearly the space and opportunity for the radical individual expression free improvisation is identified and celebrated for. Yet how is individuality retained within the 'beautiful contradiction' of large group activity in free improvisation? In the following long extract we can see a particular skill in identifying how the needs of any given individual may be reconciled with overall group activity, that may be potentially quite different in character.

> I remember this saxophone player who used to come … into the London one … he'd creep into the back … – and suddenly there's be this absolute blast!!! Absolutely deafening sound … everyone would have a knee jerk reaction, so the drummers if they were there they would start hammering away – and then there was no space … and I thought well how would it be if we didn't change what we were doing, when he started, what would happen and we tried that, and do you know something, the actual way he was playing was that he would do this blast and then he would leave this enormous space. So in actual fact he wasn't the problem, it was everybody else thinking Oh, right, we'll all pile in now even though they didn't want to. So it's that thing of being authentic, if you're truly authentic, I do believe that sooner or later it creates a space for everybody … he needed to play like that but he was also incredibly sensitive because he would play like that and we'd all, we wouldn't change what we were doing if we didn't feel like that. So that was a real lesson for me … Being strong in your own centre, being really totally committed energetically to what you're doing. And then whatever anyone else is doing won't throw you off balance. And that's a lifetimes practice. (LM, p. 13, l. 25)

Within the stated intention of 'everyone's creative – no negotiation' there is a real challenge in finding ways to incorporate and value others who may need to play differently. This extract illustrates an approach to creating the conditions for heterogeneity as a valued ingredient of improvisation. Furthermore, this process was understood as a necessary part of development in large group improvisation interaction.

> you'd get a period where it would be the same people and it would get incredibly coherent, almost insular, almost to the point where it was stagnating. It was so perfect, it was so beautiful everybody knew each other so well. And then somebody would come that would just completely disrupt just everything. (LM, p. 17, l. 3)

Disruption of the 'so perfect … so beautiful' may appear as counter to the group's aim; however, within the commitment to 'Everyone's creative – no negotiation', there is an awareness of the need to respond to difference and recognition of individual expression. This can be further expressed in terms of heterogeneity: histories of free improvisation vividly demonstrate its creative foundations in heterogeneity, with strong individuality expressed through different musical backgrounds and experimentalism. With improvisation as a social practice there is a focus upon: 'Mixed ability virtuosity. That has its own particular power' (LM). The heterogeneous character of improvisation lends itself to diversity, as Lyotard[19] states: 'consensus is only a particular state of discussion, not its end. Its end, on the contrary is paralogy'. (Remaining open to new creativity and the different forms in which it may emerge.) Attempting to too closely prescribe improvisation is undesirable, as an imposition of limitations occurs in the process; recalling SG's 'agility in the term' is helpful. Non-predetermined improvisational performance can occur in radically differing circumstances. This extract is from GB's interview.

> The way we started the concerts were sort of composed because the Pope had just put out a record. Pope John Paul ... it was on Sony ... reading psalms and giving homilies over this sort of ambient, world beat grooves ... I immediately thought OK, so we need to sample the Pope. I mean we're Pantiechrist. I wanted to put out another CD entitled "Pantiechrist: the Pope remix" (laughs). The way the concert started was that Ottomo and I went on stage first and made this big noise, blaaaa, and it gradually sort of settled down into a drone, it became quieter and quieter and the lights would go down until the stage was dark and there was just this drone and then we'd have this white down spot come on, with nobody in and then you'd hear the Pope's voice say (it was from the record) – "the man who does bad things avoids the light, for fear that his bad deeds will be exposed. But the man who does good things walks into the light". And Justin walks into the light where he just sort of has a grouchy schoolteacher outfit on looking very angry with a cocktail. Walks up to the mike and says "welcome to Bitter Mummy's Club Ariola" (laughs) and that's how the concert began and from there on it was improvised, no idea what was going to happen. (GB, p. 10, l. 3)

By using these two lengthy quotations it is intended that the potential diversity and inclusiveness offered through improvisation/real-time composition are clearly illustrated. The radically different setting in the above account is a description is of a pre-composed introduction to a professional performance: the group comprises a drag artist from the USA, voice; an improviser from Japan, electronics; and GB, also from the USA, sampler. Beyond the pre-composed introduction, the entire set is freely improvised and the theme of creating music through heterogeneity, described in SM's extract, remains constant. Improvisation as real-time composition provides the means for radical, intercultural performing experiences.

Below we continue to explore the theme of learning in real-time composition by discussing kinaesthetic learning in improvisation. Learning through the body is clearly inseparable from embodied knowledge and benefits here from discreet discussion.

---

[19] Jean-Francois Lyotard, *The Postmodern Condition: A Report on Knowledge* (Minneapolis, MN, 1984).

> Because I'm a wind player it's something that is going to be quite naturally centred in the diaphragm area. So there's going to be feeling coming from that centre of my body, there's sort of, of a grrrrr! (makes sound), that really gets me, and that's really what I want to do. (KM, p. 6, l. 27)

This extract presents a precise description of the relationship between the experience of the body and the impetus for producing the music: 'that really gets me and that's really what I want to do'. It is strongly suggestive of understanding of learning through the body. Although views vary of what has become known as 'learning styles' (Visual Audio Kinesthetic) and 'multiple intelligences',[20] kinaesthetic learning, or learning by doing, is probably widely under-acknowledged as traditions in education and the development of knowledge remain overly focussed upon textually orientated teaching and learning employing a largely visual bias. As well as clearly identifying the physical location for the activity of improvisation, the extract above describes this physical basis as significantly motivational: 'that's really what I want to do'. The joy arising from engaging physically is easily overlooked; in this case, the excitement derived from the act of free improvisation in music is clearly expressed.

> It's the speed and the speed is part of the excitement. To be able to do things almost ahead of your self, that's really fucking exciting. I love that.(KM, p. 7, l. 19)

Typically, professional improvising musicians have a shared intuitive understanding of the benefits of not allowing the music/playing to become overly analysed before it has taken place, and as previously discussed there is a close link between the non-predetermined form and allowing the body to lead. UP's practice is further informed by a developed understanding of how the body perceives and responds before the thought has taken place.

> In any sensory experience the body takes one tenth of a second. If you take part in highly specialized training, it can be reduced to one eightieth of a second.
>
> SR: Is that to do with Lester Ingber and "attentional processes"?
>
> Yes, Lester Ingber was my teacher for some time … It's really essential, it's really important. It's what is. (UP, p. 6, l. 6)
>
> … you're sounding before you know what you're sounding – there is delay … about half a second. (UP, p. 4, l. 40)

---

[20]   Howard Gardner, *Multiple Intelligences: The Theory in Practice* (New York, 1983).

A grounded understanding of the physics of auditory processes and the characteristics of human response inform UP's emphasis on the primacy of the body in improvisation. This understanding of the body's listening and responding leads to a personal, systematic approach for developing such abilities in music improvisation.

Summary

In order to understand improvisation's role in the formation of real-time composition we described the development of real-time composition in Part 1. 'The Practice of Improvisation in Music' explored improvisation in music's ubiquity and understandings of the term. 'A Background to Real-time Composition: Developments in Improvisation' described the recent history of improvisation and explored the interdisciplinary character of improvisation. In 'Improvisation and Hegemonic Power Structures' we explored the socio-political dynamics of improvisation in music. In order to better understand the phenomenon of improvisation, its experience and processes, in the formation of real-time composition, Part 2 explored themes of improvisation. Here we presented ideas developed from the analysis (IPA) of ten interview transcripts with experienced musicians for whom improvisation was of central importance. The themes reflect an idiographic approach to the data, in which a double hermeneutic retains primacy for individual's accounts. Selected themes were: 'The Improviser as Composer', 'Embodied Knowledge', 'The Relationship of Improvisation to Language' and 'The Development of Learning in Real-time Composition'. 'The Improviser as Composer' discussed the particular ways in which the interviewees refer to themselves as composers and their practice as composition. 'Embodied Knowledge' explored the particular importance of the body as the site for improvisation/real-time composition. The ways in which this revealed itself through the interviews included listening, improvisation in music as physical performance, and the unifying experience of improvisation and bodily engagement leading to trans-disciplinary performance. In 'The Relationship of Improvisation to Language', the proximity of talk and discussion, in relation to playing, forming real-time composition, was explored. 'The Development of Learning in Real-time Composition' discussed the themes of continuous learning in improvisation, improvisation as a socio-musical location, inclusive improvisation, diversity and improvisation and kinaesthetic learning.

Conclusion

In 'The Improviser as Composer', personal accounts expressing the idea of composing and composition by means of improvisation pervade the interviews. This led to a questioning of the separation of the activities of composing and improvising and why such a distinction occurred. Part 1 went some way to addressing this by exploring the socio-political field in which improvisation figures.

In the exploration of the forming of real-time composition through the act of improvisation, the 'Embodied Knowledge' theme became encapsulating. It is the 'real-time' aspect of improvisation that marks it out, what is often also referred to as being 'in the moment', leading to an emphasis on the body. Real-time composition becomes realised by means of the body and embodied knowledge and the body can be thought of as the site of improvisation. Moreover, it is an inter-subjective[21] experience: the particular manner in which improvising musicians creatively, simultaneously interact has attracted interest from a variety of other areas of study such as business systems and computing, as well as psychology in attempts at better understanding human processes. The embodied, inter-subjective character of improvising connects to newer forms of understanding cognition, leading to a particular resonance for education.

In 'The Relationship of Improvisation to Language', the importance of creating awareness of how discussion may help or hinder the creative act of forming composition through playing was discussed. Views differed as to the place of such discussion and the relative benefits of discussion in the course of creating real-time composition, but a high degree of sensitivity to the potential of discussion in relation to creative playing was apparent. This was suggestive of ways in which groups may wish to frame group improvisation activity. Within this theme it is also suggested that there is a profound level of communication, other than in language, through participation in improvisation in music, which could occur effectively, and at a high level, without relying upon language.

Through the theme of 'The Development of Learning in Real-time Composition', learning became synonymous with the activity of improvisation, creating real-time composition. This seemed, in part, to stem from the demands created by the nature of creating music at the point of performance. Regardless of expertise, there seemed to be a continuous process of increasing awareness and knowledge of possibilities for creating music in real-time. The theme of learning was also apparent through personal philosophies revealed in improvisation, such as the 'socio-musical location' of music and improvisation as a potentially socially inclusive activity.

While we have presented selected themes of improvisation, we are not attempting to overly define improvisation in the formation of real-time composition, but rather describe and interpret experiences and processes in improvisation presented by interviewees. As mentioned previously, improvisation exists in different ways, simultaneously; thinking about real-time composition in terms of *co-presence* relieves the tendency to overly 'pin down' and foreshorten understanding of the phenomenon. We acknowledge that several inter-related processes are intrinsic to real-time composition and that different interpretations are of particular value in understanding improvisation as real-time composition. We do, however, present

---

[21]   Lev S. Vygotsky, *The Collected Works of L.S. Vygotsky* (New York, 1987).

a challenge to the hierarchical construct of difference between improvisation forming real-time composition, and other forms of compositional approach, and question the value of such a continued separation of these activities.

References

Artuard, A., *The Theatre and its Double* (New York, USA: Grove Press, 1958).

Attali, J., *Noise: The Political Economy of Music* (Minneapolis, MN: The University of Minnesota Press, 1985).

Bailey, D., *Improvisation: Its Nature and Practice in Music* (London: Da Capo Press, 1992).

Biasutti, M. and L. Frezza, 'Dimensions of music improvisation', *Creativity Research Journal*, 21(2) (2009) , 232–42.

Borgo, D., 'Free jazz in the classroom: An ecological approach to music education', *Jazz Perspectives*, 1/1 (2007), 61–88; doi: 0.1080/17494060601061030; http://dx.doi.org/10.1080/17494060601061030.

Boudrieu, M.C. and D. Robey, 'Enacting integrated information technology: A human agency perspective', *Organization Science*, 16/1 (2005), 3–18; doi: 10.1287/orsc.1040.0103.

Braxton, A., *Triaxium Writings* (Lebanon, NH: Frog Peak Music, 1985).

Brook, P., *The Empty Space* (London: Simon and Schuster, 1968).

Brooke, R., *Jung and Phenomenology* (London: Routledge, 1991).

Ciborra, C., 'Improvisation and information technology in organizations', *ICIS 1996 Proceedings*, paper 26 (1996), http://aisel.aisnet.org/icis1996/26.

Craft, A., 'Studying collaborative creativity: Implications for education', *Thinking Skills and Creativity*, 3 (2008), 241–5.

Csikszentmihalyi, M. *Flow: The Psychology of Optimal Experience* (New York: HarperCollins, 1991).

Dean, R., 'Book review – playing ad lib: Improvisatory music in Australia 1836–1970', *Critical Studies in Improvisation/Études critiques en improvisation*, 1/3 (2006), http://www.improvcommunity.ca/about/research.

Dreyfus, H. and H. Hall, *Heidegger: A Critical Reader* (Oxford: Blackwell, 1992).

Foucault, Michel, *Discipline and Punish: The Birth of the Prison* (London: Penguin Books, 1977).

Foucault, Michel, *Power/Knowledge: Selected Interviews and Other Writings 1972–1977*, ed. Colin Gordon (New York: Pantheon, 1980).

Friere, P., *Pedagogy of the Oppressed* (New York: Continuum, 2006).

Gardner, Howard, *Multiple Intelligences: The Theory in Practice* (New York: Basic Books, 1993).

Grotowski, J., *Towards a Poor Theatre* (New York: Simon and Schuster, 1968).

Habermas, J., *Legitimation Crisis* (London: Heinemann, 1976).

Habermas, J., *Communication and the Evolution of Society* (London: Heinemann, 1979).

Hargreaves, D.J., R.A.R. MacDonald and D. Miell, Musical identities mediate musical development. In: G.F. Welch and G. MacPherson (eds), *Oxford Handbook of Music Education* (Oxford: Oxford University Press, 2002).

Hickey, M., 'Can improvisation be "taught"? A call for free improvisation in our schools', *International Journal of Music Education*, 27(4) (2009), 285–99.

Johnstone, K., *Impro for Storytellers* (New York: Routledge/Theatre Arts Books, 1999).

Kenny, B.J. and M. Gellrich, 'Improvisation'. In: R.P.G.E. McPherson (ed.), *The Science and Psychology of Music Performance: Creative Strategies for Teaching and Learning* (Oxford: Oxford University Press (2002), 117–34.

Lewis, G.E., 'Improvised music after 1950: Afrological and Eurological perspectives', *Black Music Research Journal*, 16/1 (1996), 91–122.

Lewis, G., 'Teaching improvised music: An ethnographic memoir'. In: J. Zorn (ed.), *Arcana: Musicians on Music* (New York: Granary Books/Hips Road, 2000), 78–107.

Lewis, G., *A Power Stronger than Itself: The AACM and American Experimental Music* (Chicago, IL: University of Chicago Press, 2008).

Lewis, G.E., 'Improvisation and pedagogy: Background and focus of inquiry', *Critical Studies in Improvisation/Études critiques en improvisation*, 3/2 (2008), http://www.improvcommunity.ca/about/research.

Litweiler, J., *Ornette Coleman: A Harmolodic Life* (New York: Morrow, 1992).

Lock, G., *Forces in Motion* (New York: Da Capo Press, 1988).

Lock, G., '"What I call a sound": Anthony Braxton's synaesthetic ideal and notations for improvisers', *Critical Studies in Improvisation/Études critiques en improvisation*, 4/1 (2008), http://www.improvcommunity.ca/about/research.

Lyotard, J.-F., *The Postmodern Condition: A Report on Knowledge* (Minneapolis, MN: Minnesota Press, 1984).

MacDonald, R.A.R. and G.B. Wilson, 'The musical identities of professional jazz musicians: A focus group investigation', *The Psychology of Music*, 33(4) (2005), 395–419.

MacDonald, R.A.R. and G.B. Wilson, 'Constructions of jazz: How jazz musicians present their collaborative musical practice', *Musicae Scientiae*, 10(1) (2006), 59–85.

MacDonald, A.R., D.H. Hargreaves and D. Miell, *Musical Identities* (Oxford: Oxford University Press, 2002).

Mazzola, G. and P.B. Cherlin, *Flow Gesture and Spaces in Free Jazz* (Heildelberg: Springer, 2009).

Nettl, B. and M. Russel (eds), *In the Course of Performance* (Chicago, IL: University of Chicago Press, 1998).

Oliveros, P., 'Tripping on wires: The wireless body: Who is improvising?', *Critical Studies in Improvisation/Études critiques en improvisation*, 1/1 (2004), http://www.improvcommunity.ca/about/research.

Pallant, C., *Contact Improvisation: An Introduction to a Vitalizing Dance form* (Jefferson, NC: McFarland, 2006).

Prevost, E., *No Sound is Innocent* (Small Press Distribution, 1997).

Rogers, C., *On Becoming a Person. A Therapist's View of Psychotherapy* (London: Constable, 1988).

Rose, S., 'Articulating perspectives of free improvisation for education', unpublished Master's thesis (Middlesex University, 2008).

Rose, S.D., 'Free improvisation phenomenon: A site of developing knowledge', unpublished PhD thesis (Glasgow Caledonian University, 2011).

Sawyer, R.K., 'Improvisation and teaching', *Critical Studies in Improvisation/ Études critiques en improvisation*, 3/2 (2008), http://www.improvcommunity. ca/about/research.

Schlicht, U., '"I feel my true colors began to show": Designing and teaching a course on improvisation', *Critical Studies in Improvisation/Études critiques en improvisation*, 3/2 (2008), http://www.improvcommunity.ca/about/research

Small, C., *Music, Society, Education* (London: John Calder, 1977).

Smith, J.A., P. Flowers and M. Larkin, *Interpretative Phenomenological Analysis Theory, Method and Research* (London: Sage, 2009).

Stanislavski, C., *An Actor Prepares* (New York: Routledge, 1936).

Stanyeck, J., 'Diasporic improvisation and the articulation of intercultural music', unpublished PhD dissertation (University of California, San Diego, CA, 2004).

Stanyek, J., 'Transmissions of an interculture: Pan-African jazz and intercultural improvisation'. In: D. Fischlin and A. Heble (eds), *The Other Side of Nowhere: Jazz, Improvisation, and Communities in Dialogue* (Middletown, CT: Wesleyan University Press, 2004), 87–130.

Stevens, J., *Search and Reflect* (London: Rockschool, 1985).

Straus, A and J. Corbin, *Grounded Theory in Practice* (London: Sage, 1997).

The Drama Review, 54/3 (T207) (Fall 2010), 123–35; posted online 25 August 2010, doi: 10.1162/DRAM_a_00007.

Tilbury, John, *Cornelius Cardew: A Life Unfinished* (Harlow: Copula, 2008).

Tucker, S., 'When did jazz go straight? A queer question for jazz studies', *Critical Studies in Improvisation/Études critiques en improvisation*, 4/2 (2008), http:// www.improvcommunity.ca/about/research (20 October 2011).

Vygotsky, L.S., *The Collected Works of L.S. Vygotsky* (New York: Plenum Press, 1987).

Wigram, T., *Improvisation: Methods and Techniques for Music Therapy Clinicians, Educators and Students* (London: Jessica Kingsley, 2007).

Wilson, G.B. and R.A.R. MacDonald, 'The meaning of the blues: Musical identities in talk about jazz', *Qualitative Research in Psychology*, 2 (2005), 341–63.

Winnicot, D.W., *Playing and Reality* (London: Routledge, 1999).

Wong, D., 'Asian American improvisation in Chicago: Tatsu Aoki and the "New" Japanese American Taiko', *Critical Studies in Improvisation/Études critiques en improvisation*, 1/3 (2006), http://www.improvcommunity.ca/about/research.

Chapter 9
On Computer-aided Composition, Musical Creativity and Brain Asymmetry

Eduardo Reck Miranda

Continuing developments of computing technology are increasingly giving composers unprecedented access to sophisticated software for symbolic processing and automation. However, whereas computing technology plays an important role in the compositional practice of a number of composers, there are a fair number of musicians who still object to the notion of using a computer as a creative partner in the compositional process. Paradoxically, despite the fact that computers are now ubiquitous in a number of creative tasks, computer-aided composition and/or computer-generated music are still largely referred to as being artificial, mechanical, non-musical, anti-creative and unemotional.

It is undeniable that music involves the artistic expression of emotions and is often regarded as the outcome of inspiration, intuition, transcendence, and so on, but by the same token one also cannot deny that reason plays an important role in music composition, especially in western Europe. One of the finest examples of early rational approaches to music composition appeared in the eleventh century, when Guido d'Arezzo proposed a lookup chart for assigning pitch to the syllables of religious hymns. Nine-hundred years later, the trajectory of such rational approaches – with a musical history full of many and varied systematisations – led to today's use of computers to generate musical compositions. In 1956, Lejaren Hiller composed *The Illiac Suite for String Quartet*, which was probably the first composition to contain computer-generated materials. Hiller teamed up with mathematician Leonard Isaacson to program the mainframe computer ILLIAC at the University of Illinois, USA, to compose the music, the first movement of which was generated using rules of counterpoint and the fourth movement was generated using a probabilistic technique known as Markov chains. Hiller and Isaacson transcribed the output of the computer into traditional notation to be played by a string quartet. The use of the computer as a composition tool[1] thus continues a tradition of western musical thought that was initiated over a thousand years ago.

---

[1] Gerard Assayag, 'Computer assisted composition today'. In: *Proceedings of 1st Symposiumon Music and Computers* (Corfu, 1998), Paul Berg, 'Composing sound structures with rules', *Contemporary Music Review*, 28/1(2009), 75–87. David Cope, *Computer Models of Musical Creativity* (Cambridge, MA, 2005). Eduardo Reck Miranda, *Composing Music with Computers* (Oxford, 2001). Curtis Roads, *The Computer*

Any attempt at distinguishing the rational from the intuitive in musical composition would probably need to take into account the music technology of the time; thus a pertinent question might be, to what extent would composers think differently when composing with computers as opposed to using other compositional practices, such as working at the piano with pencil and stave paper? When engineers use a computer to calculate complex equations, the machine frees their minds to concentrate on the problem at hand, rather than dwelling on the particulars of its equations. This certainly applies to composers as well, but surely there are other issues to be considered in the case of musical composition with computers, since composers may actually rely on them to make compositional decisions, and perhaps even aesthetic ones, on their behalf.

The role of the computer in my own compositional practice has oscillated between two extremes; on the one hand, I have simply assumed the authorship of compositions that were entirely generated by a computer, albeit programmed to follow my instructions. On the other hand, I have composed with pencil on stave paper, using the computer only to typeset the final score. I shall argue that these approaches to composition are not incompatible, but are manifestations of creative processes that are becoming progressively more polarised owing to increasingly sophisticated technology. The rest of this chapter unpacks this notion through introspection into two instances of my own compositional process.

Approaching Composition with Computers

Two major approaches to working with a computer as an active partner for composition can be identified: *bottom-up* and *top-down*. The bottom-up approach is for the composer to engage in improvisation and experimentation with the machine and store promising musical materials; at a later stage, these materials are developed into larger passages, musical structures and so forth. I call this a bottom-up approach since short passages created by or with the computer function as components for building larger musical sections, which are then developed into a fully fledged piece of music.[2] Conversely, composers might prefer a top-down approach, that is, to start by developing an overall compositional plan or algorithm beforehand and proceed by refining it. This approach forces the composer to be creative within self-imposed formal constraints,[3] such as, for example, the number of sections, the length and character of each, types of generative processes for each section, tonal development, rhythmic structure, and so on. The composer may

---

Music Tutorial (Cambridge, MA, 1996). Heinrich Taube, *Notes from the Metalevel* (London, 2004).

[2]   This later development of musical material may or may not involve the aid of a computer.

[3]   The specification of such constraints certainly embodies creative musical thought at the higher level of the top-down process.

choose to honour these limits or may prefer to change the approach if they turn out to be inadequate. In this case, the composition process results from interactions with high-level compositional constraints enforced by a computer.

Even though I often adopt a combination of the bottom-up and top-down approaches, I habitually use the computer as a generator of musical materials for my compositions. I often do not have a larger plan for my pieces; musical form emerges as I work with the compositional materials. By and large, most of my computer-generated materials are discarded and I would normally amend or adjust selected ones in order to fit particular compositional contexts and aims. Ultimately, my ear has the final say. However, the dynamics of this compositional process beg further understanding. Why do I find it exciting working with computer-generated materials? If I discard most of the materials generated by the computer and often edit the ones that I select for a particular piece anyway, why do I not write these materials myself instead?

One thread that I am currently contemplating to address the questions posed above explores an idea suggested by the nineteenth-century philosopher Friedrich Nietzsche[4] and which has recently been re-introduced by Ian McGilchrist.[5] In a brief summary of his ideas, Nietzsche suggested that great artistic creations could only result from the articulation of the mythological dichotomy referred to as the *Apollonian* and *Dionysian*. In ancient Greek mythology, Apollo was the god of the sun, music and poetry and associated with rational and logical thinking, self-control and order. Conversely, Dionysus was the god of intoxication and ecstacy and associated with irrationalism, intuition, passion and anarchy. In Greek mythology these two gods represented two conflicting creative drives, constantly stimulating and provoking one another. As I understand it, this process leads to increasingly high levels of artistic and scientific achievements. In my own artistic practice I observe one side of me as very methodical and objective, keen to use automatically generated music, computers systems, formalisms and models. Conversely, another side of me is anarchic, ironic, intuitive and metaphorical. Each side has it own agenda, so to speak, but I feel that they are not unrestrained. They tend to inhibit each other: the more I swing to the Apollonian side, the stronger is the Dionysian force that pulls me to the opposite side, and vice-versa. Nietzsche would not be my philosopher of first choice to seek enlightenment on cognitive processes, but it turns out that the nineteenth-century Apollonian/Dionysian dichotomy resonates remarkably well with current theories of brain functioning. There are parts of the human brain that are undeniably Apollonian, whereas others are outrageously Dionysian. This phenomenon is generally referred to as *brain asymmetry*.[6]

---

[4] Friedrich Nietzsche, *The Birth of Tragedy out of the Spirit of Music* (London, 2003).

[5] Ian McGilchrist, *The Master and His Emissary: The Divided Brain and the Making of the Western World* (New Haven, CT, 2009).

[6] Richard Davidson and Kenneth Hugdahl (eds), *Brain Asymmetry* (Cambridge, MA, 1995). Sally P. Springer and Georg Deutsch, *Left Brain, Right Brain: Perspectives from*

The Apollonian brain includes largely the frontal lobe of the cortex and the left hemisphere. Generally, these areas are in charge of focusing attention on detail, seeing wholes in terms of their constituents and making abstractions: they are systematic and logical. The Dionysian brain includes sub-cortical areas, which are much older in the evolutionary timeline and located in the right hemisphere. The Dionysian brain is more connected to our emotions. It perceives the world holistically and pushes us towards unfocused general views. The Apollonian brain is concerned with unilateral meanings, whereas the Dionysian brain tends to forge connections between allegedly unrelated concepts.

Left–right asymmetry is present in the brains of most animals: competition and collaboration between the two hemispheres of the brain enables them to specialise and operate more efficiently. As a rough example, when you speak with someone, the left side of the brain will be processing the verbal language, while the right side will be processing the prosody (tone and inflection). The fact that prosody of speech is processed by the right hemisphere of the brain suggests that this hemisphere might be more musical than the left one,[7] and while there have been a few studies on brain asymmetry and music processing in the brain,[8] the relationship between brain asymmetry and musical creativity remains largely elusive in the neuroscience literature with the majority of research into cognitive neuroscience of music focussing on music perception rather than composition.[9]

The notion that the Apollonian and the Dionysian tend to inhibit each other reminds me of the way in which the brain functions at all levels. In fact, inhibitory processes seem to pervade the functioning of our brain, from the microscopic level of neurones communicating with one another, to the macroscopic level of interaction between larger networks of millions of neurones. In this context, I have come to believe that the further my Apollonian brain pushes me to approach composition according to its 'agenda', the stronger the pull of my Dionysian brain to approach it differently. Accordingly, computer technology is

---

Cognitive Neuroscience (New York, 1998). Kenneth Hugdahl and Rene Westerhausen (eds), *The Two Halves of the Brain* (Cambridge, MA, 2010).

[7]   Dennis L. Molfese, 'Cerebral asymmetry in infants, children, and adults: auditory evoked responses to speech and music stimuli', *Journal of Acoustic Society of America*, 53/1 (1973), 363. Pascal Belin, Monica Zilbovicius, Sophie Crozier, Lioneel Thivard and Anne Fontaine, 'Lateralization of speech and auditory temporal processing', *Journal of Cognitive Neuroscience*, 10/4 (1998), 536–40.

[8]   Isabelle Peretz and Robert J. Zatorre, 'Brain organization for music processing', *Annual Review of Psychology*, 56 (2004), 89–114. Gottfried Schlaug, 'The brain of musicians', *Annals of the New York Academy of Sciences – The Biological Foundations of Music*, 930 (2001), 281–99. Gottfried Schlaug, L. Jancke, Y. Huang and H. Steinmetz, 'In vivo evidence of structural brain asymmetry in musicians', Science 267(5198) (1995), 699–701.

[9]   Isabelle Peretz and Roberto Zatorre (eds), *The Cognitive Neuroscience of Music* (Oxford, 2003).

of foremost importance for my *métier* since it allows me to stretch my Apollonian musical side far beyond my ability to do so by hand, prompting my Dionysian side to counteract accordingly. I would say that this cognitive push-and-pull is a vital driving force behind my musical creativity. However, it should be noted that the software I generate music with is, with very few exceptions, of my own design. The design of the software and the generative models it embodies also involves intuition and inspiration. Therefore, as it will be demonstrated, there are Dionysian aspects already embodied in my Apollonian tools. The case studies below focus on two movements of *Mind Pieces*, a five-movement-long symphonic piece for orchestra, percussion and prepared piano, which was premiered in 2011.[10]

Case Study 1: *Automata*

Automata is the fourth movement of *Mind Pieces*, generated with a cellular automaton known as the Game of Life. I devised a method to generate musical sequences with the automaton, which is explained below, but before I explain the method, I will briefly introduce the basics of cellular automata, abbreviated as CA, with a view on demonstrating why I find them inspiring. CA are tools for computational modelling widely used to model systems that change some features with time. When I saw a CA model working for the first time in the 1980s, I immediately thought that CA could be used to model music. What triggered my musical imagination then was the fact that CA produces large amounts of patterned data. At the time, I had been contemplating the notion of music composition as being based on pattern propagation following rules of development. I envisaged building a CA-based musical system in which a finite set of discrete values representing musical notes and rhythms would evolve into patterns in space and time according to mathematical rules.

Cellular automata were originally introduced in the 1960s by John von Neumann and Stanislaw Ulam as a model of a self-reproduction machine:[11] they wanted to know if it would be possible for an abstract machine to reproduce, that is, to automatically construct a copy of itself. As a result, they devised an automaton consisting of a two-dimensional grid of cells, each cell of which could assume a number of states, representing the components of the so called 'self-reproducing machine'. Completely controlled by a set of rules, the machine[12] was able to create several copies of itself by reproducing identical patterns of cells at another location on the grid. Since then, CA have been repeatedly reintroduced and applied to a considerable variety of purposes, from biomedical

---

[10] Peninsula Arts Contemporary Music Festival, on 12 February 2011 in Plymouth, by Ten Tors Orchestra, conducted by Simon Ible.

[11] Edgard F. Cood, *Cellular Automata* (London, 1968).

[12] The machine was represented as a pattern of cells on the grid.

image processing[13] to areas such as biology[14] and sociology.[15] The notion that CA could model life forms caught my imagination.

A cellular automaton consists of an array or matrix of elements, referred to as cells, to which transition rules are applied. The behaviour of the automaton is bestowed by these transition rules, which are repeatedly applied simultaneously to all cells. The rules normally take into account the states of the neighbourhood of each cell. All cells are updated simultaneously, so that the state of the automaton (that is, the values of the cells) as a whole advances in discrete time steps after each application of the rule. The value of each cell is normally associated with a colour, which facilitates the visualisation of the behaviour of the matrix like an animated film (Figure 9.1). The following paragraphs focus on Game of Life,[16] which is the automaton I used to build *Camus*,[17] the system with which I composed *Automata*.

The Game of Life automaton consists of a finite $[m \times n]$ matrix of cells, each of which can be in one of two possible states: alive, represented by the number 1, or dead represented by the number 0. On the computer screen, living cells are coloured black and dead cells are coloured white (Figure 9.1).

The state of a cell as time progresses is determined by the state of its eight nearest neighbouring cells, as follows:

- Birth – a cell that is dead at time t becomes alive at time $t + 1$ if exactly three of its neighbours are alive at time t.
- Death by overcrowding – a cell that is alive at time t will die at time $t + 1$ if four or more of its neighbours are alive at time t.
- Death by exposure – a cell that is alive at time t will die at time $t + 1$ if it has one or no live neighbours at time t.
- Survival – a cell that is alive at time t will remain alive at time $t + 1$ only if it has either two or three live neighbours at time t.

---

[13]   Kendall Preston and Michael J. B. Duff, *Modern Cellular Automata: Theory and Applications* (New York, 1984).

[14]   G. Bard Ermentrout and Leah Edelstein-Keshet, 'Cellular automata approaches to biological modeling', *Journal of Theoretical Biology*, 160 (1963), 97–133.

[15]   Joshua M. Epstein and Robert L. Axtell, *Growing Artificial Societies: Social Science from the Bottom Up* (Cambridge, MA, 1996).

[16]   Game of Life is a two-dimensional automaton invented by John Conway, who was 'fascinated by the way in which a combination of a few simple rules could produce patterns that would expand, change shape or die out unpredictably. He wanted to find the simplest possible set of rules that would give such an interesting behaviour'. Greg Wilson, 'The life and times of cellular automata', *New Scientist* (October 1988), 44.

[17]   Peter M. Tood and Eduardo Reck Miranda, 'Putting some (artificial) life into models of musical creativity', in Irène Deliège and Geraint A. Wiggins (eds), *Musical Creativity* (Hove, 2006), 376–95. Eduardo Reck Miranda and Alexis Kirke, 'Game of Life music', in Andrew Adamatzky (ed.), *Game of Life Cellular Automata* (London, 2010), 489–501.

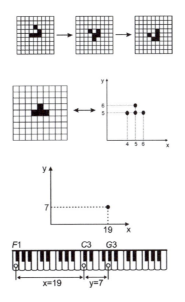

Figure 9.1   A pattern sequence generated by Game of Life is shown at the top. Given a reference note, *Camus* generates a set of three notes for each live cell.

In order to build *Camus*, I mapped Game of Life's matrix of cells onto a Cartesian plane, where each point represents an ordered set of three notes, which are defined in terms of the intervals between them. Given a reference note, the *x*-coordinate represents the interval between the reference note and the second note of the set. The *y*-coordinate represents the interval between the second note and the third. For instance, consider a live cell at coordinates (19, 7). Given a reference note, *Camus* generates two notes: one that is 19 semitones above the reference note, and another 7 semitones above the previously generated note (Figure 9.1).

To begin with, the matrix of cells is set up with a given initial configuration of cell states. The system is set to run and the cells are analysed column by column each time the CA rules have been applied. When *Camus* arrives at a live cell, its co-ordinates are used to calculate a set of three notes, from a set of given reference notes.[18] Although the cell updates occur at each time step in parallel, *Camus* sequences live cells column by column, from top to bottom. Each of these musical cells has its own timing, but the notes within a cell can be of different durations and can be triggered at different times. The method for staggering the starting and ending times of the notes of a cell (*x*, *y*) considers the states of its respective neighbouring cells. *Camus* computes a set of values from the states of the neighbours, the value being equal to 1 if a neighbour is alive and 0 if it is dead, as follows:

---

18   These notes are defined beforehand.

$a = \text{cell}\ (x, y - 1)$
$b = \text{cell}\ (x, y + 1)$
$c = \text{cell}\ (x + 1, y)$
$d = \text{cell}\ (x - 1, y)$
$m = \text{cell}\ (x - 1, y - 1)$
$n = \text{cell}\ (x + 1, y + 1)$
$o = \text{cell}\ (x + 1, y - 1)$
$p = \text{cell}\ (x - 1, y + 1)$

Then, the system forms four 4-bit words as follows: *abcd, dcba, mnop* and *ponm*. Next, it performs a bit-wise inclusive OR operation to generate two four-bit words: *Tgg* and *Dur*:

Tgg = abcd|dcba
Dur = mnop|ponm

Camus derives trigger information for the notes from *Tgg*, and duration information from *Dur*, and with each relevant four-bit word it associates a code to represent time-forms where B denotes the reference note, M the middle note (which was generated by the abscissa of the cartesian plane), and U the upper one (which was generated by the ordinate). The square brackets are used to indicate that the note events contained within that bracket occur simultaneously. The codes are as follows:

0000 = B[UM]
0001 = [UMB]
0010 = BUM
0011 = UMB
0101 = BMU
0110 = UBM
0111 = MBU
1001 = U[MB]
1011 = MUB
1111 = M[UB]

Pairs of time-forms define a temporal morphology for the cells. At the top of Figure 9.2 is an example of a temporal morphology starting with MBU and ending with B[MU], and at the bottom of the figure is a rendering of this morphology into musical notation. The notes are written to a MIDI file and/or sent directly to a MIDI sampler or synthesiser to be played.

For the composition of *Automata*, I saved the output of *Camus* into a MIDI file, which I subsequently loaded into a music notation editor. I manually deleted a few passages that did not sound interesting (to my Dionysian ears) and worked with the ones that remained. Overall the edits and changes were mostly on pitches

Figure 9.2   *Top*: temporal morphology starting with MBU and ending with B[MU]. *Bottom*: possible rendering of this morphology into musical notation.

and instrumentation rather than on rhythm and, while I edited the remaining materials, I observed my Apollonian side insisting on preserving the order of the events. My Dionysian side, however, metaphorically considered the computer-generated music as a long mesh-like structure with musical notes attached, which I intervened in by tweaking its shape and the position of the notes. Example 9.1 shows the score of a typical passage from the output of *Camus* and Example 9.2 shows an excerpt from *Automata*. I have not documented the exact changes I made to the original materials and therefore Example 9.2 does not necessarily correspond to Example 9.1. The only clue available is timing; both begin at their respective eleventh bar. Nevertheless, I still feel that the score in Example 9.2 preserves the 'structural qualia', some sort of structural identity, of the original *Camus* output. The impossibility of reverse engineering the resulting piece back to its origins should not be a predicament. Certain 'missing links' in the compositional process

Example 9.1   A sample of *Camus*-generated materials

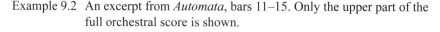

Example 9.2 An excerpt from *Automata*, bars 11–15. Only the upper part of the full orchestral score is shown.

should remain implicit and, on behalf of my Dionysian side, I would argue that computers are better kept out of this domain. The aforementioned preservation of qualia is probably due to Apollonian processes hijacking my memory as an attempt to make sense of my Dionysian bewilderment.

Case Study II: *Evolve*

Evolve is the second movement of *Mind Pieces* composed on top of a rhythmic structure generated with an Artificial Life system; the wider field of Artificial Life (A-life) arose out of my investigation into composing music with CA. A-life aims at the study, through computer modelling, wetware–hardware hybrids and other artificial media, of all phenomena characteristic of natural living systems. Its scope ranges from the investigation of the emergence of cognitive processes in natural or artificial systems to the development of life or lifelike properties from inorganic components. As a natural progression from my work with CA, I started to look into building systems for composition using A-Life models of cultural development and interacting autonomous software agents. I collaborated with João Martins, then a doctoral student at Plymouth University's Interdisciplinary Centre for Computer Music Research (ICCMR), to develop *A-rhythms*, an A-life-based system to compose rhythms based on a paradigm that we have been working with at ICCMR, known as *imitation games*.[19] In a nutshell, we developed a system whereby a group of software agents evolve repertoires of rhythms by interacting with each other. Software agents are virtual entities, or software robots, programmed to execute tasks. They are often embedded with some form of intelligence and can perform tasks independently from each other, without supervision from a central control.

In *A-rhythms*, the agents were programmed to create and play rhythmic sequences, listen to each other's sequences and perform operations on those sequences, according to an algorithm referred to as the *rules of the game*. To begin with, each agent is set up with an initial rhythm stored in its memory. These initial rhythms are randomly generated and are different for each agent. As the agents interact with each other, they can add new rhythms to and/or erase rhythms from their memories, as well as modifying existing rhythms. The aim of the game is to develop a shared lexicon of rhythmic patterns collectively and, as the interactions take place, each agent develops a repertoire of rhythms similar to the repertoires of its peers. The agents interact in pairs and at each round one of the agents plays the role of a *player* and the other the role of a *listener*. The agents count the number of times they play each rhythm stored in their memories. This counter is referred to as the *popularity* of the rhythm. The following algorithm is the core of the rules of the game:

Player:

P1 Pick a rhythm from its memory and play it.

Listener:

L1 Search the memory for a rhythm that is identical to the rhythm produced by the agent player.

L2 If an identical rhythm is found, then increase its popularity and give a positive feedback to the agent player.

L3 If an identical rhythm is not found, then add this rhythm to the memory and give a negative feedback to the agent player.

---

[19] Eduardo Reck Miranda, 'Mimetic development of intonation'. In: *Proceedings of the 2nd International Conference on Music and Artificial Intelligence*. Lecture Notes on Artificial Intelligence (London, 2002).

Player:

P2   If the listener's feedback was positive, then increase the popularity of the played rhythm.

P3   If feedback is negative, then decrease the popularity of the played rhythm.

P4   Perform memory updates.

After each interaction, the player peforms a number of updates. For instance, from time to time, the agent may delete the rhythm in question if its popularity y remains below a minimum threshold for a given period of time. This means that other agents probably do not share this rhythm and therefore should no longer be used. Also, from time to time the agent may transform the rhythm. This decision is based on a number of factors; for example there is a variable, referred to as the transformation counter, which is updated in terms of its popularity; the more popular a rhythm is, the more likely it is that the agent will transform it. Furthermore, the agents are programmed with a memory loss mechanism, whereby after each interaction all the rhythms have their popularity decreased by a specified amount. The agents store rhythms as a sequence of inter-onset intervals, represented in terms of small integer ratios of an isochronous pulse (Figure 9.3).

At the core of the mechanism by which the agents develop rhythmic sequences are transformation operations. The transformation operations are as follows:

- Divide a rhythmic figure by two (e.g. $\frac{1}{2} = \frac{1}{4} + \frac{1}{4}$).
- Merge two rhythmic figures (e.g. $\frac{1}{2} + \frac{1}{2} = 1$).
- Add one element to the sequence.
- Remove one element from the sequence.

The agents are programmed with the ability to measure the degree of similarity of two rhythmic sequences. This measurement is used when a listener searches for identical rhythms in its repertoire. Thus, if the degree of similarity of two rhythms is within a given threshold then the rhythms are considered identical. This threshold is set beforehand. Therefore, two rhythmic sequences do not necessarily need to be exactly equal to be considered identical.[20]

Figure 9.3   Standard music notation of a rhythmic sequence and its corresponding inter-onset representation

[20]   João Martins, Marcelo Gimenes, Jonatas Manzolli and Adolfo Maia Jr, 'Similarity measures for rhythmic sequences'. In: *Proceedings of the 10th Brazilian Symposium on Computer Music (SBCM)* (Belo Horizonte, Brazil, 2004).

We ran *A-rhythms* systematically with different parametric values in order to observe the behaviour of the agents under a number of different conditions, and observed the emergence of repertoires across the agents, some of which were more coherent than others. Additionally, the size of the repertoires varied according to the number of agents in a group, and the thresholds for probing the popularity and transformation counters mentioned earlier.[21] For the composition of *Evolve*, Martins and I ran simulations with three, 10 and 50 agents, for 5000 or so interactions each. At the end of the simulations we opened the memories of the agents and picked out the common rhythmic patterns that had evolved. Subsequently, these patterns were loaded into a music notation editor and sequenced. I had no plans for how the composition would develop from here, so I auditioned the sequences with various timbres hoping for an idea to emerge. When I played them on a synthetic snare drum, my Dionysian brain somehow connected it to Maurice Ravel's orchestral piece *Boléro* and made a split-second decision: to use the rhythmic sequence to form the backbone of the entire movement and to base the orchestration of the entire movement on that of *Boléro*. As my Apollonian side strived to be as systematic as possible, following the orchestration scheme laid out by Ravel, my Dionysian brain brought in melodic lines and themes whose origins I am unable to ascertain. I speculate that they were musical ideas lurking deep in my memory. Example 9.3 shows an excerpt of *Evolve*. The computer-generated rhythm played on the snare drum (S.D.) is doubled by the saxophones (Ten. Sax.), bassoons (Bsn.1) and trumpets (C Tpt.).

Concluding Remarks

Our brains evolved (and probably are still evolving) for optimal performance of rational tasks. Moreover, we are continuously developing computers, which emulate the basic requirements to perform such tasks, with varying degrees of success. Therefore, in theory computers can compose music of fairly convincing quality if programmed accordingly. Metaphorically, Apollo would be able to compose music in his own right, although the music would certainly not be compelling. Conversely, Dionysus would not able to do so on his own; he needs the help of Apollo. In the book *The Master and His Emissary: The Divided Brain and the Making of the Western World*, Ian McGilchrist discusses the tension between the sides of the divided brain through the history of western culture. He takes us on a journey through the thought of writers and artists, from philosophers of ancient Greece to twentieth-century painters. He argues that the left, Apollonian brain is increasingly taking precedence in the contemporary world at our peril. However, I am not particularly convinced that any sides are

---

[21]   João Martins and Eduardo Reck Miranda, 'Engineering the Role of Social Pressure: A New Artificial Life Approach to Software for Generative Music', *Journal of Software Engineering*, 2/3 (2008), 31–42.

Example 9.3   An excerpt from *Evolve*, bars 234–9. Only the upper part of the
full orchestral score is shown.

taking precedence as such. If anything I believe the right – or Dionysian – brain
is far from being superseded.

As to the question 'To what extent would composers think differently when
composing with computers?' the answer is not trivial. The computer certainly
bestows practices that were not possible in the past, but how does this relate to

thinking creatively? There have been a number of attempts at addressing this question,[22] but I fail to find matching accounts; there are as many answers as authors addressing it. This chapter contributes yet another account, that is, the notion that creativity in musical composition is a byproduct of brain asymmetry, an account that is a rather personal one. In reality, composers think differently from each other simply because human beings are different from each other. Composers of different epochs have had access to different technologies, but the extent to which they have influenced the evolution of musical creativity is doubtful. The complexity of John Sebastian Bach's music comes to mind here; would his music have been different if computers had been available? My hunch is that it would probably not be so different.

At least in my case, there clearly is a cognitive push-and-pull driving force behind musical creativity, which is embodied by the dichotomy of reason and intuition. The computer only exacerbates this dichotomy in my compositional practice; for instance, I would probably never have had the idea of basing the orchestration of *Evolve* on that of Ravel's *Boléro* if I had not worked with those computer-generated rhythms discussed earlier. Computers allow me to stretch my Apollonian musical side far beyond my ability to do so by hand, prompting my Dionysian side to counteract accordingly. In the examples discussed above, this push-and-pull process took place at all levels and stages of the compositional process, from software design to orchestration.

So, why do I find it exciting working with computer-generated materials? Computer-generated music often prompts me to flush out my musical imagination in surprising ways. I find this exciting and different. This is for me what makes composing with computers running generative music software different from composing with a musical instrument and pencil and stave paper. With a computer I seldom need to wait for capricious inspiration to emerge. However, it is possible that what I said above about my creative process is wrong: I am left-handed.

References

Adamatzky, Andrew (ed.), *Game of Life Cellular Automata* (London: Springer, 2010).

Assayag, Gerard, 'Computer assisted composition today'. In: *Proceedings of 1st Symposium on Music and Computers* (Corfu, 1998).

Ball, Phillip, *Music Instinct: How music works and why we can't do without it* (London: Bodley Head, 2010).

---

[22]   Francois Pachet. 'Enhancing individual creativity with interactive musical reflexive systems'. In: Irène Deliège and Geraint A. Wiggins (eds), *Musical Creativity* (Hove, 2006), 357–75. Cope, *Computer Models of Musical Creativity*. Scott Watson, *Using Technology to Unlock Musical Creativity* (New York, 2011).

Belin, Pascal, Monica Zilbovicius, Sophie Crozier, Lionel Thivard and Anne Fontaine, 'Lateralization of speech and auditory temporal processing', *Journal of Cognitive Neuroscience*, 10/4 (1998), 536–40.

Berg, Paul, 'Composing sound structures with rules', *Contemporary Music Review*, 28/1 (2009).

Cood, Edgar, *Cellular Automata* (London: Academic Press, 1968).

Cope, David, *Computer Models of Musical Creativity* (Cambridge, MA: MIT Press, 2005).

Davidson, Richard and Kenneth Hugdahl (eds), *Brain Assymetry* (Cambridge, MA: MIT Press, 1995).

Dean, Roger (ed.), *The Oxford Handbook of Computer Music* (Oxford: Oxford University Press, 2009).

Deliege, Irene and Geraint Wiggins (eds), *Music Creativity* (Hove: Psychology Press, 2006).

Epstein, Joshua and Robert Axtell, *Growing Artificial Societies: Social Science From The Bottom Up* (Cambridge, MA: MIT Press, 1996).

Ermentrout, Bard and Leah Edelstein-Keshet, 'Cellular automata approaches to biological modeling', *Journal of Theoretical Biology*, 160 (1963), 97–133.

Hugdahl Kenneth and Rene Westerhausen (eds), *The Two Halves of The Brain* (Cambridge, MA: MIT Press, 2010).

Martins, João and Eduardo Reck Miranda, 'Engineering the role of social pressure: a new artificial life approach to software for generative music', *Journal of Software Engineering*, 2/3 (2008), 31–42.

Martins, João, Marcelo Gimenes, Jonatas Manzolli and Adolfo Maia Jr, 'Similarity measures for rhythmic sequences'. In: *Proceedings of the 10th Brazillian Symposium on Computer Music (SBCM)* (Bello Horizont, Brazil, 2005).

McGilchrist, Ian *The Master and his Emissary: The Divided Brain and the Making of the Western World* (New Haven, CT: Yale University Press, 2009).

Miller, Paul (ed.), *Sound on Bound* (Cambridge, MA: MIT Press, 2008).

Miranda, Eduardo Reck, *Composing Music with Computers* (Oxford: Focal Press, 2001).

Miranda, Eduardo Reck, 'Mimetic development intonation', *Proceedings of the 2nd International Conference on Music and Artificial Intelligence*. Lecture Notes on Artificial Intelligence (London: Springer, 2002).

Miranda, Eduardo Reck (ed.), *A-Life For Music: Music and Computer Models of Living Systems* (Middleton, WI: A-R Additions, 2011).

Miranda, Eduardo Reck, *Mozart Reloaded* (Baldock: Sargasso, 2011).

Miranda, Eduardo Reck and A. Kirke, 'Game of Life music'. In: Andrew Adamatzky (ed.), *Game of Life Cellular Automata* (London: Springer, 2010), 489–501.

Molfese, Dennis, 'Cerebral asymmetry in infants, children and adults: Auditory evoked responses to speech and music stimuli', *Journal of Acoustic Society of America*, 53/1 (1973), 363.

Nehamas, Alexander, *Nietzsche: Life as Literature* (Cambridge, MA: Harvard University Press, 1985).

Nietzsche, Friedrich, *The Birth of Tragedy out of the Spirit of Music* (London: Penguin, 2003).

Pachet, Francois, 'Enhancing individual creativity with interactive musical reflective systems'. In: Irene Deliege and Geraint A. Wiggins (eds), *Musical Creativity* (Hove: Psychology Press/Taylor and Francis, 2006), 357–75.

Peretz, Isabelle and Robert Zatorre (eds), *The Cognitive Neuroscience of Music* (Oxford: Oxford University Press, 2003).

Peretz, Isabelle and Robert Zatorre, 'Brain organisation for music processing', *Annual Review of Psychology*, 56 (2004), 89–114.

Preston, Kendall and Michael Duff, *Modern Cellular Automata: Theory and Applications* (New York, Plenum, 1984).

Roads, Curtis, *The Computer Music Tutorial* (Cambridge, MA: The MIT Press, 1996).

Schlaug, Gottfried, 'The brain of musicians', *Annals of The New York Academy of Sciences – The Biological Foundations of Music*, 930 (2001), 281–99.

Schlaug, Gottfried, Lutz Jancke, Yi Huang and Helmuth Steinmetz, 'In vivo evidence of structural brain asymmetry in musicians', *Science*, 267/5198 (1995), 699–701.

Springer, Sally and Georg Deutsch, *Left Brain, Right Brain: Perspectives from Cognitive Neuroscience* (New York: W.H. Freemen, 1998).

Taube, Heinrich, *Notes from the Metalevel* (London: Taylor and Francis, 2004).

Tood, Peter and Eduardo Reck Miranda, 'Putting some (artificial) life into models of musical creativity'. In: Irene Deliege and Gerainte Wiggins (eds), *Musical Creativity* (Hove: Psychology Press/Taylor and Francis, 2006), 376–95.

Watson, Scott, *Using Technology to Unlock Musical Creativity* (New York: Oxford University Press, 2011).

Weiss, Piero and Richard Taruskan, *Music in the Western World* (Florence, KY: Wadsworth, 2007).

Wilson, Greg, 'The life and times of cellular automata', *News Scientist* (October 1988), 44.

Young, Julian, *Nietzsche's Philosophy of Art* (Cambridge: Cambridge University Press, 1992).

Chapter 10

Defining Inspiration? Modelling the Non-conscious Creative Process

Geraint A. Wiggins

What Composers Do

The title of this collection, 'The Act of Musical Composition: Studies in the Creative Process', might be taken to carry with it some suppositions about the nature of possible answers to the questions it implies. The purpose of this chapter is to deconstruct some aspects of those suppositions and to tease apart the tangled and inscrutable network of happenings that constitute the construction of a piece of music by a musician. The narrative here is intended to propose a hypothesis accounting for human musical creativity, which is a large-scale endeavour. For that reason, I do not present detail of the computational mechanisms on which I rely for evidence, nor of the empirical work done to validate them as cognitive models. The interested reader is invited to learn about the detail in the various published papers that I cite along the way.

My colleagues and I have argued elsewhere[1] that music needs to be studied as a primarily psychological construct, for it is from the psychology that music's equally important social, sociological and shared aesthetic aspects emerge. This requirement, I claim, holds no less for composition than for any other aspect of musical behaviour; indeed, it is easiest to identify in the Romantic notion of the composer struggling alone in his[2] artistic garret, for he is abstracted from all social context other than that encoded in his memory, in his chosen notation, and perhaps that implicit in the design of his instrument, if he uses one. My approach, therefore, begins from psychology.

Composers are often placed on metaphorical pedestals, even by the most extraordinarily gifted instrumentalists, at least in the non-Popular music world. As a composer myself, I have often been asked, 'How can you *do* that?' However, the only answer I can give, which is no answer at all, is 'How can you *not* do

---

[1] Geraint A. Wiggins, 'Semantic gap?? Schemantic Schmap!! Methodological considerations in the scientific study of music'. In: *Proceedings of 11th IEEE International Symposium on Multimedia* (IEEE, 2009), 477–82. Geraint A. Wiggins, Daniel Müllensiefen, and Marcus T. Pearce, 'On the non-existence of music: Why music theory is a figment of the imagination', *Musicae Scientiae, Discussion Forum 5* (ESCOM, 2010), 231–55.

[2] Romantic notions are rarely gender-neutral.

that?', by which I mean that to generate new pieces of music is so fundamentally a part of my nature that I can no more imagine not doing it than I can imagine not tasting food or not feeling the keyboard on which I am currently typing. The British composer Richard Rodney Bennett concurs: 'I didn't ever decide I was going to be a composer. It was like being tall. It's what I was. It's what I did'.[3] Of course, there is a more detailed answer, which says, 'I take my ideas and then work them through into finished pieces of music, using such-and-such an approach', and I could discuss the nature of the ideas, which might be motivic, timbral, structural, metaphorical or any combination of these. My point here is that, for me, at least, the generation of musical ideas, of one kind or another, is on-going, involuntary and fundamental to my being. It follows logically that many such ideas lie abandoned, forgotten amidst the turmoil of everyday existence, although I cannot be sure of this, because it is I who have forgotten them.

One supposition implied by the current volume's title might be that there is a single identifiable Act of musical creation, which is part of a single, universal – 'the' – Creative Process. According with that position, there are myths about Wolfgang Amadeus Mozart being able to 'see' the entirety of a composition in one creative flash. However, these stories are probably derived from an inaccurate précis of Mozart's own introspective description:

> When I am, as it were, completely myself, entirely alone, and of good cheer – say traveling in a carriage, or walking after a good meal, or during the night when I cannot sleep; it is on such occasions that my ideas flow best and most abundantly. Whence and how they come, I know not; nor can I force them. Those ideas that please me I retain in memory, and am accustomed, as I have been told, to hum them to myself.
>
> All this fires my soul, and provided I am not disturbed, my subject enlarges itself, becomes methodized and defined, and the whole, though it be long, stands almost completed and finished in my mind, so that I can survey it, like a fine picture or a beautiful statue, at a glance. Nor do I hear in my imagination the parts successively, but I hear them, as it were, all at once. What a delight this is I cannot tell! All this inventing, this producing takes place in a pleasing lively dream. Still the actual hearing of the toutensemble is after all the best. What has been thus produced I do not easily forget, and this is perhaps the best gift I have my Divine Maker to thank for.[4]

In this account, there is no single creative flash, but rather the spontaneous emergence of initial ideas over a period of time, occurring when Mozart is in the

---

[3]   Nick Wroe, 'A life in music: Richard Rodney Bennett', *The Guardian* (London, 22 July 2011).

[4]   Edward Holmes, *The Life of Mozart: Including his Correspondence*, Cambridge Library Collection (Cambridge, 2009), 317–18.

right emotional state, and when he is undistracted. These ideas are either selected or discarded and, when retained in memory over some unspecified time, form (again spontaneously?) into completed compositions.

Mozart mentions his prodigious memory, and there is objective evidence of this elsewhere: he was able to transcribe Allegri's *Miserere* from memory after only one hearing, only checking it on the second. His transcription was verified by one of the performers.[5] Mozart identifies his memory as 'perhaps' his 'best gift', maybe a surprising insight for one so consumed by the sound of music. So, arguably, this composer maintained a particular advantage over those endowed with weaker recall: he was capable of conceptualising and then memorising a piece in enough detail that he could 'hear … the parts … all at once'. Nevertheless, he writes clearly that imagining is not as good as 'actual hearing'. There are many possible reasons why this might be so, but one plausible account is that there is further elaboration to do as part of the notation process.

For many composers (myself included), it does not come that easily. The definition of genius, commonly attributed to Thomas Edison, as being 5 per cent inspiration and 95 per cent perspiration is often subverted to describe composition; for example, Steven Stuckey writes:

> You don't make music with ideas, or poetic dreams or wishful thinking. You make it with notes – with technique, with hard work, with Edison's 95 percent perspiration. It is technique that paints paintings, writes poems, builds buildings.[6]

So Stuckey seems to disregard spontaneous, imaginative creativity entirely, not even mentioning the 5 per cent, although one ought to remark that, in context, this may be for polemic effect. In any case, Mozart's and Stuckey's respective positions serve as proxies for two extremes of a spectrum of opinion: on the one hand, composition is entirely inspiration, and music is born in the mind of the composer (although not necessarily in a single flash of insight); on the other, it is derived from hard graft at the piano or on the page by entirely conscious, reasoned acts of deduction.[7]

Peter Warlock presents a third, different view of composition, placed somewhere between these two poles:

---

[5]   Ibid., 66–7.

[6]   Steven Stuckey, 'Creating music of geometry and longing', *Cornell University Arts and Sciences Newsletter*, 18/1 (Cornell University, 1996).

[7]   An interesting question, which I will expand later, is whether that technique necessarily has to be explicit and conscious, or whether implicit, non-conscious 'technique' – if it can even be called that – is sufficient, as Mozart seems to suggest: for him, musical form apparently 'just happened' without (much) conscious intervention, in the same way as the core ideas.

If I *had* ideas, I could not write them down without a piano! The sum total of my "compositions" – (I ought to say "compilations" for they were all "discovered" at the piano ...).[8]

In Warlock's approach, ideas are 'discovered' at the piano, maybe by improvising in a relatively uncontrolled way and then identifying the 'good', much as Mozart selects some of his imagined ideas and discards others; or maybe by using the piano as a sounding board to work out what the ideas that are imagined actually are in terms of notes. Arguably, *pacet* Stuckey, this is not *only* technique – one might say that the technique visible here is Warlock's 'compilation', and that he is also using his piano to explore the range of imagined possibilities as Mozart's imagination does. So Warlock can be placed on a spectrum somewhere between Mozart and Stuckey. This spectrum allows us to make distinctions between conscious creation in the deliberate planning of a formalist composer, the semi-spontaneous but cooperative and partly planned creation of the jazz improviser in a trio, and the entirely spontaneous whistling in the street of the same people that Schoenberg famously hoped and failed to convince of his 12-note 'tunes'.[9] It is important to note that a non-polar position on this spectrum necessarily entails a *mixture* of explicit technique and implicit imagination: there is not a smooth transition in kind between the two.

Therefore, the hypothesis that I shall put forward in the rest of this chapter proposes two separable, but interacting, cognitive mechanisms involved in composing music, which coexist in such a way as to account for the range of thinking expressed in the spectrum.[10]

Studying Creativity

Before beginning the discussion it will be useful to lay out some theoretical tools. Several general models of creative cognition have been proposed in the past century;[11] each has its own virtue, but for the current purpose, that of Boden is

---

[8]   Barry Smith (ed.), *Frederick Delius and Peter Warlock: A Friendship Revealed* (Oxford, 2000).

[9]   Arnold Schoenberg, *Letters*, ed. Erwin Stein (London, 1974); trans. from the original German by Eithne Wilkins and Ernst Kaiser. The word 'tunes' is quoted here because it is Schoenberg's own usage, not because I intend to question its propriety.

[10]   There ought, of course, to be a relationship with improvisation, as variously practised by organists, jazz performers and others, but I shall omit reference to this here, to keep the argument linear.

[11]   Graham Wallas, *The Art of Thought* (New York, 1926). Arthur Koestler, *The Act of Creation* (London, 1976). Margaret Boden, *The Creative Mind: Myths and Mechanisms*

most useful, partly because it can be operationalised mathematically,[12] but also because it provides a context in which the other theories, in particular that of Koestler, may be placed.

Boden's model of creativity revolves around her notion of a *conceptual space* and the exploration of such a space by creative agents – their exact nature is unspecified in the theory: they may be people, computer programs, or other as-yet-unimagined things. The conceptual space is a set of artefacts (in Boden's terms, *concepts*), which are in some quasi-syntactic sense deemed to be acceptable as examples of whatever is being created, so we might take the conceptual space as similar to the set of a certain kind of thing: that which is to be created. Implicitly, the conceptual space may include partially defined artefacts too. *Exploratory creativity* is the process of exploring a given conceptual space, or of selecting an item within it (for example, the range of possible frisbees: different colours, patterns, materials, shapes); *transformational creativity* is the process of changing the rules that delimit the conceptual space (for example, subverting the frisbee to serve as a dinner plate or a hat, or vice versa). Boden[13] also makes an important distinction between mere membership of a conceptual space and the *value* of a member of the space, which is extrinsically defined, but imprecisely. This distinction is easy to see in music: most people can point to pieces of music that they are content to *identify* as such, but which they do not *value* as such; that personal notion of value is also easily extended into a collective social construct.

An important philosophical point is that the mere existence of the conceptual space does not imply that its contents are known, much as a mathematician's knowledge of the existence of the infinite set of integer numbers does not entail that they have all been written down. Knowledge of the conceptual space is *intensional*,[14] expressible in terms of properties and constraints rather than by example, and needs to be *extended* to realise concepts from their intensional specification. Given this, exploration of the space becomes something more than mere enumeration of things that are known: it is a little akin to route-finding on a map, in the dark, with a very small torch – one knows the invisible territory exists, but one does not know its form, except by redirecting the torch and looking; on doing this, one can no longer see where one has been.

(London, 1990). Jacob W. Getzels and Mihaly Csikszentmihalyi, *The Creative Vision: A Longitudinal Study of Problem Finding in Art* (New York, 1976).

[12]   Geraint A. Wiggins, 'A preliminary framework for description, analysis and comparison of creative systems', *Journal of Knowledge Based Systems*, 19/7 (2006), 449–58. Geraint A. Wiggins, 'Searching for computational creativity', *New Generation Computing*, 24/73 (2006), 209–22.

[13]   Margaret Boden, 'Creativity and artificial intelligence', *Artificial Intelligence Journal*, 103 (1998), 347–56.

[14]   This is the converse of *extensional* and not semantically related to *intentional*.

Bundy[15] and Buchanan[16] join Boden in citing *reflection*, and hence reasoning *about* the conceptual space, rather than *within* it, as a requirement for 'real' or 'significant' creativity (although the definition of such creativity is so far left imprecise). I have shown elsewhere that, in terms of my Creative Systems Framework at least, transformational creativity is precisely exploratory creativity in the conceptual space of conceptual spaces.[17] So transformational creativity is precisely creativity *about* conceptual spaces. For completeness, I also mention here that there are other views: Ritchie,[18] for example, presents a completely different account of what is going on in 'transformational' creativity, in which the notion of transformation is not so clearly present. Nevertheless, Boden's notion of conceptual space is very helpful to the current discussion.

It is also important not to confuse the dimension of exploratory vs transformational (or object-level vs meta-level[19]) with the dimension of conscious vs non-conscious[20] thought. As a species, humans generally believe they are in much more conscious control than is actually the case. For example, there is evidence that conscious awareness of the intention to speak arises somewhat *after* the commencement of activity associated with generation of linguistic utterances in the brain.[21] Broadly speaking, much of cognition is a good deal less conscious than we tend to think it is, on the basis of introspection, and of course we can only know that which is conscious by definition, so we *would* think that way.

In the computational creativity literature,[22] this introspective bias provides a straw man to sceptics. Proposed mechanisms which might well work at a cognitive level unavailable to conscious introspection, are often derided by human creators because they 'obviously' do not describe what is going on – for example, they say, inspiration, introspected upon, is 'clearly not' the product of systematic enumeration of possibilities. However, the straw man is fireproof, because a majority of cognitive process is not available to introspection. What is needed is, firstly, to explicitly locate creative cognition with respect to conscious awareness

---

[15] Alan Bundy, 'What is the difference between real creativity and mere novelty?', *Behavioural and Brain Sciences*, 17/3 (1994), 533–4.

[16] Bruce Buchanan, 'Creativity at the metalevel', *AI Magazine*, 22/3 (2001), 13–28 [AAAI-2000 presidential address].

[17] Wiggins, 'A preliminary framework for description, analysis and comparison of creative systems'.

[18] Graeme Ritchie, 'Some empirical criteria for attributing creativity to a computer program', *Minds and Machines*, 17/1 (2007), 67–99.

[19] Wiggins, 'Searching for computational creativity'.

[20] I avoid 'subconscious' to forefend unintended Freudian associations.

[21] Francesca Carota, Andres Posada, Sylvain Harquel, Claude Delpuech, Olivier Bertrand, and Angela Sirigu, 'Neural Dynamics of the Intention to Speak', *Cerebral Cortex*, 20/8 (2010), 1891–7.

[22] See www.computationalcreativity.net.

and, secondly, to demystify creativity, accepting that many of the human activities studied in cognitive science are to some extent creative, even if that extent is so small that everyone does it all the time. At this point, we take the controversial step of knocking creativity off its Romantic pedestal.

In this chapter, I use Boden's notion of conceptual space, as characterised above, to capture the set of possible musical compositions. Evidently, this space may be decomposed into smaller spaces capturing different styles, genres or whatever, and I will focus mostly on the conceptual space of tonal melody. Importantly, in my formalisation,[23] the space contains the *empty concept*, a concept with no features at all, which may be thought of as the frame on which all concepts hang, and it also explicitly contains partially defined concepts, which may safely be thought of as pieces in various stages of completeness, although this must be tempered with the acknowledgement that one composer's finished piece may be another's unfinished one. In this way of thinking, a particular compositional path might be described as a point-to-point trajectory from the empty concept (the blank page) to whatever concept corresponds with the final piece. Equally, the trajectory might, star-like, draw together a number of points in the space, each of which begins at a non-empty concept. Here, we are allowing the notion of spontaneous generation of motifs (of whatever kind). In that case, the question must be asked, 'Whence come those initial points?' This is the key question that this chapter aims to answer and the subsequent question begged is, 'How do the points get joined together?' I tentatively propose an account for that also. First, however, we must ask whence comes the conceptual space, for each individual?

Learning and Creativity

To find the source of the conceptual space, we must examine the human capacity to learn. To deny this relation would be to deny the evidence observed by every parent in history: we are not born with a full understanding of the world around us, but we must learn it. The vast majority of learning, however, is not done explicitly at school or from books, but implicitly, from direct experience of the world itself. In the musical context, even capacities such as the perception of relative pitch (as distinct from the trained ability to name the interval classes thus formed) are implicitly learned,[24] and are learned with surprising efficiency, given exposure to the necessary stimuli. Musical style is self-evidently learned too: an individual enculturated in Africa, for example, has a different internal model of musical style

---

[23]   Wiggins, 'A preliminary framework for description, analysis and comparison of creative systems'.

[24]   Jenny Saffran and Gregory Griepentrog, 'Absolute pitch in infant auditory learning: Evidence for developmental reorganization', *Developmental Psychology*, 37/1 (2001), 74–85.

from an individual extensively and exclusively exposed to European music.[25] In the complete absence of evidence for genetic encoding of musical style, and given the substantial and increasing body of evidence for implicit musical learning, it is the latter hypothesis that is more convincing. The existential, evolutionary value of the voracious human capacity to learn[26] is based in its affordance of expectation: a massively enhanced ability to manage the world,[27] which is strictly necessary for such a frail organism.

It is a property of the human mind to generalise from examples: indeed, the tendency is so strong as sometimes to lead us astray in quite simple logic. At the non-conscious perceptual level, generalisation allows us to capture the essential properties of events and objects in the world around us, and serves to protect us from threats that are similar to, but not the same as, threats previously encountered and survived. In the case of music, as we are exposed to more and more examples, the more we tend to generalise the style, the more we learn about it, and the more we develop efficient ways of hearing and remembering it. For example, experienced listeners to music of the Classical period can develop a very strong sense of tonal structure, and are able to hear movement around the various tonal functions; this is not the same as being taught the music-theoretic tonal functions and knowing about them. The two kinds of knowledge are quite independent. Learning, for example, what a dominant sounds like is cognitively useful in the face of large quantities of tonal data because it helps promote cognitively efficient classification and recall of that sound data, even if the learner–perceiver does not know that this is called 'dominant' by music theorists. It follows that someone never previously exposed to a particular style is probably cognitively incapable of hearing the finer-grained aspects of that style that an experienced listener enjoys.

In the context of Boden's theory, this implicitly learned, generalised perceptual mental model of music is one candidate to supply the conceptual space. The other candidate is a theoretically acquired, explicitly learned model of music, as taught in music theory classes across the western world. On the compositional level, these two possibilities correspond with the two ends of my compositional spectrum, introduced earlier; the former is at the Mozart-like, spontaneous end, while the latter is Stuckey-like, relying on technique and knowledge *about* music, rather than implicit musical imagination. As might be expected, a mixture of the two can produce a Warlock-amalgam of behaviours, where explicit and implicit knowledge interact. However, when we are learning

---

[25]   Petri Toiviainen, and Tuomas Eerola, 'Where is the beat?: Comparison of Finnish and South-African listeners'. In: Reinhard Kopiez, Andreas Lehmann, Irving Wolther and Christian Wolf (eds), *Proceedings of the 5th Triennial ESCOM Conference* (ESCOM, 2005).

[26]   Irving Biederman and Edward Vessel, 'Perceptual pleasure and the brain', *American Scientist*, 94 (2006), 247–53.

[27]   Marcus T. Pearce and Geraint A. Wiggins, 'Auditory expectation: The information dynamics of music perception and cognition', *Topics in Cognitive Science* (Wiley, 2012).

to *hear* music, there is only the perceptually learned model: the music-theoretic account is meaningless, in a literal sense, if one has not learned the necessary cognitive representations for the style in question. It is an interesting point to note that this meaninglessness does not prevent the successful application of theoretical rules, at least at a simple level. This is the same property that allows logical calculi to propose solutions to problems in reasoning: their syntax directly encodes their semantics.

A Model of Musical Learning that Can Perhaps Create

One way to provide evidence for the hypothesis developed here as an account of human creativity is to build computer models of it, and demonstrate that behaviour of such models predicts that of human creators. To do so, we must begin with a model of learning – here, I use that proposed, implemented and evaluated by Pearce,[28] a complex and detailed model of auditory sequence learning, embodied in a computer program. The detail of the model and the program that embodies it are not relevant to the current argument, except in the following. The model has no programmed rules about musical style, although it has the simulated capacity to perceive[29] various musical constructs, such as scale degree and key note. The model is exposed to a large body of tonal melodies from which it learns, merely by counting the number of occurrences of each kind of event in sequence, in the context of what preceded it, using various different representations (for example, absolute pitch, scale degree, note duration) simultaneously to do so. The different representations predict separately, but their predictions are combined into one for each note, using Shannon's mathematical information theory.[30] Finally, and crucially, the model is able to generalise, to accommodate events that it has not previously encountered;[31] again the detail of how is not relevant here. Once learning is complete, the model is able to predict the expectations of listeners enculturated into western music to a surprising degree of accuracy: in statistical

---

[28] Marcus T. Pearce, 'The construction and evaluation of statistical models of melodic structure in music perception and composition', PhD thesis (Department of Computing, City University, London, 2005).

[29] Avoiding anthropomorphism in this kind of discussion, as would be ideal, entails awkward and continual circumlocution, or at best an excess of quotation marks. It clearest simply to use the anthropomorphic terminology while reminding ourselves that all of these quasi-human traits are *simulated*.

[30] Claude Shannon, 'A mathematical theory of communication', *Bell System Technical Journal*, 27 (1948), 379–423, 623–56; Marcus T. Pearce, Darrell Conklin and Geraint A. Wiggins, 'Methods for combining statistical models of music'. In: Uffe Kock Wiil (ed.), *Computer Music Modelling and Retrieval* (Heidelberg: Springer, 2005), 295–312.

[31] Marcus T. Pearce and Geraint A. Wiggins, 'Expectation in melody: The influence of context and learning', *Music Perception*, 23/5 (2006), 377–405.

terms, it accounts for up to 81% of the variance in human responses[32] (of course, not all listeners respond identically, so there is no single correct answer). The model is also able to predict *segmentation* of musical melody – the points at which phrase boundaries are perceived by listeners – from its learned data alone, to a degree comparable with explicitly music-theoretical approaches.[33]

Because it is capable of successful application to these tasks, I hypothesise that the model may serve as a simulated conceptual space for the melodies it learns, and, further, that the simulation is of a human conceptual space, not an arbitrary computational one. This claim is underpinned by the empirical evidence cited here for the behaviour of the model as a model of perception, and by the well-supported hypothesis that a key feature of human conceptual spaces is their close relationship with perception.[34] This model, however, is rather abstract; it is not a direct model of the neural behaviour of the brain (although it does seem to have certain neural correlates[35]). This, however, does not undermine its status as a model of cognitive *function*: the proof is in its demonstrable ability to predict human behaviour. Because it does so by counting observed occurrences it is, in essence, a statistical model. This means that, in principle, standard methods from statistics can be used to sample from the model's memory, to produce complete melodies in the broad style that the model has learned. This has been shown to work, to a minimal level of acceptability, for melodies in the style of those harmonised as chorales by Johann Sebastian Bach.[36] The melodies are rarely good, but they are recognisable as melodies, when rigorously evaluated by independent observers. The one selected as best by our observers is reproduced in Example 10.1.

Whorley has developed a more advanced statistical system[37] that is capable of harmonising hymn tunes to a reasonably high musical level, demonstrating the generality of the ideas beyond melody alone; I give an example in Example 10.2. Substantial work remains to be done before strong claims can be made, however.

---

[32]   Ibid.

[33]   Marcus T. Pearce, Daniel Müllensiefen and Geraint A. Wiggins, 'The role of expectation and probabilistic learning in auditory boundary perception: A model comparison', *Perception*, 9 (2010), 1367–91.

[34]   Peter Gärdenfors, *Conceptual Spaces: the Geometry of Thought* (Cambridge, MA, 2000).

[35]   Marcus T. Pearce, Maria Herrojo Ruiz, Selina Kapasi, Geraint A. Wiggins and Joydeep Bhattacharya, 'Unsupervised statistical learning underpins computational, behavioural and neural manifestations of musical expectation', *NeuroImage*, 50/1 (2010), 303–14.

[36]   Marcus T. Pearce and Geraint A. Wiggins, 'Evaluating cognitive models of musical composition'. In: Amílcar Cardoso and Geraint A. Wiggins (eds), *Proceedings of the 4th International Joint Workshop on Computational Creativity* (2007), 73–80.

[37]   Raymond Whorley, Marcus T. Pearce and Geraint A. Wiggins, 'Computational modelling of the cognition of harmonic movement'. In: *Proceedings of the 10th International Conference on Music Perception and Cognition*, Sapporo, Japan (2008). Raymond Whorley,

Example 10.1   A statistically generated chorale melody, deemed acceptable by human listeners. The rhythm is taken from *Jesu, meiner Seelen Wonne* (BWV 359); pitches are generated by our statistical model without human intervention.

Example 10.2   A harmonisation by Whorley's statistical harmonisation system, again without human intervention. The tune is a French church melody, from *Chants Ordinaires de l'Office Divin* (Paris, 1881); it is reprinted as Hymn No. 33, *Grafton*, in the 1993 edition of the English Hymnal.

Returning briefly to my compositional spectrum, the sampling approach described above is an extreme case of the Mozart myth, in that it supposes a complete melody appearing in one flash of sampled inspiration, equivalent to picking a completed piece out of the conceptual space as one point, fully formed, as Minerva from the forehead of Jove. Therefore, I do not propose it as a representative model of human composition. A closer simulation of Mozart's

Geraint A. Wiggins, Christophe Rhodes and Marcus T. Pearce, 'Development of techniques for the computational modelling of harmony'. In: Ventura et al. (eds), *Proceedings of the First International Conference on Computational Creativity* (2010).

self-reported approach would be the statistical generation of melodic fragments, or motifs, which are glued together by subsequent traversal of the conceptual space – the star-shaped creative trajectory mentioned in an earlier section. Yet how can statistical sampling (over whole pieces or fragments) be justified as a cognitive model of creativity?

I have already mentioned the human property of expectation, casting it in general as a device for managing the world. However, what is the relation between statistical memory of musical melody and expectation? The answer is quite simple: one non-consciously predicts what happens next on the basis of what one has experienced in the immediate past. This is a very efficient way of managing information in the world, because relevant memories can be accessed in advance, priming us to be ready for what is next. What is more, appropriate cognitive processing power can be applied: something that is expected needs less processing – less attention – than something that is not, because we already know what it is. So, simply put, we expect things more in a given context if we have heard something similar in a similar context before; we are non-consciously, continually guessing what comes next. This simple idea (which is more complicated to implement) seems to underlie several aspects of speech processing as well – indeed, the model proposed here is capable of segmenting speech into morphemes, using the same method it uses for phrase segmentation.[38] Most importantly, predicting what comes next helps us communicate more efficiently. Therefore, it is established that, when listening to music and speech, there is a cognitive process that continually predicts what is coming next. It is entirely reasonable to propose that this process is equally capable of responding to internal (imagined) musical phenomena as external (heard) ones, and so it is not hard to imagine a situation where any sound, real or remembered, might trigger the expectation mechanism, suggesting a continuation into a sequence. Given the position that learning is an essentially statistical process, to do with correlations of co-occurrence in observed events, the expectation mechanism can be thought of as statistical sampling: the generation of instances from a statistical model. Crucially, the involvement of generalisation means that it is possible to sample instances that the model has not specifically observed.

In this more incremental view, we might see small sections of music – motifs – appearing, note by note, rather than as a whole, pre-formed melody. As a result we can generate small units, and consider their likelihood in terms of the extant model, the non-conscious correlate of this latter activity being the ability to 'see' (that is, without conscious consideration) how a motif might fit into one or another context. Following the *hedonic curve* of Wilhelm Wundt[39] (see Figure 10.1), we

---

[38]   Geraint A. Wiggins, '"I let the music speak": cross-domain application of a cognitive model of musical learning'. In: Patrick Rebuschat and John Williams (eds), *Statistical Learning and Language Acquisition* (Amsterdam, 2011).

[39]   Wilhelm Wundt, *Grundzüge der physiologischen Psychologie* (W. Engelman, 1874), transl. into English as Wilhelm Wundt and Edward Titchener, *Principles of*

find that very likely units are dull, while very unlikely ones are difficult to relate to the conceptual space – exactly as we might expect from the corresponding probabilities. There is a balance to be struck between novelty and stylistic conformity. Each of these units corresponds with a point, a non-empty concept, in the conceptual space, just as Mozart's initial ideas gave him starting points for musical imagination. This, then, is a hypothetical account of how inspiration, at the level of motivic ideas, might happen. The next step in my argument is to propose why it happens in the cognitive context.

The Chattering Crowd of Mind

For decades, in artificial intelligence, the notion of collective, agent-based models of mind has been current – for example, Marvin Minsky's famous Society of Mind.[40] Here the massively parallel nature of cognitive processing is captured in systems that consist of interacting processes, whose combined emergent properties are then complex and unpredictable. Within this broad category, Bernard Baars has proposed Global Workspace Theory,[41] a convincing theory of consciousness based on information production by large numbers of cognitive processes, which may operate in various degrees of synchrony, and high synchrony is associated with conscious awareness. Murray Shanahan gives neurophysiological underpinning for the theory.[42] It is impossible to give a complete account of these wide-ranging, subtle and elegant ideas in the space available here, so I summarise instead by analogy. Human cognition may be conceptualised as a crowd of book-makers,[43] each of whom continually shouts the odds of informational tips from data provided by sensory mechanisms and memory. Some of the tips make it as far as the Global Workspace, where they can be heard by everyone, but some of them are lost on the way, in the constant babble of shouting book-makers. When a tip from one bookie appears in the Global Workspace, it becomes accessible, not only to all the others, but also to consciousness, by a process that remains somewhat obscure – but that is not the focus of the current argument.

To match the theory against Mozart's reported creative experience, a point-by-point summary is useful. To deal with the world, we constantly predict from models built statistically from experience. Prediction is continual, multiple and

---

Physiological Psychology, Vol. 1 of Principles of Physiological Psychology (Sonnenschein, 1904). Elizabeth Margulis and Andrew Beatty, 'Musical style, psychoaesthetics, and prospects for entropy as an analytic tool', *Computer Music Journal*, 32/4 (2008), 64–78.

[40]   Marvin Minsky, *The Society of Mind* (New York, 1985).

[41]   Bernard Baars, *A cognitive theory of consciousness* (Cambridge, 1988).

[42]   Murray Shanahan, *Embodiment and the Inner Life: Cognition and Consciousness in the Space of Possible Minds* (Oxford, 2010).

[43]   That is to say, not publishers, but people who give the odds, take bets and offer 'tips' – not gratuities, but suggestions for promising bets – on horse races.

in parallel. Predicted items are selected, and made available to consciousness, so there is a notion of competition between predictors. When a prediction is selected, the new information becomes available to all predictors. Now, let us compare this sequence of events with Mozart's report. When he is 'completely himself', when nothing is distracting him, and his mind is open, so there is relatively little to compete with musical predictors, ideas 'come', spontaneously (he 'cannot force them'). The ideas cannot be 'forced', so the essence of the process is non-conscious. Some of the ideas formed do not 'please' him, and are deliberately discarded, so we may hypothesise that whatever non-conscious 'selection' is applied at this stage of Mozart's compositional process is not a complete determinant of musical value, just like our experimental melody creators, mentioned above.

Having been selected, first by the mysterious Global Workspace selection mechanism, and then by Mozart's own idiosyncratic hedonic assessment (the details of which are inscrutable, since it passed away with its owner), the chosen ideas are consciously memorised and therefore available to all predictors in the Global Workspace. Given the overwhelming tendency to predict, what would be more natural than to predict musical structures that include these multiple smaller units, appropriately connected together? In this way, each prediction can step towards a completed composition, guided but not restricted by the hypothetical composer's generalised statistical model of style, with the composer selecting or manipulating at each cycle: 'my subject enlarges itself, becomes methodized and defined'. One can also speculate that a composer with Mozart's capacious and punctilious memory might be able to remember the process as well as the outcome; and the sequence of events proposed here does seem to match his introspective description, although, of course, there may be other candidates, and the question of which really is correct cannot be answered.

There remain two outstanding aspects of the current matter for which I have not proposed hypothetical solutions: first, the conscious selection of potentially usable motifs on the basis of idiosyncratic quality; and, second, the non-conscious restriction of the predictors' output.

We can seek a solution to the first of these in the relatively new field of neuroaesthetics, where, for example, Biederman and Vessel[44] have given convincing proposals and evidence as to how somatic hedonic responses may be derived from the process of learning about perceived objects. This work is in its infancy, and is an area where great scientific contributions to the understanding of humankind are to be made. We can, also, in more conscious contexts (for example, the deliberate construction of rock 'anthems'), imagine a rule-based selector, working on the basis of stylistic similarity to analytically identified key features of other music of the target kind.

A candidate solution for the second question (of how non-conscious selection is applied) can be given directly, in terms of the operation of the statistics of the

---

[44]   Biederman and Vessel, 'Perceptual pleasure and the brain' and later work.

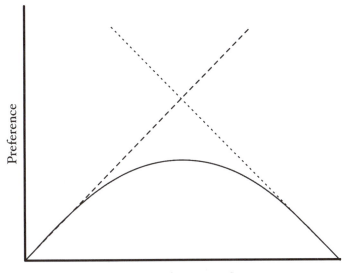

Likelihood/Information Content

Figure 10.1   The Wundt curve (solid) is formed by the multiplication of two linear functions: the likelihood of a generated item (dashed) and the number of generators likely to agree on an item, according to its likelihood (dotted).

predictors, in terms of their memory models, but also in terms of the collective crowd. There are two factors involved here. The first is the probability of the item being predicted and, relatedly, the amount of information it carries. As one is sampling continually, and more probable items are likely to be selected more frequently, so we might expect the Workspace to be cluttered with banal rubbish. However, Wundt[45] tells us that likely items are less interesting than unlikely ones; in terms of Shannon's[46] information theory, they do not carry much information. So part of my candidate solution is that there needs to be a certain amount of information in a prediction before it is allowed through into the global workspace. This is philosophically reasonable: there would be little value in conscious awareness of prediction if it were not to isolate the unexpected; valued cognitive resources would be wasted. There is empirical evidence for this in perception: we[47] have shown that there is indeed increased global synchrony (which, I noted above, corresponds in Global Workspace Theory with conscious awareness) in

[45]   Wundt, *Grundzüge der physiologischen Psychologie*.

[46]   Shannon, 'A mathematical theory of communication'.

[47]   Pearce et al., 'Unsupervised statistical learning underpins computational, behavioural and neural manifestations of musical expectation'.

beta-band neural activity, in response to improbable melodic notes, as compared with probable ones. I propose that the same mechanism operates on produced items as on perceived ones.[48] Thus, information-heavy predictions are preferred over information-light ones.

The second part of this second solution emerges straightforwardly from the statistical dynamics of the system. According to Shanahan,[49] the synchrony that corresponds with availability to consciousness can be thought of as multiple predictors producing a particular solution simultaneously. At any given time, and given a large number of randomly sampling predictors, likely predictions will be more common in the population; unlikely ones, which contain more information, will be less common, and outrageously obscure ones very rare indeed. Therefore, it is less likely that sufficient synchrony will be achieved for conscious awareness, by the less likely outcomes, simply because it is less likely that they will be selected. This gives us two opposing trends, which are linear functions of likelihood, one positive and one negative, as illustrated in Figure 10.1. The multiplicative combination of these two, motivated by the usual combination of independent likelihoods in probability theory, gives (one version of) the Wundt curve, as shown in the figure. This explanation is powerful, because it needs no mechanism other than that already proposed above and elsewhere for other purposes. At this stage, I have proposed a hypothetical mechanistic cognitive framework in which inspiration, or, more objectively, *spontaneous creativity*, can take place.

Technique, Structure and How to 'See the Truth'

At this stage, I have proposed a hypothetical mechanistic cognitive framework in which inspiration (or spontaneous creativity) can take place. I now return to the question of technique, and its opposition to inspiration. However, the first question to ask is: 'Are these two really in opposition?' To help consider this question, imagine, on the one hand, a music freshman laboriously harmonising a melody in the style of Bach according to taught rules on paper, and, on the other, an expert organist, harmonising the same melody in the same style, live at the keyboard, during a Sunday service. While the organist certainly has knowledge of the rules that the student is applying, she does not need to think very hard, if at all, about them: she simply *feels* what comes next, to the extent that her fingers almost seem to work independently from conscious intervention.

---

[48]   Here, as elsewhere, I appeal to Occam's razor, a scientific precept owing to William of Ockham: a simple theory is better than a complicated one. In the current case, one mechanism applicable in two instances is simpler than two different mechanisms, one for each instance.

[49]   Shanahan, *Embodiment and the Inner Life: Cognition and Consciousness in the Space of Possible Minds*.

Karmiloff-Smith[50] identifies three cognitive stages of learning: a data-driven acquisition phase, where representations are independently stored and used, with no internal representational change; a middle phase of internal representational change, during internalisation of knowledge; and finally, reconcilation of the new internal representations with the external knowledge, which includes reflection. Our student is at the first, following rules, while our organist has reached the third, where knowledge is encoded so deeply in the non-conscious system that the effect of using it is encoded in common parlance ... in other words, she has the music 'under her fingers'. Mozart, it appears, was at this level in terms of imagining music. Warlock, on the other hand, possibly used his implicit deep knowledge of piano technique to guide his 'discovery' of new musical ideas, but without Mozart's level of imagination of music. Again, it is regrettably too late to test this proposal.

Karmiloff-Smith's three stages of learning constitute a comparator against which a given individual's capacity at a given task can be measured, broadly summarised as the range between completely explicit reasoning (conscious, rule-based) and completely implicit reasoning (non-conscious, intuitive). For the music freshman with the necessary inclination, diligence and core ability, there is a trajectory to the level of the organist, moving along this spectrum – and that is the original point of the theory.

The Stuckey-end of my compositional spectrum seems at first sight to correspond to some degree with Karmiloff-Smith's first level (conscious application of rules), but this is misleading – it is altogether more complicated. Compositional technique (as distinct from harmonisation exercises where rules are predefined) is not merely about the application of given rules; it also entails intuition or design of the rules to be applied, and their effective application. These actions are transformational, in Boden's sense, so may be considered 'more' creative than mere application of taught rules.

Computational rule-based systems have been applied extensively to compositional tasks in the past,[51] sometimes explicitly from the point of view of *search control*,[52] which may be thought of as technique: 'Which rule(s) should I apply at each point?' The problem, though, with such methods, is that one always needs to start from somewhere: even given an initial empty concept, a first step

[50]   Annette Karmiloff-Smith, *Beyond Modularity: A Developmental Perspective on Cognitive Science* (Cambridge, MA, 1995).

[51]   David Cope, *Computers and Musical Style* (Oxford, 1991). George Papadopoulos and Geraint A. Wiggins, 'AI methods for algorithmic composition: A survey, a critical view and future prospects'. In: *Proceedings of the AISB'99 Symposium on Musical Creativity* (Brighton, 1999), 110–17.

[52]   Kemal Ebcioğlu, 'An expert system for harmonizing four-part chorales', *Computer Music Journal*, 12/3 (1988), 43–51. Geraint A. Wiggins, George Papadopoulos, Somnuk Phon-Amnuaisuk and Andrew Tuson, 'Evolutionary methods for musical composition', *International Journal of Computing Anticipatory Systems* (1999).

has to be taken. In harmonisation examples, there is the given melody and all the implicit framing-information it brings with it (key, tonality, and so on). In David Cope's Experiments in Musical Intelligence program (EMI), it seems that structure from human-composed music supplies the basis.[53] It is hard to see indeed how a rule-based system can start from a blank page, unless it is by fiat from a programmer (so the seed of creativity is coming from a human, not the program, and therefore the program is not embodying a complete theory of creativity) or by random selection, as practised (usually with a non-uniform distribution, derived from prior musical knowledge) in evolutionary music generation.[54]

Towards an Objective Account of Spontaneous Creativity

This idea brings us full circle, since biased random sampling, followed by selection, is precisely the cognitive mechanism proposed above. I have cited some preliminary empirical evidence for the mechanisms proposed, too, suggesting that one can have at least some confidence in the proposal – there is no pretence at this stage of more than hypothetical claims.

Given such a hypothesis, one can in principle begin to build a veridical simulation of the creative mechanisms proposed here, and music is an ideal domain in which to work, being untrammelled by the reasoning about the real world that makes linguistic and non-abstract visual art difficult for creative computer systems. Most importantly, from these precepts, we can at last begin to give an account of spontaneous human creativity in music, in terms of conscious and non-conscious processes, some of which are so banal as to go unnoticed every day, and some of which can produce humankind's greatest art.

References

Baars, Bernard J. *A Cognitive Theory of Consciousness* (Cambridge: Cambridge University Press, 1988).

Biederman, Irving and Edward A. Vessel, 'Perceptual pleasure and the brain', *American Scientist*, 94 (2006), 247–53.

Boden, Margaret A., *The Creative Mind: Myths and Mechanisms* (London: Weidenfield and Nicholson, 1990).

Boden, Margaret A., 'Creativity and artificial intelligence', *Artificial Intelligence Journal*, 103 (1998), 347–56.

Buchanan, Bruce G., 'Creativity at the metalevel', *AI Magazine*, 22/3 (2001), 13–28 [AAAI-2000 presidential address].

---

[53] David Cope *Virtual Music: Computer Synthesis of Musical Style* (Cambridge, MA, 2004).

[54] Wiggins et al., 'Evolutionary methods for musical composition'.

Bundy, Alan, 'What is the difference between real creativity and mere novelty?', *Behavioural and Brain Sciences*, 17/3 (1994), 533–4.

Carota, Francesca, Andres Posada, Sylvain Harquel, Claude Delpuech, Olivier Bertrand and Angela Sirigu, 'Neural dynamics of the intention to speak', *Cerebral Cortex*, 20/8 (2010), 1891–7.

Cope, David, *Computers and Musical Style* (Oxford: Oxford University Press, 1991).

Cope, David, *Virtual Music: Computer Synthesis of Musical Style* (Cambridge, MA: The MIT Press, 2004).

Ebcioğlu, Kemal, 'An expert system for harmonizing four-part chorales', *Computer Music Journal*, 12/3 (1988), 43–51.

Gärdenfors, Peter, *Conceptual Spaces: the Geometry of Thought* (Cambridge, MA: The MIT Press, 2000).

Getzels, Jacob and Mihalyi Csikszentmihalyi, *The Creative Vision: A Longitudinal Study of Problem Finding in Art* (New York: Wiley, 1976).

Holmes, Edward, *The Life of Mozart: Including his Correspondence*, Cambridge Library Collection (Cambridge: Cambridge University Press, 2009).

Karmiloff-Smith, Annette, *Beyond Modularity: A Developmental Perspective on Cognitive Science* (Cambridge, MA: The MIT Press,1995).

Koestler, Arthur, *The Act of Creation* (London, UK: Hutchinson, 1976).

Margulis, Elizabeth H. and Andrew P. Beatty, 'Musical style, psychoaesthetics, and prospects for entropy as an analytic tool', *Computer Music Journal*, 32/4 (2008), 64–78.

Minsky, Marvin, *The Society of Mind* (New York: Simon and Schuster Inc., 1985).

Papadopoulos, George and Geraint A. Wiggins, 'AI methods for algorithmic composition: A survey, a critical view and future prospects'. In: *Proceedings of the AISB'99 Symposium on Musical Creativity* (Brighton: SSAISB, 1999), 110–17.

Pearce, Marcus T., 'The construction and evaluation of statistical models of melodic structure in music perception and composition', PhD thesis (Department of Computing, City University, London, 2005).

Pearce, Marcus T., Darrell Conklin and Geraint A. Wiggins, 'Methods for combining statistical models of music'. In: Uffe Kock Wiil (ed.), *Computer Music Modelling and Retrieval* (Heidelberg: Springer, 2005), 295–312.

Pearce, Marcus T., Maria Herrojo Ruiz, Selina Kapasi, Geraint A. Wiggins and Joydeep Bhattacharya, 'Unsupervised statistical learning underpins computational, behavioural and neural manifestations of musical expectation', *NeuroImage*, 50/1 (2010), 303–14.

Pearce, Marcus T. and Geraint A. Wiggins, 'Expectation in melody: The influence of context and learning', *Music Perception*, 23/5 (2006), 377–405.

Pearce, Marcus T. and Geraint A. Wiggins, 'Evaluating cognitive models of musical composition'. In: Amìlcar Cardoso and Geraint A. Wiggins (eds), *Proceedings of the 4th International Joint Workshop on Computational Creativity* (2007), 73–80.

Pearce, Marcus T., Daniel Müllensiefen, and Geraint A. Wiggins, 'The role of expectation and probabilistic learning in auditory boundary perception: A model comparison', *Perception*, 9 (2010), 1367–91.

Pearce, Marcus T. and Geraint A. Wiggins, 'Auditory expectation: The information dynamics of music perception and cognition', *Topics in Cognitive Science* (2012, in press).

Phon-Amnuaisuk, Somnuk, Alan Smaill and Geraint A. Wiggins 'Chorale harmonization: A view from a search control perspective', *Journal of New Music Research*, 35/4 (2006), 279–305.

Ritchie, Graeme, 'Some empirical criteria for attributing creativity to a computer program', *Minds and Machines*, 17/1 (2007), 67–99.

Saffran, Jenny R. and Gregory J. Griepentrog, 'Absolute pitch in infant auditory learning: Evidence for developmental reorganization', *Developmental Psychology*, 37/1 (2001), 74–85.

Schoenberg, Arnold, *Letters*, ed. Erwin Stein (London: Faber, 1974); trans. from the original German by Eithne Wilkins and Ernst Kaiser.

Shanahan, Murray, *Embodiment and the Inner Life: Cognition and Consciousness in the Space of Possible Minds* (Oxford: Oxford University Press, 2010).

Shannon, Claude, 'A mathematical theory of communication', *Bell Systems Technical Journal*, 27 (1948), 379–423, 623–56.

Smith, Barry (ed.). *Frederick Delius and Peter Warlock: A Friendship Revealed* (Oxford: Oxford University Press, 2000).

Stuckey, Steven, 'Creating music of geometry and longing', *Cornell University Arts and Sciences Newsletter*, 18/1 (1996), http://www.arts.cornell.edu/newsletr/fall96/stucky.htm.

Toiviainen, Petri and Tuomas Eerola, 'Where is the beat?: Comparison of Finnish and South-African listeners'. In: Reinhard Kopiez, Andreas C. Lehmann, Irving Wolther and Christian Wolf (eds), *Proceedings of the 5th Triennial ESCOM Conference* (ESCOM, 2005).

Wallas, Graham, *The Art of Thought* (New York: Harcourt Brace, 1926).

Whorley, Raymond, Marcus T. Pearce and Geraint A. Wiggins, 'Computational modelling of the cognition of harmonic movement'. In: *Proceedings of the 10th International Conference on Music Perception and Cognition* (2008), Sapporo, Japan.

Whorley, Raymond, Geraint A. Wiggins, Christophe Rhodes and Marcus T. Pearce, 'Development of techniques for the computational modelling of harmony'. In: Ventura et al. (eds), *Proceedings of the First International Conference on Computational Creativity* (2010).

Wiggins, Geraint A., 'A preliminary framework for description, analysis and comparison of creative systems', *Journal of Knowledge Based Systems*, 19/7 (2006), 449–58.

Wiggins, Geraint A., 'Searching for computational creativity', *New Generation Computing*, 24/3 (2006), 209–22.

Wiggins, Geraint A., 'Semantic gap?? Schemantic Schmap!! Methodological considerations in the scientific study of music'. In: *Proceedings of 11th IEEE International Symposium on Multimedia* (2009), 477–82.

Wiggins, Geraint A., '"I let the music speak": Cross-domain application of a cognitive model of musical learning'. In: Patrick Rebuschat and John Williams (eds), *Statistical Learning and Language Acquisition* (Amsterdam: Mouton De Gruyter, 2011).

Wiggins, Geraint A., George Papadopoulos, Somnuk Phon-Amnuaisuk and Andrew Tuson, 'Evolutionary methods for musical composition', *International Journal of Computing Anticipatory Systems* (1999), http://www2.ulg.ac.be/mathgen/CHAOS/IJCAS/IJCAS_CONTENT.htm#.

Wiggins, Geraint A., Daniel Müllensiefen and Marcus T. Pearce, 'On the non-existence of music: Why music theory is a figment of the imagination', *Musicae Scientiae*, Discussion Forum 5 (2010), 231–55.

Wroe, Nick, ' A life in music: Richard Rodney Bennett', *The Guardian* (22 July 2011), http://www.guardian.co.uk/culture/2011/jul/22/richard-rodney-bennett-life-music-film.

Wundt, Wilhelm, *Grundzüge der physiologischen Psychologie* (W. Engelman, 1874).

Wundt, Wilhelm and Edward Titchener, *Principles of Physiological Psychology*, Vol. 1 (Sonnenschein, 1904).

Chapter 11

Rules, Tactics and Strategies for Composing Music

David Cope

Background

During my teen years, my parents sent me to art school, determined, I imagine, to broaden my horizons beyond chess, astronomy and music, the subjects that occupied most of my time during those years. While creating visual art for three hours a week for seven consecutive years, I learned the basic techniques of different media, fewer in number then since this predated the digital age. For four of my years at this school, I worked with the 'blank canvas' – drawing, watercolours and oils. While I produced several competent examples in each genre, I found the process itself difficult to master. For example, imitating nature in the raw or in the studio seemed like a poor substitute for photography, which even in its infancy then produced better results, I thought. Abstractions were more inventive, but facing the blank canvas often produced a similar blank canvas inside of my head. In my fifth year of art school, however, the instructors introduced me to pottery wheels, dumping moist lumps of clay in the centre of a pedal-controlled, horizontally positioned circular wheel. By simply guiding my hands over this clay in certain ways as the wheel moved, I could create all manner of fascinating forms, gradually correcting errors as I went.

Pottery turned to carving plaster-of-Paris, wood and other materials, and I soon found myself in artist utopia. My ultimate sculptures already existed in the geometric solids with which I began. All I had to do was find them – an extraordinary opportunity it seemed. The blank canvas disappeared immediately from my creative approach. I flourished in this medium and made new discoveries; even mistakes often caused me to re-think goals and consider the occasional surprises better than my original conception. I had definitely found my creative milieu and produced literally dozens of interesting pieces during my final years in art school. It took several years of my musical life to realise the possibility that sculptural techniques could be as useful to me as a composer as they had been to me as a nascent visual artist. This fact became particularly obvious as I discovered algorithmic composing. I could program computers to produce my musical clay, wood and plaster-of-Paris substitutes, and sculpt the results in much the same ways as I had as a young man in art school.

What follows here, then, is a detailed account of how I use my early studies in art, along with game theory and decision-making, as a major source of my composing processes. I include game theory and decision-making to ensure that my initial musical 'blobs of clay', wood or plaster geometric solids not only consist of every possible pitch, but also have suggestive forms and structures from which to build my completed musical works.

Concept

Composers use many different processes to compose their music. Some of these processes have intuitive or subconscious sources and thus cannot be easily explained. Other processes can be articulated more clearly, even to laypersons. In recent decades, several composers have used techniques of artificial intelligence (AI) to create music, either as complete pieces or as sections of pieces. Of these, stochasticism (and other mathematical processes), Markov techniques, genetic algorithms and various networks (neural, associative, and so on) stand out. I have also used data-driven algorithms such as recombination with some success. However, game theory (discrete mathematics) and game trees (AI) have not received the same kind of interest, apart from Iannis Xenakis, who stands out as one of the few to have used such processes to compose music, especially in his works *Duel* (1959) and *Stratégie* (1962), both for two orchestras. The otherwise general lack of interest in game theory may be due to the perception of the inherent nature of games as leisure-time entertainments rather than serious sources of musical creativity. Those involved in the study of games, however, believe that game fundamentals underlie much of what we as humans do, and much of what the universe does. I, too, take such game studies seriously and, as I will shortly demonstrate, base a good deal of my personal composition on the principles and processes of these studies.

As an example of the seriousness with which many take the study of games, John Holland, often described as the father of genetic algorithms, assesses the value of board games (in particular) as follows:

> Board Games are not usually accorded the same primacy as numbers, but to my mind they are an equally important cornerstone in the scientific endeavor. In particular, I think board games as well as numbers, mark a watershed in human perception of the world.[1]

Morton Davis further notes that, 'by viewing a complex situation as a game, you can translate the intuitive insights of an experienced observer into a quantitative model. This allows you to make subtle quantitative inferences that are far from obvious'.[2] As someone devoted to playing and creating board games for over 50

---

[1]	John Holland, *Emergence* (Cambridge, 1998), 202–3.

[2]	Morton Davis, *Game Theory: A Nontechnical Introduction* (New York, 1983), XV.

years, I find such comments particularly apropos to the manner in which I think about my life and my work. Certainly composing represents one possible 'complex situation' to which Davis refers, and I often find parallels while playing board games. Such parallels often lead to the development of new ideas or solutions to problems, and even direct me towards unique approaches in my compositions. The eminent music theorist Leonard Meyer comments,

> The implied analogy to games may serve to illuminate something about the nature of appreciation. In works of art, as well as in games, what we enjoy and respond to is not our knowledge of governing principles or rules but the peculiar relationships discerned in a specific composition or the idiosyncratic play of a particular game. And just as our delight in the play of a particular game of football depends in crucial ways on our understanding of the constraints governing the game – the established rules, prevalent strategies, physical circumstances, and so on – so our enjoyment and evaluation of art depends on our knowledge (which may be tacit) of the constraints that governed the choices made by the artist and, hence, the relationships presented in the work of art.[3]

Rules, tactics and strategies (RTS) represent some of the most important basic processes used by those playing games and composers when they compose music. Rules, whether conscious or not, constrain the number and type of choices available. Tactics solve immediate problems created by such rules, and provide successful local control of the compositional environment. Strategies involve more global goals, indicating where, and to some extent how, a game player or a composer can achieve these goals. Since such concepts seem more typically and traditionally associated with game playing,[4] I here present a computer program showing how RTS can be used to successfully play board games, and follow this by using a strikingly similar program to compose music. Note that my differentiation between the terms tactics and strategies here does not necessarily conform to their uses in game theory, where these terms can be used interchangeably, or one at the exclusion of the other.

One convenient way to explain how rules, tactics and strategies can accomplish winning objectives in board games and, ultimately, in music is by applying them to what is often called the Knight's Tour, a variant of chess. In brief, the Knight's Tour uses only an empty chessboard and one chess piece, the knight. The game involves a single player who must, beginning on any square,

---

[3]   Leonard Meyer, *The Spheres of Music: A Gathering of Essays* (Chicago, IL, 2000), 193.

[4]   Philip Straffin, *Game Theory and Strategy* (Washington, DC, 1996). Duncan R. Luce and Howard Raiffa, *Games and Decisions: Introduction and Critical Survey* (New York, 1989). John von Neumann and Oskar Morgenstern, *Theory of Games and Economic Behavior* (Princeton, NJ, 1947). Joel Watson, *Strategy: An Introduction to Game Theory* (New York, 2007).

move this knight to every other square on the board, landing on each square *one time only*. This represents the Rules of the game. Moving the knight to an empty square with at least one empty square available for a successive move represents the Tactics of the game. Having a plan for how to accomplish the full task at hand, an overall pattern of moves that guarantees that you will not dead-end until all spaces have been touched once, represents the Strategy of the game. Each successive level of the process, rules, tactics and strategies, builds on the previous level(s).

A musical parallel to the Knight's Tour might be a 64-pitch row, where necessary repeating pitches occur in different registers so that no two notes are identical. The rules of pitch selection from this collection could be described as no consecutive pitches in the row being separated by an interval larger than a major sixth in either direction, nor any actual pitch of the 64 being repeated before all others have been stated. This is not an unreasonable restriction given similar, at least in terms of rigour, rules for isorhythmic motets, fugues, fourth-species counterpoint, serialism, and so on. In each of these cases, including the 64-pitch rule, both tactics and strategies are required for achieving a proper conclusion, that is, before finding oneself in a situation with no new pitch possible. While I have little desire to learn the Knights Tour or create a 64-pitch-rule work, both processes represent simple examples of how RTS can successfully complete both games and musical compositions.

The game-playing and composition-creating software I will now present differs from programs I have described elsewhere. For example, those readers familiar with other of my algorithmic composing programs will know that my Experiments in Musical Intelligence program (EMI) composes entire works based on a stylistic inheritance algorithm. My Alice program is more interactive than Emmy, representing both a composer's tool and a composing program. Emily Howell has both interactive and style components. With the exception of each being data-driven, the program I describe here differs in its ability to create its own rules.

Game Basics

I have for many years designed board games. These games do not require programming and in a broad sense resemble games such as checkers, chess and go, games that require physical boards with pieces moved about on their surfaces by the players. Watching two people play one of my games and enjoying themselves comes very close to the joy I get from watching two or more people playing or listening to my music and enjoying themselves. My penchant for creating games comes from a youthful obsession with chess, and feeling that, if I could create a game only half as extraordinary, I would have achieved one of the goals in my life. Suffice it to say, I have not achieved this goal, nor do I have any real expectation of ever doing so. However, in the process of creating my games, and of studying mathematical and AI game theory and game trees, I have come to believe that such board games provide a model for almost everything we do in life, including composing music.

To understand how games can produce such a model, we need to understand a little more about game space, in other words, what kinds of possibilities games present to players. For example Claude Shannon, a pioneer of mathematical information theory, computed the number of possible legal moves in chess at roughly 10 to the power of 120,[5] a number so large that it dwarfs the predicted number of atoms in the known universe. To compute these numbers of moves, Shannon used a 'game-tree' model, in which each move creates a larger set of possible successive moves and thus resembles a tree-like structure, with longer limbs and more foliage – and thus more choices – towards the bottom of the tree as one progresses down its metaphorical trunk. Game-tree structures can represent any activity that proceeds over time from a single beginning towards destinations that themselves create numerous new possibilities.

Of course, many of the moves that Shannon computed for chess prove ridiculous to a skilled player; the possible *legal* moves far outnumber the possible *logical* moves. Shannon might argue, however, that the number of logical moves, something that he could not compute, would still be staggeringly large. He could even argue further that some of the apparently illogical moves might themselves prove logical to an intuitive mind looking ahead in a game. Thus, game-trees can model any situation where new choices occur after an initial choice is made. Musical composition, for example, resembles chess in that, once chosen, a first pitch can lead to numerous second-pitch choices that, in turn, lead to even more numerous third-pitch choices, and so on. Computing a musical composition game-tree would prove enormously difficult, far larger than the chess model, given the number of possible choices and the wide number of variables: what instrument, what dynamic, what articulation, what duration and so on, a composer might choose for each new pitch. Nonetheless, a game-tree could be constructed for composing a piece of music, virtual or not, where the size of the tree would be limited only by the constraints inhibiting the possible choices available to the composer (the rules).

The question one then confronts is how, in fact, do humans negotiate games of chess and the creation of new music faced with such staggeringly large numbers of possibilities following each and every game move or musical choice? The answer to this question would seem that chess players and composers focus on the here and now, the smaller number of immediate choices and possibly a few moves ahead (rules and tactics), and use more general principles (strategies) to focus on the larger goals of winning their games or completing their compositions. These principles allow the player or the composer to proceed through a maze of local possibilities, while achieving a more global goal – staying as close to the trunk of the game-tree as possible – while necessarily having to move out on limbs to solve temporary problems.

---

[5]   Claude E. Shannon, 'Programming a Computer for Playing Chess', *Philosophical Magazine*, 41/314 (1950).

Tic-tac-toe and Tactic-toe

I begin my discussion of games with tic-tac-toe, a simple game occasionally played with pieces on a board, but easy enough to play with Xs and Os using pencil and paper. While it may seem to some readers that I have chosen a game highly inappropriate for modelling music composition, I use such a simple model in order to present the ideas and programming concepts within a small game space and using few words. To indicate the power of these processes, I follow this with a brief discussion of the same concepts for playing chess. The rules as I present them here consist of parenthetical lists resulting from my use of Lisp (LISt Processing), one of the oldest computer languages in use today and still a favourite of the artificial intelligence community. While I use Lisp to program the software I describe here, reading these lists does not require any knowledge of Lisp on the reader's part.

Tic-tac-toe (also called Noughts and Crosses) requires two players alternately marking Xs and Os in the spaces of a three-by-three matrix. The player who first succeeds in placing three equivalent marks in a horizontal, vertical or diagonal row wins the game. The simplicity of tic-tac-toe is ideal for teaching the concepts of combinational game theory and the branch of artificial intelligence that deals with game-tree searches. While simple to play, there are actually 255,168 possible tic-tac-toe games. Without eliminating symmetries (rotations and reflections), 131,184 games can be won by the player moving first, 77,904 games can be won by the player moving second, and 46,080 games end in a draw. Eliminating symmetries produces only 138 unique games, with 91 games won by the player moving first, 44 games won by the player moving second, and three games ending in a draw. While simple in concept, tic-tac-toe provides an excellent opportunity for demonstrating computational learning processes.

Many computational versions of tic-tac-toe exist. Some play themselves, some require one human user, some extend the game beyond a three-by-three matrix to various other sizes, and so on. Most of these computational versions use commonly known artificial intelligence techniques; in other words, they play their human counterparts directly out of the box. The program I describe here differs from these versions in that it has no initial knowledge of how to play tic-tac-toe at all, and will undoubtedly lose most if not all of its initial games. However, using experience only, this program slowly develops skills that rival and eventually surpass any opponent, human or computational, every time it plays.

Players playing tic-tac-toe attempt to align their own Xs or Os for a win, while simultaneously trying to block their opponents from succeeding. Thus, tactics can become fairly complex, even in this simple game. However, eventually players of equal abilities tie, making it less interesting to those pursuing more intellectually stimulating activities. The player with the first move in tic-tac-toe has the advantage; after all, if the game fills the board, the player beginning the game has five moves to the opponent's four moves. First-move players typically attempt to create *forks* (pieces or marks in three of the four corners) thus producing two ways to win in their subsequent move. These attempts can place second-moving players on the defensive, and at a disadvantage. The self-learning, heuristic algorithm I describe here for playing tic-tac-toe, called Tactic-Toe, uses rules derived from example games, and tactics and strategies derived from playing games using these rules, where the fewer the strategies necessary to win, the greater the cohesion, and vice versa. These processes can then play more complex board games and, ultimately, with a few alterations, compose more interesting and cohesive music.

The computer program called Tactic-Toe, of which I now present an overview, plays tic-tac-toe until it is obvious it has learned the rules properly. Tactic-Toe then returns a percentage of wins and ties by O, the learning player, and the one making the second move. In this completely automated version of the game, the O player initially has no idea how to play the game, just that the two players move alternately and can only choose vacant squares. In order to learn the game, and thus have a chance to win, Tactic-Toe originally trains with a virtual opponent that plays randomly but according to the rules so player O can learn them. Thus, while games initially end quite evenly with X, O and D (for draw) appearing in roughly equal numbers, as the number of games increases, player O wins increasingly more games. Eventually the percentage of wins for O never reaches 100% no matter how many games are played; this results from the manner in which Tactic-Toe learns – simple tactics gleaned from previously won or lost games. These simple tactics involve no look-ahead techniques necessary to thwart the fork problem mentioned earlier. The program also does not reach a higher level of performance owing to the incredible number of games required of it to do so. In order for the program to actually find all the possible tactics for winning or tying games, it must play at least 125,168 games. Additionally, many of these games repeat, thus increasing the number of games necessary to complete all possibilities. Interestingly, even at 555 games, the program typically approximates a 90–100 per cent success rate; that is, the program either wins or ties its randomly playing opponent 90–100 per cent of the time.

To understand how Tactic-Toe works in more detail requires some simple examples. Tactics in the computer game of Tactic-Toe take the form shown in Figure 11.1. As mentioned earlier, Tactic-Toe is written in Lisp, and thus the need for parentheses is important for the list component of this language. Tactics appear in right to left order in Tactic-Toe and require that two moves be present. In Figure 11.1, we see two moves defined by the two sub-parentheses. The first move shown here, the one on the bottom and shown in the legend as ((O 2 2) (X X nil nil O nil O nil nil)), contains two sub-parentheses. The sub-parenthesis to the left represents the move itself with (O 2 2) indicating that player O has moved to the coordinates

```
(((X 1 3) (X X X nil O nil O nil nil))
 ((O 2 2) (X X nil nil O nil O nil nil)))
```

Figure 11.1   A tactic in Tactic-Toe

2, 2 (the centre of the board, with rows and columns numbered from 1). The second sub-parenthesis presents the board in nine parts by row from bottom to top, after the move to the left here has been made. Thus, the board at this point in the game looks like that shown in Figure 11.2.

The move represented by the top group of sub-parentheses in Figure 11.1 has not yet been entered in Figure 11.2. This move represents X's win as shown in the first sub-parenthesis in Figure 11.1, and an X entered to the lower right bottom row of Figure 11.2. With more games played, Tactic-Toe will move as X has moved here in order to win or block similar moves by X such that, whenever encountering a position of two Xs in a row, the program will automatically take X's next move as its own move blocking X's win. This simple tactic works quite well with the exception that it only succeeds when no other X pieces appear on the board. In other words, the snapshot that Tactic-Toe takes of the board (using X's piece only) must be precisely the same or the tactic will not apply. Thus, several tactics need to exist to cover the various layouts with X still winning by linking three Xs across the bottom of the board. Certainly having a tactic in the game that only concentrates on three Xs in a row solves this problem. However, as stated earlier, Tactic-Toe does not initially have any information on how to play the game: having such a programmer-added tactic would spoil the computational heuristic learning process.

Tactic-Toe collects two types of tactics: first, the protect tactic just described, and second, the attack tactic I will describe shortly. The protect tactics in Tactic-Toe attempt to make it impossible for X to win a game by collecting every possible case where X wins in order for O to look ahead one move and thwart that win. This brute-force approach is matched by a similar set of win tactics. With win tactics, Tactic-Toe saves moves prior to and including its wins, and attempts – by consulting these tactics – to win in like manner in any relevant future game. Before each move, Tactic-Toe first checks to see if it can win (no reason to protect if a win is imminent), and then consults its protect tactics. In cases where neither consultation produces a win possibility, O continues to play randomly like X.

Obviously, this simple approach does not in any way parallel what we imagine intelligent beings do when faced with learning to play a new game without any information on how to win. Intelligence would, within but a few games, glean that it takes three of the same piece-type in a row to win, and develop principles to

$$
\begin{array}{ccc}
O & - & - \\
- & O & - \\
X & X & -
\end{array}
$$

Figure 11.2   The board (X X nil nil O nil O nil nil) in Tactic-Toe

avoid having to play thousands of games to learn this. However, tactics represent just the first step in computer game-playing techniques. The strategies I now describe more aptly model intelligent processes.

Strategies result from pattern matching: discarding non-essential aspects of board contents and concentrating on the layouts that winning positions have in common. For example, Figure 11.3 shows eight board positions representing the eight ways in which X can win a game – three across, three top to bottom and two diagonal.

Finding patterns in common between these eight boards requires that we first eliminate the irrelevant Os from the board. The eight boards now look like that shown in Figure 11.4. The pattern matcher of our heuristic program discounts any entirely nil patterns as these represent non-relevant squares. These nils may exist as a part of patterns containing Xs, but cannot represent a winning pattern in themselves. Patterns in this matcher consist of three elements since the rules require three in a row to win. Instead of having several thousand protect and attack tactics then, we need only six strategies as shown in Figure 11.5, with the additional caveat that, whenever one of these tactics appears minus one of its elements, for either side, Tactic-Toe attempts to either thwart (in the case of X moving next) or complete (in the case of O moving next).

Thus, within a very small number of games (say, 10 or 12), Tactic-Toe, by using RTS, begins to create tactics and develop its six strategies, and begins playing seriously against its opponent. In order to create strategies, Tactic-Toe must produce composites of many winning boards from its simple tactics. For

(X X X nil O nil O nil nil)

(nil O nil X X X O nil nil)

(nil O nil O nil nil X X X)

(X nil O X nil nil X O nil)

(O X nil nil X nil O X nil)

(nil O X nil nil X nil O X)

(X nil O nil X nil nil O X)

(O nil X nil X nil X O nil)

Figure 11.3   Eight board positions representing the eight ways in which X can win a game in tic-tac-toe (three across, three top to bottom and two diagonal)

```
(X X X nil nil nil nil nil nil)

(nil nil nil X X X nil nil nil)

(nil nil nil nil nil nil X X X)

(X nil nil X nil nil X nil nil)

(nil X nil nil X nil nil X nil)

(nil nil X nil nil X nil nil X)

(X nil nil nil X nil nil nil X)

(nil nil X nil X nil X nil nil)
```

Figure 11.4   Eight boards without Os in Tactic-Toe

```
(
  (X X X)                                 ;3 left to right
  (X nil nil)                             ;3 in left column
  (nil X nil)                             ;3 in center column
  (nil nil X)                             ;3 in right column
  ((X nil nil)(nil X nil)(nil nil X))     ;3 in L/R diagonal
  ((nil nil X)(nil X nil)(X nil nil))     ;3 in R/L diagonal
)
```

Figure 11.5   Six strategies drawn from several thousand simple tactics
               in Tactic-Toe

example, a board such as (nil nil X nil nil X nil nil X), which represents a top-down win in column three for X, also matches boards of (nil nil X X nil X nil nil X) or (nil nil X nil nil X nil X X), both of which represent a win for X. This particular type of pattern matching produces reinforcements of winning boards.

However implementing strategies can also pose problems. For example, strategies will not account for the forks that I mentioned earlier, unless the pattern-matching program hunts for combinational patterns, that is, patterns that produce two simultaneous ways of winning. For example, a simple board layout of a fork showing Xs appears in Figure 11.6, here shown in both graphic and computational formats.

```
- - -
X - -
X X -
```

(X X nil X nil nil nil nil nil)

Figure 11.6   A fork in graphic and Tactic-Toe formats

The fork here demonstrates the (X X nil) lowest pattern ready for a row win, and the (X X nil) and (X nil nil) patterns ready for a bottom-left to upper-left first-column win. With these patterns 'learned' by Tactic-Toe, the program can simply avoid them in its previous move by placing an O in one of the positions here before X moves there. What is more, these combinational strategies make it possible for Tactic-Toe to actually attempt forks on its own.

Strategies can further evolve into higher-level strategies. With Tactic-Toe, this means grouping all left-to-right strategies together as (X X X), all vertical strategies together as (X nil nil), and both diagonals together as symmetries, creating three meta-strategies. Eventually, these meta-strategies could themselves evolve into yet higher-level strategies, such as any straight line in any direction wins. In other words, the strategies reduce from eight, to three, to one in number. This process produces more than just efficiency, it produces a process of organisation that allows the program to group and recombine ideas at progressively higher and higher hierarchical levels, not having to deal with the details of lower levels. More importantly, this process more closely resembles the one that humans use as they abstract basic principles from detailed examples. Thus, strategies make learning faster, more efficient and more comprehensive. Using strategies, Tactic-Toe achieves 100 per cent wins or ties within 100 games with both machine and human opponents. Combining simple learning processes with higher-level pattern matching achieves goals that neither one of these processes alone could achieve.

At this point in the process, after the Tactic-Toe program has learned the rules, tactics and strategies of the game, its playing partner switches from random choices to a robust algorithm capable of high-level performance. Choosing Minimax for this role (an algorithm for choosing next moves in two-player games) seems natural given its stature in the AI game-playing community, and the fact that most humans rarely beat such programs, only tie or lose to them. John von Neumann, originator of the Minimax Theorem, says

> as far as I can see, there could be no theory of games ... until the *Minimax Theorem* was proved.[6]

[6]   John L. Casti, *Five Gold Rules: Great Theories of 20th-Century Mathematics – And Why They Matter* (Upper Saddle River, NJ, 1996).

As such, Minimax *mini*mises possible losses while *maximising* potential gains and works by associating values for each move with each game state, typically computed by means of a position evaluation function. The program then makes moves that maximise the minimum value of a position resulting from the opponent's possible subsequent moves. Originally formulated for two-player zero-sum game theory, Minimax can play simple as well as complex games and participate in general decision-making.

Figure 11.7 – a zero-sum game where A and B make simultaneous moves – illustrates Minimax solutions, where each player has three choices as shown here in the payoff matrix for A. Assuming that the payoff matrix for player B uses the same matrix as player A with the signs reversed (that is, if the choices are A1 and B1, then B pays 3 to A), then the Minimax choice for A would be A2, since the worst possible result gives away one point, while its best result returns four points. The Minimax choice for B would be B2, since the worst possible result it could receive would be no payment at all, but it could gain as many as three points. However, if B believes A will choose A2, then B might choose B1 to gain one point. If A believes B will choose B1, then A might choose A1 to gain three points. To create a more stable solution, some choices are *dominated* by others, and these can be eliminated. For example, A will not choose A3 since either A1 or A2 produces better results, no matter what B chooses. Additionally, B will not choose B3, since B2 produces a better result, no matter what A chooses.

The Minimax algorithm will also look ahead a certain number of moves in a game. Called the *look-ahead*, this process is measured in *plies*. Supplying a heuristic evaluation function gives values to these non-final game states without considering all the possible ensuing sequences. This limits the necessity of Minimax having to look all the way to game's end. For example, Deep Blue, the chess-playing computer program that beat Garry Kasparov (1997),[7] looked ahead 12 plies and then applied a heuristic evaluation function.

In Tactic-Toe, a standard Minimax model opponent takes X and makes the first move. Tactic-Toe, the O player, makes the second move and follows the RTS

	B chooses B1	B chooses B2	B chooses B3
A chooses A1	+3	-2	+2
A chooses A2	-1	0	+4
A chooses A3	-4	-3	+1

Figure 11.7   The payoff matrix for player A for a simultaneous-move game

---

[7]   Feng-hsiung Hsu, *Behind Deep Blue: Building the Computer that Defeated the World Chess Champion* (Princeton, NJ: Princeton University Press, 2004).

heuristic learning model described previously. This gives the Minimax algorithm the advantage in all the games played, thus making wins by RTS that much more difficult. In head-to-head contests between an 'educated' version of Tactic-Toe and a well-programmed Minimax algorithm moving first, Tactic-Toe always wins or ties and never loses. This striking result proves the robustness of the Tactic-Toe RTS process, particularly given the robustness of Minimax.

Chess

For those readers believing Tic-tac-toe represents a much too simplistic model for music composition, no matter how effective Tactic-toe is in tying or defeating a well-known high-level computer algorithm, I present here a similar program for chess. Figure 11.8 shows two in-progress chess game boards in both visual (a and c) and strategy (b and d) notations. These two game boards provide apparently quite different situations.

As can be seen in this figure, the two board layouts have only two piece-positions in common (pawns at e5 and h7). However, as initially improbable as it may seem, the patterns match. Players who use positional chess tactics may recognise how this is so. In both cases, White plays first and wins in two moves. In Figure 11.8a, White moves knight at d5 to f6, placing Black's king in check. This move also uncovers White's bishop at c4, pinning Black's rook at f7. Since Black's king cannot move itself out of check, Black's queen at d8 must take White's knight at f6, relieving the check. With Black's queen moved, White can now move its queen at h6 to f8 for checkmate. Figure 11.8c produces a nearly identical win for White, although at first glance this similarity may not be obvious. To make this clear, I quote the above passage, and bracket the changed positions: 'White moves knight at [e7] to [c6], placing Black's king in check. This move also uncovers White's bishop at [f8], pinning Black's rook at [c5]. Since Black's king cannot move itself out of check, Black's queen at [e4] must take White's knight at [c6], relieving the check. With Black's queen moved, White can now move queen at [a6] to [c4] for checkmate'. Removing all the irrelevant pieces from each board and comparing the results by analysing the move types makes this comparison more clear. Figure 11.9a and c presents a slimmed down version of Figure 11.8a and c, respectively.

The reason for the difference in number of pieces of the boards here, eight vs eleven, results from the fact that, in Figure 11.9a, Black's king rests against the board edge, where in Figure 11.9c Black's king has pieces behind it to create the same lack of available reverse motion. Sliding Black down to the edge of the board creates an eight-piece equivalency as shown in Figure 11.10. Now, inverting the board in Figure 11.10 bottom to top and left to right makes the relationship even clearer, as shown in Figure 11.11.

Comparing Figure 11.11 with the reduced layout of the original game layout of Figure 11.9a proves the equivalency of the two positions. Only one actual piece differs between the two boards, a rook vs a pawn in h7, a difference with no

a)

```
8 BR -- BB BQ -- -- BK --
7 BP BP BP -- -- BR -- BP
6 -- -- BN BP -- BP WN WQ
5 -- -- BB WN BP BP -- --
4 -- -- WB -- WP -- -- --
3 -- -- -- WP -- -- -- --
2 WP WP WP -- -- WP WP WP
1 WR -- -- -- WK -- -- WR
   A  B  C  D  E  F  G  H
```

b)

```
((R*  nil B*  Q*  nil nil K*  nil)
 (P*  P*  P*  nil nil R*  nil P*)
 (nil nil N*  P*  nil P*  N+  Q+)
 (nil nil B*  N+  P*  P*  nil nil)
 (nil nil B+  nil P+  nil nil nil)
 (nil nil nil P+  nil nil nil nil)
 (P+  P+  P+  nil nil P+  P+  P+)
 (R+  nil nil nil K+  nil nil R+))
```

c)

```
8 -- -- -- -- -- WB -- --
7 -- -- -- -- WN BP BP BP
6 WQ WN -- -- -- -- -- --
5 BR -- BR -- BP -- -- --
4 -- BK -- -- BQ -- WP --
3 BP BP BB -- -- -- -- --
2 -- -- -- WP WP -- -- --
1 WK -- -- -- -- -- -- --
   A  B  C  D  E  F  G  H
```

d)

```
((nil nil nil nil nil B+  nil nil)
 (nil nil nil nil N+  P*  P*  P*)
 (Q+  N+  nil nil nil nil nil nil)
 (R*  nil R*  nil P*  nil nil nil)
 (nil K*  nil nil Q*  nil P+  nil)
 (P*  P*  B*  nil nil nil nil nil)
 (nil nil nil P+  P+  nil nil nil)
 (K+  nil nil nil nil nil nil nil))
```

Figure 11.8   Two chess games in both visual (a and c) and computational (b and d)
notation with White indicated by '+' and Black by '*'

a)

```
8 -- -- -- BQ -- -- BK --
7 -- -- -- -- -- BR -- BP
6 -- -- -- -- -- -- WN WQ
5 -- -- -- WN -- -- -- --
4 -- -- WB -- -- -- -- --
3 -- -- -- -- -- -- -- --
2 -- -- -- -- -- -- -- --
1 -- -- -- -- -- -- -- --
  A  B  C  D  E  F  G  H
```

b)

```
((nil nil nil Q*  nil nil K*  nil)
 (nil nil nil nil nil R*  nil P*)
 (nil nil nil nil nil nil N+  Q+)
 (nil nil nil N+  nil nil nil nil)
 (nil nil B+  nil nil nil nil nil)
 (nil nil nil nil nil nil nil nil)
 (nil nil nil nil nil nil nil nil)
 (nil nil nil nil nil nil nil nil))
```

c)

```
8 -- -- -- -- -- WB -- --
7 -- -- -- -- WN -- -- --
6 WQ WN -- -- -- -- -- --
5 BR -- BR -- -- -- -- --
4 -- BK -- -- BQ -- -- --
3 BP BP BB -- -- -- -- --
2 -- -- -- -- -- -- -- --
1 -- -- -- -- -- -- -- --
  A  B  C  D  E  F  G  H
```

d)

```
((nil nil nil nil nil B+  nil nil)
 (nil nil nil nil N+  nil nil nil)
 (Q+  N+  nil nil nil nil nil nil)
 (R*  nil R*  nil nil nil nil nil)
 (nil K*  nil nil Q*  nil nil nil)
 (P*  P*  B*  nil nil nil nil nil)
 (nil nil nil nil nil nil nil nil)
 (nil nil nil nil nil nil nil nil))
```

Figure 11.9   Slimmed down version of Figure 11.8a and c along with computational notations (b and d)

```
8  --  --  --  --  --  --  --  --
7  --  --  --  --  --  --  --  --
6  --  --  --  --  --  --  --  --
5  --  --  --  --  --  WB  --  --
4  --  --  --  --  WN  --  --  --
3  WQ  WN  --  --  --  --  --  --
2  BR  --  BR  --  --  --  --  --
1  --  BK  --  --  BQ  --  --  --
   A   B   C   D   E   F   G   H
```

Figure 11.10   Sliding pieces down to the edge of the board to create an eight-piece mirror of the board in Figure 11.9c

```
8  --  --  --  BQ  --  --  BK  --
7  --  --  --  --  --  BR  --  BR
6  --  --  --  --  --  --  WN  WQ
5  --  --  --  WN  --  --  --  --
4  --  --  WB  --  --  --  --  --
3  --  --  --  --  --  --  --  --
2  --  --  --  --  --  --  --  --
1  --  --  --  --  --  --  --  --
   A   B   C   D   E   F   G   H
```

Figure 11.11   Inverting the board in Figure 11.10 to make its relationship to Figure 11.9a clearer

consequence to the inevitable outcome of the game. Accomplished chess players routinely use such positional references to win games. In fact, were it not for these types of relationships, every situation would pose a new circumstance and require many more brute-force mental computations than necessary. Moreover, not only is relating board configurations that initially appear very different elpful for reducing the amount to time in playing, it also helps avoid mistakes and, worse, mistaken opportunities. Obviously, knowing how to play chess well, working in the real world of pieces and boards, being able to visualise the board from many different virtual and real angles, momentarily eliminating irrelevant pieces, and so on, aids human players in relating patterns that apparently differ dramatically. For humans, the ability to coalesce mental and physical information along with acquired skills obtained from extensive experience makes such successful reductions of different patterns not only possible, but, in many ways, easy. Philip Ross notes that 'Studies of the mental processes of chess grand masters have revealed clues to how people become experts in other fields as well … just as a master can recall all the moves in a game he has played, so can an accomplished musician often reconstruct the score to a sonata heard just once'.[8] A computer program can thus learn tactics of games and develop skills relatively easily. Gained information about these tactics then helps such programs use basic pattern recognition to reduce out irrelevant pieces and to transpose piece locations for positional comparisons. Developing strategies and meta-strategies then add the development of skills necessary to defeat opponents of very high calibre (for example, RTS).

I do not here differentiate between Tactic-Toe and my chess-playing program, preferring instead to continue using Tactic-Toe whenever I reference game-playing programs. I do this in an effort to keep the processes themselves as simple and as clear as possible. Examples of strategies in chess, even simple examples, would require enormous amounts of explanation, when, in fact, they typically reduce to much the same type of game states.

Musical Examples

In order to demonstrate the RTS processes described here for composing music, I now provide several examples in the creation of a movement for a string quartet. While this movement does not currently belong to any string quartet of mine, I find the music here engaging and, even though produced especially for this presentation, I may include it in a future work.

The first step in composing a new passage, movement, or work using algorithmic game-playing techniques involves creating a database of music from which the program can derive rules for how to create further such music and how, eventually, to succeed I here begin with a scale. There are precisely 2^{11} or 2048 possible scales in the equal tempered tuning system. Of these, fewer than 10 per cent have been used commonly, with the other 90 per cent occurring rarely if at all, and then only as a result of chromatic embellishments in music predominantly consisting of other scales. Example 11.1 provides the scale I will use here to algorithmically create the new string quartet movement. While I cannot assure readers that this scale does not have a name, or has not been used previously, I can guarantee that it was new to me when I devised it. Note the four half-steps (scale-degrees 1–2, 4–5, 6–7, 8–1) and the two half-steps occurring successively (scale-degrees 8–1 and 1–2), both tending to separate it from more commonly used scales.

---

[8]   Philip E. Ross, 'The expert mind', *Scientific American*, 295/2 (2006), 64–71.

Example 11.1   A scale for use as data in algorithmically creating a new string
quartet movement

Example 11.2 provides a small section of a database of music (what I call the
medium) created algorithmically using the above-described scale. Note that this
music uses only the pitches of this scale and, thus, four pitches (D, E, G and Bb)
never occur. Obviously, I could use these pitches to make the music here more
interesting. However, I do not want to confuse the analysis that takes place next in
the composing process. I can always add chromatic pitches as needed in the latter
stages of composition. For now, I want a clean four-part texture with all pitches
belonging to the scale just described.

Example 11.2   A small part of a database or *medium* created algorithmically
using the scale in Example 11.1

The algorithm used to create the medium music in Example 11.2 consists of three simple rules. First, each instrument plays only four pitches from the scale. Second, these pitches taken together include all the pitches of the scale in use. Third, the upper two lines and the lower two lines have the same pitch sets, but separated by one octave. These rules allow for several different harmonies to occur, even the possibility of a single doubled-at-the-octave pitch. While homorhythmic, the duration choices are random, having no particular regard for the metre. The reason for these freedoms is that I am particularly interested in having the small program creating this medium explore the fullest range of possibilities of the raw material, and thus also create a broad set of rules, or probabilities if you wish, for the game program to discover. This program can then derive tactics and strategies for producing what sculptors call *foundations* for my new compositions. The rules derived from the music of Example 11.2 appear in the matrix shown in Figure 11.12, the available pitches without their registers for each of the four string instruments.

In computational rule terms, this matrix can be expressed as shown in Figure 11.13, indicating, in this case, the pitches C, Eb, B and Db moving to the pitches B, Gb, A and Eb (from bottom to top, and from Vc up to V1 without their associated registral indications).

There are 4^4 or 256 possible arrangements of the four vertical pitch groupings in this matrix and therefore possible rules for governing their motions. However, as one can see by analysing the music in Example 11.2, this number has not been approached here, nor will it, even with several times this number of measures

V1	–	**Db**	**Eb**	**F**	**Gb**
V2	–	**Ab**	**A**	**B**	**C**
Va	–	**Db**	**Eb**	**F**	**Gb**
Vc	–	**Ab**	**A**	**B**	**C**

Figure 11.12   The pitches for each instrument in the music of Example 11.2 without registers

```
(
((nil nil X nil) (nil nil nil X) (nil X nil nil) (nil X nil nil))
((nil nil nil X) (nil X nil nil) (nil nil X nil) (X nil nil nil))
)
```

Figure 11.13   A matrix in computational rule terms

of such music, since many situations will repeat. The rules gathered from this database then constitute the basis for generating both tactics and strategies for creating new music. Studying the first phrase of the quartet shown in Example 11.3 provides readers with a sense of how the game processes create music based on the same principles as the RTS of games such as tic-tac-toe and chess. Note, however, that the example of database music in Example 11.2 represents just that, an example, and not the entire database, which would be prohibitive to fully reproduce here. I want the algorithmic music from this RTS program, what I call the *foundations*, to be as close as possible to my end product in order to avoid having to make too many changes. Therefore, I carefully choose music for the medium that will produce music more to my liking for the foundations.

The distinctions between the medium and the foundation here are very important. *Media* – and I might use or discard many of these – represent raw materials that I judge in terms of resources rather than in terms of musical value. *Foundations*, on the other hand – and again I might use or discard many of these – must sound roughly like what I anticipate a final result sounding. Foundations must have shape, a semblance of structure, and directions towards goals, the win if you will. *Transformations*, a subject I tackle next, hone the foundations, much as the foundations hone the medium, with each step in the process bringing a work, movement or passage that much closer to my objective.

Transformations

The transformational portion of the music-composing program consists of four basic algorithms that accomplish the following:

> Modulation
> Non-modulatory chromaticism
> Rhythm variations
> Entry offset.

Each of these basic processes can be used individually or in combination with one or more of the other three processes. These basic transformations also have several sub-categories, the number of which varies according to the music being transformed. For example, Entry Offset may include different settings for precisely when the various voices enter. Non-modulatory chromaticism may add one or more out-of-scale pitches, with the number of pitches determined by the number of diatonic pitches in the scale in use. Suffice it to say, that even a very conservative estimate of the possible overlays of categories and sub-categories numbers in the millions. The transformational program decides which and how many categories and sub-categories to use based on an analysis of the number and types of tactics and strategies it uncovers in the music that RTS produces from its medium. In every case, the purpose of the transformations is to increase the diversity of its output compared to its input. Thus, a very simple diatonic piece with little rhythmic or chromatic interest can evoke many transformation modules linked to these parameters. In contrast, a complex scale of, say, nine pitches, and a rhythm consisting of many different durations may not require any transformation at all.

The results of these processes make the eventual output of the program often surprising, but never random. Since the transformation program assumes that discarded output indicates user dissatisfaction with its choices, the program will select different transformational categories and subcategories for subsequent creation. Surprises result from the large number of possibilities available for transforming the music, and my lack of ability to predict from that number what I might expect to hear. This transformational program is therefore data-dependant, to a degree at least, as are most of my other composing programs. However, the choices of the categories and sub-categories are limited to the parameters with which the composing process deals almost exclusively, namely, pitch and rhythm. Obviously dozens of other potentially valuable transformational categories can substitute for or add to the ones I describe above. I have limited my program to four categories here because of space limitations and to indicate to readers those that have proven most successful in my composition during the past few years.

Example 11.3 presents a complete version of a new movement created by the previously described program with my addition of dynamics, phrasing, spelling changes for the performers, tempo, and other markings to make performance possible. (For those not willing or able to hear this music otherwise, I have placed it, and all of the other musical figures, in MP3 format on my website[9]).

The first phrase of Example 11.3 (mm. 1–21) demonstrates clear short-range move-by-move tactics, and longer-range strategies as shown in the cadence here. The results, to my mind, while bearing a strong similarity to the database medium upon which my game-playing program trained, has differences as well, ones that I find attractive. The second phrase of the string quartet (mm. 22–48) shows a staggered entrance version of another output of the game software. This variation is the result of the transformational program that attempts to produce more interesting results. The individual lines here follow the same pitches of the original first phrase, but with independence from the program's static rhythmic nature, one move following another in synchronicity. The third phrase of the string quartet (mm. 49–97) presents a radically different variation of the original medium, also the result of the transformational process. I have transposed this section to provide all but one of the missing pitches (Bb) of the original scale, and ensure that the music remains within the ranges of the instruments in use. The missing Bb intrigues me, and so I do not mind its absence.

The final aspect of the composing process I describe in this chapter is the addition of dynamics, articulations, special effects, tempo markings, and so on. In this final stage, I may change pitches, re-write entire sections, and/or eliminate

---

[9]   http:// arts.ucsc.edu/faculty/cope/downloads.

material as I see fit. In short, nothing remains safe from my alteration or censure. However, I typically make few changes and, as is the case here, often make no changes at all, just adding performance markings. Were I to rewrite this movement, I would most likely create transitions between the three sections and add other logical pitches.

Example 11.3   A completed version of a new movement with added dynamics, phrasing, spelling changes, tempo and other markings

Example 11.3 (continued)

Example 11.3 (continued)

Example 11.3 (continued)

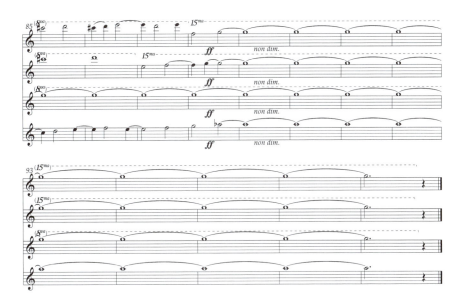

Summation

Considering board games as illustrating the processes of rules, tactics and strategies, they offer many parallels to musical composition. First, games may have one player (solitaire, as in monophony), two or more players moving at different times (as in counterpoint), and two or more players moving simultaneously (as in homophony). Second, the processes of playing games and composing music, as different as they may initially seem, resemble one another in that they both require the learning of rules, the gaining of expertise in using those rules, and then the application of those rules to achieve their respective ends. Third, both game playing and composing music require a *medium* (for example, board, pieces, instruments, scales), a *foundation* (long-range strategy, rough draft) and a *transformation* (winning meta-strategies) in order to succeed (win, complete the work). In both game playing and composing, one must be constantly aware of the current environment and envision many possible future environments to come.

Overall, these apparently divergent and disparate processes, sculptural concepts, game theory, RTS, and music composition, can integrate, forming useful composing techniques. I leave it to readers to determine whether or not my various approaches have gelled in ways that create interesting if not successful compositions. Ultimately, however, as composer, I am the final arbiter of what wins musically for me, and I find that these processes coalesce to create extraordinarily useful results.

References

Casti, John L., *Five Gold Rules: Great Theories of 20th-Century Mathematics – And Why They Matter* (Upper Saddle River, NJ: Prentice-Hall, 1996).

Cope, David, *Computers and Musical Style* (Madison, WI: A-R Editions, 1991).

Cope, David, *Experiments in Musical Intelligence* (Madison, WI: A-R Editions, 1996).

Cope, David, *The Algorithmic Composer* (Madison, WI: A-R Editions, 2000).

Cope, David, *Virtual Music* (Cambridge, MA: MIT Press, 2001).

Cope, David, 'A musical learning algorithm', *Computer Music Journal*, 28/3 (2004), 12–27.

Cope, David, *Computer Models of Musical Creativity* (Cambridge, MA: MIT Press, 2005).

Cope, David, *Hidden Structure* (Madison, WI: A-R Editions, 2007).

Davis, Morton D., *Game Theory: A Nontechnical Introduction* (New York: Basic Books, 1983).

Hardy, G.H., *A Mathematician's Apology* (Cambridge: Cambridge University Press, 1940).

Holland, John, *Emergence* (Cambridge, MA: Perseus Books, 1998).

Hsu, Feng-hsiung, *Behind Deep Blue: Building the Computer that Defeated the World Chess Champion* (Princeton, NJ: Princeton University Press, 2004).

Luce, R. Duncan and Howard Raiffa, *Games and Decisions: Introduction and Critical Survey* (New York: Dover, 1989).

Meyer, Leonard, *The Spheres of Music: A Gathering of Essays* (Chicago, IL: The University of Chicago Press, 2000).

Ross, Philip E., 'The expert mind', *Scientific American*, 295/2 (2006), 64–71.

Shannon, Claude E., 'Programming a computer for playing chess', *Philosophical Magazine*, 41/314 (1950), 256–75.

Straffin, Philip, *Game Theory and Strategy* (Washington, DC: Mathematical Association of America Textbooks, 1996).

von Neumann, John and Oskar Morgenstern, *Theory of Games and Economic Behavior*, 2nd edn (Princeton, NJ: Princeton University Press, 1947).

Watson, Joel, *Strategy: An Introduction to Game Theory*, 2nd edn (New York: W.W. Norton, 2007).

Xenakis, Iannis, *Formalized Music: Thought and Mathematics in Composition*, Harmonologia Series, no. 6 (Hillsdale, NY: Pendragon Press, 2001).

Index

Page numbers referring to figures are *italic*, music examples are **bold** and tables are ***bold italic***.